Fourth Edition

Understanding
Human Communication

◆ **Speech is civilization itself. The word, even the most contradictory word, preserves contact—it is silence which isolates.**

Thomas Mann
The Magic Mountain

Fourth Edition

Understanding Human Communication

Ronald B. Adler
Santa Barbara City College

George Rodman
Brooklyn College
City University of New York

Harcourt Brace Jovanovich College Publishers
Fort Worth   Philadelphia   San Diego   New York   Orlando   Austin   San Antonio
Toronto   Montreal   London   Sydney   Tokyo

Publisher:	Ted Buchholz
Acquisitions Editor:	Janet Wilhite
Developmental Editor:	Kathryn Lang
Senior Project Editor:	Dawn Youngblood
Production Manager:	Kathleen Ferguson
Art & Design Supervisor:	Vicki McAlindon Horton
Text Designer:	Janet Bollow
Cover Designer:	Rhonda Campbell
Cover Artist:	Bill Reed/Palmworks Studio

LIBRARY OF CONGRESS CATALOGING-IN-PUBLICATION DATA

Adler, Ronald B. (Ronald Brian), 1946–
 Understanding human communication.

 Includes bibliographies and index.
 I. Communication. I. Rodman, George R., 1948–
II. Title.
P90.A32 1991 302.2—dc20 90-4092

ISBN 0-03-049727-2

Address Editorial Correspondence to: 301 Commerce Street, Suite 3700
 Fort Worth, TX 76102

Address Orders to: 6277 Sea Harbor Drive,
 Orlando, FL 32887
 1-800-782-4479, or
 1-800-433-0001 (in Florida)

Printed in the United States of America

 2 3 4   0 3 9   9 8 7 6 5

Harcourt Brace Jovanovich, Inc.
The Dryden Press
Saunders College Publishing

Copyright Acknowledgments begin on page 469.

PREFACE

It is hard to imagine an academic subject more appealing than human communication. Students may complain about calculus, balk at biology, or even hate the humanities; but almost no one disputes the value of understanding how people communicate and learning how to do a better job.

Understanding Human Communication attempts to harness this interest by providing a comprehensive, inviting introduction to the field of communication. It is aimed at two audiences: nonmajors for whom this will be the only systematic look at the discipline, and students who are using the course as an overview that precedes more detailed study in future courses.

Theory and Skills

Like its predecessors, this edition of *Understanding Human Communication* refuses to take sides in the "theory vs. skills" debate that seems to rage endlessly within the discipline. The cognitive and behavioral goals that open each chapter show that students will cover both domains of the subject, learning more about theory and research on face-to-face communication *and* developing skills that will help them communicate more effectively in their lives. Activities in every chapter give students a chance to develop their understanding of communication principles and practice communication skills.

Pedagogical Approach

All this information is presented in a way that experience has shown has high student appeal. Along with the readable text and attractive design, the material is illustrated by a variety of epigrams, brief readings, and sophisticated cartoons. Thought-provoking photographs suggest themes in the text rather than presenting them literally, challenging students to consider topics in new ways. Three editions of praise from professors and students have endorsed the fact that these materials illustrate principles in a way that is often more interesting, amusing, and eloquent than even the best academic prose.

Changes in This Edition

Several changes distinguish this edition from its predecessors. Most noticeably, there are two new chapters. Chapter 7, "Communicating with Family and Friends" describes the unique forms of communication that distinguish these important relationships. Chapter 10, "Communicating on the Job" examines the kinds of communication readers will experience at work, and offers guidelines for working more effectively with the people who can make or break their career.

To keep the length of the book manageable for a one-term course, Chapter 6, "Understanding and Improving Interpersonal Relationships" consolidates material that was spread over two chapters in the previous edition. Chapter 15, "Persuasive Speaking," has been reorganized to clarify strategies for influencing an audience's beliefs and actions and to emphasize the nature and importance of ethical persuasion.

Student activities in this edition have a new look. They are integrated within each chapter where they will be most accessible to readers, and where their relationship to textual material is clearest. Many of these activities are designed to develop communication skills; others will increase the students' understanding of communication concepts.

In addition to these prominent changes, every chapter of *Understanding Human Communication* has been revised, modified, and updated to keep the material interesting, clear, and up-to-date. For example, there is new treatment of the influence of culture on person perception (Chapter 2), time as a dimension of nonverbal communication (Chapter 5), impersonal and interpersonal communication (Chapter 6), when to use groups for problem-solving and stages of problem-solving discussions (Chapter 9), and there are several new sample speeches (Chapters 11, 12, 14, and 15).

Ancillary Instructional Material

Understanding Human Communication is accompanied by a package of instructional support materials that will make the process of instruction easier and more effective for instructors.

◆ A comprehensive *Instructor's Manual,* authored by Mary Bozik, provides a wealth of teaching strategies, class schedules, and testing options that should prove useful for both new and experienced instructors.
◆ *Transparency masters* contained in the Instructor's Manual illustrate key concepts and figures in the text, making it easier for instructors and students to discuss them during class sessions.
◆ A *computerized test bank* with over 750 questions makes it easy for instructors to create and edit exams.

◆ A set of three *videotapes,* created by David Hudson and Sharon Ratliffe, of Golden West College, illustrate how communication principles operate beyond the classroom. Tapes on interpersonal, group, and public communication make this package among the most complete in the field.

Acknowledgments

We are grateful to the colleagues from around the country who offered constructive suggestions about how to improve this edition of *Understanding Human Communication*: Martha Atkins, Iowa State University; Alice Bante, St. Louis Community College at Meramec; Dan Chandler, New York City College/SUNY; Susan Coffey, Central Virginia Community College; Elizabeth Coughlin, Northern Virginia Community College; Judy Goldberg, Arapahoe Community College; Suzanne Hagen, University of Wisconsin at River Falls; Janet Hartman, Kirkwood Community College; and Jo Young Switzer, Purdue University.

We continue to appreciate the comments of those people who reviewed previous editions of *Understanding Human Communication*. Their ideas continue to prove useful here: Richard Arthur, Montana State University; Ruth Aurelius, Des Moines Area Community College; Ann E. Busse, Northern Illinois University; Daniel Canary, Portland Community College; Robert T. Dixon, St. Louis Community College; Carley Dodd, Abilene Christian University; Diane M. Harney, Florida State University; David Hough, Vincennes University; Albert Katz, University of Wisconsin–Superior; Melba Kop, Chaminade University of Honolulu; Paul D. Krivonos, California State University–Northridge; Judith Litterst, St. Cloud State University; Don Morlan, University of Dayton; Kaye J. Nubel, Saddleback College; Gwenn D. Schultz, Portland State University; John P. Sprowl, University of Connecticut; Charlotte Toguchi, Kapiolani Community College; and Barbara Willard, Florida State University.

We wish to extend thanks to the following members of our focus group from St. Louis Community College at Meramec: Alice Bante, Linda Bianca, Dianne Breitwieser, Chris Carenza, Marilyn Davis, Bob Dixon, Jim Greer, Phil Hanson, Jan Mirikitani, Ray Sikes, and Sue Stanton.

A personal thank you is extended to Sharon Ratliffe and David Hudson for their hard work and attention to detail in producing the interpersonal, small group, and public speaking video tapes which enhance the text. We appreciate their professionalism and good humor.

We are also grateful to the team of professionals at Holt, Rinehart and Winston whose skill and goodwill have made this project a pleasure to work on: Janet Wilhite, Kathryn Lang, Dawn Youngblood, Kathy Ferguson, and Vicki McAlindon Horton. As always, we owe a tremendous debt to Janet Bollow for transforming a dog-eared manuscript into such a handsome book.

Ronald B. Adler
George Rodman

Preface

BRIEF CONTENTS

CONTENTS

Contents

CHAPTER 4 LISTENING 89

CHAPTER 5 NONVERBAL COMMUNICATION 117

Contents

Contents

Contents

CHAPTER 9 SOLVING PROBLEMS IN GROUPS 245

CHAPTER 10 COMMUNICATING ON THE JOB 275

Contents

Contents

Contents

ELEMENTS OF COMMUNICATION

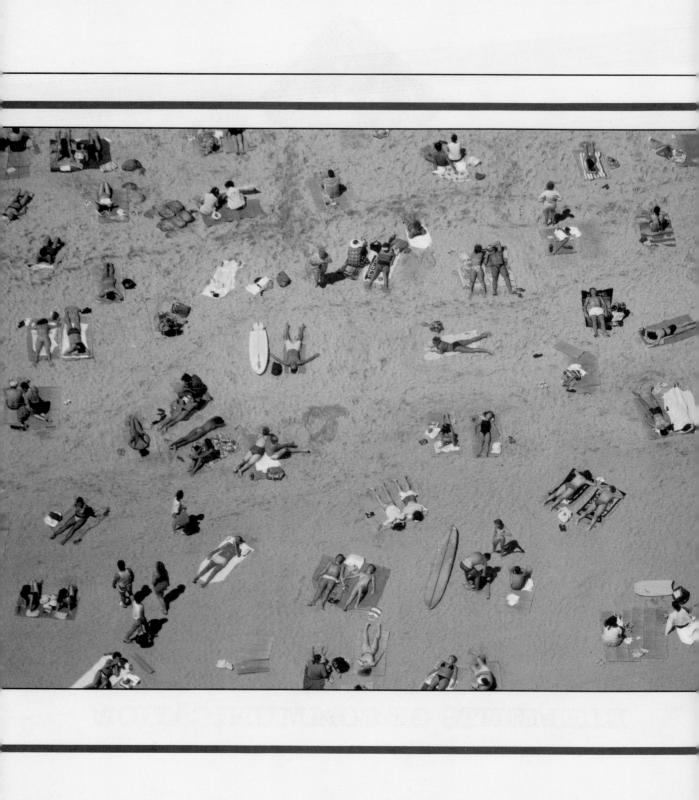

After reading this chapter, you should understand the following:

1. The working definition of communication used in *Understanding Human Communication.*

2. The types of communication discussed in this book.

3. The needs satisfied by communication.

4. The value of a communication model.

5. The elements of the transactional communication model introduced in this chapter.

6. Five common misconceptions about communication.

You should be able to do the following:

1. Give specific examples of the various types of needs you attempt to satisfy by communicating.

2. Identify the elements of the communication model in this chapter as they apply to an incident in your life.

3. Identify the misconceptions about communication you have held and suggest a more accurate belief for each.

KEY TERMS

affection
channel
communication
control
decoding
dyadic
  communication
encoding
environment
external noise
feedback
inclusion
interactive
  communication
  model
intrapersonal
  communication
linear communication
  model

message
model
noise
physical need
physiological noise
psychological noise
public communication
receiver
safety need
self-actualization
  need
self-esteem need
small group
  communication
social need
symbol
transactional
  communication
  model

Human Communication: What and Why

Because this is a book about communication, it makes sense to begin by defining that term. This is not as simple as it might seem, for people use the word in a variety of ways that are only vaguely related:

◆ Family members, coworkers, and friends make such statements about their relationships as "We just can't communicate" or "We communicate perfectly."

◆ Business people talk about "office communications systems" consisting of computers, telephones, printers, and so on.

◆ Scientists study and describe communication among ants, dolphins, and other animals.

◆ Certain organizations label themselves "communications conglomerates," publishing newspapers, books, and magazines and owning radio and television stations.

There is clearly some relationship among uses such as these, but we need to narrow our focus before going on. A look at the Table of Contents of this book shows that it obviously doesn't deal with animals, computers, or newspapers. Neither is it about Holy Communion, the bestowing of a material thing, or many of the other subjects mentioned in the *Oxford English Dictionary*'s 1,200-word definition of communication.

What, then, *are* we talking about when we use the term *communication*? A survey of the ways in which scholars use the word will show that there is no single, universally accepted usage.[1] Some definitions are long and complex whereas others are brief and simple. This isn't the place to explore the differences between these conceptions or to defend one against the others. What we need is a working definition that will help us in our study. For our purposes we will say that **communication** refers to *the process of human beings responding to the face-to-face symbolic behavior of other persons.*

A point-by-point examination of this definition reveals some important characteristics of communication as we will be studying it.

Communication Is Human

In this book we'll be discussing communication between human beings. Animals clearly do communicate: Bees instruct their hive-mates about the location of food by a meaning-laden dance. Chimpanzees have been taught to express themselves with the same sign language used by deaf humans, and a few have developed impressive vocabularies. And on a more commonplace level, pet owners can testify to the variety of messages their animals can express. Although this subject of animal communication is a fascinating and an important one, it goes beyond the scope of this book.

Communication Is a Face-to-Face Activity

Written messages, like books and letters, do not require face-to-face inter-action; neither do mass media messages delivered by radio, television, or film. These types of communication are certainly important—so important that they deserve full treatment elsewhere. In this book we will focus on communication between persons who are in each other's presence.

Communication Is a Process

We often talk about communication as if it occurred in discrete, individual acts. In fact, communication is truly a continuous, ongoing process. Consider, for example, a friend's compliment about your appearance. Your interpretation of those words will depend on a long series of experiences stretching far back in time: How have others judged your appearance? How do you feel about your looks? How honest has your friend been in the past? How have you been feeling about one another recently? All this history will help shape your response to the other person's remark. In turn, the words you speak and the way you say them will shape the way your friend behaves toward you and others—both in this situation and in the future.

This simple example shows that it's inaccurate to talk about "acts" of communication as if they occurred in isolation. To put it differently, communi-cation isn't a series of incidents pasted together like photographs in a scrapbook; instead, it is more like a motion picture in which the meaning comes from the unfolding of an interrelated series of images.

Communication Is Symbolic

Symbols are used to represent things, processes, ideas, or events in ways that make communication possible. Chapter 3 discusses the nature of symbols in detail, but this idea is so important that it needs an introduction now. The most significant feature of symbols is their *arbitrary* nature. For example, there's no logical reason why the letters in *book* should stand for the object you're reading now. Speakers of Spanish would call it a *libro* whereas Germans would label it a *Buch*. Even in English, another term would work just as well as long as everyone agreed to use it in the same way. We overcome the arbitrary nature of symbols by linguistic rules and customs. Effective communication depends on agreement among people about these rules. This is easiest to see when we observe people who don't follow linguistic conventions. For example, recall how unusual the speech of children and nonnative speakers of a language often sounds.

We've already talked about words as one type of symbol. In addition, nonverbal behavior can have symbolic meaning. As with words, some nonverbal behaviors, though arbitrary, have clearly agreed-upon meanings.

The Many Meanings of "Communication"

Few words have as many meanings as *communication*. The term can refer to everything from messages on T-shirts to presidential speeches, from computer code to chimpanzee behavior. Communication has been the professional concern of philosophers, scientists (social, biological, and physical), poets, politicians, and entertainers, to name a few. Responding to this diversity, Brent Rubin asked, "How does being interested in communication differ from being interested in life?"

There are several reasons why the term *communication* has so many different meanings. Understanding them will help explain how and why this word refers to a broad range of subjects.

Interdisciplinary Heritage   Unlike most subjects, communication has captured the interest of scholars from a wide range of fields. Ever since classical times, philosophers have studied the meaning and significance of messages. In the twentieth century, social scientists have joined the field: Psychologists examine the causes and effects of communication as it relates to individuals. Sociologists and anthropologists examine how communication operates within and between societies and cultures. Political scientists explore the ways communication influences political behavior. Engineers use their skill to devise methods of conveying messages electronically. Zoologists focus on communication between animals. With this kind of diversity, it's no surprise that *communication* can be a broad and sometimes confusing term.

Field and Activity   Sometimes the word communication refers to a field of study (of nonverbal messages or effects of televised violence on children, for example). In other cases it denotes an activity that people do. This confusion doesn't exist in most disciplines. People may study history or sociology, but they don't "historicate" or "sociologize." Having only one word that refers to both the field of study and the activity that it examines leads to confusion.

Humanity and Social Science   Unlike most disciplines, communication straddles two very different academic domains. It has one foot firmly planted in the humanities, where it shares concerns with disciplines like English and philosophy. At the same time, other scholars in the field take an approach like their colleagues in the social sciences like psychology, sociology, and anthropology. And to confuse matters even further, communication is sometimes associated with the performing arts, especially in the area of oral interpretation of literature.

Natural and Professional   Communication is a natural activity that we all engage in unconsciously. At the same time, there are professional communication experts whose specialized duties require training and skill. Careers such as marketing, public relations, broadcasting, speechmaking, counseling, journalism, and management all call for talent that goes far beyond what is required for everyday speaking and listening.

Communication and Communications   Even the name of the field is confusing. Traditionally *Communications* (with an "s") has been used when referring to activities involving technology and the mass media. *Communication* is typically used to describe face-to-face and written messages, as well as to the field as a whole. With the growth of communication technology, the two terms are being used interchangeably more often.

Communication and Human Behavior, 2d ed.
by Brent Rubin

For example, to most North Americans, placement of a thumb and first finger together while facing the palm of the hand outward stands for the idea of something being "OK." But even more than words, nonverbal behaviors are ambiguous. Does a frown signify anger or unhappiness? Does a hug stand for a friendly greeting or a symbol of the hugger's romantic interest in you? One can't always be sure. We'll discuss the nature of nonverbal communication in Chapter 5.

Communication Requires the Response of a Receiver

Sending by itself isn't sufficient to create an act of communication: There needs to be some response to a message as well. To understand this point, think of a radio station broadcasting late at night without a single listener tuned in. One needn't argue about trees falling in an unpopulated forest to agree that no communication has occurred here. In the same way, a speaker talking at one or more people who aren't listening isn't communicating—at least by our definition.

Ideally we hope that others receive and understand our messages exactly as we intend them; but for our purposes we'll say that this doesn't have to occur for communication to take place. There are many other types of receiver response that qualify as part of the communication process. Sometimes a person who isn't your target receives a message, as when a bystander overhears you muttering about matters that weren't intended for others' ears. In other cases, the intended receiver does, in fact, pick up a message but interprets it incorrectly, as when an overly sensitive friend takes your joking insults seriously. Finally, there are cases where no one seems to have received your message, but where your behavior has created an internal, unobservable response in someone else. We have known students who appeared to be daydreaming through our lecture but who, when questioned, prove to have been listening carefully.

◆ TYPES OF COMMUNICATION

Within the domain of face-to-face human interaction, there are several types of communication. Each occurs in a different context. Despite the features all share, each has its own characteristics.

Intrapersonal Communication

By definition, **intrapersonal communication** means communicating with oneself. You can tune into one way that each of us communicates internally by listening to the little voice that lives in your mind. Take a moment and listen to what it is saying. Try it now, before reading on. Did you hear it? It may have been saying something like "What little voice? I don't have any little voice!" This voice is the "sound" of your thinking.

Drawing by W. Miller © 1984 The New Yorker Magazine, Inc.

We don't always think in verbal terms, but whether the process is apparent or not, the way we mentally process information influences our interaction with others. Thus, even though intrapersonal communication doesn't fit the "face-to-face" element of our definition of communication, it does affect those forms of interaction. You can understand the role of intrapersonal communication by imagining your thoughts in each of the following situations.

◆ You are planning to approach a stranger who you would like to get to know better.

◆ You pause a minute and look at the audience before beginning a ten-minute speech.

◆ The boss yawns while you are asking for a raise.

◆ A friend seems irritated lately, and you're not sure whether you are responsible.

The way you handle all of these situations would depend on the intrapersonal communication that precedes or accompanies your overt behavior. Much of Chapter 2 deals with the perception process in everyday situations, and part of Chapter 13 focuses on the intrapersonal communication that can minimize anxiety when you deliver a speech.

Dyadic Communication

Social scientists call two persons interacting a **dyad,** and they often use the adjective **dyadic** to describe this type of communication.[2] Dyadic communication is often called *interpersonal,* but not all two-person interaction meets the definition of that term that you will read in Chapter 6. In fact, you will learn that the qualities that characterize interpersonal communication aren't limited to twosomes. They can be present in threesomes, or even in small groups.

Dyads are the most common communication setting. One study revealed that college students spend almost half of their total communication time interacting with one other person.[3] Observations in a variety of settings ranging from playgrounds, train depots, shopping malls, and other settings shows that most communication is dyadic in nature.[4] Even communication within larger groups (think of classrooms, parties, and families as examples) consists of multiple, often shifting dyadic encounters.

Small Group Communication

In **small group communication** every person can participate actively with the other members. Small groups are a common fixture of everyday life. Your family is a group. So is an athletic team, a collection of fellow workers, and a group of students working on a class project.

Whatever their makeup, small groups possess characteristics that are not present in a dyad.[5] For instance, two or more members of a group can form a coalition to defend their position against other members, while in a dyad the members face each other on their own, without support from others. In a group, the majority of members can put pressure on those in the minority to conform, either consciously or unconsciously; but in a dyad no such pressures exist. Conformity pressures can also be comforting, leading group members to take risks that they would not dare if they were alone or in a dyad. With their greater size, groups also have the ability to be more creative than dyads. Finally, communication in groups is affected strongly by the type of leader who is in a position of authority. Groups are such an important communication setting that Chapters 8 and 9 focus exclusively on them. In addition, part of Chapter 7 describes how communication operates in family groups, and Chapter 10 discusses communication on the job, where working in groups is common.

Public Communication

Public communication occurs when a group becomes too large for all members to contribute. One characteristic of public communication is an unequal amount of speaking. One or more people are likely to deliver their remarks to the remaining members, who act as an audience. This leads to a second characteristic of public settings: limited verbal feedback. The audience isn't able to talk back a two-way conversation the way they might in a dyadic or small group setting. This doesn't mean that speakers operate in a vacuum when delivering their remarks. Audiences often have a chance to ask questions and offer brief comments, and their nonverbal reactions offer a wide range of clues about their reception of the speaker's remarks.

Public speakers usually have a greater chance to plan and structure their remarks than do communicators in smaller settings. For this reason, several chapters of *Understanding Human Communication* describe the steps you can take to prepare and deliver an effective speech.

◆ FUNCTIONS OF COMMUNICATION

Now that we have a working understanding of the term *communication,* it is important to discuss why we will spend so much time exploring this subject. Perhaps the strongest argument for studying communication is its central role in our lives. The amount of time we spend communicating is staggering. In one study, researchers measured the amount of time a sample group of college students spent on various activities.[6] They found that the subjects spent an average of over 61 percent of their waking hours engaged in some form of communication. Whatever one's occupation, the results of such a study would not be too different. Most of us are surrounded by others, trying to understand them and hoping that they understand us: family, friends, coworkers, teachers, and strangers.

There's a good reason why we speak, listen, read, and write so much: Communication satisfies most of our needs.

Elements of Communication

Physical Needs

Communication is so important that it is necessary for physical health. In fact, evidence suggests that an absence of satisfying communication can even jeopardize life itself. Medical researchers have identified a wide range of hazards that result from a lack of close relationships. For instance:

1. Socially isolated people are two to three times more likely to die prematurely than are those with strong social ties. The type of relationship doesn't seem to matter: Marriages, friendship, religious and community ties all seem to increase longevity.[7]
2. Divorced men (before age seventy) die from heart disease, cancer, and strokes at double the rate of married men. Three times as many die from hypertension; five times as many commit suicide; seven times as many die from cirrhosis of the liver; and ten times as many die from tuberculosis.[8]
3. The rate of all types of cancer is as much as five times higher for divorced men and women, compared to their single counterparts.[9]
4. Poor communication can contribute to coronary disease. One Swedish study examined thirty-two pairs of identical twins. One sibling in each pair had heart disease whereas the other was healthy. The researchers found that the obesity, smoking habits, and cholesterol levels of the healthy and sick twins did not differ significantly. Among the significant differences, however, were "poor childhood and adult interpersonal relationships": the ability to resolve conflicts and the degree of emotional support given by others.[10]
5. The likelihood of death increases when a close relative dies. In one Welsh village, citizens who had lost a close relative died within one year at a rate more than five times greater than those who had not suffered from a relative's death.[11]

Research like this demonstrates the importance of satisfying personal relationships. Remember: Not everyone needs the same amount of contact, and the quality of communication is almost certainly as important as the quantity. The important point here is that personal communication is essential for our well-being. In other words, "people who need people" aren't "the luckiest people in the world" . . . they're the *only* people!

Ego Needs

Communication does more than enable us to survive. It is the way—indeed, the *only* way we learn who we are. As you'll read in Chapter 2, our sense of identity comes from the way we interact with other people. Are we smart or stupid, attractive or ugly, skillful or inept? The answers to these questions don't come from looking in the mirror. We decide who we are based on how others react to us.

Deprived of communication with others, we would have no sense of identity. In his book *Bridges, Not Walls*, John Stewart dramatically illustrates this fact by citing the case of the famous "Wild Boy of Aveyron," who spent his early

◆ Whether the consequence of a mental attitude or a living condition, loneliness affects millions, usually for the worse. Death certificates read heart attack, cancer, or suicide; but coroners are missing the point. With no one to love or to love us, we tend to smoke, drink, brood, or simply cry ourselves into earlier graves.

Don E. Hamachek
Encounters with Others

childhood without any apparent human contact. The boy was discovered in January 1800 while digging for vegetables in a French village garden. He showed no behaviors one would expect in a social human. The boy could not speak but uttered only weird cries. More significant than this absence of social skills was his lack of any identity as a human being. As author Roger Shattuck put it, "The boy had no human sense of being in the world. He had no sense of himself as a person related to other persons."[12] Only after the influence of a loving "mother" did the boy begin to behave—and, we can imagine, think of himself as a human.

Like the boy of Aveyron, each of us enters the world with little or no sense of identity. We gain an idea of who we are from the way others define us. As Chapter 2 explains, the messages we receive in early childhood are the strongest, but the influence of others continues throughout life.

List the needs you have attempted to satisfy by communicating during a recent twenty-four hour period. Because describing every need-satisfying act would call for writing a small book, choose a sample of incidents representing each of the categories described in this chapter.

a. What encounters may have affected your physical health, either positively or negatively?
b. What messages have helped shape your identity, either confirming or changing your self-concept?
c. What exchanges have satisfied your social needs for inclusion, control, and affection?
d. What practical needs have you met by communicating with others?

Social Needs

Besides helping define who we are, communication is the way we relate socially with others. Psychologist William Schutz describes three types of social needs we strive to fulfill by communicating.[13] The first is **inclusion,** the need to feel a sense of belonging to some personal relationship. Inclusion needs are sometimes satisfied by informal alliances: the friends who study together, a group of runners, or neighbors who help one another with yard work. In other cases, we get a sense of belonging from formal relationships: everything from religious congregations to a job to marriage.

A second type of social need is the desire for **control**—the desire each of us has to influence others, to feel some sense of power over our world. Some types of control are obvious, such as the boss or team captain whose directions make things happen. Much control, however, is more subtle. Experts in child development tell us that preschoolers who insist on staying up past bedtime or having a treat in the supermarket may be less concerned with the issue at hand than with knowing that they have at least some ability to make things happen.[14] In this case, even driving a parent crazy can satisfy the need for control. This answers the parent's question "Why are you being so stubborn?"

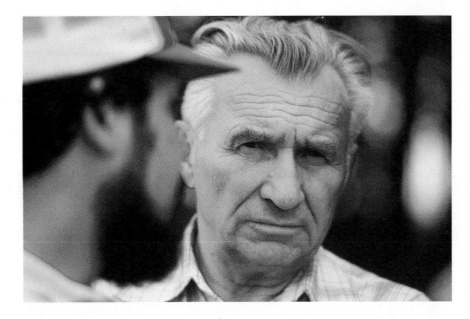

◆ *See that man over there?*
Yes.
Well, I hate him.
But you don't know him.
That's why I hate him.

Gordon Allport
The Nature of Prejudice

The third social need is **affection**—a desire to care for others and know that they care for us. Affection, of course, is critical for most of us. Being included and having power aren't very satisfying if the important people in our lives don't care for us.

Practical Needs

We shouldn't overlook the everyday, important functions communication serves. Communication is the tool that lets us tell the hair stylist to take just a little off the sides, the doctor where it hurts, and the plumber that the broken pipe needs attention *now!* Communication is the means of learning important information in school.[15] It is the method you use to convince a prospective employer that you're the best candidate for a job, and it is the way to persuade the boss you deserve a raise. The list of common but critical jobs performed by communicating goes on and on, and it's worth noticing that the inability to express yourself clearly and effectively in every one of the preceding examples can prevent you from achieving your goal.

Psychologist Abraham Maslow suggested that human needs such as the preceding ones fall into five categories, each of which must be satisfied before we concern ourselves with the following ones.[16] As you read on, think about the ways in which communication is often necessary to satisfy each need. The most basic of these needs are **physical:** sufficient air, water, food, and rest and the ability to reproduce as a species. The second of Maslow's needs involves **safety:** protection from threats to our well-being. Beyond physical and safety concerns are the **social** needs we have mentioned already. Even beyond these, Maslow suggests that each of us has **self-esteem** needs: the desire to

**Human Communication:
What and Why**

believe that we are worthwhile, valuable people. The final category of needs described by Maslow involves **self-actualization:** the desire to develop our potential to the maximum, to become the best person we can be.

◆ MODELING COMMUNICATION

So far we have introduced a basic definition of communication and seen the functions communication performs. This information is useful, but it only begins to describe the subject. One way to understand more about communication is to examine a model of that process.

Why Use Models?

A **model** is a simplified representation of some process. For instance, consider what a model of "digestion" might look like. At one end of a page we could draw a mouth with food going into it, followed by tubes running into a baglike object representing the stomach. To represent the intestines, we could draw a coiled hose connected at the top end to the stomach.

   Whereas this representation may begin to tell us something about digestion, it also tells us a great deal about the following characteristics of models:

1. *Models can represent the relevant elements of a process.* Even though our diagram is crude, it does provide a good introduction to the basic parts of the digestive tract.
2. *Models organize the parts of a process and indicate how they are related to each other.* For example, an uninformed viewer would learn from our drawing that the stomach is below the esophagus and above the intestines.
3. *Models simplify a complex event.* This simplification helps promote understanding. It's certainly easier for an uninitiated learner to start exploring the digestion process with a simple model than by looking into the entire process in all its complexity.
4. *Models provide an opportunity to look at a familiar process in a new way.* By doing so, models sometimes make us aware that we've been operating on misconceptions. For instance, adding an explanation of what goes on in each part of our digestion model makes clear how little digestion actually goes on in the stomach, contrary to the belief of many people.

Whereas models clearly offer several advantages, they also suffer from a number of potential drawbacks. First, in an attempt to make a complex event simple, a model may oversimplify and lead viewers into thinking that the event itself is simple. This mistaken assumption has the highest probability of occurring if a learner has little information on what the event is really like. For instance, someone not versed in physics might actually believe that an atom is quite similar in form and motion to marbles spinning around a grapefruit.

   It's also important to remember that a model is an analogy, nothing more. The danger of confusing the map with the territory is illustrated by the story of an elementary school child who, having studied geography by using the classroom map, was surprised to discover that Spain was not a pink country, France green, and so on.

Finally, a model can cause us to stop thinking about the process that it represents and can cause us to conclude that we know everything significant about the subject. This mistake is termed *premature closure* and, of course, should be avoided.

A Communication Model

Keeping the advantages and dangers of models in mind, we can begin to build a representation of what goes on in the process of communication. Because we need to begin somewhere, let's start with your wanting to express an idea (see Figure 1–1). If you think about it for a moment, you'll realize that most ideas you have don't come to you already put into words. Rather, they're more like mental images, often consisting of unverbalized feelings (anger, excitement, and the like), intentions (wants, desires, needs), or even mental pictures (such as how you want a job to look when it is finished). We can represent your mental image in Figure 1–1 like this:

FIGURE 1–1

Because people aren't mind readers, you have to translate this mental image into symbols (usually words) that others can understand. No doubt you can recall times when you actually shuffled through a mental list of words to pick exactly the right ones to explain an idea. This process, called **encoding,** goes on every time we speak (see Figure 1–2). Chapter 3 will deal in some detail with the problems and skills of being an effective encoder.

FIGURE 1–2

Once you have encoded an idea, the next step is to send it. We call this step the **message** phase of our model. The message includes both the speaker's planned words and actions and the unplanned, sometimes unconscious signals sent. There are a number of ways a message can be delivered. For instance, you might express yourself in a letter, over the telephone or in a face-to-face conversation. In this sense, writing, telecommunication, and speaking are three of the **channels** through which we send messages (see Figure 1–3). In addition to these channels, we transfer our thoughts and

FIGURE 1–3

feelings by touch, posture, gestures, distance, clothing, and many other ways described in Chapter 5.

All communication channels aren't equal: The method of communication often influences the type of interaction that occurs between people. For instance, one study revealed that students were more likely to ask questions of professors through computer networks than in person.[17] Another showed that some discussions carried on by computer hookups are more argumentative than face-to-face sessions, but also more equal in terms of shared discussion time and decision making.[18]

When your message reaches another person, much the same process we described earlier occurs in reverse (see Figure 1–4). The **receiver** must make some sense out of the symbols you've sent by **decoding** them back into feelings, intentions, or thoughts that mean something.

FIGURE 1–4

A **linear communication model** characterizes communication as a one-way activity in which information flows from sender to receiver. In a linear model, communication seems like something that an active sender "does" to a passive receiver. A linear model suggests that messages exist in a sender and that conveying meaning is the sender's role alone. As some scholars metaphorically suggest, a linear model implies that communication is like giving or getting an inoculation: Ideas and feelings are prepared in some form of message and then injected in a straight line into a receiver. Although some types of messages (print and broadcast media, for example) appear to flow in a one-way manner, a linear model is not a complete or accurate representation of any type of communication, especially the interpersonal variety. What's missing? The model we've just examined ignores the fact that receivers *react* to messages.

Consider, for instance, the significance of a friend's yawn as you describe your vacation exploits. Imagine the blush you might see as a listener's response to one of your raunchier jokes. Nonverbal behaviors like these show that most communication—especially in interpersonal situations—is two-way. The discernible response of a receiver to a sender's message is called **feedback.** Not all feedback is nonverbal, of course. Sometimes it is oral, as when you ask questions to clarify a speaker's remarks. In other cases, it can be written, as when you demonstrate your knowledge of this material to your instructor on an examination. When we add the element of feedback, we have an image of communication as pictured in the **interactive communication model** in Figure 1–5. A sender formulates and transmits a message to a receiver, who, in turn, formulates and sends a response.

The interactive model suggests that, after a period of interaction, the mental images of the sender and receiver ought to match. If this happens, we can say that an act of successful communication has occurred. However, as

Elements of Communication

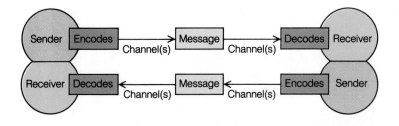

FIGURE 1—5

you know from your own experience, things often go wrong somewhere between the sender and the receiver. For instance,

Your constructive suggestion is taken as criticism.

Your carefully phrased question is misunderstood.

Your friendly joke is taken as an insult.

Your hinted request is missed entirely.

And so it often goes. Why do such misunderstandings occur? To answer this question, we need to add more details to our model. We recognize that, without several more crucial elements, our model would not represent the world.

First, it's important to recognize that communication always takes place in an **environment.** By this term we do not mean simply a physical location but also the personal history that each person brings to a conversation. The problem here is that each of us has a different environment because of our differing backgrounds. Although we certainly have some experiences in common, we also see each situation in a unique way. For instance, consider how two individuals' environments would differ if

A were well rested and *B* were exhausted;

A were rich and *B* were poor;

A were rushed and *B* had nowhere special to go;

A had lived a long, eventful life and *B* were young and inexperienced; or

A were passionately concerned with the subject and *B* were indifferent to it.

Obviously this list could go on and on. The problem of differing environments is critical to effective communication. Even now, though, you can see from just these few items that the world is a different place for sender and receiver. We can represent this idea in Figure 1—6 with a revised model.

Notice that the environments of *A* and *B* overlap. This overlapping represents those things that our communicators have in common. This point is important because it is through our shared knowledge and experiences that we are able to communicate. For example, you are able at least partially to understand the messages we are writing on these pages because we share the same language, however imprecise it often may be.

Different environments aren't the only cause of ineffective communication. Social scientists use the term **noise** to label other forces that interfere with the process and point out that it can occur in every stage. There are three types of

Human Communication: What and Why

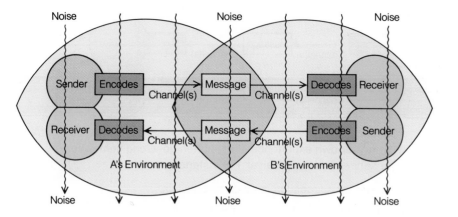

FIGURE 1—6

noise that can block communication—external, physiological, and psychological. **External noise** includes those factors outside the receiver that make it difficult to hear, as well as many other kinds of distractions. For instance, too much cigarette smoke in a crowded room might make it hard for you to pay attention to another person, and sitting in the rear of an auditorium might make a speaker's remarks unclear. External noise can disrupt communication almost anywhere in our model—in the sender, channel, message, or receiver. **Physiological noise** involves biological factors in the receiver that interfere with accurate reception: hearing loss, illness, and so on.

Psychological noise refers to forces within a communicator that interfere with the ability to express or understand a message accurately. For instance, an outdoor person might exaggerate the size and number of the fish he caught in order to convince himself and others of his talents. In the same way, a student might become so upset upon learning that she failed a test that she would be unable (perhaps *unwilling* is a better word) to understand clearly where she went wrong. Psychological noise is such an important communication problem that we have devoted much of Chapter 10 to investigating its most common form, defensiveness.

Even with the addition of these new elements our model isn't completely satisfactory. Notice that the preceding discussion portrays communication as a static activity. It suggests that there are discrete "acts" of communication that begin and end in identifiable places and that a sender's message "causes" some "effect" in a receiver. Furthermore, it suggests that at any given moment a person is either sending or receiving.

In fact, none of these characterizations is valid for interpersonal communication. The activity of communicating is usually not interactive but transactional. A **transactional communication model** differs from the more simplistic ones we've already discussed in several ways.

First, a transactional model reveals that communicators usually send and receive messages simultaneously, so that the images of sender and receiver should not be separated as if a person were doing only one or the other, but rather, superimposed and redefined as "participants."[19] At a given moment, we are capable of receiving, decoding, and responding to another person's

Elements of Communication

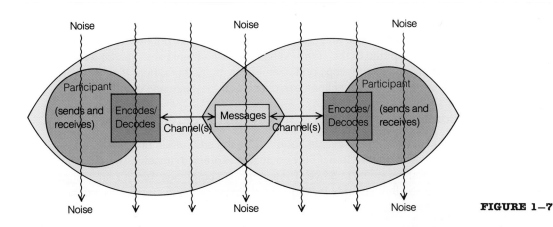

FIGURE 1—7

behavior while at the same time that other person is receiving and responding to ours. Consider, for example, what might occur when you and a housemate negotiate household chores. As soon as you begin to hear (receive) the words sent by your partner, "I want to talk about cleaning the bathroom . . . " you grimace and clench your jaw (sending a nonverbal message of your own while receiving the verbal one). This reaction causes your partner to interrupt himself, defensively sending a new message: "Now wait a minute . . . ."

Besides illustrating the simultaneous nature of face-to-face interaction, this example reminds us that it's difficult to isolate a single discrete "act" of communication from the events that precede and follow it. Your partner's comment about cleaning the bathroom (and the way it was presented) probably grew from exchanges you had in the past. Likewise, the way you'll act toward one another in the future depends on the outcome of this conversation. Although Figure 1—7 does a fair job of picturing the phenomenon we call communication, an animated version, in which the environments, communicators, and messages constantly changed, would be an even better way of capturing the process. You can also see that communication is not something that people do *to* one another but a process in which they create a relationship by interacting *with* each other.

◆ CLARIFYING MISCONCEPTIONS ABOUT COMMUNICATION

Having spent time talking about what communication is, we ought also identify some things it is not.[20] Recognizing these misconceptions is important, not only because they ought to be avoided by anyone knowledgeable about the subject, but also because following them can get you into personal trouble.

Communication Is Not Always a Good Thing

For most people, belief in the value of communication rates somewhere close to motherhood in their hierarchy of important values. In truth, communication is neither good nor bad in itself. Rather, its value comes from the way it is used.

Human Communication: What and Why

In this sense, communication is similar to fire: Flames in the fireplace on a cold night keep you warm and create a cozy atmosphere, but the same flames can kill if they spread to the surrounding room. Communication can be a tool for expressing warm feelings and useful facts, but under different circumstances the same words and actions can cause both physical and emotional pain.

Communication Will Not Solve All Problems

"If I could just communicate better . . . " is the sad refrain of many unhappy people who believe that if they could just express themselves better, their relationships would improve. Though this is sometimes true, it's an exaggeration to say that communicating—even communicating clearly—is a guaranteed panacea.

Use your understanding of the elements in the communication process to increase the chances of success in your own life. Identify an important message that you would like to communicate within the next week. Describe

a. The idea you want to convey and the various ways you could encode it.
b. The channels by which you could send your message.
c. The ways in which your receiver might decode the message.
d. Possible differences between your environment and that of the receiver that might make it difficult for your message to be accurately understood.
e. Likely sources of external, physiological, and psychological noise that might interfere with the communication transaction.
f. Types of feedback you can use to see whether or not you have succeeded in having your message understood.

Based upon your answers to these questions, describe the steps you can take to construct and deliver your message in the way that gives it the greatest chance of being accurately received.

More Communication Is Not Always Better

Although it's certainly true that not communicating enough is a mistake, there are also situations when *too much* communication is a mistake. Sometimes excessive communication simply is unproductive, as when we "talk a problem to death," going over the same ground again and again without making any headway. And there are times when communicating too much can actually aggravate a problem. We've all had the experience of "talking ourselves into a hole"—making a bad situation worse by pursuing it too far. As McCroskey and Wheeless put it, "More and more negative communication merely leads to more and more negative results."[21]

There are even times when *no* communication is the best course. Any good salesperson will tell you that it's often best to stop talking and let the customer think about the product. And when two people are angry and hurt, they may

"I'm so glad we've had this little talk, Earl!"

Drawing by Gahan Wilson, © 1986 The New Yorker Magazine, Inc.

say things they don't mean and will later regret. At times like these it's probably best to spend a little time cooling off, thinking about what to say and how to say it.

One key to successful communication, then, is to share an *adequate* amount of information in a *skillful* manner. Teaching you how to decide what information is adequate and what constitutes skillful behavior is one major goal of this book.

Avoid falling for the common misconceptions about communication by recalling situations described below.

a. An incident in which communication was used "skillfully" for unethical or malicious goals.

b. A problem that even the best communication could not solve.

c. A situation where more communication made matters worse, not better.

d. An incident in which two (or more) people had different meanings for the same message.

e. A situation that required highly developed communication skills to resolve.

Meanings Rest in People, Not Words

We already hinted that meanings rest in people, not in words, when we said earlier that the symbols we use to communicate are arbitrary. It's a mistake to think that, just because you use a word in one way, others will do so too. Sometimes differing interpretations of symbols are easily caught, as when we might first take the statement "He's gay" to mean the subject has homosexual preferences, only to find out that he is cheerful—and straight. In other cases, however, the ambiguity of words and nonverbal behaviors isn't so apparent . . . and thus has more far-reaching consequences. Remember, for instance, a time when someone said to you, "I'll be honest . . . ," and only later did you learn that those words hid precisely the opposite fact. In Chapter 3 you'll read a great deal more about the problems that come from mistakenly assuming that meanings rest in words.

Communication Is Not Simple

Most people assume that communication is an aptitude that people develop without the need for training—rather like breathing. After all, we've been swapping ideas with one another since early childhood, and there are lots of people who communicate pretty well without ever having had a class on the subject. Though this picture of communication as a natural ability seems accurate, it's actually a gross oversimplification.

Throughout history there have been cases of infants raised without human contact. In all these instances the children were initially unable to communicate with others when brought into society. Only after extensive teaching (and not even then in some cases) were they able to speak and understand language in ways we take for granted. But what about the more common cases of effective communicators who have had no formal training yet are skillful at creating and understanding messages? The answer to this question lies in the fact that not all education occurs in a classroom: Many people learn to communicate skillfully because they have been exposed to models of such behavior by those around them. This principle of modeling explains why children who grow up in homes with stable relationships between family members have a greater chance of developing such relationships themselves. They know how to do so because they've seen effective communication in action.

Does the existence of these good communicators mean that certain people don't need courses like the one you're taking? Hardly. Even the best communicators aren't perfect: They often suffer the frustration of being unable to get a message across effectively, and they frequently misunderstand others. Furthermore, even the most successful people you know can probably identify ways in which their relationships could profit by better communication. These facts show that communication skills are rather like athletic ability: Even the most inept of us can learn to be more effective with training and practice, and those who are talented can always become better.

◆ SUMMARY

This chapter introduced some key concepts that provide a foundation for the material that follows in the rest of the book. It explained the nature of communication as it will be studied here: a face-to-face symbolic process between human beings, in which the receiver is involved. It introduced the four types of communication that will be discussed in this book: intrapersonal, dyadic, small group, and public. The chapter described several types of needs communication satisfies: physical, ego, social, and practical.

The chapter explained the value of models as a way of understanding any process and introduced a model of human communication. It also introduced several misconceptions about communication.

◆ NOTES

1. For a survey of various perspectives on the study of communication, see *Human Communication as a Field of Study,* edited by S.S. King (Albany, N.Y.: State University of New York Press, 1989).
2. For a comprehensive discussion of dyadic communication, see W. Wilmot, *Dyadic Communication,* 3d ed. (New York: Random House, 1987).
3. L. Wheeler and J. Nelek, "Sex Differences in Social Participation," *Journal of Personality and Social Psychology* 35 (1977): 742–754.
4. J. John, "The Distribution of Free-Forming Small Group Size," *American Sociological Review* 18 (1953): 569–570.
5. F. Williams, *The New Communications,* 2d ed. (Belmont, Calif.: Wadsworth, 1989), pp. 164–165.
6. Rudolph Verderber, Ann Elder, and Ernest Weiler, "A Study of Communication Time Usage Among College Students," unpublished study, University of Cincinnati, 1976.
7. R. Narem, "Try a Little TLC," research reported in *Science* 80: 1 (1980): 15.
8. J. Lynch, *The Broken Heart: The Medical Consequences of Loneliness* (New York: Basic Books, 1977), pp. 239–242.
9. Ibid.
10. E. A. Liljefors and R. H. Rahe, "Psychosocial Characteristics of Subjects with Myocardial Infarction in Stockholm," in E. K. Gunderson and R. H. Rahe (eds.), *Life Stress Illness* (Springfield, Ill.: Charles C. Thomas, 1974), pp. 90–104.
11. W. D. Rees and S. G. Lutkins, "Mortality of Bereavement," *British Medical Journal* 4 (1967): 13.
12. R. Shattuck, *The Forbidden Experiment: The Story of the Wild Boy of Aveyron* (New York: Farrar, Straus & Giroux, 1980), p. 37.
13. W. Schutz, *The Interpersonal Underworld* (Palo Alto, Calif.: Science and Behavior Books, 1966).
14. E. H. Erikson, *Childhood and Society* (New York: Norton, 1963).
15. R. B. Rubin and E. E. Graham, "Communication Correlates of College Success: An Exploratory Investigation," *Communication Education* 37 (1988): 14–27.
16. A. H. Maslow, *Toward a Psychology of Being* (New York: Van Nostrand Reinhold, 1968).
17. D. Goleman, "The Electronic Rorschach," *Psychology Today* 17:2 (February 1983): 42.
18. Ibid., p. 41.
19. E. M. Rogers and D. L. Kincaid, *Communication Networks: Toward a New Paradigm for Research* (New York: Free Press, 1981), pp. 43–48, 63–66.
20. Adapted from J. C. McCroskey and L. R. Wheeless, *Introduction to Human Communication* (Boston: Allyn and Bacon, 1976), pp. 3–10.
21. Ibid., p. 5.

After reading this chapter, you should understand the following:

1. The communicative influences that shape the self-concept.

2. The three elements of the perception process.

3. The perceptual errors that distort perception of others.

4. The ways that culture can influence perceptions of others.

5. The importance of empathy in improving communication.

6. How self-fulfilling prophecies can influence behavior.

7. The requirements for changing one's self-concept.

You should be able to do the following:

1. Identify the ways you influence the self-concept of others and the ways significant others influence your self-concept.

2. Describe the different ways that you and at least one other person perceive an event, showing how selection, organization, and interpretation lead to the differing perceptions.

3. Identify the errors listed in this chapter that have led you to develop distorted perceptions of others.

4. Use perception checking to become more accurate in your perceptions of others' behavior.

5. Identify communication-related, self-fulfilling prophecies that you have imposed on yourself, that others have imposed on you, and that you have imposed on others.

6. List the steps you could take to change an important part of your self-concept that affects your communication.

KEY TERMS

empathy	reflected appraisal
interpretation	selection
organization	self-concept
perception checking	self-fulfilling prophecy
personality	significant other
punctuation	

Perception and the Self

A student is practicing his first assigned speech with several friends.

"This is a stupid topic," he laments. The other students sincerely assure him that the topic is an interesting one and that the speech sounds good.

Despite these reassurances, the student remains unconvinced. Later in class he becomes flustered because he believes that his speech is no good. As a result of his unenthusiastic delivery, the student receives a low grade on the assignment.

Despite her nervousness, a job candidate does her best in a job interview. She leaves the session convinced that she botched her big chance. A few days later she is surprised to receive a job offer.

At a party several guests have been emptying a keg of beer with great gusto. They are now engaged in conversation that they think is witty, but that a sober observer would find foolish. However, as there are no sober observers present, the reality of the situation is lost on the participants.

Stories like these are probably familiar to you. Yet behind this familiarity lie principles that are perhaps the most important ones in this book:

1. Two or more people often perceive an event in radically different ways.
2. The beliefs each of us holds about ourselves—our self-concept—have a powerful effect on our behavior, even when these beliefs are inaccurate.

These simple truths play a role in virtually all the important messages we send and receive. The goal of this chapter is to demonstrate the significance of these principles by describing the nature of perception and showing how it influences the way we view ourselves and how we relate to others.

◆ UNDERSTANDING THE SELF-CONCEPT

We will begin our study by examining the nature of the self-concept. We will first define that term and next go on to explore how the self-concept develops. Then after looking at the role of perception in human interaction, we will discuss how the self-concept affects communication.

Self-Concept Defined

The **self-concept** is a set of relatively stable perceptions each of us holds about ourselves. The self-concept includes our conception about what is unique about us and what makes us both similar to, and different from, others.[1] To put it differently, the self-concept is rather like a mental mirror that reflects how we view ourselves: not only physical features, but also emotional states, talents, likes and dislikes, values, and roles.

We will have more to say about the nature of the self-concept shortly, but first you will find it valuable to gain a personal understanding of how this theoretical construct applies to you. You can do so by answering a simple question: "Who are you?"

How do you define yourself? As a student? A man or woman? By your age? Your religion? Occupation?

There are many ways of identifying yourself. Take a few more moments, and list as many ways as you can to identify who you are. You'll need this list later in this chapter, so be sure to complete it now. Try to include all the characteristics that describe you:

your moods or feelings
your appearance and physical condition
your social traits
talents you possess or lack

your intellectual capacity
your strong beliefs
your social roles

Even a list of twenty or thirty terms would be only a partial description. To make this written self-portrait complete, your list would have to be hundreds—or even thousands—of words long.

Of course, not every item on such a list would be equally important. For example, the most significant part of one person's self-concept might consist of social roles whereas for another it could consist of physical appearance, health, friendships, accomplishments, or skills.

You can begin to see how important these elements are by continuing this personal experiment. Pick the ten items from your list that describe the most fundamental aspects of who you are. Rank these ten items so that the most fundamental one is in first place, with the others following in order of declining importance. Now, beginning with the tenth item, imagine what would happen if each characteristic in turn disappeared from your makeup. How would you be different? How would you feel?

For most people, this exercise dramatically illustrates just how fundamental the self-concept is. Even when the item being abandoned is an unpleasant one, it's often hard to give it up. And when they are asked to let go of their most central feelings or thoughts, most people balk. "I wouldn't be *me* without that," they insist. Of course, this proves our point: The self-concept is perhaps our most fundamental possession. Knowing who we are is essential, for without a self-concept it would be impossible to relate to the world.

◆ **Retrospectively, one can ask "Who am I?" But in practice, the answer has come before the question.**

J. M. Yinger

Communication and Development of the Self

So far we've talked about what the self-concept is; but at this point you may be asking what it has to do with the study of human communication. We can begin to answer this question by looking at how you came to possess your own self-concept.

Newborn babies come into the world with very little sense of self.[2] In the first months of life infants have no awareness of their bodies as being separate from the rest of the environment. At eight months of age, for example, a child will be surprised when a toy grabbed from the grip of another child "resists." Not until somewhere between their first and second birthday are children most able to recognize their own reflections in a mirror.[3]

Perception and the Self

You can appreciate the importance of significant others in shaping a self-concept by completing this exercise.

a. Recall an incident that occurred either recently or in the past when a person helped enhance your self-esteem by acting in a way that made you feel accepted, competent, worthwhile, important, attractive, or valued in some other way. The incident needn't have been a major one: The self-concept can be shaped by many tiny nudges as well as by a smaller number of major events.

b. Recall an incident when another person's actions lowered your self-esteem in a large or small way. The other person needn't have been acting maliciously. Behaviors often affect another's self-concept without the actor having any awareness of the act.

c. Now that you have considered how others shape your self-concept, consider an incident in which your behavior—either deliberate or unintentional—boosted another person's self-esteem. You may need the help of others to answer this question.

d. Finally, recall an incident when your actions diminished the self-esteem of another person. Were you aware of the effect of your behavior at the time?

◆ **Premier Artiste**

Watch me perform!
I walk a tightrope of
** unique design.**
I teeter, falter, recover
** And bow.**
**   You applaud.**
I run forward, backward,
** hesitate**
** And bow.**
**   You applaud.**
If you don't applaud
** I'll fall.**
Cheer me! Hurray me!
Or you push me
Down.

Lenni Shender Goldstein

**Elements of
Communication**

How does this rudimentary sense of identity grow into the rich, multidimensional self-concept you identified in the preceding section? It develops almost exclusively from communication with others. As psychologists Arthur Combs and Donald Snygg put it:

> The self is essentially a social product arising out of experience with people.... We learn the most significant and fundamental facts about ourselves from ... "reflected appraisals," inferences about ourselves made as a consequence of the ways we perceive others behaving toward us.[4]

The term **reflected appraisal,** coined by Harry Stack Sullivan,[5] is a good one, for it metaphorically describes the fact that we develop an image of ourselves from the way we think others view us. This notion of the "looking-glass self" was first introduced in 1902 by Charles H. Cooley, who suggested that we put ourselves in the position of other people and then, in our mind's eye, view ourselves as we imagine they see us.[6] In other words, we interpret (or "decode," to use the terminology of our communication model) the behavior of others, assuming that this interpretation is an accurate representation of how they view us.

The stream of messages about who we are begins early in life, long before we have developed sufficiently to think about them in any systematic way. During this prelinguistic stage the messages are nonverbal. The amount of time parents allow their infant to cry before responding can, over time, communicate how important the child is to them. Their method of handling the baby also speaks volumes: Do they affectionately play with it, joggling it gently and holding it close, or do they treat it like so much baggage, changing diapers and

Drawing by Modell; © 1985 The New Yorker Magazine, Inc.

feeding and bathing it in a brusque, impersonal manner? Does the tone of voice they use express love and enjoyment or disappointment and irritation?

As the youngster learns to speak and understand language, verbal messages—both positive and negative—also contribute to the developing self-concept. These messages continue later in life, especially when they come from what social scientists term **significant others**—people whose opinions we especially value. A teacher from long ago, a special friend or relative, or perhaps a barely known acquaintance whom you respected can all leave an imprint on how you view yourself. To see the importance of significant others, ask yourself how you arrived at your opinion of you as a student . . . as a person attractive to the opposite sex . . . as a competent worker . . . and you will see that these self-evaluations were probably influenced by the way others regarded you.

Research supports the importance of reflected appraisals. One study identified the relationship between adult attitudes toward children and the children's self-concepts.[7] The researcher first established that parents and teachers expect children from higher socioeconomic backgrounds to do better academically than socioeconomically disadvantaged youngsters. In other words, parents and teachers have higher expectations for socioeconomically advantaged students. Interestingly, when children from a higher socioeconomic class performed poorly in school their self-esteem dropped; but children from less advantaged backgrounds did not lose self-esteem. Why was there this difference? Because the parents and teachers sent messages about their disappointment to the higher status children whereas no such messages went to their less-advantaged counterparts.

Later in life the influence of significant others is less powerful.[8] The evaluations of others still influence beliefs about the self in some areas, such as physical attractiveness and popularity. In other areas, however, the looking glass of the self-concept has become distorted, so that it shapes the input of others to make it conform with our existing beliefs. For example, if your

◆ I am not what I think I am. I am not what you think I am. I am what I think you think I am.

Aaron Bleiberg and Harry Leubling

Perception and the Self

self-concept includes the element "poor student," you might respond to a high grade by thinking "I was just lucky" or "The professor must be an easy grader."

You might argue that not every part of one's self-concept is shaped by others, insisting there are certain objective facts that are recognizable by self-observation. After all, nobody needs to tell you that you are taller than others, speak with an accent, can run quickly, and so on. These facts are obvious.

Though it's true that some features of the self are immediately apparent, the *significance* we attach to them—the rank we assign them in the hierarchy of our list and the interpretation we give them—depends greatly on the opinions of others. After all, there are many of your features that are readily observable, yet you don't find them important at all because nobody has regarded them as significant.

Recently we heard a woman in her eighties describing her youth. "When I was a girl," she declared, "we didn't worry about weight. Some people were skinny and others were plump, and we pretty much accepted the bodies God gave us." Compare this attitude with what you find today: It's seldom that you pick up a popular magazine or visit a bookstore without reading about the latest diet fads, and television ads are filled with scenes of slender, happy people. As a result, you'll find many people who complain about their need to "lose a few pounds." The reason for such concern has more to do with the attention paid to slimness these days than with any increase in the number of people in the population who are overweight. Furthermore, the interpretation of characteristics such as weight depends on the way people important to us regard them. We generally see fat as undesirable because others tell us it is. In a society where obesity is the ideal (and there are such societies), a heavy person would feel beautiful. In the same way, the fact that one is single or married, solitary or sociable, aggressive or passive, takes on meaning depending on the interpretation society attaches to those traits. Thus, the importance of a given characteristic in your self-concept has as much to do with the significance you and others attach to it as with the existence of the characteristic.

The Self-Concept, Personality, and Communication

While the self-concept is an internal image we hold of ourselves, the personality is the view others hold of us. We use the notion of **personality** to describe a relatively consistent set of traits people exhibit across a variety of situations.[9] We use the notion of personality to characterize others as friendly or aloof, energetic or lazy, smart or stupid, and in literally thousands of other ways. In fact, one survey revealed almost 18,000 trait words in the English language that can be used to describe a personality.[10] People do seem to possess some innate personality traits. Psychologist Jerome Kagan reports that 10 percent of all children appear to be born with a biological disposition toward shyness.[11] Babies who stop playing when a stranger enters the room, for example, are more likely than others to be reticent and introverted as adolescents. Likewise, Kagan found that another 10 percent of infants seem to be born with especially sociable dispositions. Research with twins also suggests that personality may be at least partially a matter of physical destiny.[12]

Biologically identical twins are much more similar in sociability than are fraternal twins. These similarities are apparent not only in infancy but also when the twins have grown to adulthood, and are noticeable even when the siblings have had different experiences.

Despite its common use, the term "personality" is often an oversimplification. Much of our behavior isn't consistent. Rather, it varies from one situation to another. You may be quiet around strangers and gregarious with friends and family. You might be optimistic about your schoolwork or career and pessimistic about your romantic prospects. The term "easygoing" might describe your behavior at home, while you might be a fanatic at work. This kind of diversity isn't only common; it's often desirable. The argumentative style you use with friends wouldn't be well received by the judge in traffic court when you appeal a citation. Likewise, the affectionate behavior you enjoy with a romantic partner at home probably wouldn't be appropriate in public. As you read in Chapter 1, a wide range of behaviors is an important ingredient of communication competence. In this sense, a consistent personality can be more of a drawback than an asset—unless that personality is "flexible."

Figure 2–1 pictures the relationship between the self-concept and behavior. It illustrates how the self-concept both shapes much of our communication behavior and is affected by it. We can begin to examine the process by considering the self-concept you bring to an event.[13] Suppose, for example, that one element of your self-concept is "nervous with authority figures." That image probably comes from the evaluations of significant others in the past—perhaps teachers or former employers. If you view yourself as nervous with authority figures like these, you will probably behave in nervous ways when you encounter them in the future—in a teacher-student conference or a job interview. That nervous behavior is likely to influence how others view your personality, which in turn will shape how they respond to you—probably in ways that reinforce the self-concept you brought to the event. Finally, the responses of others will affect the way you interpret future events: other job

FIGURE 2–1
The self-concept and communication: A cyclic process. The interaction between the self-concept and communication with others can operate in both positive and negative ways.

SELF-CONCEPT Nervous with authority figures		SELF-CONCEPT Confident with authority figures
PERCEPTION OF EVENTS "They didn't think much of me."	BEHAVIOR Stammer Blush	PERCEPTION OF EVENTS "I handled that situation well."
OTHERS' RESPONSES Disapproval Unresponsive		BEHAVIOR Speak calmly and fluently
		OTHERS' RESPONSES Approval Cooperation

interviews, meetings with professors, and so on. This cycle illustrates the chicken-and-egg nature of the self-concept, which is shaped by significant others in the past, helps to govern your present behavior, and influences the way others view you.

Using Figure 2–1 on page 31 as a model, describe two patterns in your life—one positive, the other negative—that illustrate the cyclical relationship between your self-concept, behavior, others' responses, and your perception of events. For each pattern, describe

a. The way you select, organize, and interpret certain stimuli and ignore others.

b. The way you organize and punctuate the stimuli you have selected.

c. The interpretations you attach to the stimuli. Describe at least one alternate way of interpreting the same situation.

◆ PERCEPTION AND COMMUNICATION

By now it should be clear that the self-concept is not an objective characteristic, like height or hair color. Sometimes an individual's self-evaluation is unrealistically high. You might, for instance, see yourself as a witty joke teller when others can barely tolerate your attempts at humor; or you might consider yourself an excellent worker, in contrast to the employer who is thinking about firing you. In other cases, people view themselves more harshly than objective facts suggest. You may have known people, for instance, who insist they are unattractive or incompetent in spite of your honest insistence to the contrary.

Because we react to ourselves and others according to the perceptions we hold rather than objective events themselves, it is important to take a look at the process of perception and see how it influences communication.

The Perception Process

We need to begin our discussion of perception by talking about the gap between "what is" and what we know. Our idea of reality is only a partial one: The world contains far more than we are able to experience with our limited senses. Infrared photos, electron microscopes, and other technological tools reveal a world our ancestors never imagined. Certain animals can hear sounds and detect scents not apparent to humans.

Even within the realm of our senses we are only aware of a small part of what is going on around us. For instance, most people who live in large cities find that the noises of traffic, people, and construction soon fade out of awareness. Others can take a walk through the forest without distinguishing one bird's call from another or noticing the differences between various types of vegetation. On a personal level we have all had the experience of failing to notice something unusual about a friend—perhaps a new hairstyle or a sad expression—until it's called to our attention.

**Elements of
Communication**

Sometimes our failure to recognize some events while noticing others comes from not paying attention to important information. But in other cases it simply isn't possible to be aware of everything, no matter how attentive we might be: There is just too much going on.

William James said that "to the infant the world is just a big, blooming, buzzing confusion." One reason for this is the fact that infants are not yet able to sort out the myriad impressions with which we're all bombarded. As we grow, we learn to manage all this information, and as we do so, we begin to make sense out of the world.

Because this ability to organize our perceptions in a useful way is such a critical factor in our ability to function, we need to begin our study of perception by taking a closer look at this process. We can do so by examining the three steps by which we attach meaning to our experiences.[14]

◆ **For the most part we do not see first and then define; we define first and then see.**

Walter Lippmann

SELECTION As we are exposed to more input than we can possibly manage, the first step in perceiving is **selection,** the act of attending to certain stimuli in the environment. There are several factors that cause us to notice some messages and ignore others.

Stimuli that are *intense* often attract our attention. Something that is louder, larger, or brighter stands out. This explains why—other things being equal—we're more likely to remember extremely tall or short people and why someone who laughs or talks loudly at a party attracts more attention (not always favorable) than do more quiet guests.

Repetitious stimuli, repetitious stimuli, repetitious stimuli, repetitious stimuli, repetitious stimuli, repetitious stimuli also attract attention.[15] Just as a quiet but steadily dripping faucet can come to dominate our awareness, people to whom we're frequently exposed become noticeable.

ATTENTION IS ALSO FREQUENTLY RELATED TO contrast OR change IN STIMULATION. Put differently, unchanging people or things become less noticeable. This principle gives an explanation (excuse?) for why we come to take wonderful people for granted when we interact with them frequently. It's only when they stop being so wonderful or go away that we appreciate them.

Motives also determine what information we select from our environment. If you're anxious about being late for a date, you'll notice whatever clocks may be around you; and if you're hungry, you'll become aware of any restaurants, markets, and billboards advertising food in your path. Motives also determine how we perceive people. For example, someone on the lookout for a romantic adventure will be especially aware of attractive potential partners whereas the same person at a different time might be oblivious to anyone but police or medical personnel in an emergency.

ORGANIZATION After selecting information from the environment, we must **organize** it by arranging those data in some meaningful way. Many messages are ambiguous and can be organized in more than one manner. For example, consider Figure 2–2. How many ways can you view the boxes? Most people have a hard time finding more than one perspective. (There are four.) If you can't find all of them, turn to Figure 2–3 for some help.

FIGURE 2–2

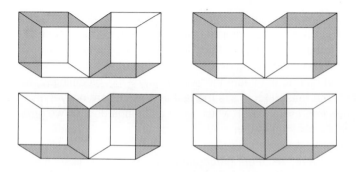

FIGURE 2—3

We can see the principle of alternative organizing patterns in human inter-action. Young children usually don't classify people according to their skin color. They are just as likely to identify a black person, for example, as being tall, wearing glasses, or being a certain age. As they become more socialized, however, they learn that one common organizing principle in today's society is race, and then their perceptions of others change.

Many interpersonal disputes arise from the different ways people organize the cause-and-effect relationship in a series of events.[16] This process of **punctuation** is easy to see in a conflict between two friends (see Figure 2—4). One says, "I get quiet when you ask me so many personal questions," while the other says, "I ask you so many personal questions because you're so quiet." Likewise, one partner might say, "I get mad because you tease me so much," while the other would say, "I tease you because you get mad so often." In situations like these, the definition of cause and effect can give the same situation a completely different appearance.

FIGURE 2—4
Punctuation. The same event can be organized in more than one way.

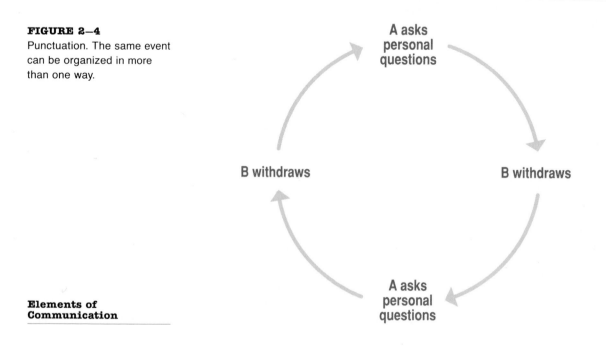

INTERPRETATION   Having organized data, we give them meaning in the process of **interpretation.** There are many ways to interpret a single event. Is the person who smiles at you across a crowded room interested in romance or simply being polite? Is a friend's kidding a sign of affection or an indication of irritation? Should you take an invitation to "Drop by any time" literally or not?

There are several factors that cause us to interpret an event in one way or another:

1. **Past Experience.** What meanings have similar events held? If, for example, you've been gouged by landlords in the past, you might be skeptical about an apartment manager's assurances that careful house-keeping will ensure the refund of your cleaning deposit.

2. **Assumptions About Human Behavior.** "People generally do as little work as possible to get by." "In spite of their mistakes, people are doing the best they can." Beliefs like these will shape the way we interpret another's actions.

3. **Expectations.** Anticipation shapes interpretations. If you imagine that your boss is unhappy with your work, you'll probably feel threatened by a request to "see me in my office first thing Monday morning." On the other hand, if you imagine that your work will be rewarded, your weekend will probably be a pleasant one as you anticipate a reward from the boss.

4. **Knowledge.** If you know that a friend has just been jilted by a lover or been fired from a job, you'll interpret her aloof behavior differently than if you were unaware of what had happened. If you know that an instructor speaks sarcastically to all students, then you won't be as likely to take any such remarks personally.

5. **Personal Moods.** When you're feeling insecure, the world is a very different place from what it is when you're confident. The same goes for happiness and sadness or any other opposing emotions. The way we feel determines how we interpret events.

Accuracy and Inaccuracy in Person Perception

Not all interpretations are accurate. Research has uncovered several common perceptual errors we need to guard against if we are to gain a clear under-standing of ourselves and others.[17]

WE ARE INFLUENCED BY WHAT IS MOST OBVIOUS   The error of being influenced by what is most obvious is understandable. As you read earlier, we select stimuli from our environment that are noticeable: intense, repetitious, unusual, or otherwise attention-grabbing. The problem is that the most obvious factor is not necessarily the only cause—or the most significant one for an event. For example:

◆ When two children (or adults, for that matter) fight, it may be a mistake to blame the one who lashes out first. Perhaps the other one was at least equally responsible, teasing or refusing to cooperate.

Perception and the Self

◆ You might complain about an acquaintance whose malicious gossiping or arguing has become a bother, forgetting that, by putting up with that kind of behavior, you have been at least partially responsible.

◆ You might blame an unhappy working situation on the boss, overlooking other factors beyond her control such as a change in the economy, the policy of higher management, or demands of customers or other workers.

WE CLING TO FIRST IMPRESSIONS, EVEN IF WRONG Labeling people according to our first impressions is an inevitable part of the perception process. These labels are a way of making interpretations. "She seems cheerful." "He seems sincere." "They sound awfully conceited."

If they're accurate, impressions like these can be useful ways of deciding how to respond best to people in the future. Problems arise, however, when the labels we attach are inaccurate; for once we form an opinion of someone, we tend to hang onto it and make any conflicting information fit our image.

Suppose, for instance, you mention the name of your new neighbor to a friend. "Oh, I know him," your friend replies. "He seems nice at first, but it's all an act." Perhaps this appraisal is off-base. The neighbor may have changed since your friend knew him, or perhaps your friend's judgment is simply unfair. Whether the judgment is accurate or not, once you accept your friend's evaluation, it will probably influence the way you respond to the neighbor. You'll look for examples of the insincerity you've heard about . . . and you'll probably find them. Even if the neighbor were a saint, you would be likely to interpret his behavior in ways that fit your expectations. "Sure he *seems* nice," you might think, "but it's probably just a front." Of course, this sort of suspicion can create a self-fulfilling prophecy, transforming a genuinely nice person into someone who truly becomes an undesirable neighbor.

Given the almost unavoidable tendency to form first impressions, the best advice we can offer is to keep an open mind and be willing to change your opinion as events prove that the first impressions were mistaken.

WE TEND TO ASSUME OTHERS ARE SIMILAR TO US People commonly imagine others possess the same attitudes and motives that they do. For example, research shows that people with low self-esteem imagine that others view them unfavorably whereas people who like themselves imagine that others like them too.[18] The frequently mistaken assumption that others' views are similar to our own applies in a wide range of situations. For example:

◆ You've heard a raunchy joke that you found funny. You might assume that it won't offend a somewhat straight friend. It does.

◆ You've been bothered by an instructor's tendency to get off the subject during lectures. If you were a professor, you'd want to know if anything you were doing was creating problems for your students, so you decide that your instructor will probably be grateful for some constructive criticism. Unfortunately, you're wrong.

◆ You lost your temper with a friend a week ago and said some things you regret. In fact, if someone said those things to you, you would consider the relationship was finished. Imagining that your friend feels the same way, you avoid making contact. In fact, your friend feels that he was partly responsible and has avoided you because he thinks you're the one who wants to end things.

Examples like these show that others don't always think or feel the way we do and that assuming similarities exist can lead to problems. How can you find out the other person's real position? Sometimes by asking directly, sometimes by checking with others, and sometimes by making an educated guess after you've thought the matter out. All these alternatives are better than simply assuming everyone would react the way you do.

WE TEND TO FAVOR NEGATIVE IMPRESSIONS OVER POSITIVE ONES   What do you think about Harvey? He's handsome, hardworking, intelligent, and honest. He's also very conceited.

Did the last quality make a difference in your evaluation? If it did, you're not alone. Research shows that when people are aware of both the positive and

THE SATURDAY EVENING POST

"The truth is, Cauldwell, we never
see ourselves as others see us."

Perception and the Self

negative characteristics of another, they tend to be more influenced by the undesirable traits. In one study, for example, researchers found that job interviewers were likely to reject candidates who revealed negative information even when the total amount of information was highly positive.[19]

Sometimes this attitude makes sense. If the negative quality clearly outweighs any positive ones, you'd be foolish to ignore it. A surgeon with shaky hands and a teacher who hates children, for example, would be unsuitable for their jobs whatever their other virtues. But much of the time it's a bad idea to pay excessive attention to negative qualities and overlook good ones. This is the mistake some people make when screening potential friends or dates. They find some who are too outgoing or too reserved, others who aren't intelligent enough, and still others who have the wrong sense of humor. Of course, it's important to find people you truly enjoy, but expecting perfection can lead to much unnecessary loneliness.

WE BLAME INNOCENT VICTIMS FOR THEIR MISFORTUNES The blame we assign for misfortune depends on who the victim is. When others suffer, we often blame the problem on their personal qualities. On the other hand, when we're the victims, we find explanations outside ourselves. Consider a few examples:

◆ When *they* botch a job, we might think they weren't listening well or trying hard enough; when *we* make the mistake, the problem was unclear directions or not enough time.

◆ When *he* lashes out angrily, we say he's being moody or too sensitive; when *we* blow off steam, it's because of the pressure we've been under.

◆ When *she* gets caught speeding, we say she should have been more careful; when *we* get the ticket, we deny we were driving too fast or say, "Everybody does it."

There are at least two explanations for this kind of behavior. As most of us want other people to approve of us, we defend ourselves by finding explanations for our own problems that make us look good. Basically what we're doing here is saying, "It's not *my* fault." And because looking good is so often a personal goal, putting others down can be a cheap way to boost our own self-esteem, stating in effect, "I'm better than he is."

Don't misunderstand: We don't always commit the kind of perceptual errors described in this section. Sometimes, for instance, people *are* responsible for their misfortunes, and our problems are not our fault. Likewise, the most the 7x9.6obvious interpretation of a situation may be the correct one. Nonetheless, a large amount of research has proved again and again that our perceptions of others are often distorted in the ways listed here. The moral, then, is clear: Don't assume that your first judgment of a person is accurate.

Perception and Culture

Perceptual differences make communication challenging enough between members of the same culture. But when communicators come from different backgrounds, the potential for misunderstandings is even greater. Culture provides a perceptual filter that influences the way we interpret even the most simple events. This fact was demonstrated in studies exploring the domination of vision in one eye over the other.[20] Researchers used a binocular-like device that projects different images to each eye. The subjects were twelve natives of the United States and twelve Mexicans. Each was presented with ten pairs of photographs, each pair containing one picture from U.S. culture (e.g., a baseball game) and one from Mexican culture (e.g., a bullfight). After viewing each pair of images, the subjects reported what they saw. The results clearly indicated the power of culture to influence perceptions: Subjects had a strong tendency to see the image from their own background.

The same principle causes people from different cultures to interpret the same event in different ways. Blinking while another person talks may be hardly noticeable to North Americans, but the same behavior is considered impolite in Taiwan. A "V" made with fingers means victory in most of the Western world . . . as long as the palm is facing out. But in some European countries the same sign with the palm facing in roughly means "Shove it." The beckoning finger motion that is familiar to Americans is an insulting gesture in most Middle and Far Eastern countries.

Even beliefs about the very value of talk differ from one culture to another.[21] North American culture views talk as desirable and uses it for social purposes as well as to perform tasks. Silence has a negative value in this culture. It is likely to be interpreted as lack of interest, unwillingness to communicate, hostility, anxiety, shyness, or a sign of interpersonal incompatibility. Westerners are uncomfortable with silence, which they find embarrassing and awkward. Furthermore, the *kind* of talk Westerners admire is characterized by

◆ When I meet someone from another culture, I behave in the way that is natural to me, while the other behaves in the way that is natural to him or her. The only problem is that our "natural" ways do not coincide.

Raymonde Carroll

Perception and the Self

◆ When Bob, who is from Detroit, talks to his colleagues from New York City, he keeps getting interrupted because he waits longer than they between turns. But in conversations with Athabaskan Indians in Alaska, where he works, he finds that he is doing all the talking—because Athabaskans expect longer pauses between turns than he does. With New Yorkers, Bob is a slow talker; with Athabaskans, he's a fast talker.

A woman from Texas went to Washington D.C. for a job in dormitory administration. When the dorm staff got together for meetings, she kept searching for the right time to break in—and never found it. Although back home she was considered outgoing and confident, in Washington she was perceived as shy and retiring. When she was evaluated at the end of a year, she was told to take an assertiveness-training course because of her inability to speak up.

That's why slight differences in conversational style—tiny little things like microseconds of a pause—can have enormous impact on your life. These little signals make up the mechanics of conversation, and when they're even slightly off, conversation is thrown off—or even cut off. The result in this case was a judgment of psychological problems—even in the mind of the woman herself, who really wondered what was wrong with her and signed up for assertiveness training.

Deborah Tannen
That's Not What I Meant

---

straightforwardness and honesty. Being indirect or vague—"beating around the bush," it might be labeled—has a negative connotation.

On the other hand, most Asian cultures discourage the expression of thoughts and feelings. Silence is valued, as Taoist sayings indicate: "In much talk there is great weariness," or "One who speaks does not know; one who knows does not speak." Unlike Westerners who are uncomfortable with silence, Japanese and Chinese believe that remaining quiet is the proper state when there is nothing to be said. To Easterners a talkative person is often considered a show-off or insincere. And when an Asian does speak up on social matters, the message is likely to be phrased indirectly to "save face" for the recipient.

It is easy to see how these different views of speech and silence can lead to communication problems when people from different cultures meet. Both the talkative Westerner and the silent Asian are behaving in ways they believe are proper, yet each views the other with disapproval and mistrust. Only when they recognize the different standards of behavior can they adapt to one another, or at least understand and respect their differences.

Perceptual differences are just as important right at home when members of different subcultures interact. Failure to recognize subcultural differences can lead to unfortunate and unnecessary misunderstandings. For example, an uninformed Anglo teacher or police officer might interpret the downcast expression of a Latino female as a sign of avoidance, or even dishonesty, when in fact this is the proper behavior in her culture for a female being addressed by an older man. To make direct eye contact in such a case would be considered undue brashness or even a sexual come-on.

Elements of Communication

Eye contact also differs in traditional black and white cultures. Whereas whites tend to look away from a conversational partner while speaking and at the other person while listening, blacks do just the opposite, looking at their companion more when talking and less when listening.[22] This difference can cause communication problems without either person's realizing the cause. For instance, whites are likely to use eye contact as a measure of how closely the other person is listening: The more others look, the more they seem to be paying attention. A white speaker, therefore, might interpret a black partner's lack of eye contact as a sign of inattention or rudeness when quite the opposite could be true.

Subcultural differences can be quite subtle. For example, when meeting with academic counselors, Latinos expressed a desire to be respected as members of their own culture as well as individuals. On the other hand, blacks preferred to be acknowledged as individuals rather than being identified as members of an ethnic group.[23]

Interview a member of another culture or subculture. Find out how that person views communication with a member of your culture or subculture in each of the following situations:

a. Being stopped by a police officer for a traffic violation.
b. Being asked for a date.
c. Encountering one another on a lonely, dark street at night.
d. Being asked by a professor to stay after class.
e. Being assigned as partners for a six-week class project.

Ask how your partner would view each of these situations differently if the other person involved was a member of the same culture or subculture.

Empathy Defined

Empathy is the ability to recreate another person's perspective; to experience the world from the other's point of view. As we'll use the term here, empathy involves two dimensions. On the cognitive level, empathy means *understanding* the other's perspective—not as a judge or critic, but from the same point of view as the person holding it. This kind of understanding requires a suspension of judgment, so that for the moment you set aside your own opinions and take on those of the other person. Besides cognitive understanding, empathy has an *emotional* dimension. An empathic communicator momentarily feels as the other person does. In other words, empathy requires you to *experience* the other's perception—in effect, to become that person temporarily.*

It is easy to confuse empathy with sympathy, but the concepts are different in two important ways. First, sympathy means you feel compassion *for* another person in his or her predicament, whereas empathy means you have a per-

---

*Technically speaking, *empathy* is the ability to experience *emotions* similar to another person's whereas *decentering* or *role taking* is the ability to experience the other's thoughts as well. In practice, however, *empathy* is used as the global, all-purpose term.

BLOOM COUNTY by Berke Breathed © 1989, Washington Post Writers Group. Reprinted with permission.

sonal sense of what that predicament is like. Consider the difference between sympathizing with an unwed mother or a homeless person and empathizing with them—imagining what it would be like to be in their position. Despite your concern, sympathy lacks the degree of identification that empathy entails. When you sympathize it is the other's confusion, joy, or pain. When you empathize, the experience becomes your own, at least for the moment. Both perspectives are important ones, but empathy is clearly the more complete of the two.

Empathy is different from sympathy in another way. We only sympathize with people whom we pity, whereas it's possible to empathize without feeling sympathy. You can empathize with a difficult relative, a rude stranger, or even a criminal, without feeling much sympathy for them. Empathizing allows you to understand another person's motives without requiring you to agree with them. After empathizing, you will almost certainly understand them better, but sympathy won't always follow.

Total empathy is impossible to achieve. Completely understanding another person's point of view is simply too difficult a task for humans with different backgrounds and limited communication skills. Nonetheless, it is possible to get a strong sense of what the world looks like through another person's eyes.

The value of empathy is demonstrated by the results of a simple experiment.[24] In this study, college students were asked to list their impression of people either shown in a videotaped discussion or described in a short story. Half the students were instructed to empathize with the person as much as possible, and the other half were not given any instructions about empathizing. The results were impressive: The students who did not practice empathy were prone to explain the person's behavior in terms of personality characteristics. For example, they might have explained a cruel statement by saying that the speaker was mean, or they might have attributed a divorce to the partners' lack of understanding. The empathic students, on the other hand, were more aware of possible elements in the situation that might have contributed to the reaction. For instance, they might have explained a person's unkind behavior in terms of job pressures or personal difficulties. In other words, practicing empathy seems to make people more tolerant.

Elements of Communication

Choose a disagreement you presently have with another person or group. The disagreement might be a personal one—such as an argument about how to settle a financial problem or who is to blame for a present state of affairs—or it might be a dispute over a contemporary public issue, such as the right of women to obtain abortions on demand or the value of capital punishment.

a. In 300 words or so, describe your side of the issue. State why you believe as you do, just as if you were presenting your position to an important jury.

b. Now take 300 words or so to describe in the first-person singular how the other person sees the same issue. For instance, if you are a religious person, write this section as if you were an atheist: For a short while get in touch with how the other person feels and thinks.

c. Now show the description you wrote in step b to your "opponent," the person whose beliefs are different from yours. Have that person read your account and correct any statements that don't reflect his or her position accurately. Remember, you're doing this so that you can more clearly understand how the issue looks to the other person.

d. Make any necessary corrections in the account you wrote in step c, and again show it to your partner. When your partner agrees that you understand his or her position, have your partner sign your paper to indicate this.

e. Now record your conclusions to this experiment. Has this perceptual shift made any difference in how you view the issue or how you feel about your partner?

You might argue here, "Why should I be more tolerant? Maybe behavior I disapprove of *is* due to the other person's personality defects and not just a result of outside factors. Maybe people are selfish, lazy, or stupid much of the time." Perhaps so, but research clearly shows that we are much more charitable when finding explanations for our own behavior.[25] When explaining our actions, we are quick to suggest situational causes: "I was tired." "She started it." "The instructions weren't clear." In other words, we often excuse ourselves by saying, "It wasn't my fault!" As we've already said, we're less forgiving when we judge others. Perhaps becoming more empathetic can help even the score a bit, enabling us to treat others at least as kindly as we treat ourselves.

REQUIREMENTS FOR EMPATHY   Empathy may be valuable, but it isn't always easy. In fact, research shows that it's hardest to empathize with people who are different from us radically: in age, sex, socioeconomic status, intelligence, and so forth.[26] In order to make the kind of perceptual leaps we are talking about, you need to develop several skills and attitudes.

Open-mindedness   Perhaps the most important ingredient of empathy is the ability and disposition to be open-minded—to set aside for the moment your own beliefs, attitudes, and values and consider those of the other person.

Perception and the Self

TRYING ON OLD AGE

How would you like to travel through time? That is, how would you like a glimpse into your golden years? That's the opportunity students are getting in psychologist Randall Wight's class on aging and human development.

Wight asked students at Ouachita Baptist University to put together a costume that would make them look like senior citizens to casual observers. To create the illusion of age, Wight suggested wearing earplugs to reduce hearing, wrapping joints with elastic bandages to create stiffness and using or discarding glasses to impair eyesight.

The students put in five hours of role-playing as older versions of themselves. They also submitted descriptions and ratings of the exercise as well as photographs of how they looked before and after donning their costumes.

Most of the students gained valuable insights during their sojourn in old age. Even such mundane activities as walking across the street took on new meanings, as one student observed: "With our legs wrapped, we walked considerably slower than most people. Inevitably, cars had to wait on us . . . not only do you feel a bother to other people, you worry about your life."

One student described how it felt to be ignored, while another was accosted by a group of boys in a passing car who screamed insults and demanded money.

Not all the experiences were frightening, however. One student was asked when he had last eaten and was offered $10 as he pretended to rummage in a garbage can for food. Another male student said that "the highlight of my experiment came when a little old lady on the opposite bench winked at me."

Holly Hall
Psychology Today

This is especially difficult when the other person's position is radically different from your own. The temptation is to think (and sometimes say), "That's crazy!" "How can you believe that?" or "I'd do it this way . . . ." Of course, attitudes like these aren't helpful even if your position is correct.

Being open-minded is frequently difficult because people confuse *understanding* another's position with *accepting* it. These are quite different matters. To understand why a friend might disagree with you, for example, doesn't mean you have to give up your position and accept hers.

Imagination   Being open-minded often isn't enough to allow empathy. You also need enough imagination to be able to picture another person's background and thoughts. A happily married or single person needs imagination to empathize with the problems of a friend considering divorce. A young person needs it to empathize with a parent facing retirement. A teacher needs it to understand fully the problems facing students, just as those students can't be empathetic without having enough imagination to understand how their instructor feels.

Commitment   Because empathizing is often difficult, a third necessary quality is the sincere desire to understand the other person. Listening to unfamiliar, often confusing information takes time and isn't always fun. If you aim to be empathetic, it's realistic to be willing to face the challenge.

Elements of Communication

So far in this chapter we've talked about two important factors that influence communication: the self-concept and the perception process. Now we are ready to look at how these two factors influence each other.

How the Self-Concept Influences Perception

You have already seen that we learn about ourselves through the reflected appraisal of others. But *what* others? And *what* appraisals? Every day we are bombarded with information about ourselves that is often contradictory. A letter from your family says, "We're proud of your work at school," whereas an instructor's comments suggest you're doing poorly. An old friend's phone call implies that you're important and valued, but a potential date's rejection of your invitation suggests the opposite.

Although it would be theoretically possible to incorporate contradictory messages like these into a single self-concept, in reality this usually doesn't happen. Rather than juggle conflicting messages, we strive for *simplicity* and *consistency* in our self-perception.[27]

You can verify the drive for consistency in your own life by looking at the self-concept list you developed on page 27. You will almost certainly find that it describes you in relatively simple, consistent terms: either intelligent or unintelligent, attractive or ugly, industrious or lazy, and so on.

Because messages about ourselves aren't consistent, we build and maintain a self-concept by creating perceptual filters that allow us to view the world in a way that fits our beliefs. We said earlier that perception is selective; now we see that our selection is guided by this desire for consistency.

Our perceptual filters maintain a consistent self-concept in two ways: by selecting and by distorting information. To see how the process of *selection* operates, imagine that the person with whom you live accuses you of being a slob and not doing your share of the housework. Unless your self-concept fits this description, you might defend yourself by pointing out all the neat, helpful things you've done while forgetting to remember the chores you've left unfinished. It's important to realize that in cases like this you probably wouldn't be lying, but rather remembering selectively.

Because your housemate's perceptions aren't limited by the need to maintain an image of you as conscientious and tidy, your selective memory would probably be met with a reminder of all the unfinished and sloppy housekeeping you forgot to mention. At this point the second perceptual filter, namely *distortion,* might come into play. You could protest that it really wasn't your fault you failed to do your share of the work; that illness, schoolwork . . . anything but your unwanted habits were responsible for the undone chores. Although distortions like these probably wouldn't impress your housemate, they would serve the purpose of maintaining your self-image as a responsible, reasonably neat person. Distortions like these often take the form of defense mechanisms; as you can imagine, they can lead to troublesome conflicts.

Perception and the Self

◆ **It has become something of a cliché to observe that if we do not love ourselves, we cannot love anyone else. This is true enough, but it is only part of the picture. If we do not love ourselves, it is almost impossible to believe fully that we *are loved* by someone else. It is almost impossible to *accept* love. It is almost impossible to *receive* love. No matter what our partner does to show that he or she cares, we do not experience the devotion as convincing because we do not feel lovable to ourselves.**

Nathaniel Branden
The Psychology of Romantic Love

The egocentric tendency to rate ourselves more favorably than others see us has been demonstrated experimentally.[28] In one study, a random sample of men were asked to rank themselves on their ability to get along with others.[29] Defying mathematical laws, all subjects—every last one—put themselves in the top half of the population. Sixty percent rated themselves in the top 10 percent of the population, and an amazing 25 percent believed they were in the top 1 percent. In the same study, 70 percent of the men ranked their leadership in the top quarter of the population whereas only 2 percent thought they were below average. Sixty percent said they were in the top quarter in athletic abilities whereas only 6 percent viewed themselves as below average.

Distortions like these usually revolve around the desire to maintain a self-concept that has been threatened. The desire to maintain a favorable presenting image is often strong. If you want to view yourself as a good student or musician, for example, an instructor who gives you a poor grade or a critic who doesn't appreciate your music *must* be wrong, and you'll find evidence to show it. If you want to think of yourself as a good worker or parent, you'll find explanations for the problems in your job or family that shift the responsibility

Elements of Communication

away from you. Of course, the same principle works for people with excessively negative self-images: They'll go out of the way to explain any information that's favorable to them in terms that show they really are incompetent or undesirable.

The self-concept not only influences our perceptions of ourselves. It also affects the way we judge others (see Table 2–1). Extensive research shows that a person with high self-esteem is more likely to think well of others whereas someone with low self-esteem is likely to have a poor opinion of others.[30] Your own experience may bear this out: Persons with low self-esteem are often cynical and quick to ascribe the worst possible motives to others whereas those who feel good about themselves are disposed to think favorably about the people they encounter. As one writer put it, "What we find 'out there' is what we put there with our unconscious projections. When we think we are looking out a window, it may be, more often than we realize, that we are really gazing into a looking glass."[31]

Perception Checking to Prevent Misunderstandings

By now it is apparent that our perceptions of others are often distorted. The problems that can arise when we act on these distorted perceptions are

TABLE 2–1 Self-esteem Affects Perceptions of Others

PERSONS WITH HIGH SELF-ESTEEM	PERSONS WITH LOW SELF-ESTEEM
1. Likely to think well of others.	**1.** Likely to disapprove of others.
2. Expect to be accepted by others.	**2.** Expect to be rejected by others.
3. Evaluate their own performance more favorably than people with low self-esteem.	**3.** Evaluate their own performance less favorably than people with high self-esteem.
4. Perform well when being watched: not afraid of others' reactions.	**4.** Perform poorly when being watched: sensitive to possible negative reaction.
5. Work harder for people who demand high standards of performance.	**5.** Work harder for undemanding, less critical people.
6. Inclined to feel comfortable with others they view as superior in some way.	**6.** Feel threatened by people they view as superior in some way.
7. Able to defend themselves against negative comments of others.	**7.** Have difficulty defending themselves against others' negative comments; more easily influenced.

Reported in D. E. Hamachek, *Encounters with Others: Interpersonal Relationships and You* (New York: Holt, Rinehart and Winston, 1982), pp. 3–5.

Perception and the Self

obvious. Like most people, you probably resent others' jumping to conclusions about the reasons for your behavior:

"Why are you mad at me?" (Who said you were?)

"What's the matter with you?" (Who said anything was the matter?)

"Come on now. Tell the truth." (Who said you were lying?)

Even if your interpretation is correct, a dogmatic, mind-reading statement is likely to generate defensiveness.

The skill of **perception checking** provides a better way to handle your interpretations. A perception check has three parts:

A description of the behavior you have noticed.

At least two possible interpretations of the behavior.

A request for feedback about how to interpret the behavior correctly.

Perception checks for the preceding three examples would look like this:

"When you stomped out of the room and slammed the door, I wasn't sure whether you were mad at me, or whether you were just in a hurry. How *did* you feel?"

"You haven't laughed much in the last couple of days. It makes me wonder whether something's bothering you or whether you're just feeling quiet. What's up?"

"You said you really liked the job I did, but there was something about your voice that made me think you may not like it. How do you really feel?"

Perception checking statements like these will keep you from jumping to false conclusions. Not only will they prevent the hard feelings that come from mis-interpreting others' actions and motives; they can also help bring your self-concept more in line with reality. The following activity will give you practice in developing perception checking statements.

Practice your perception checking ability by developing three-part verifications for the following situations:

a. You made what you thought was an excellent suggestion to an instructor. The professor looked uninterested but said she would check on the matter right away. Three weeks have passed and nothing has changed.

b. A neighbor and good friend has not responded to your "Good morning" for three days in a row. This person is usually friendly.

c. You haven't noticed the usual weekly phone call from the folks back home in over a month. The last time you spoke, you had an argument about where to spend the holidays.

d. An old friend with whom you have shared the problems of your love life for years has recently changed when around you: The formerly casual hugs and kisses have become longer and stronger; and the occasions where you "accidentally" brush up against one another, more frequent.

The Self-Fulfilling Prophecy

The self-concept is such a powerful force on the personality that it not only determines how we communicate in the present, but it can actually influence our future behavior and that of others. Such occurrences come about through a phenomenon called the self-fulfilling prophecy.

◆ There is an old joke about a man who was asked if he could play a violin and answered, "I don't know. I've never tried." This is psychologically a very wise reply. Those who have never tried to play a violin really do not know whether they can or not. Those who say too early in life and too firmly, "No, I'm not at all musical," shut themselves off prematurely from whole areas of life that might have proved rewarding. In each of us there are unknown possibilities, undiscovered potentialities—and one big advantage of having an open self-concept rather than a rigid one is that we shall continue to discover more and more about ourselves as we grow older.

S. I. Hayakawa

A **self-fulfilling prophecy** occurs when a person's expectation of an event makes the outcome more likely to occur than would otherwise have been true. Self-fulfilling prophecies occur all the time although you might never have given them that label. For example, think of some instances you may have known:

◆ You expected to become nervous and botch a job interview and later did so.
◆ You anticipated having a good (or terrible) time at a social affair and found your expectations being met.
◆ A teacher or boss explained a new task to you, saying that you probably wouldn't do well at first. You did not do well.
◆ A friend described someone you were about to meet, saying that you wouldn't like the person. The prediction turned out to be correct—you didn't like the new acquaintance.

In each of these cases, there is a good chance that the event happened because it was predicted to occur. You needn't have botched the interview, the party might have been boring only because you helped make it so, you might have done better on the job if your boss hadn't spoken up, and you might have liked the new acquaintance if your friend hadn't given you preconceptions. In other words, what helped make each event occur was the expectation that it would happen.

There are two types of self-fulfilling prophecies. The first occurs when your own expectations influence your behavior. Like the job interview and the party described earlier, there are many times when an event that needn't have occurred does happen because you expect it to. In sports you have probably psyched yourself into playing either better or worse than usual, so that the only explanation for your unusual performance was your attitude that you would behave differently. Similarly, you have probably faced an audience at one time or another with a fearful attitude and forgotten your remarks, not because you were unprepared, but because you said to yourself, "I know I'll blow it." (Chapter 15 offers more advice on overcoming this kind of stage fright.)

A second type of self-fulfilling prophecy occurs when the expectations of one person govern another's actions. The classic example was demonstrated by Robert Rosenthal and Lenore Jacobson:

> Twenty percent of the children in a certain elementary school were reported to their teachers as showing unusual potential for intellectual growth. The names of these 20 percent were drawn by means of a table of random numbers, which is to say that the names were drawn out of a hat. Eight months later these unusual or "magic" children showed significantly greater gains in IQ than did the remaining children who had not been singled out for the teachers' attention. The change in the teachers' expectations regarding the intellectual performance of these allegedly "special" children had led to an actual change in the intellectual performance of these randomly selected children.[32]

How do self-fulfilling prophecies affect your communication?

a. Identify three communication-related self-fulfilling prophecies you impose on yourself. For each, explain the prediction you make, how that prediction affects your communication, and whether you are satisfied with the results of the prediction. If you are not satisfied, describe how you could eliminate this self-fulfilling prophecy from your life.

b. Identify three communication-related self-fulfilling prophecies you communicate to others. For each, explain the prediction you convey, and how that prediction affects the other person's behavior. If you are not satisfied with the results of your communication in each situation, describe how you could handle it differently.

In other words, some children may do better in school, not because they are any more intelligent than their classmates, but because they learn that their teacher, a significant other, believes they can achieve.

To put this phenomenon in context with the self-concept, we can say that when a teacher communicates to students the message, "I think you're bright," they accept that evaluation and change their self-concepts to include that evaluation. Unfortunately, we can assume that the same principle holds for those students whose teachers send the message, "I think you're stupid."

This type of self-fulfilling prophecy has been shown to be a powerful force for shaping the self-concept and thus the behavior of people in a wide range of settings outside the schools. In medicine, patients who unknowingly use placebos—substances such as injections of sterile water or doses of sugar pills that have no curative value—often respond just as favorably to treatment as people who actually received a drug. The patients believe they have taken a substance that will help them feel better, and this belief actually brings about a "cure." In psychotherapy, Rosenthal and Jacobson describe several studies that suggest that patients who believe they will benefit from treatment do so, regardless of the type of treatment they receive. In the same vein, when a

Perception and the Self

doctor believes a patient will improve, the patient may do so precisely because of this expectation, whereas another person for whom the physician has little hope often fails to recover. Apparently the patient's self-concept as sick or well—as shaped by the doctor—plays an important role in determining the actual state of health.

The self-fulfilling prophecy operates in families as well. If parents tell their children long enough that they can't do anything right, the children's self-concepts will soon incorporate this idea, and they will fail at many or most of the tasks they attempt. On the other hand, if children are told they are capable or lovable or kind persons, there is a much greater chance of their behaving accordingly.

The self-fulfilling prophecy is an important force in communication, but it doesn't explain all behavior. There are certainly times when the expectation of an event's outcome won't bring about that occurrence. Your hope of drawing an ace in a card game won't in any way affect the chance of that card's turning up in an already shuffled deck, and your belief that good weather is coming won't stop the rain from falling. In the same way, believing you'll do well in a job interview when you're clearly not qualified for the position is unrealistic. Similarly, there will probably be people you don't like and occasions you won't enjoy, no matter what your attitude. To connect the self-fulfilling prophecy with the "power of positive thinking" is an oversimplification.

In other cases, your expectations will be borne out because you are a good predictor and not because of the self-fulfilling prophecy. For example, children are not equally well equipped to do well in school, and in such cases it would be wrong to say that a child's performance was shaped by a parent or teacher even though the behavior did match what was expected. In the same way, some workers excel and others fail, some patients recover and others don't—all according to our predictions but not because of them.

As we keep these qualifications in mind, it's important to recognize the tremendous influence that self-fulfilling prophecies play in our lives. To a great extent we are what we believe we are. In this sense we and those around us constantly create our self-concepts and thus ourselves.

◆ CHANGING THE SELF-CONCEPT

◆ **The only person who behaves sensibly is my tailor. He makes new measurements every time he sees me. All the rest go on with the old measurements.**

George Bernard Shaw

Having read this far, you know more clearly just what the self-concept is, how it is formed, and how it affects communication. But we still haven't focused on what may be the most important question of all: How can you change the parts of your self-concept with which you aren't happy? Sometimes the answer involves changing your *self* (for example, getting a responsible job or losing weight), and sometimes it means changing your *beliefs* (recognizing your strengths or decreasing self-criticism). Neither of these processes is simple, for there's usually no quick method for becoming the person you'd like to be: Personal growth and self-improvement are lifelong activities. But there are several suggestions that can help you move closer to your goals.

Have Realistic Expectations

It's extremely important to realize that some of your dissatisfaction might come from expecting too much of yourself. If you demand that you handle every act of communication perfectly, you're bound to be disappointed. Nobody is able to handle every conflict productively, to be totally relaxed and skillful in conversations, to ask consistently perceptive questions, or to be 100 percent helpful when others have problems. Expecting yourself to reach such unrealistic goals is to doom yourself to unhappiness at the start.

How committed are you to changing your self-concept? You can find out by responding to the steps that follow.

a. Choose a partner and for five minutes or so take turns making and listing statements that begin with "I can't..." Try to focus your statements on your relationships with family, friends, co-workers and students, and even strangers: whomever you have a hard time communicating with.

    Sample statements:
"I can't be myself with strangers I'd like to get to know at parties."
"I can't tell a friend how much I care about her."
"I can't bring myself to ask my supervisor for the raise I think I
   deserve."
"I can't ask questions in class."

b. Notice the feelings you experience as you make each statement: self-pity, regret, concern, frustration, and so on; and share these with your partner.

c. Now go back and repeat aloud each statement you've just made, but this time change each *can't* to a *won't*. After each sentence, share with your partner whatever thoughts you have about what you've just said.

d. After you've finished, decide whether "can't" or "won't" is more appropriate for each item, and explain your choice to your partner.

e. Are there any instances of the self-fulfilling prophecy in your list—times when your decision that you "couldn't" do something was the only force keeping you from doing it?

Sometimes it's easy to be hard on yourself because all those around you seem to be handling themselves so much better than you. It's important to realize that much of what seems like confidence and skill in others is a front to hide uncertainty. They may be suffering from the same self-imposed demands of perfection that you place on yourself.

Even in cases where others definitely seem more competent than you, it's important to judge yourself in terms of your own growth, not against the behavior of others. Rather than feeling miserable because you're not as talented as an expert, realize that you probably are a better, wiser, or more skillful person than you used to be and that this is a legitimate source of satisfaction. Perfection is fine as an ideal, but you're being unfair to yourself if you expect actually to reach that state.

Perception and the Self

Have a Realistic Perception of Yourself

One source of a poor self-concept is an inaccurate self-perception. As you've already read, such unrealistic pictures sometimes come from being overly harsh on yourself, believing that you're worse than the facts indicate. By sharing the self-concept list you recorded on page 27, you will be able to see whether you have been selling yourself short. Of course, it would be foolish to deny that you could be a better person than you are, but it's also important to recognize your strengths.

An unrealistically poor self-concept can also come from the inaccurate feedback of others. Perhaps you are in an environment where you receive an excessive number of "downer" messages, many of which are undeserved, and a minimum of upper messages. We have known many women, for example, who have returned to college after many years spent in homemaking where they received virtually no recognition for their intellectual strengths. It's amazing that these women have the courage to come to college at all, so low is their self-esteem; but come they do, and most are thrilled to find that they are much brighter and more competent intellectually than they suspected. In the same way, workers with overly critical supervisors, children with cruel "friends," and students with unsupportive teachers all are prone to suffering from low self-concepts owing to excessively negative feedback.

If you fall into this category, it's important to put the unrealistic evaluations you receive into perspective and then to seek out more supportive people who will acknowledge your assets as well as point out your shortcomings. Doing so is often a quick and sure boost to self-esteem.

Have the Will to Change

Often we claim we want to change, but we aren't willing to do the necessary work. You might, for instance, decide that you'd like to become a better conversationalist. Taking the advice offered in the next section of this book, you ask your instructor or some other communication adviser how to reach this goal. Suppose you receive two suggestions: first, to spend the next three weeks observing people who handle themselves well in conversations and to record exactly what they do that makes them so skillful; second, to read several books on the subject of conversational skills. You begin these tasks with the best intentions, but after a few days the task of recording conversations becomes a burden—it would be so much easier just to listen to others talk. And your diligent reading program becomes bogged down as the press of other work fills up your time. In other words, you find you just "can't" fit the self-improvement plan into your busy schedule.

Let's be realistic. Becoming a better communicator is probably one of many goals in your life. It's possible that you'll find other needs more pressing, which is completely reasonable. However, you should realize that changing your self-concept often requires a good deal of effort, and without that effort your good intentions alone probably won't get you much closer to this goal. In communication, as in most other aspects of life, "there's no such thing as a free lunch."

Have the Skill Needed to Change

Often trying isn't enough. There are some cases where you would change if you knew of a way to do so. To see if this is the case for you, check the list of *can'ts* and *won'ts* from the exercise on page 53, and see if any items there are more appropriately "don't know hows." If so, then the way to change is to learn how. You can do so in two ways.

First, you can seek advice—from books such as this one, from the references listed at the end of each chapter, and from other printed sources. You can also get suggestions from instructors, counselors, and other experts, as well as from friends. Of course, not all the advice you receive will be useful, but if you read widely and talk to enough people, you have a good chance of learning the things you want to know.

A second method of learning how to change is to observe models—people who handle themselves in the ways you would like to master. It's often been said that people learn more from models than in any other way, and by taking advantage of this principle you will find that the world is full of teachers who can show you how to communicate more successfully. Become a careful observer. Watch what people you admire do and say, not so that you can copy them, but so that you can adapt their behavior to fit your own personal style.

At this point you might be overwhelmed at the difficulty of changing the way you think about yourself and the way you act. Remember, we never said that this would be easy (although it sometimes is). But even when change is difficult, you know that it's possible if you are serious. You don't need to be perfect, but you can improve your self-concept if you choose to.

◆ SUMMARY

The chapter began by introducing the role of the self in communication. It defined the self-concept and described the forces contributing to its development. The next section described the relationship between the self-concept and the personality, emphasizing the cyclical relationship between self-concept, behavior, responses of others, and one's perception of events. "Personality" was shown to be an inaccurate concept in many cases, since a person's behavior often changes over time and in different situations.

The chapter next examined the nature of perception, both of oneself and others. It began by introducing the steps in the perception process: selection, organization, and interpretation. It listed several common errors in person perception, and then described the influences of cultural background on perceptual differences. Next, the notion of empathy was defined, and the requirements for becoming more empathic were described.

The final section of the chapter showed how the self-concept influences perception. It discussed the desire for consistency and explained how this leads people to interpret events in ways that fit with their existing beliefs and attitudes. It showed how self-fulfilling prophecies can influence both one's own communication and the behavior of others. Finally, the chapter suggested ways of changing the self-concept.

◆ NOTES

1. Anthony G. Athos and John J. Gabarro, *Interpersonal Behavior: Communication and Understanding in Relationships* (Englewood Cliffs, N.J.: Prentice-Hall, 1978), p. 140.

2. Kathleen S. Berger, *The Developing Person* (New York: Worth, 1980), pp. 243–244.

3. Michael Lewis and Jeanne Brooks, "Self-knowledge and Emotional Development," in Michael Lewis and Leonard A. Rosenblum (eds.), *The Development of Affect* (New York: Plenum, 1978), pp. 205–226.

4. Arthur W. Combs and Donald Snygg, *Individual Behavior,* rev. ed. (New York: Harper & Row, 1959), p. 134.

5. Harry S. Sullivan, *The Interpersonal Theory of Psychiatry* (New York: Norton, 1953).

6. Charles H. Cooley, *Human Nature and the Social Order* (New York: Scribner's, 1902).

7. Monte D. Smith, S. A. Zingalc, and J. M. Coleman, "The Influence of Adult Expectations/Child Performance Discrepancies upon Children's Self-Concepts," *American Educational Research Journal* 15 (1978): 259–265.

8. G. J. McCall, "The Self-Concept and Interpersonal Communication," in M. E. Roloff and G. R. Miller (eds.), *Interpersonal Processes: New Directions in Communication Research* (Newbury Park, Calif.: Sage, 1987).

9. T. M. Steinfatt, "Personality and Communication: Classical Approaches," in J. C. McCroskey and J. A. Daly (eds.), *Personality and Interpersonal Communication* (Newbury Park, Calif.: Sage, 1987), p. 42.

10. G. W. Allport and H. W. Odbert, "Trait Names, A Psychological Study," *Psychological Monographs* 47 (1936).

11. J. Kagan, *The Nature of the Child* (New York: Basic Books, 1984).

12. J. C. McCroskey and V. Richmond, *The Quiet Ones: Communication Apprehension and Shyness* (Dubuque, Iowa: Gorsuch Scarisbrick, 1980).

13. Adapted from J. W. Krinch, "A Formalized Theory of the Self-Concept," in J. Manis and B. N. Meltzer (eds.), *Symbolic Interaction,* 2d ed. (Boston: Allyn and Bacon, 1972), pp. 245–252.

14. D. Coon, *Introduction to Psychology,* 4th ed. (St. Paul, Minn.: West, 1987).

15. Ibid.

16. Paul Watzlawick, Janet Beavin, and Don D. Jackson, *Pragmatics of Human Communication* (New York: Norton, 1967).

17. Summarized in Don E. Hamachek, *Encounters with Others* (New York: Holt, Rinehart and Winston, 1982), pp. 23–30.

18. See, for example, Penny Baron, "Self-Esteem, Ingratiation, and Evaluation of Unknown Others," *Journal of Personality and Social Psychology* 30 (1974): 104–109; and Elaine Walster, "The Effect of Self-Esteem on Romantic Liking," *Journal of Experimental and Social Psychology* 1 (1965): 184–197.

19. See, for example, D. E. Kanouse and L. R. Hanson, "Negativity in Evaluations," in E. E. Jones, D. E. Kanouse, H. H. Kelley, R. E. Nisbett, S. Valins, and B. Weiner (eds.), *Attribution: Perceiving the Causes of Behavior* (Morristown, N.J.: General Learning Press, 1972).

20. J. W. Bagby, "A Cross-Cultural Study of Perceptual Predominance in Binocular Rivalry," *Journal of Abnormal and Social Psychology* 54 (1957): 331–334.

21. S. Ting-Toomey, "Rhetorical Sensitivity Style in Three Cultures: France, Japan and the United States," *Central States Speech Journal* 39 (Spring 1988): 28–36. J. M. Wiemann, V. Chase, and H. Giles, "Beliefs About Talk and Silence in a Cultural Context," paper presented at the annual meeting of the Speech Communication Association, Chicago, 1986.

22. J. Horn, "Conversational Breakdowns: As Different as Black and White," *Psychology Today* 8 (May 1974): 30.

23. Mary Jane Collier, "Rule Violations in Intercultural/Ethnic Advisement Contexts," paper presented at the annual meeting of the Western Speech Communication Association, Tucson, Arizona, 1986.

24. D. T. Regan and J. Totten, "Empathy and Attribution: Turning Observers into Actors," *Journal of Personality and Social Psychology* 35 (1975): 850–856.

25. Hamachek, op. cit., pp. 23–24.

26. G. Cronkhite, *Communication and Awareness* (Menlo Park, Calif.: Cummings, 1976), p. 82.

27. See F. Heider, *The Psychology of Interpersonal Relations* (New York: Wiley, 1968); C. Osgood and P. Tannenbaum, "The Principle of Congruity in the Prediction of Attitude Change," *Psychological Review* 62 (1955): 42–55; and L. Festinger, *A Theory of Cognitive Dissonance* (Stanford, Calif.: Stanford University Press, 1957).

28. B. Sypher and H. E. Sypher, "Seeing Ourselves as Others See Us," *Communication Research* 11 (January 1984): 97–115.

29. Reported by D. Myers, "The Inflated Self," *Psychology Today* 14 (May 1980): 16.

30. See, for example, P. Baron, "Self-Esteem, Ingratiation, and Evaluation of Unknown Others," *Journal of Personality and Social Psychology* 30 (1974): 104–109.

31. Hamachek, op. cit., p. 3.

32. Robert Rosenthal and Lenore Jacobson, *Pygmalion in the Classroom* (New York: Holt, Rinehart and Winston, 1968).

3

After reading this chapter, you should understand the following:

1. The symbolic, person-centered nature of language.
2. The syntactic and semantic characteristics of language.
3. The ways in which language shapes the perceptions of users.
4. How language reflects the attitudes of users.
5. The types of linguistic misunderstandings listed in this chapter.
6. The relationship between language use and gender.

You should be able to do the following:

1. Identify at least two ways in which language has shaped your perceptions of a person, object, or event.
2. Identify at least two ways in which your language reflects your attitudes about a person, object, or event.
3. Identify and correct the linguistic misunderstandings listed in this chapter in a conversation or written text.
4. Translate overly abstract problems, goals, appreciations, complaints, and requests into more specific, behavioral terms.

KEY TERMS

abstraction ladder	inferential statement
abstract language	language
behavioral description	phonological rules
connotation	regulative rules
denotation	relative words
emotive language	semantic rules
equivocal words	sex role
euphemism	syntactic rules
factual statement	Whorf-Sapir hypothesis

Language

◆ ...words strain,
Crack and sometimes break, under the burden
Under the tension, slip, slide, perish,
Decay with imprecision, will not stay in one place,
Will not stay still.

T. S. Eliot
"Burnt Norton"
in *Four Quartets*

At one time or another every one of us has suffered the limits and traps of language. Even though we are using familiar words, it's clear that we don't understand others, and they don't appreciate us.

In the following pages we will explore the nature of linguistic communication. By the time you have finished reading this chapter, you will better appreciate the complexity of language, its power to shape our perception of people and events, and its potential for incomplete and inaccurate communication. Perhaps more importantly, you will be better equipped to prevent or correct misunderstandings—to use the tool of language more skillfully.

◆ THE NATURE OF LANGUAGE

Humans speak about 10,000 different languages and dialects.[1] Despite their differences, all share the same characteristics of **language:** a collection of symbols, governed by rules, and used to convey messages between individuals. A closer look at this definition can help explain why language works as well as it does, and why it often fails to communicate effectively.

Language Is Symbolic

All languages contain elements which can be combined in various ways to create meaning, much like bricks and mortar can be combined in a number of ways to create different structures. The elements of the English language consist of the letters of our alphabet along with punctuation marks, such as commas, periods, and so on. In the language of mathematics the elements are the integers zero through nine plus other symbols, such as plus and minus signs. The Morse code has only two elements—dots and dashes.

The elements of a language usually have no meaning by themselves. And in many combinations they are also meaningless. But they can be combined to create symbols—representations that stand for objects, things, ideas, or activities. For example, the letters "t," "r," and "a" are meaningless, but when combined in different ways they create the symbols "art," "rat," and "tar." In spoken and written languages, most symbols are words. But there are other kinds of linguistic symbols. For example, American Sign Language expresses messages by using the hands and body.

Elements of
Communication

Language Is Rule-Governed

Languages contain several types of rules. **Phonological rules** govern how sounds are combined to form words. For instance, the words "champagne," "double," and "occasion" have the same meaning in French and English, but all are pronounced differently.

Syntactic rules govern the ways symbols can be arranged. For example, correct English syntax requires that every word contain at least one vowel and prohibits sentences such as "Have you the cookies brought?" which is a perfectly acceptable word order in a language such as German. Although most of us aren't able to describe the rules that govern our language, it's easy to recognize the existence of such rules by noting how odd a statement that violates them appears.

Semantic rules also govern our use of the language. But where syntax deals with structure, semantics governs meaning. Semantic rules reflect the ways in which speakers of a language respond to a particular symbol. Semantic rules are what make it possible for us to agree that "bikes" are for riding and "books" are for reading; they also help us to know who we will and won't encounter when we use rooms marked "Men" or "Women." Without semantic rules, communication would be impossible, for each of us would use symbols in unique ways, unintelligible to one another.

After reading the last sentence, you might object, thinking about the many cases in which people don't follow the same semantic rules. Of course, you would be correct, for there are many times when a single word has different meanings for different people. This is possible because words, being symbols, have no meaning in themselves. Ogden and Richards have illustrated this point graphically in their well-known "triangle of meaning" (Figure 3–1).[2] This

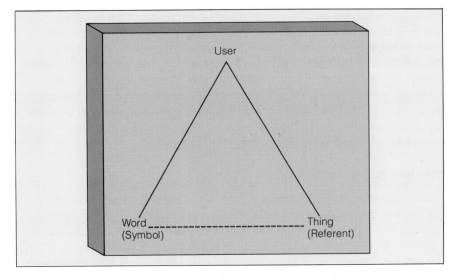

FIGURE 3–1
Ogden and Richards' triangle of meaning

*Some of these "things" or referents do not exist in the physical world. For instance, some referents are mythical (such as unicorns), some are no longer tangible (such as the deceased Mr. Smith), and others are abstract ideas (such as "love").

Language

triangle shows that there is only an indirect relationship—indicated by a broken line—between a word and the thing it claims to represent.* Problems arise when people mistakenly believe that words automatically represent things or when we assume that our meaning for a word is the same as someone else's. We will spend most of this chapter discussing how to avoid such linguistic problems.

Interview someone who is familiar with a language besides English. (If you speak a second language, use your own experience to complete this exercise.) For each area below, identify examples of the differences between English and the other language:

a. phonological rules
b. syntactic rules
c. semantic rules
d. regulative rules

Are there any cases when one or more types of these rules vary *within* the same language?

Semantic rules help us understand the meaning of individual words, but they often don't explain how language operates in everyday life. Consider the statement, "Let's get together tomorrow." The semantic meaning of the words in this sentence is clear enough, yet the statement could be taken in several ways. It could be a request ("I hope we can get together"), a polite command ("I want to see you"), an empty cliché ("I don't really mean it"). We learn to distinguish the accurate meanings of such speech acts through **regulative rules,** which tell us what interpretation of a message is appropriate in a given context. These rules—usually understood by all players in the language game—help us understand the speaker's intention. For example, the relationship between the communicators plays a large role in defining many statements. Our example, "I want to see you" is likely to mean one thing when uttered by your boss, and another entirely when it comes from your lover. Likewise, the situation in which the statement is made plays a role. Saying, "I want to see you" at the office will probably have a different meaning than the same words uttered at a cocktail party. Of course, the nonverbal behaviors that accompany a statement also help explain its meaning.

Meanings Are in People, Not Words

Show a dozen people the same symbol and ask them what it means, and you are likely to get twelve different answers. Does an American flag bring up associations of soldiers giving their lives for their country? Fourth of July parades? Mom's apple pie? How about a cross: What does it represent? The gentleness and wisdom of Jesus Christ? Fire-lit rallies of Ku Klux Klansmen? Your childhood Sunday school? The necklace your sister always wears?

Like these symbols, words can be interpreted in many different ways. And, of course, this is the basis for many misunderstandings. It's possible to have an argument about *feminism* without ever realizing that you and the other person are using the word to represent entirely different things. The same goes for *communism, Republicans, rock music,* and thousands upon thousands of other symbols. Words don't mean; people do—and often in widely different ways.

It might seem as if one remedy to misunderstandings like these would be to have more respect for the dictionary meanings of words. After all, you might think, if people would just consult a dictionary whenever they send or receive a potentially confusing message, there would be little problem.

This approach has three shortcomings. First, dictionaries show that many words have multiple definitions, and it isn't always clear which one applies in a given situation. The 500 words most commonly used in everyday communication have over 14,000 dictionary definitions, which should give you an idea of the limitations of this approach.

A second problem is that people often use words in ways you would never be able to look up. Sometimes the misuse of words is due to a lack of knowledge, as when you might ask your auto parts dealer for a new generator when you really need an alternator.

The third shortcoming of dictionaries is that they define most words in terms of *other* words, and this process often won't tell you any more about a term than you already know. In fact, it's possible to talk endlessly about a subject and sound very knowledgeable without ever having the slightest idea of what

◆ **The spoken word belongs half to the one who speaks and half to the one who hears.**

French proverb

◆ **"I don't know what you mean by 'glory,' " Alice said.**

Humpty Dumpty smiled contemptuously. "Of course you don't—till I tell you. I meant 'there's a nice knock-down argument for you!' "

"But 'glory' doesn't mean 'a nice knock-down argument,' " Alice objected.

"When _I_ use a word," Humpty Dumpty said, in a rather scornful tone, "it means just what I choose it to mean—neither more nor less."

"The question is," said Alice, "whether you _can_ make words mean so many different things."

"The question is," said Humpty Dumpty, "which is to be master—that's all."

Lewis Carroll
Through the Looking Glass

---

your words refer to. Jessica Davidson's quiz is an example of this. Read the paragraph; then see if you can answer the questions:

> Because public opinion is sometimes marsiflate, empetricious insoculences are frequently zophilimized. Nevertheless, it cannot be overemphasized that carpoflansibles are highly traculate.

1. In the author's opinion, carpoflansibles are
   a. empetricious
   b. traculate
   c. zophilimized
2. Public opinion is sometimes
   a. insoculent
   b. variable
   c. marsiflate
3. According to the text, insoculences are zophilimized
   a. often
   b. never
   c. sometimes[3]

You can see that the correct answers are 1(b), 2(c), and 3(a). But even if you scored perfectly on the quiz, do you know the meaning of the paragraph? Of course not, for the words are gibberish. But if you look closely, you'll find that many people use their own language in the same way, talking in terms they can define only by other terms.

Despite the potential for linguistic problems, the situation isn't hopeless. We do, after all, communicate with one another reasonably well most of the time. And with enough effort, we can clear up most of the misunderstandings that do occur. The key to more accurate use of language is to avoid assuming that others interpret words the same way we do. In truth, successful communication occurs when we _negotiate_ the meaning of a statement. By working to clarify the way language is used, we move closer to a shared understanding:

The need to negotiate meanings highlights both the shortcomings and strengths of language. On one hand, it is an imprecise tool for communicating. In any interchange we are likely to be misunderstood, and the odds are great that our understanding of others is flawed. On the other hand, the same language that works so imperfectly allows us to discover and clarify problems of understanding when they occur.

Language Shapes Attitudes

Language does far more than describe the world. On a more fundamental level, the labels we use shape the way we look at the world and, in so doing, influence the way we behave.

CULTURE Many social scientists believe that the structure of a culture's language shapes the world view of its members. This idea is articulated most clearly in the **Whorf-Sapir hypothesis.**[4]

After spending several years with various North American Indian cultures, Benjamin Whorf found that their patterns of thinking were shaped by the language they spoke. For example, Nootka, a language spoken on Vancouver Island, contains no distinction between nouns and verbs. The Indians who speak Nootka view the entire world as being constantly in process. Whereas English speakers see something as fixed or constant (noun), Nootka speakers view it as constantly changing. Therefore, the Nootka speaker might label a "fire" as a "burning," or a house as a "house-ing." In this sense, our language operates much like a snapshot camera whereas Nootka works more like a moving-picture camera.

What does this difference have to do with communication? Because of the static, unchanging nature of our grammar, we often regard people and things as never changing. Someone who spoke a more process-oriented language would view people quite differently, assuming their changeable nature. Some cultures, for example, allow their members to change names whenever they wish. We can speculate that this practice might make it easier to see that others change over time, and in the same way it might make it easier for individuals to escape the inhibiting effects of an obsolete self-concept.

A look at more familiar languages also shows how the linguistic world we inhabit can subtly shape our attitudes. English-speaking parents often label the mischievous pranks of their children as "bad," implying that there is something immoral about acting wild. "Be good!" they are inclined to say. On the other hand, French adults are more likely to say, *"Sois sage!"*—"Be wise." The linguistic implication is that misbehaving is an act of foolishness. Swedes would correct the same action with the words *"Var snell!"*—"Be friendly. Be kind." By contrast, German adults use the command *"Sei Artig!"*—literally "Be of your own kind"—in other words, get back in step, conform to your role as a child.[5]

Although the Whorf-Sapir hypothesis originally focused on foreign languages, Neil Postman illustrates the principle with an example closer to home. He describes a culture where physicians identify patients they treat as "doing" arthritis and other diseases instead of "having" them and where criminals are diagnosed as "having" cases of criminality instead of "being" criminals.[6]

The implications of such a linguistic difference are profound. We believe that characteristics people "have"—what they "are"—are beyond their control whereas they are responsible for what they "do." If we changed our view of what people "have" and what they "do," our attitudes would most likely change as well. Postman illustrates the consequences of this linguistic difference as applied to education:

Language

◆ **Words do not label things already there. Words are like the knife of the carver: They free the idea, the thing, from the general formlessness of the outside. As a man speaks, not only is his language in a state of birth, but also the very thing about which he is talking.**

Edmund Carpenter

In schools, for instance, we find that tests are given to determine how smart someone is or, more precisely, how much smartness someone "has." If one child scores a 138, and another a 106, the first is thought to "have" more smartness than the other. But this seems to me a strange conception—every bit as strange as "doing" arthritis or "having" criminality. I do not know anyone who *has* smartness. The people I know sometimes *do* smart things (as far as I can judge) and sometimes *do* stupid things— depending on what circumstances they are in, and how much they know about a situation, and how interested they are. "Smartness," so it seems to me, is a specific performance, done in a particular set of circumstances. It is not something you *are* or have in measurable quantities. In fact, the assumption that smartness is something you *have* has led to such nonsensical ideas as "over-" and "underachievers." As I understand it, an overachiever is someone who doesn't *have* much smartness but does a lot of smart things. An underachiever is someone who *has* a lot of smartness but does a lot of stupid things.

In any case, I am not prepared here to argue the matter through. Although I have not heard of them, there may be good reasons to imagine that smartness or honesty or sensitivity are "qualities" that people *have* in measurable proportions and that exist independently of what people actually do. What I am driving at is this: All language is metaphorical, and often in the subtlest ways. In the simplest sentence, sometimes in the simplest word, we do more than merely express ourselves. We construct reality along certain lines. We make the world according to our own imagery.[7]

The Sapir-Whorf hypothesis has never been conclusively proved or disproved. In spite of its intellectual appeal, some critics point out that it is possible to conceive of flux even in static languages like English. They suggest that Sapir and Whorf overstated the importance of their idea. Supporters of the hypothesis respond that though it is *possible* to conceptualize an idea in different languages, some languages make it much easier to recognize a term than do others.

NAMING   The power of language is so great that it even extends to personal names. Research shows that these names are more than just a simple means of identification; that, in fact, they shape the way others think of us, the way we view ourselves, and the way we act.[8]

Different names have different connotations. In one study, psychologists asked college students to rate over a thousand names according to their likability, how active or passive they seemed, and their masculinity or femininity. In spite of the large number of subjects, the responses were quite similar. Michael, John, and Wendy were likable and active and were rated as possessing the masculine or feminine traits of their sex. Percival, Isadore, and Alfreda were less likable, and their sexuality was more suspect. Other research also suggests that names have strong connotative meanings. More common names

Elements of Communication

A Fred by Any Other Name

Fred Daniel says it started back in grade school. Schoolmates made fun of his name, calling "Hey, Fray-yud!" as if he were a dumb kid in overalls chewing on a long straw.

It was downhill from there.

Girls he met in high school humiliated him by saying, "Your name is Fred? Really?" and then laughing out loud.

"Anti-Fred" stereotypes only made it worse: comedian Red Skelton's Freddie the Freeloader, cartoon caveman Fred Flintstone, the bumbling character of Fred Mertz on "I Love Lucy," and the Freddy, a semi-popular dance of the '60s resembling calisthenics. Today's TV commercials have produced "Fred Rated," a character who advertises home entertainment equipment in Groucho glasses and silly disguises, and the Milquetoast who cowers behind the water cooler while his boss snidely remarks, "Should have used Federal Express, don't you think, Fred?"

Enough was enough. Three years ago, Daniel formed the Fred Society, now a national organization of 160 members. The point, he said, is to "recognize and promote Freds," letting the world know "that not every Fred is a dumb caveman named Fred Flintstone with a wife named Wilma."

Daniel, 31, is a freelance graphic artist with a sense of humor as dry as the Mojave Desert where he was reared. A homemade palm tree, real cacti, and framed drawings of the desert decorate his Santa Ana apartment, where the national headquarters of the Fred Society is located right off the kitchen.

A life-size poster of Fred Astaire—a positive role model—hangs over his drawing table where Daniel designs a line of Fred pride accessories he calls Fredrobilia.

There are bumper stickers that proclaim: "Fred and Proud," "I Brake for Freds," "Better Fred Than Dead," and "When All Else Fails Hug Your Freddy."

"Here's the epitome of what people think of Freds," he said, holding a cartoon of "Fred's Computerlot" with a salesman in a checkered coat, funny glasses, and mismatched socks. Another shows three bums on a bench. One says: "And Fred here, he's in marketing. Remember the new Coke?"

He pulled out a copy of a page from a personal computer instruction manual. To explain how to correct mistakes, the name "FREDD" was used as an example. "There's this assumption that someone named Fred would misspell his name," Daniel said.

"There are a lot of dogs named Fred," he said. "Here's a mule named Fred," he added, waving a snapshot of a sad-looking animal. "He belongs to my uncle in Fresno."

Daniel figures less than 1 percent of the population is named Fred, and most of them are older men.

"They're really dwindling right up there with the California condor," Daniel said. One of his bumper stickers reads, "Name Your Next Child Fred."

In September, a woman came by his booth at a swap meet with an infant she had named Fred. "I know at least there's one little Fred out there."

Daniel and his wife, Sue, have been married six months and plan to become parents in a few years. If they have a son, his wife adamantly refuses to name him Fred, Daniel said, because it "sounds like an old man's name."

"She wants something a little more acceptable like Steve or Shaun. Well, they don't hold a candle to Fred."

Lynn Smith
The Los Angeles Times

"B.C." by permission of Johnny Hart and Creators Syndicate.

are generally viewed as being more active, stronger, and better than unusual ones.

The preconceptions we hold about people because of their names influence our behavior toward them. In another well-known study, researchers asked a number of teachers to read several essays supposedly written by fifth-grade students. The researchers found that certain names—generally the most popular ones such as Lisa, Michael, and Karen—received higher grades regardless of which essay they were attached to whereas other less popular names—Elmer, Bertha, Hubert—were consistently graded as inferior. There was one exception to the link between popular names and high grades: Unpopular Adelle received the highest evaluation of all. The researchers speculated that the teachers saw her as more "scholarly."

It's not surprising to find that the attitudes others hold toward a person because of his or her name have an effect on that person's self-concept. Over forty years ago, researchers found that students at Harvard who had unusual names were more likely to be neurotic and to flunk out of school. The negative effect of unusual names seems to be more damaging to men than women, perhaps owing to our social convention that makes such labels acceptable for females. At any rate, research such as this makes it clear that the question "What shall we name the baby?" is an important one for more than aesthetic reasons.

CREDIBILITY Scholarly speaking is a good example of how speech style influences perception. We refer to what has been called the Dr. Fox hypothesis.[9] "An apparently legitimate speaker who utters an unintelligible message will be judged competent by an audience in the speaker's area of apparent expertise." The Dr. Fox hypothesis got its name from one Dr. Myron L. Fox, who delivered a talk followed by a half-hour discussion on "Mathematical Game Theory as Applied to Physical Education." The audience included psychiatrists, psychologists, social workers, and educators. Questionnaires collected after the session revealed that these educated listeners found the lecture clear and stimulating.

Despite his warm reception by this learned audience, Fox was a complete fraud. He was a professional actor whom researchers had coached to deliver a lecture of double-talk—a patchwork of information from a *Scientific American* article mixed with jokes, non sequiturs, contradictory statements, and meaningless references to unrelated topics. When wrapped in a linguistic package of high-level professional jargon, however, the meaningless gobbledygook was judged as important information. In other words, Fox's credibility came more from his style of speaking than from the ideas he expressed.

The same principle seems to hold for academic writing.[10] A group of thirty-two management professors rated material according to its complexity rather than its content. When a message about consumer behavior was loaded with unnecessary words and long, complex sentences, the academics rated it highly. When the same message was translated into more readable English, with shorter words and clearer sentences, the professors judged the same research as less competent.

STATUS   In the stage classic *My Fair Lady,* Professor Henry Higgins transformed Eliza Doolittle from a lowly flower girl into a high-society woman by replacing her Cockney accent with an upper-crust speaking style. The power of speech to influence status is a real-life fact. British researcher Howard Giles conducted experiments that conclusively demonstrated (if any proof were necessary) that, in Britain, judgments of attractiveness and status are strongly influenced by style of speech.[11] The same principle operates in the New World. For instance, speakers of Black English, a distinctive language with its own accent, grammar, syntax, and semantic rules are rated as less intelligent, professionally capable, socially acceptable, and employable by speakers of standard English.[12]

SELF-ESTEEM   The words we use to describe people's roles or functions in society can also shape the way they feel about themselves. Much of people's self-esteem is derived from the importance they feel their work has, a perception that often comes from the titles of their roles. For example, a theater owner had trouble keeping ushers working for more than a week or two. The ushers tired quickly of their work, which consisted mostly of taking tickets, selling popcorn, and showing people to their seats. Then, with only one change, the personnel problems ended. The manager simply "promoted" all the ushers to the "new" position of "assistant manager." Believe it or not, the new title was sufficient to make the employees happy. The new name encouraged them to think more highly of themselves and to take new pride in their work.

The significance of words in shaping our self-concept goes beyond job titles. Racist and sexist language greatly affects the self-concepts of those facing discrimination. Casey Miller and Kate Swift point out some of the aspects of our language that suggest women are of lower status than men. Miller and Swift write that, except for words referring to females by definition, such as *mother* and *actress,* English defines many nonsexual concepts as male. The underlying assumption is that people in general are men. Also, words associated with males have positive connotations, such as *manly, virile, courageous, direct, strong,* and *independent* whereas words related to females

◆ **On the television screen, a teacher of first-graders who has just won a national award is describing her way of teaching. "You take each child where you find him," she says. "You watch to see what he's interested in, and then you build on his interests."**

A five-year-old looking at the program asks her mother, "Do only boys go to that school?"

"No," her mother begins, "she's talking about girls too, but—"

But what? The teacher being interviewed on television is speaking correct English. What can the mother tell her daughter about why a child, in any generalization, is always *he* rather than *she?* How does a five-year-old comprehend the generic personal pronoun?

Casey Miller and Kate Swift

Language

"Sticks and stones may break my bones, but names can give me an inferiority complex."

are fewer and have less positive connotations, such as *feminine wiles* and *womanish tears.*[13]

Most dictionaries, in fact, define *effeminate* as the opposite of *masculine* although the opposite of *feminine* is closer to *unfeminine.* Any language expressing stereotyped sexual attitudes or assuming the superiority of one sex over another is sexist, so adding feminine endings to nonsexual words, such as *poetess* for female poet, is as sexist as *separate but equal* is racist.

Whereas sexist language usually defines the world as made up of superior men and inferior women, racist language usually defines it as composed of superior whites and other, inferior racial groups. Words and images associated with *white* are usually positive, whether it's the hero-cowboy in white or connotations of white as *pure, clean, honorable, innocent, bright,* and *shiny.* The words and images associated with black are often negative, a concept that reaches from the clothes of the villain-cowboy to connotations such as *decay, dirt, smudge, dismal, wicked, unwashed,* and *sinister.*

To the extent that our language is both sexist and racist, our view of the world is affected. For example, men are given more opportunity than women to see themselves as "good," and in the same way whites are given more opportunity than blacks. Language shapes the self-concepts of those it labels in such a way that members of the linguistically slighted group see themselves as inferior.

Many linguistic changes beginning in the late 1960s were aimed primarily at teaching speakers and writers a new vocabulary to change the destructive connotations that accompany many of our words. For example, "black is beautiful" is an effort to reduce perceived differences in status among blacks and whites.

Changes in writing style were also designed to counter the sexual prejudices inherent in language, particularly eliminating the constant use of *he* and introducing various methods either to eliminate reference to a particular sex or to refer to both sexes. Words that use *man* generically to refer to humanity at large often pose problems, but only to the unimaginative. Consider the following substitutions: *Mankind* may be replaced by *humanity, human beings, human race,* and *people; man-made* may be replaced by *artificial, manufactured,* and *synthetic; manpower* may be replaced by *human power, workers,* and *work force;* and *manhood* may be replaced by *adulthood.*

Congressmen are *members of Congress.*

Firemen are *fire fighters.*

Chairmen are *presiding officers, leaders,* and *chairs.*

Foremen are *supervisors.*

Policemen and *policewomen* are both *police officers.*

Stewardesses and *stewards* are both *flight attendants.*

Throughout this book we have used a number of techniques for avoiding sexist language: switching to the sexual neutral plural (*they*), occasionally using the passive voice to eliminate sexed pronouns, employing the *he or she* structure, carefully balancing individual masculine and feminine pronouns in illustrative material, and even totally rewriting some parts to delete conceptual sexual bias.

Language Reflects Attitudes

Besides shaping the way we view ourselves and others, language reflects our attitudes. Feelings of control, attraction, commitment, responsibility . . . all these and more are reflected in the way we use language.

POWER   Communication researchers have identified a number of language patterns that add to, or detract from, a speaker's ability to influence others, as well as reflecting how a speaker feels about his or her degree of control over a situation.[14] Table 3–1 summarizes some of these findings by listing several types of "powerless" language.

You can see the difference between powerful and powerless language by comparing the following statements:

◆ **For tens, and perhaps hundreds, of thousands of years, people regarded language as a holy instrument that let them look out upon the world in wonder and fear and joy. "In the beginning was the Word" is the reassuring first line of the Gospel According to St. John. Only in the last few decades have people suspected that their window on the world has a glass that gives a distorted view.**

Peter Farb
Word Play

Language

TABLE 3-1 Examples of Powerless Language

Hedges	"I'm *kinda* disappointed…"
	"I *think* we should…"
	"I *guess* I'd like to…"
Hesitations	"*Uh,* can I have a minute of your time?"
	"*Well,* we could try this idea…"
	"I wish you would—*er*—try to be on time."
Intensifiers	"*So* that's how I feel…"
	"I'm not *very* hungry."
Polite forms	"Excuse me, *sir*…"
Tag questions	"It's about time we got started, *isn't it?*"
	"*Don't you think* we should give it another try?"
Disclaimers	"*I probably shouldn't say this, but…*"
	"*I'm not really sure but…*"

"Excuse me, sir, I hate to say this, but I…uh…I guess I won't be able to turn in the assignment on time. I had a personal emergency and…well…it was just impossible to finish it by today. I'll have it in your mailbox on Monday, okay?"

"I won't be able to turn in the assignment on time. I had a personal emergency, and it was impossible to finish it by today. I'll have it in your mailbox on Monday."

Whether or not the professor finds the excuse acceptable, it's clear that the second speaker feels confident whereas the first one is apologetic and uncertain. The first statement is a classic example of what social scientists have come to call "one-down" communication.[15]

Some relationships are characterized by what social scientists term *complementary* communication, in which one partner uses consistently powerful language while the other responds with powerless speech. A demanding boss and compliant employees or the stereotypically tyrannical husband and submissive wife are examples of complementary relationships. In other relationships, called *symmetrical,* the power is distributed more evenly between the partners: Both may use equally powerful or powerless speech. The locus of power isn't constant: As relationships pass through different stages, the distribution of power shifts, and so do the speech patterns of the partners.[16] You can test this principle for yourself. Recall situations in which you were feeling especially vulnerable, uncertain, confused, or powerless. Did your language include the characteristics listed in Table 3-1? Did these characteristics disappear when you felt more safe, confident, or powerful? What factors led to these changes? The subject being discussed? Your feelings about yourself at the moment? The way the other person was treating you?

Simply counting the number of powerful or powerless statements won't always reveal who has the most control in a relationship. Social rules often mask the real distribution of power. A boss who wants to be pleasant might say to a secretary, "Would you mind retyping this letter?" In truth, both boss and

Couple Weds So They Know What To Call Each Other

This piece will use names of two people, Pietro and Tess.

For three years Pietro and Tess lived together without marrying. Such an arrangement had ceased to be scandalous when they took it up, had even become fashionable. It expressed the partners' reevaluation of the culture, or their liberation from tired old values, or something. It doesn't matter what. Pietro and Tess did it.

They were married a few weeks ago.

The canker in the love nest was the English language. Though English is the world's most commodious tongue, it provided no words to define their relationship satisfactorily to strangers. When Tess took Pietro to meet her parents the problem became troublesome. Presenting Pietro, she said, "Mommy and daddy, this is my lover, Pietro."

Pietro was not amused. "It made me sound like a sex object," he said.

A few weeks later they were invited to meet the president. Entering the reception line, Pietro was asked by the protocol officer for their names. "Pietro," he said. "And this is my mate."

As they came abreast of the president, the officer turned to Mr. Reagan and said, "Pietro and his mate."

"I felt like the supporting actress in a Tarzan movie," said Tess. It took Pietro three nights of sleeping at the YMCA to repair their relationship.

Back to the drawing board, on which they kept the dictionary.

For a while they tried "my friend." One night at a glamorous party Pietro introduced Tess to a marrying millionaire with the words, "This is my friend, Tess." To which the marrying millionaire replied, "Let's jet down to the Caribbean, Tess, and tie the knot."

"You don't understand," said Pietro. "Tess is my *friend.*"

"So don't you like seeing your friends headed for big alimony?" asked the marrying millionaire.

"She's not that kind of friend," said Pietro.

"I'm his *friend,*" said Tess.

"Ah," said the matrimonialist, upon whom the dawn was slowly breaking, "Ah—your—*friend.*"

As Tess explained at the wedding, they couldn't spend the rest of their lives rolling their eyeballs suggestively every time they said "friend." There was only one way out. "The simple thing," Pietro suggested, "would be for me to introduce you as 'my wife.' "

"And for me," said Tess, "to say, 'This is my husband, Pietro.' "

And so they were wed, victims of a failure in language.

Russell Baker
The New York Times

secretary know this is an order and not a request, but the questioning form makes the medicine less bitter.[17] Therefore, a knowledge of the context and the personalities of the speakers is necessary before it's safe to make any assumptions about who controls whom.

ATTRACTION AND INTEREST Social customs discourage us from expressing like or dislike in many situations. Only a clod would respond to the question "What do you think of the cake I baked for you?" by saying, "It's terrible." Bashful or cautious suitors might not admit their attraction to a

Language

potential partner. Even when people are reluctant to speak candidly, the language they use can suggest their degree of interest and attraction toward a person, object, or idea. Morton Weiner and Albert Mehrabian outline a number of linguistic clues that reveal these attitudes.[18]

◆ *Demonstrative pronoun choice.*
These people want our help (positive) vs. *Those* people want our help (less positive).

◆ *Negation.*
It's *good* (positive) vs. It's *not bad* (less positive).

◆ *Sequential placement.*
Dick and Jane (Dick is more important) vs. Jane and Dick (Jane is more important).*

RESPONSIBILITY   In addition to suggesting liking and importance, language can also reveal the speaker's willingness to accept responsibility for a message.

◆ *"It" vs. "I" statements.*
It's not finished (less responsible) vs. *I* didn't finish it (more responsible).

◆ *"You" vs. "I" statements.*
Sometimes *you* wonder if he's honest (less responsible) vs. Sometimes *I* wonder if he's honest (more responsible).

◆ *"But" statements.*
It's a good idea, *but* it won't work. You're really terrific, *but* I think we ought to spend less time together. (*But* cancels everything that went before the word.)

◆ *Questions vs. statements.*
Do you think we ought to do that? (less responsible) vs. I don't think we ought to do that (more responsible).

◆ THE LANGUAGE OF MISUNDERSTANDINGS

After reading this far, you should understand that language isn't the simple tool for expressing ideas that it first seems to be. Some terms have especially high potential for being misunderstood. By becoming more aware of them, your chances for communicating accurately will grow.

Equivocal Language

Equivocal words have more than one correct dictionary definition. Some equivocal misunderstandings are simple and humorous. Not long ago we were ordering dinner in a Mexican restaurant and noticed that the menu described each item as coming with rice or beans. We asked the waitress for "a tostada with beans," but when the order arrived, we were surprised to find that instead

*Sequential placement isn't always significant. You may put "toilet bowl cleaner" at the top of your shopping list simply because it's closer to the market door than champagne.

of a beef tostada with beans on the side as we expected, the waitress had brought a tostada *filled* with beans. Looking back on the incident, it's obvious that the order was an equivocal one.

Other equivocal misunderstandings are more serious. A nurse once told her patient that he "wouldn't be needing" the materials he requested from home. He interpreted the statement to mean he was near death when the nurse meant he would be going home soon. A colleague of ours mistakenly sent some confidential materials to the wrong person after his boss told him to "send them to Richard," without specifying *which* Richard.

As we mentioned earlier, most of the words people use can be interpreted in a number of ways. A good rule to remember if you want to keep misunderstandings to a minimum is "If a word can be interpreted in more than one way, it probably will be." The paraphrasing and questioning skills you will learn in Chapter 4 can help overcome equivocal misunderstandings.

Relative Terms

Relative words gain their meaning by comparison. For example, is the school you attend large or small? This depends on what you compare it to: Alongside a campus like UCLA, with its almost 33,000 students, it probably looks small; but compared with a smaller institution, it might seem quite large. In the same way relative words like *fast* and *slow, smart* and *stupid, short* and *long* depend for their meaning upon what they're compared to. (The "large" size can of olives is the smallest you can buy; the larger ones are "giant," "colossal," and "super-colossal.")

Some relative terms are so common that we mistakenly assume that they have a clear meaning. In one study, graduate students were asked to assign numerical values to terms such as "doubtful," "toss-up," "likely," "probable," "good chance," and "unlikely."[19] There was a tremendous variation in the meaning of most of these terms. For example, the responses for "possible" ranged from 0 to 99 percent. "Good chance meant between 35 and 90 percent, while "unlikely" fell between 0 and 40 percent.

Using relative terms without explaining them can lead to communication problems. Have you ever responded to someone's question about the weather by saying it was warm, only to find out that what was warm to you was cold to the other person? Or have you followed a friend's advice and gone to a "cheap" restaurant, only to find that it was twice as expensive as you expected? Have you been disappointed to learn that classes you've heard were "easy" turned out to be hard, that journeys you were told would be "short" were long, that "unusual" ideas were really quite ordinary? The problem in each case came from failing to anchor the relative term used to a more precisely measurable term.

Emotive Language

To understand how emotive language works, we need to distinguish between **denotation** and **connotation.** A denotative definition describes an event in

◆ The little second grader's family had just moved and she was going to her school for the first time. When she came home that afternoon she said to her mother, "What's sex?" Her mother had been expecting that question for some time and she was ready for her tiny daughter. So, for the next half hour she explained about the birds and the bees. Then she said to her, "Now, do you understand what I have been telling you?" "Yes," her daughter said, "I think I do." Then she showed her mother a school registration card that she had brought home from school and said, "But how am I going to get all of that into this little square?"

Winston K. Pendelton

Language

◆ **How to Tell a Businessman from a Businesswoman**

A businessman is aggressive; a businesswoman is pushy.

He is careful about details; she's picky.

He loses his temper because he's so involved in his job; she's bitchy.

He's depressed (or hung over), so everyone tiptoes past his office; she's moody, so it must be her time of the month.

He follows through; she doesn't know when to quit.

He's firm; she's stubborn.

He makes wise judgments; she reveals her prejudices.

He is a man of the world; she's been around.

He isn't afraid to say what he thinks; she's opinionated.

He exercises authority; she's tyrannical.

He's discreet; she's secretive.

He's a stern taskmaster; she's difficult to work for.

---

purely objective terms, whereas connotative interpretations contain an emotional element. Consider, for example, the term *pregnant.* The denotative meaning of this word involves a condition in which a female is carrying her offspring during a gestation period. When used in this purely biological sense, most people could hear the term without a strong emotional reaction. But imagine the additional turmoil this word would create when an unmarried teenage couple find it stamped on the young woman's lab report. Certainly the meaning to these people would go far beyond the dictionary definition.

Some words have little or no connotative meaning: *the, it, as,* and so on. Others are likely to evoke both denotative and connotative reactions: *cancer, income tax,* and *final examination,* for example. There are also terms that are almost exclusively connotative, such as the *damn!* (or other oath) you would probably utter if you hammered your thumb instead of a nail.

Connotative meanings are a necessary and important part of human communication. It's a fact of life that people, as creatures with emotions, will use some words that will evoke strong reactions. Without connotative meanings, we'd be unable to describe our feelings fully.

Problems occur, however, when people claim to use words in a purely denotative way when they are really expressing their attitudes. **Emotive language,** then, contains words that sound as if they're describing something when they are really announcing the speaker's attitude toward something. Do you like that old picture frame? If so, you would probably call it "an antique," but if you think it's ugly, you would likely describe it as "a piece of junk." Now whether the picture frame belongs on the mantel or in the garbage can is a matter of opinion, not fact, but it's easy to forget this when emotive words are used. Emotive words may sound like statements of fact but are always opinions. The humorous guide "How to Tell a Businessman from a Businesswoman" illustrates how emotive language indirectly expresses the speaker's attitude.

As this list suggests, problems occur when people use emotive terms without labeling them as such. You might, for instance, have a long and bitter argument with a friend about whether a third person was "assertive" or "obnoxious," when a more accurate and peaceable way to handle the issue would be to acknowledge that one of you approves of the behavior and the other doesn't.

Test your ability to identify emotive language by playing the following word game.

a. Take an action, object, or characteristic and show how it can be viewed either favorably or unfavorably, according to the label it is given. For example:

I'm casual
You're careless
He's a slob

I read love stories
You read erotic literature
She reads pornography

b. Now create three-part descriptions of your own, using the following statements as a start:

(1) I'm tactful
(2) I'm conservative
(3) I'm quiet
(4) She's a liar
(5) You have a high opinion of yourself
(6) You're pessimistic

c. Now recall two situations in which you used emotive language as if it were a description of fact. How might the results have differed if you had used more objective language?

FACT-INFERENCE CONFUSION   Some statements refer to things or acts we can observe ("She is driving a Volkswagen"), and some refer to things we can't observe directly ("She is seething with rage"). Although the two types of statements are grammatically identical, they are quite different semantically. **Factual statements** are based on direct observation and are usually easy to verify. **Inferential statements** are interpretations of sense data.

There's nothing wrong with making inferences as long as you identify them as such: "She stomped out and slammed the door. It looked to me as if she were seething with rage." The danger comes when we confuse inferences with facts and make them sound like the absolute truth.

One way to avoid fact-inference confusion is to use the perception checking skill described in Chapter 2 to test the accuracy of your inferences. Recall that a perception check has three parts: a description of the behavior being discussed, your interpretation of that behavior, and a request for verification. For instance, instead of saying, "Why are you laughing at me?" you could say, "When you laugh like that [description of behavior], I get the idea you think something I did was stupid [interpretation]. *Are* you laughing at me [question]?"

Language

EUPHEMISMS Euphemisms (from the Greek word meaning "to use words of good omen") are pleasant terms substituted for more direct but less pleasant ones. Euphemisms soften the impact of information that might be unpleasant. Unfortunately, this pulling of linguistic punches often obscures the accuracy of a message.

There are certainly cases where tactless honesty can be brutal: "What do I think of your new hairstyle? I think it's ugly!" or "How do I feel about the relationship? I can hardly wait to get away from you!" At the same time, being too indirect can leave others wondering where you stand: "What an original haircut," or "We could grow closer than we are now." When you are choosing how to broach difficult subjects, the challenge is to be as kind as possible without sacrificing either your integrity or the clarity of your message. (The guidelines for self-disclosure outlined in Chapter 6 will help you.)

Every year the National Council of Teachers of English (NCTE) bestows its 1984 Doublespeak Award on deserving people or groups who use euphemisms to obscure meaning. The awards are named after the Big Brother governmental language described in George Orwell's *1984.* They are restricted to "misuses of language with more potential to cause harm than garden-variety jargon, gobbledegook, or solecisms."

The following list recognizes some winners from recent years and offers their real-world translations.

Doublespeak	Meaning	Source
Unlawful or arbitrary deprivation of life	Killing	U.S. State Department
Uncontrolled flights into terrain	Airplane crashes	National Transportation Safety Board
Permanent pre-hostility	Peace	U.S. Defense Department
Crew transfer containers	Coffins for space shuttle Challenger crew members	NASA

Explore your everyday use of abstract language by following these steps:

a. Complete each of these sentences:
- (1) Women are...
- (2) Men are...
- (3) In my opinion, conservatives...
- (4) Minorities in America...
- (5) This college is...

b. Share your results with another person who has also completed each of these sentences. Notice any differences in the way each of you used the same terms.

c. Now go back over your list, reducing the subject of each sentence to whatever lower-level abstractions better describe the original idea.

d. Reflect on the unnecessarily abstract terms you use in your everyday communication. In what ways are those terms inaccurate? What misunderstandings do they cause?

Overly Abstract Language

Most objects, events, and ideas can be described with varying degrees of specificity. Consider the material you are reading. You could call it:

A book

A textbook

A communication textbook

Understanding Human Communication

Chapter 3 of *Understanding Human Communication*

Page 79 of Chapter 3 of *Understanding Human Communication*

In each case your description would be more and more specific. Semanticist S. I. Hayakawa created an **abstraction ladder** to describe this process.[20] This ladder consists of a number of descriptions of the same person, object, or event. Lower items focus specifically on the thing under discussion, and higher terms are generalizations that include the subject as a member of a larger class. These higher-level generalizations are absolutely necessary, for without them language would be too cumbersome to be useful. But though higher level abstractions allow us to focus on similarities, they also cause us to ignore differences between the objects being discussed in the category. Thus, overly abstract language can lead to several problems.

1. **Stereotyping.** Imagine someone who has had a bad experience while traveling abroad and, as a result, blames an entire country. "Yeah, those damn Hottentots are a bunch of thieves. If you're not careful, they'll steal you blind. I know because one of 'em stole my camera last year." You can see here how lumping people into highly abstract categories ignores the fact that for every thieving Hottentot there are probably 100 honest ones. It's this kind of thinking that leads to mistaken assumptions that keep people apart: "None of those kids are any damn good!" "You can't trust anybody in business." "Those cops are all a bunch of goons." Each of these statements ignores the very important fact that sometimes our descriptions are too general; that they say more than we really mean.

DOONESBURY   **by Garry Trudeau**

Doonesbury copyright 1982 G. B. Trudeau. Reprinted with permission. All rights reserved.

When you think about examples like these, you begin to see how thinking in abstract terms can lead to ignoring individual differences, which can be as important as similarities. In this sense, semantics isn't "just" a matter of words. People in the habit of using highly abstract language begin to *think* in generalities, ignoring uniqueness. And as we discussed in Chapter 2, expecting people to be a certain way can become a self-fulfilling prophecy. If I think all police officers are brutal, I'm more likely to react in a defensive, hostile way toward them, which, in turn, increases the chance that they'll react to me as a threat. If I think that no teachers care about their classes, then my defensive indifference is likely to make a potentially helpful instructor into someone who truly doesn't care.

2. Confusing others. Imagine the lack of understanding that results from imprecise language in situations like this:

A: "We never do anything that's fun anymore."
B: "What do you mean?"
A: "We used to do lots of unusual things, but now it's the same old stuff, over and over."
B: "But last week we went on that camping trip, and tomorrow we're going to that party where we'll meet all sorts of new people. Those are new things."
A: "That's not what I mean. I'm talking about *really* unusual stuff."
B: *(becoming confused and a little impatient)* "Like what? Taking hard drugs or going over Niagara Falls in a barrel?"
A: "Don't be stupid. All I'm saying is that we're in a rut. We should be living more exciting lives."
B: "Well, I don't know what you want."

Overly **abstract language** also leads to confusing directions:

Professor: "I hope you'll do a thorough job on this paper."
Student: "When you say thorough, how long should it be?"
P: "Long enough to cover the topic thoroughly."
S: "How many sources should I look at when I'm researching it?"
P: "You should use several—enough to show me that you've really explored the subject."
S: "And what style should I use to write it?"
P: "One that's scholarly but not too formal."
S: "Arrgh!!!"

Along with unclear complaints and vague instructions, even appreciations can suffer from being expressed in overly abstract terms. Psychologists have established that behaviors that are reinforced will recur with increased frequency. This means that your statements of appreciation will encourage others to keep acting in ways you like. But if they don't know just what it is that you appreciate, the chances of that behavior's being repeated are lessened. There's a big difference between "I appreciate your being so nice" and "I appreciate the way you spent that time talking to me when I was upset."

The best way to avoid this sort of overly abstract language is to use **behavioral descriptions** instead. See Table 3.2. Behavioral descriptions

TABLE 3-2 Abstract and Behavioral Descriptions

	ABSTRACT DESCRIPTION	BEHAVIORAL DESCRIPTION			REMARKS
		Who is involved	In what circumstances	Specific behaviors	
Problem	"I'm no good at meeting strangers."	People I'd like to date	When I meet them at parties or at school	Think to myself, "They'd never want to date me." Also, I don't originate conversations.	Behavioral description more clearly identifies thoughts and behaviors to change.
Goal	"I'd like to be more assertive."	Telephone and door-to-door solicitors	When I don't want the product or can't afford it	Instead of apologizing or explaining, say, "I'm not interested" and keep repeating this until they go away.	Behavioral description clearly outlines how to act; abstract description doesn't.
Appreciation	"You've been a great boss."	(no clarification necessary)	When I've needed to change my schedule because of school exams or assignments	"You've rearranged my hours cheerfully."	Give both abstract and behavioral descriptions for best results.
Complaint	"I don't like some of the instructors around here."	Professors A and B	In class when students ask questions the professors think are stupid.	Either answer in a sarcastic voice (you might demonstrate) or accuse us of not studying hard enough.	If talking to A or B, use only behavioral description. With others, use both abstract and behavioral descriptions.
Request	"Quit bothering me!"	You and your friends X and Y	When I'm studying for exams	Instead of asking me over and over to party with you, I wish you'd accept my comments that I need to study and leave me to do it.	Behavioral description will reduce defensiveness and make it clear that you don't *always* want to be left alone.

clarify the speaker's meaning whether the message describes a problem, goal, appreciation, complaint, or request. They do so by moving down the abstraction ladder to identify the specific, observable phenomenon being discussed. A thorough description should contain three elements:

1. **Who Is Involved?** Are you speaking for just yourself or for others as well? Are you talking about a group of people ("the neighbors," "women") or specific individuals ("the people next door with the barking dog," "Lola and Lizzie")?

2. **In What Circumstances Does the Behavior Occur?** Where does it occur?: Everywhere or in specific places (at parties, at work, in public)? When does it occur?: When you're tired? When a certain subject comes up?

   The behavior you are describing probably doesn't occur all the time. In order to be understood, you need to pin down what circumstances set this situation apart from other ones.

3. **What Behaviors Are Involved?** Though terms such as "more cooperative" and "helpful" might sound like concrete descriptions of behavior, they are usually too vague to do a clear job of explaining what's on your mind. Behaviors must be *observable,* ideally both to you and to others. For instance, moving down the abstraction ladder from the relatively vague term "helpful," you might come to behaviors such as "does the dishes every other day," "volunteers to help me with my studies," or "fixes dinner once or twice a week without being asked." It's easy to see that terms like these are easier for both you and others to understand than are more vague abstractions.

   There is one exception to the rule that behaviors should be observable, and that involves the internal processes of thoughts and emotions. For instance, in describing what happens to you when a friend has kept you waiting for a long time, you might say, "My stomach felt as if it were in knots—I was really worried. I kept thinking that you had forgotten and that I wasn't important enough to you for you to remember our date." What you're doing when offering such a description is to make unobservable events clear.

Behavioral descriptions can improve communication in a wide range of situations, as Table 3–2 illustrates. Research also supports the value of specific language. One study found that well adjusted couples had just as many conflicts as poorly adjusted couples, but the way the adjusted pairs handled their problems was significantly different. Instead of blaming one another by using emotive language, the well adjusted couples expressed their complaints in behavioral terms.[21]

◆ GENDER AND LANGUAGE

Elements of Communication

So far we have discussed language use as if it were identical for both sexes. In many cases, however, there are significant differences between the way men and women speak.[22]

Content

While there's a great deal of variation within each gender, on the average men and women discuss a surprisingly different range of topics. The first research on conversational topics was conducted over sixty years ago. Despite the changes in male and female roles since then, the results of recent studies are remarkably similar.[23] In these surveys, women and men ranging in age from seventeen to eighty described the range of topics each discussed with friends of the same sex. Certain subjects were common to both sexes: work, movies, and television proved to be frequent topics for both groups. Both men and women reserved discussions of sex and sexuality for members of the same gender. The differences between men and women were more striking than the similarities. Female friends spent much more time discussing personal and domestic subjects, relationship problems, family, health and reproductive matters, weight, food and clothing, men, and other women. Men, on the other hand, were more likely to discuss music, current events, sports, business, and other men. Both men and women were equally likely to discuss personal appearance, sex, and dating in same-sex conversations. True to one common stereotype, women are more likely to gossip about close friends and family. By contrast, men spent more time gossiping about sports figures and media personalities. Women's gossip was no more derogatory than men's.

These differences can lead to frustration when men and women try to converse with one another. Researchers report that "trivial" is the word often used by both sexes to describe topics discussed by the opposite sex. "I want to talk about important things," a woman might say, "like how we're getting along. All he wants to do is talk about the news or what we'll do this weekend."

Reasons for Communicating

Men and women use language for different purposes. Men value talks with friends for their freedom, playfulness, and camaraderie. When researchers asked them what they liked best about their all-male talk, the most frequent answer was its ease. A common theme was appreciation of the practical value of conversation: new ways to solve problems about everyday matters. Some

---

Use your own experience to examine the role gender plays in language. Note differences in the language use of three men and three women you know. Include yourself in the analysis. Consider the following categories:

a. conversational content   **c.** conversational style
b. reasons for communicating   **d.** use of powerful/powerless speech

Your analysis will be most accurate if you tape record the speech of each person you analyze.

How much does gender influence speech? What role do other variables play? Consider occupational or social status, cultural background, social philosophy, competitive-cooperative orientation, and other factors in your analysis.

Language

men also mentioned enjoying the humor and rapid pace that characterized all-male conversations.

Women, on the other hand, seem to look for very different kinds of satisfaction when talking with their friends. The most common theme mentioned in surveys is a feeling of empathy or understanding—"To know you're not alone," as some put it, or "the feeling of sharing and being understood without a sexual connotation." Whereas men commonly describe same-sex conversations as something they *like*, females characterize their woman-to-woman talks as a kind of contact they *need*.

The greater frequency of female conversations reflects their importance. Nearly 50 percent of the women surveyed said they called friends at least once a week just to talk, whereas less than half as many men did so. In fact, 40 percent of the men surveyed reported that they never called another man just to chat.

Conversational Style

Women and men behave differently in conversations than do men.[24] For example, women ask more questions in mixed-sex conversations than do men—nearly three times as many, according to one study. Other research has revealed that in mixed-sex conversations, men interrupt women far more than the other way around. Some theorists have argued that differences like these result in womens' speech that is less powerful and more emotional than mens'. Research has supported these theories—at least in some cases. Even when clues about the speakers' sex were edited out, raters found clear differences between transcripts of male and female speech. In one study womens' talk was judged more aesthetic, while men were seen as more dynamic, aggressive, and strong. In another, male job applicants were rated more fluent, active, confident, and effective than females.

Other studies have revealed that men and women behave differently in certain conversational settings. For example, in mixed-sex dyads men talk longer than women, while in same-sex situations women speak for a longer time. In larger groups, men talk more, while in smaller settings women do more of the speaking.

Given these differences, it's easy to wonder how men and women manage to communicate with one another at all. One reason cross-sex conversations do run smoothly is because women accommodate to the topics men raise. Both men and women regard topics introduced by women as tentative, whereas topics that men bring up are more likely to be pursued. Thus, women seem to grease the wheels of conversation by doing more work than men in maintaining conversations. A complementary difference between men and women also promotes cross-sex conversations: Men are more likely to talk about themselves with women than with other men; and since women are willing to adapt to this topic, conversations are likely to run smoothly, if one-sidedly.

Non-Gender Variables

Despite the differences in the way men and women speak, the link between gender and language use isn't as clear-cut as it might seem. A large number of

"Now that we've learned to talk, try to speak the same language."

By Herbert Goldberg; Copyright © 1970 by Saturday Review Inc.

studies have found no significant difference between male and female speech in areas such as use of profanity, use of qualifiers such as "I guess" or "This is just my opinion," tag questions, and vocal fluency. Some on-the-job research shows that male and female supervisors in similar positions behave the same way and are equally effective. Other studies, however, have found differences between the style of men and women. Female managers were rated as providing more information, putting more emphasis on happy interpersonal relationships, and being more encouraging, receptive to new ideas, concerned, and attentive. Male managers were rated as being more dominant, direct, and quick to challenge. The researchers concluded that "male and female managers [exerted] leadership in their own distinct fashions." They also argued that females may be superior managers because their verbal communication promotes more job satisfaction.

A growing body of research explains some of the apparent contradictions between the similarity and differences between male and female speech. They have revealed other factors which influence language use as much or more than gender. For example, social philosophy plays a role. Feminist wives talk longer than their partners, while nonfeminist wives spoke less than their husbands. Orientation toward problem-solving also plays a role in conversational style. The cooperative or competitive orientations of speakers had more influence on how they interacted than does their gender.

The speaker's occupation also influences speaking style. For example, male day-care teachers' speech to their students resembles the language of female teachers more closely than it resembles the language of fathers at home. Overall, doctors interrupt their patients more often than the reverse, although male patients do interrupt female physicians more often than their male counterparts. A close study of trial transcripts showed that the speaker's experience on the witness stand and occupation had more to do with language use than did gender. If women generally use "powerless" language, this fact probably reflects their social role in society at large. As the balance of power grows more equal between men and women, we can expect many linguistic differences to shrink.

Sex Roles

Why is the research on gender differences so confusing? In some cases male and female speech seems identical, while other studies reveal important differences. As we've already said, one reason for the confusion is that other factors besides gender influence the way people speak: the setting in which conversation takes place, the expertise of the speakers, their social roles (husband/wife, boss/employee, and so on). Also, female roles are changing so rapidly that many women simply don't use the conversational styles that characterized their older sisters and mothers. But in addition to these factors, another powerful force that influences the way individual men and women speak is their **sex role**—the social orientation that governs behavior, rather than the biological gender. Researchers have identified three sex roles: masculine, feminine, and androgynous. These sex types don't always line up neatly with gender. There are "masculine" females, "feminine" males, and androgynous communicators who combine traditionally masculine and feminine characteristics.

Research shows that linguistic differences are often a function of these sex roles more than the speaker's biological sex. Masculine sex–type communicators—whether male or female—use more dominant language than either feminine or androgynous speakers. Feminine communicators have the most submissive speaking style, while androgynous speakers fall between these extremes. When two masculine communicators are in a conversation, they often engage in a one-up battle for dominance, responding to the other's bid for control with a counter-attempt to dominate the relationship. Feminine sex–type speakers are less predictable. They use dominance, submission, and equivalent behavior in an almost random fashion. Androgynous individuals are more predictable: They most frequently met another's bid for dominance with a symmetrical attempt at control, but then move quickly toward an equivalent relationship.

All this information suggests that, when it comes to communicating, "masculinity" and "femininity" are culturally recognized sex roles, and not biological traits. As opportunities for men and women become more equal, we can expect that the differences between male and female use of language will become smaller.

◆ SUMMARY

Language is both one of humanity's greatest assets and the source of many problems. This chapter highlighted the characteristics that distinguish language, and suggested methods of using it more effectively.

Any language is a collection of symbols, governed by a variety of rules, and used to convey messages between people. Because of its symbolic nature, language is not a precise tool: Meanings rest in people, and not in words themselves. In order for effective communication to occur, it is necessary to negotiate meanings for ambiguous statements.

Language not only describes events, but also shapes our perception of them. This point is true for individual labels, which create favorable or unfavorable images for the receiver. Perhaps more significantly, the structure of an entire language may shape the very way its users perceive reality.

Many types of language have potential to create misunderstandings or distort meanings. Equivocal words, relative terms, emotive descriptions, fact-inference confusion, euphemisms, and overly abstract language all need to be recognized and either qualified or avoided.

The relationship between gender and language is a confusing one. There are many differences in the way men and women speak: The content of their conversations varies, as do their reasons for communicating and their conversational style. Not all differences in language use can be accounted for by the speaker's gender, however. Occupation, social philosophy, and orientation toward problem-solving also influence the use of language, and psychological sex role can be more of an influence than biological sex.

Elements of Communication

1. William S. Y. Wang, "Language and Derivative Systems," in William S. Y. Wang (ed.), *Human Communication: Language and Its Psychobiological Basis* (San Francisco, Calif.: Freeman, 1982), p. 36.

2. C. K. Ogden and I. A. Richards, *The Meaning of Meaning* (New York: Harcourt, Brace, 1923), p.11.

3. Jessica Davidson, "How to Translate English," in Joseph Fletcher Littell (ed.), *The Language of Man,* vol. 4 (Evanston, Ill.: McDougal Littel, 1971).

4. Benjamin Lee Whorf, *Language, Thought, and Reality: Selected Writings of Benjamin Lee Whorf,* John B. Carroll (ed.) (Cambridge, Mass.: MIT Press, 1966). See also Harry Hoijer, "The Sapir-Whorf Hypothesis" in Larry A. Samovar and Richard E. Porter (eds.), *Intercultural Communication: A Reader* (Belmont, Calif.: Wadsworth, 1988), pp. 225–232.

5. L. Sinclair, ed., "A Word in Your Ear," in *Ways of Mankind* (Boston: Beacon Press, 1954), pp. 28–29.

6. Neil Postman, *Crazy Talk, Stupid Talk* (New York: Delta, 1976), p. 122.

7. Ibid., pp. 123–124.

8. Research on the following pages is cited in Mary G. Marcus, "The Power of a Name," *Psychology Today* 9 (October 1976): 75–77, 108.

9. Donald H. Naftulin, John E. Ware, Jr., and Frank A. Donnelly, "The Doctor Fox Lecture: A Paradigm of Educational Seduction," *Journal of Medical Education* 48 (July 1973): 630–635. See also C. T. Cory (ed.),"Bafflegab Pays," *Psychology Today* 13 (May 1980): 12.

10. J. Scott Armstrong, "Unintelligible Management Research and Academic Prestige," *Interfaces* 10 (1980): 80–86.

11. Faith L. Jackson and Dorothy K. Williamson-Ige, "The Effects of Black Speech on White College Students' Predictions of Speakers' Educational, Professional, and Social Success," paper presented at annual meeting of the Speech Communication Association, Chicago, 1986.

12. H. Giles and P. F. Poseland, *Speech Style and Social Evaluation* (New York: Academic Press, 1975).

13. C. Miller and K. Swift, "One Small Step for Genkind," *The New York Times Magazine,* April 16, 1972. Reprinted in J. DeVito (ed.), *Language: Concepts and Processes* (Englewood Cliffs, N.J.: Prentice-Hall, 1973), pp. 171–182.

14. See, for example, Lawrence A. Hosman, "The Evaluative Consequences of Hedges, Hesitations, and Intensifiers: Powerful and Powerless Speech Styles," *Human Communication Research* 15 (1989): 383–406.

15. P. Watzlawick, J. H. Beavin, and D. D. Jackson, *Pragmatics of Human Communication* (New York: Norton, 1967).

16. B. A. Fisher and G. R. Drecksel, "A Cyclical Model of Developing Relationships: A Study of Relational Control Interaction," *Communication Monographs* 50 (1983): 66–78.

17. J. Bradac and A. Mulac, "Attributional Consequences of Powerful and Powerless Speech Styles in a Crisis-Intervention Context," *Journal of Language and Social Psychology* 3 (1984): 1–19.

18. Morton Wiener and Albert Mehrabian, *A Language Within Language* (New York: Appleton-Century-Crofts, 1968).

19. T. Wallstein, "Measuring the Vague Meanings of Probability Terms," *Journal of Experimental Psychology: General* 115 (1986): 348–365.

20. S. I. Hayakawa, *Language in Thought and Action* (New York: Harcourt, Brace, 1964).

21. J. K. Alberts, "An Analysis of Couples' Conversational Complaints." *Communication Monographs* 55 (1988): 184–197.

22. For a detailed discussion of the relationship between gender and communication, see Barbara Bate, *Communication and the Sexes* (New York: Harper & Row, 1988) and Judy C. Pearson, *Gender and Communication* (Dubuque, Iowa: W. C. Brown, 1985).

23. See, for example, A. Haas and M. A. Sherman, "Conversational Topic as a Function of Role and Gender," *Psychological Reports* 51 (1982): 453–454; A. Haas and M. A. Sherman, "Reported Topics of Conversation Among Same-Sex Adults," *Communication Quarterly* 30 (1982): 332–342.

24. For a summary of research on difference between male and female conversational behavior, see H. Giles and R. L. Street, Jr. "Communication Characteristics and Behavior," in M. L. Knapp and G. R. Miller (eds.) *Handbook of Interpersonal Communication* (Beverly Hills, Calif.: Sage, 1985): 205–261; and A. Kohn, "Girl Talk, Guy Talk," *Psychology Today* 22 (February 1988): 65–66.

Language

4

After reading this chapter, you should understand the following:

1. The common misconceptions about listening.
2. The four components of the listening process.
3. The nine common types of listening failure.
4. The reasons why people fail to listen effectively.
5. The characteristics of informational, evaluative, and empathic listening.

You should be able to do the following:

1. Appreciate the effort required to listen effectively.
2. Identify the situations in which you listen poorly and explain the reasons for your lack of effectiveness.
3. Demonstrate your ability to follow the guidelines for effective informational, evaluative, and critical listening given in this chapter.

KEY TERMS

advising
ambushing
analyzing
attending
defensive listening
empathic listening
evaluative listening
hearing
informational listening
insensitive listening

insulated listening
judging response
listening
paraphrasing
pseudolistening
questioning
residual message
selective listening
stage hogging
supporting

Listening

In a world where almost everyone acknowledges the importance of better communication, the experience of not being listened to is all too common. The problem is especially bad when you realize that listening is the most frequent type of communication behavior. This fact was established as early as 1926, when Paul Rankin surveyed a group of businesspeople, asking them to record the percentage of time they spent speaking, reading, writing, and listening.[1] Rankin found that his subjects spent more time listening than in any other communication activity, devoting 42 percent of their time to it. Research over the past sixty years continues to show the importance of listening. A recent study (summarized in Figure 4–1) revealed that college students spent an average of 14 percent of their communicating time writing; 16 percent, speaking; 17 percent, reading; and a whopping 53 percent, listening. Listening was broken down further into listening to mass media messages, such as radio and television, and listening to face-to-face messages. Listening to media accounted for 32 percent of the students' communication time whereas listening in person accounted for 21 percent—still more than any other type of face-to-face communication.[2]

Listening, then, is one of the most frequent activities in which we engage. Despite this fact, experience shows that much of the listening we and others do is not at all effective. We misunderstand others and are misunderstood in return. We become bored and feign attention while our minds wander. We engage in a battle of interruptions where each person fights to speak without hearing the other's ideas.

As you'll soon read, some of this poor listening is inevitable. But in other cases we can be better receivers by learning a few basic listening skills. The purpose of this chapter is to help you become a better listener by giving you some important information about the subject. We'll talk about some common

FIGURE 4-1
Types of Communication
Activities

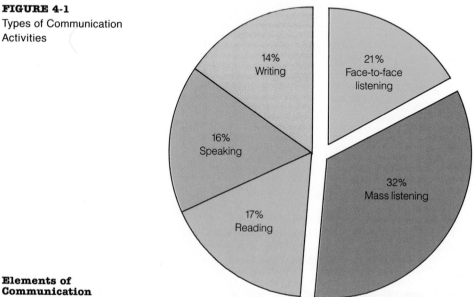

misconceptions concerning listening and show you what really happens when listening takes place. We'll discuss some poor listening habits, explain why they occur, and suggest better alternatives.

◆ MISCONCEPTIONS ABOUT LISTENING

In spite of its importance, listening is misunderstood by most people. Because these misunderstandings so greatly affect our communication, we need to take a look at four common misconceptions that many communicators hold.

Listening and Hearing Are Not the Same Thing

Hearing is the process wherein sound waves strike the eardrum and cause vibrations that are transmitted to the brain. **Listening** occurs when the brain reconstructs these electrochemical impulses into a representation of the original sound and then gives them meaning. Barring illness, injury, or earplugs, hearing cannot be stopped. Your ears will pick up sound waves and transmit them to your brain whether you want them to or not.

Listening, however, is not so automatic. Many times we hear but do not listen. Sometimes we deliberately do not listen. Instead of paying attention to words or other sounds, we avoid them. This most often occurs when we block irritating sounds, such as a neighbor's power lawn mower or the roar of nearby traffic. We also stop listening when we find a subject unimportant

◆ **I can't help hearing, but I don't always listen.**

George Burns

Listening

91

or uninteresting. Boring stories, TV commercials, and nagging complaints are common examples of messages we avoid.

There are also cases when we honestly believe we're listening even though we're merely hearing. For example, recall times when you think you've "heard it all before." It's likely that in these situations you might claim you were listening when, in fact, you had closed your mental doors to new information.

People who confuse listening with hearing often fool themselves into thinking that they're really understanding others when, in fact, they're simply receiving sounds. As you'll see by reading this chapter, true listening involves much more than the passive act of hearing.

Listening Is Not a Natural Process

Another common myth is that listening is like breathing: a natural activity that people do well. "After all," this common belief goes, "I've been listening since I was a child. Why should I have to study the subject in school?"

This attitude is understandable considering the lack of attention most schools devote to listening in comparison with other communication skills. From kindergarten to college, most students receive almost constant training in reading and writing. Every year the exposure to literature continues, from Dick and Jane through Dostoevski. Likewise, the emphasis on writing continues without break. You could probably retire if you had a dollar for every composition, essay, research paper, and bluebook you have written since the first grade. Even spoken communication gets some attention in the curriculum. It's likely that you had a chance to take a public speaking class in high school and another one in college.

Compare all this training in reading, writing, and speaking with the almost total lack of instruction in listening. Even in college there are few courses devoted exclusively to the subject. This state of affairs is especially ironic when you consider the fact that, as mentioned, over half of our communication involves listening.

The truth is that listening is a skill much like speaking: Virtually everyone listens, although few people do it well. Your own experience should prove that communication often suffers owing to poor listening. How many times have others misunderstood directions or explanations because they didn't seem to be receiving your ideas clearly? And how often have you failed to understand others accurately because you weren't receiving their thoughts accurately? The answers to these questions demonstrate the need for effective training in listening.

Listening Is Not a Passive Activity

Most people assume that listening is fundamentally a passive activity in which the receiver absorbs a speaker's ideas rather the way a sponge absorbs water. In truth, even the kind of one-way listening in the linear communication model described in Chapter 1 requires mental effort by the receiver. Probably the most familiar examples include students listening to a professor lecture or viewers paying careful attention to a television program. One-way communication also takes place in interpersonal settings as when one person dominates a conversation while the others fall into the role of audience members or when some parents lecture their children without allowing them to respond.

The most important feature of one-way communication is that it contains little or no feedback. The receiver may deliberately or unintentionally send nonverbal messages that show how the speaker's ideas are being received—nods and smiles, stifled yawns, more or less eye contact—but there's no verbal response to indicate how—or even whether—the message has been received.

Because the speaker isn't interrupted in this type of lecture-conversation, one-way communication has the advantage of being relatively quick. We've all felt like telling someone, "I'm in a hurry. Just listen carefully and don't interrupt." What we're asking for here is one-way communication.

Sometimes one-way communication is an appropriate way of listening. As you'll soon read, sometimes the best way to help people with problems is to hear them out. In many cases, they're not looking for, nor do they need, a verbal response. At times like these, when there's no input by the receiver, *anybody* who will serve as a sounding board will do as a "listener." This explains why some people find relief talking to a pet or a photograph.

One-way communication also works well when the listener wants to ease back mentally and be entertained. It would be a mistake to interrupt a good joke or story or to stand up in the middle of a play and shout out a question to the performers.

But outside of these cases, one-way listening isn't very effective for the simple reason that it almost guarantees that the listener will misunderstand at least some of the speaker's ideas. There are at least three types of misunderstandings. As you read about each of them, think about how often they occur for you.

The first kind of misunderstanding happens when a speaker sends a clear, accurate message that the receiver simply gets wrong. Somehow a quarter cup of sugar is transformed into four cups, or "I'll see you at twelve" is translated into "I'll see you at two."

In other cases, the receiver is listening carefully enough, but the speaker sends an incorrect message. These instances are the reverse of the ones just mentioned, and their results can be just as disastrous.

The third mix-up that comes from one-way communication is probably the most common. The speaker sends a message that may not be incorrect but is overly vague, and the receiver interprets the words in a manner that doesn't match the speaker's ideas. In Chapters 2 and 3 we talked about the problems that come from failing to check out interpretations. In this statement, "I'm a little confused," does "little" mean "slightly," or is it an understatement that could be translated into "very"? When a lover says, "You're my best friend," is this synonymous with the message, "Besides being such a romantic devil, I also feel comfortable with you," or does it mean, "I want to become less of a lover and more of a pal"? You could make your own personal list of confusing messages and in doing so prove the point: Your assumption that you understand another's words isn't always a sure thing. Fortunately, there's another, usually better way of listening.

Listening

All Listeners Do Not Receive the Same Message

When two or more people are listening to a speaker, we tend to assume that they are each hearing and understanding the same message. In fact, such uniform comprehension isn't the case. Communication is *proactive:* Each person involved in a transaction of ideas or feelings responds uniquely. Recall our discussion of perception in Chapter 2, where we pointed out the many factors that cause each of us to perceive an event differently. Physiological factors, social roles, cultural background, personal interests, and needs all shape and distort the raw data we hear into uniquely different messages.

◆ COMPONENTS OF LISTENING

Most communication scholars agree that the term *listening* covers four components.[3]

Hearing

As we have already discussed, *hearing* is the physiological aspect of listening. It is the nonselective process of sound waves impinging on the ear and the ear responding to those waves that fall within a certain frequency range and are sufficiently loud. Hearing is also influenced by background noise. If such noise is the same frequency as the speech sound, then the speech sound is said to be masked; however, if the background noise is of a different frequency from speech, it is called "white noise" and may or may not detract greatly from our ability to hear. Hearing is also affected by auditory fatigue, a temporary loss of hearing caused by continuous exposure to the same tone or loudness. People who spend an evening dancing to a loud band may experience auditory fatigue, and if they are exposed often enough, permanent hearing loss may result.[4]

Attending

After the sounds are converted into electrochemical impulses and transmitted to the brain, a decision—often unconscious—is made whether to focus on what was heard. Though the listening process started as a physiological one, it quickly became a psychological one of **attending.** An individual's needs, wants, desires, and interests determine what is attended to, or selected, to use the term introduced in Chapter 2. If you're hungry, you are more likely to attend to the message about restaurants in the neighborhood from the person next to you than the competing message on the importance of communication from the speaker in front of the room. Table 4–1 lists several factors that influence how closely a listener attends to a message.

> Use the information in Table 4–1 to identify the factors that influenced your ability to accurately receive a message in a recent, important situation. Describe the forces within yourself, the message, the source of that message, and the environment that led you to be an especially effective or ineffective listener.

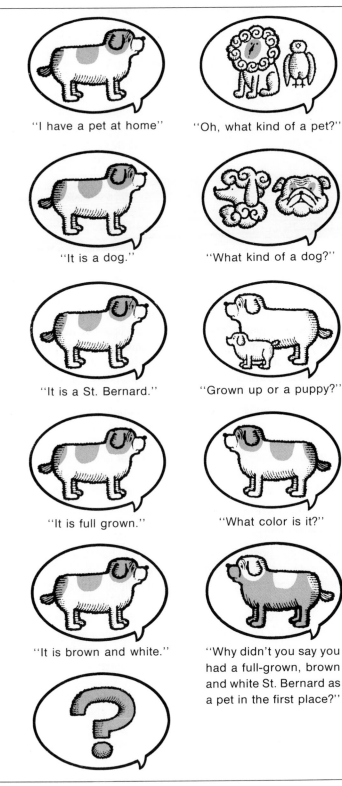

TABLE 4–1   Some Factors Affecting Information Reception

1. THE RECEIVER	**3.** SOURCE
—Needs	—Proximity
—Attitudes, beliefs, values	—Attractiveness
—Goals	—Similarity
—Experience and habit	—Credibility
—Verbal ability and intelligence	—Perceived motivation and intent
2. THE MESSAGE	—Delivery
—Channel	—Status, power, and authority
—Organization	**4.** ENVIRONMENT
—Novelty	—Social context
—Grammatical and	—Physical factors
linguistic rules	—Familiarity

Adapted from *Communication and Human Behavior,* 2d ed., by Brent Ruben (New York: Macmillan, 1988).

Understanding

The component of understanding involves interpreting a message and is composed of several elements, some of which are listed in Table 2–1. For example, understanding a message involves some recognition of the grammatical rules used to create that message. We find the children's books by Dr. Seuss amusing because he breaks the rules of grammar and spelling in interesting ways, and we are familiar enough with the rules to recognize this. Understanding also depends on our knowledge about the source of the message—whether the person is sincere, prone to lie, friendly, an adversary, and so on. *Social context* also influences the understanding of a message. The time and place, for example, help us decide whether to take a friend's insults seriously or as a joke. Understanding depends, generally, on sharing common assumptions about the world. Consider the following two sentences.[5]

1. I bought alligator shoes.
2. I bought horseshoes.

Both sentences can be interpreted the same way because they have the same grammatical structure and may be uttered by the same person (the first two components of understanding). Both could indicate that a person bought two pairs of shoes, one made from alligator, the other from horse, or that two pairs of shoes were purchased, one for an alligator, the other for a horse. However, because of the common semantic assumptions we share about the world, we understand that the first sentence refers to shoes made *from* alligator hides and that the second refers either to shoes *for* horses (or for playing a game).

Finally, understanding often depends on the ability to organize the information we hear into recognizable form. As early as 1948, Ralph Nichols related successful understanding to a large number of factors, most prominent among which were verbal ability, intelligence, and motivation.[6]

Remembering

The complaint "You didn't listen to me" often means "You didn't remember what I said."[7] The ability to recall information is a function of several factors: the number of times the information is heard or repeated, how much information there is to store in the brain, and whether the information may be "rehearsed" or not.

Research has revealed that people remember only about half of what they hear *immediately after* hearing it.[8] This is true even if people work hard at listening. This situation would probably not be too bad if the half remembered right after were retained, but it isn't. Within two months half of the half is forgotten, bringing what we remember down to about 25 percent of the original message. This loss, however, doesn't take two months: People start forgetting immediately (within eight hours the 50 percent remembered drops to about 35 percent). Given the amount of information we process every day—from instructors, friends, the radio, TV, and other sources—the **residual message** (what we remember) is a small fraction of what we hear.

◆ FAULTY LISTENING BEHAVIORS

Although it may not be necessary or desirable to listen effectively all the time, most people possess one or more bad habits that keep them from understanding truly important messages.

Pseudolistening

Pseudolistening is an imitation of the real thing. "Good" pseudolisteners give the appearance of being attentive: They look you in the eye, nod and smile at the right times, and even may answer you occasionally. Behind that appearance of interest, however, something entirely different is going on, for pseudolisteners use a polite facade to mask thoughts that have nothing to do with what the speaker is saying. Often pseudolisteners ignore you because of something on their mind that's more important to them than your remarks. Other times they may simply be bored or think that they've heard what you have to say before, and so they tune out your remarks. Whatever the reasons, the significant fact is that pseudolistening is really counterfeit communication.

Stage Hogging

Stage hogs are interested only in expressing their ideas and don't care about what anyone else has to say. These people will allow you to speak from time to time, but only so they can catch their breath, use your remarks as a basis for their own babbling, or keep you from running away. Stage hogs really aren't conversing when they dominate others—they are making a speech . . . and at the same time probably making an enemy.

◆ **Congress is so strange. A man gets up to speak and says nothing, nobody listens and then everybody disagrees.**

Will Rogers

Listening

Selective Listening

Selective listeners respond only to the parts of a speaker's remarks that interest them, rejecting everything else. All of us are selective listeners from time to time as, for instance, when we screen out media commercials and music while keeping an ear cocked for a weather report or an announcement of time. In other cases, selective listening occurs in conversations with people who expect a thorough hearing but get their partner's attention only when the subject turns to the partner's favorite topic—perhaps money, sex, a hobby, or some particular person. Unless and until you bring up one of these pet subjects, you might as well talk to a tree.

Although failing to listen is a crime we both commit and suffer from, it often goes unnoticed. Trying this activity with a partner will demonstrate its seriousness.

a. Each person, in turn, should take two minutes to discuss with the other his or her ideas about a current issue (abortion, capital punishment, or some other idea that is personally important). But, as the talker shares his or her ideas, the other person should think about the unfinished business in his or her life—incomplete assignments, on-the-job work, things to discuss with the family. The partner shouldn't be rude but should respond politely every so often to the speaker, putting on a good appearance of paying close attention. Nonetheless, the idea is to think about personal concerns, not the speaker's remarks.

b. After each partner completes the preceding step, spend some time sharing the feelings you experienced when you were talking and

Elements of Communication

being listened to by the other. Also discuss how you felt as you thought about your problems instead of listening to the speaker.

c. Next conduct a five-minute discussion with a partner in which each of you shares one personal communication problem you hope to solve. Try to be as sincere and open with your feelings as you can. But as both partners talk, each should try to keep the discussion focused on his or her own problem. Every time the other shares an idea or experience, try to turn it around to relate to your situation. Don't get sidetracked by his or her comments. Your task is to tell the other about your communication problem.

d. After your discussion, take a few minutes to talk about how you felt during the conversation—when the other person ignored your message and when you ignored his or hers.

Filling in Gaps

People who fill in the gaps like to think that what they remember makes a whole story. Because we remember half or less of what we hear, these people manufacture information so that when they retell what they listened to, they can give the impression they "got it all." Of course, filling in the gaps is as dangerous as selective listening: The message that's left is only a distorted (not merely incomplete) version of the message that could have been received.

Assimilation to Prior Messages

We all have a tendency to interpret current messages in terms of similar messages remembered from the past. This phenomenon is called *assimilation to prior input.* A problem arises for those who go overboard with this and push, pull, chop, squeeze, and in other ways mutilate messages they receive to *make sure* they are consistent with what they heard in the past. This unfortunate situation occurs when the current message is in some way uniquely different from past messages.

Insulated Listening

Insulated listeners are almost the opposite of their selective-listening cousins. Instead of looking for something, these people avoid it. Whenever a topic arises they'd rather not deal with, insulated listeners simply fail to hear it or, rather, to acknowledge it. If you remind them about a problem—perhaps an unfinished job, poor grades, or the like—they'll nod or answer you and then promptly forget what you've just said.

Defensive Listening

Defensive listeners take innocent comments as personal attacks. Teenagers who perceive parental questions about friends and activities as distrustful snooping are defensive listeners as are insecure breadwinners who explode when their mates mention money or touchy parents who view any questioning by their children as a threat to their authority and parental wisdom. It's fair to assume that many defensive listeners are suffering from shaky public images and avoid admitting this by projecting their insecurities onto others.

Ambushing

Ambushers listen carefully, but only because they are collecting information to attack what you have to say. The cross-examining prosecution attorney is a good example of an ambusher. Needless to say, using this kind of strategy will justifiably initiate defensiveness on the other's behalf.

Insensitive Listening

Insensitive listeners offer the final example of people who don't receive another person's messages clearly. People often don't express their thoughts or feelings openly but instead communicate them through subtle and unconscious choice of words or nonverbal clues or both. Insensitive listeners aren't able to look beyond the words and behavior to understand their hidden meanings. Instead, they take a speaker's remarks at face value.

It's important not to go overboard in labeling listeners as insensitive. Often a seemingly mechanical comment is perfectly appropriate. This most often occurs in situations involving *phatic* communication, in which a remark derives its meaning totally from context. For instance, the question "How are you?" doesn't call for an answer when you pass an acquaintance on the street. In this context, the statement means no more than "I acknowledge your existence, and I want to let you know that I feel friendly toward you." It is not an inquiry about the state of your health. Although insensitive listening is depressing, you would be equally discouraged to hear a litany of aches and pains every time you asked, "How's it going?"

◆ REASONS FOR POOR LISTENING

Despite the importance of good listening, people seem to get worse at the skill as they grow older.[9] Teachers at various grade levels were asked to stop their lectures periodically and ask students what they were talking about. Ninety percent of first grade children could repeat what the teacher had been saying, and 80 percent of the second graders could do so; but when the experiment was repeated with teenagers, the results were much less impressive. Only 44 percent of junior high students and 28 percent of senior high students could repeat their teachers' remarks.

Research suggests that adults listen even more poorly—at least in some important relationships. One experiment found that people listened more attentively and courteously to strangers than to their spouses. When faced with decision-making tasks, couples interrupted one another more frequently and were generally less polite than they were to strangers.[10]

What causes people to listen poorly? There are several reasons, some of which can be avoided and others which are sad but inescapable facts of life.

Effort

Listening effectively is hard work. The physical changes that occur during careful listening show the effort it takes: Heart rate quickens, respiration increases, and body temperature rises.[11] Notice that these changes are similar to the body's reaction to physical effort. This is no coincidence, for listening carefully to a speaker can be just as taxing as more obvious efforts.

Message Overload

The amount of speech most of us encounter everyday makes careful listening to everything we hear impossible. As we've already seen, many of us spend as much as one-third of the time we're awake listening to verbal messages—from teachers, coworkers, friends, family, salespeople, and total strangers. This means we often spend five hours or more a day listening to people talk. If you add this to the amount of time we tune in radio and television, you can see that it's impossible for us to keep our attention totally focused for this amount of time. Therefore, we have to let our attention wander at times.

Rapid Thought

Listening carefully is also difficult for a physiological reason. Although we are capable of understanding speech at rates up to 300 words per minute,[12] the average person speaks between 100 and 140 words per minute.[13] Thus, we have a great deal of mental "spare time" to spend while someone is talking. And the temptation is to use this time in ways that don't relate to the speaker's ideas, such as thinking about personal interests, daydreaming, planning a rebuttal, and so on. The trick is to use this spare time to understand the speaker's ideas better rather than letting your attention wander.

> Use the categories on pages 97–100 to describe the faulty listening behaviors you use in your everyday interactions. In what circumstances do you use these behaviors: Around whom? With what subjects? In what settings? At what times? What are the main reasons for your failure to listen in these circumstances? How satisfied are you with your findings? How could you change your behavior in the unsatisfying areas?

Psychological Noise

Another reason we don't always listen carefully is that we're often wrapped up in personal concerns that are of more immediate importance to us than the messages others are sending. It's hard to pay attention to someone else when you're anticipating an upcoming test or thinking about the wonderful time you had last night with good friends. Yet we still feel we have to "listen" politely to others, and so we continue with our charade.

Physical Noise

The world in which we live often presents distractions that make it hard to pay attention to others. The sound of traffic, music, others' speech, and the like interfere with our ability to hear well. Also, fatigue or other forms of discomfort can distract us from paying attention to a speaker's remarks. Consider, for example, how the efficiency of your listening decreases when you are seated in a crowded, hot, stuffy room that is surrounded by traffic and other noises. In such circumstances even the best intentions aren't enough to ensure clear understanding.

Hearing Problems

Sometimes a person's listening ability suffers from a physiological hearing problem. Once a hearing problem has been diagnosed, it's often possible to treat it. The real tragedy occurs when a hearing loss goes undetected. In such cases, both the person with the defect and others can become frustrated and annoyed at the ineffective communication that results. If you suspect that you or someone you know suffers from a hearing loss, it's wise to have a physician or audiologist perform an examination.

Faulty Assumptions

We often make incorrect assumptions that lead us to believe that we're listening attentively when quite the opposite is true. If the subject is a familiar one, it's easy to think that you've "heard it all before" when, in fact, the speaker is offering new information. A related problem arises if you assume that a speaker's thoughts are too simple or obvious to deserve careful attention when the truth is that you ought to be listening carefully. At other times, just the opposite occurs: You think that another's comments are too complex to possibly understand (as in some lectures) and so give up trying to make sense of them. A final mistake people often make is to assume that a subject is unimportant and to stop paying attention when they ought to be listening carefully.

Talking Has More Apparent Advantages

It often appears that we have more to gain by speaking than by listening. One big advantage of speaking is that it gives you a chance to control others' thoughts and actions. Whatever your goal—to have a prospective boss hire you, to convince others to vote for the candidate of your choice, or to describe the way you want your hair cut—the key to success seems to be the ability to speak well.

Another apparent advantage of speaking is the chance it provides to gain the admiration, respect, or liking of others. Tell jokes, and everyone will think you're a real wit. Offer advice, and they'll be grateful for your help. Tell them all you know, and they'll be impressed by your wisdom. But keep quiet . . . and it seems as if you'll look like a worthless nobody.

What Good Is Free Speech If No One Listens?

It is the law in this country, as in no other, that the individual has an extraordinary right to personal expression. The First Amendment to the Constitution protects the right to speak and to publish; these rights and the degree to which they are safeguarded are the distinguishing characteristics of American society.

For that we have only the courts to thank. Americans seem to be almost completely uninterested in any point of view other than their individual own. We are absolutely up to our necks in groups and blocs and religious and economic interests certain beyond all reason that they are correct and actively interested in imposing their rules and values and self-selected morals on the rest of us. They prattle about democracy, and use it when it suits them without the slightest regard or respect for what it means and costs and requires. These people are—please believe me—dangerous.

The right to speak is meaningless if no one will listen, and the right to publish is not worth having if no one will read. It is simply not enough that we reject censorship and will not countenance suppression; we have an affirmative responsibility to hear the argument before we disagree with it.

I think that you think that you agree with me, that you are fair and open-minded and good citizens. But if we put it to the test—if I make up some speeches about gun control, abortion, gay rights, racial and ethnic characteristics, political terrorism and genocide—I believe that I can make you boo and jeer or at least walk out in protest.

We cannot operate that way. It's not difficult to listen to the philosophy you agree with or don't care about. It's the one that galls that must be heard. No idea is so repugnant that it must not be advocated. If we are not free to speak heresy and utter awful thoughts, we are not free at all. And if we are unwilling to hear that with which we most violently disagree, we are no longer citizens but have become part of the mob.

Nowhere is the willingness to listen more important than at a university, and nowhere is our failure more apparent than at the university whose faculty members or students think that it's legitimate to parade their own moral or political purity by shouting down the unpopular view of the day.

It will not be a week, and certainly not a month, before you will become aware that someone in your own circle of influence is saying something or thinking something very wrong. I think you have to do something about that. I think you have to help them be heard. I think you are required to listen.

Kurt Luedtke

Finally, talking gives you the chance to release energy in a way that listening can't. When you're frustrated, the chance to talk about your problems can often help you feel better. In the same way, you can often lessen your anger by letting it out verbally. It is also helpful to share your excitement with others by talking about it, for keeping it inside often leaves you feeling as if you might burst.

Although it's true that talking does have many advantages, it's important to realize that listening can pay dividends, too. As you'll soon read, being a good listener is one way to help others with their problems; and what better way is there to have others appreciate you? As for controlling others, it may be true

Listening

103

that it's hard to be persuasive while you're listening, but your willingness to hear others out will often leave them open to thinking about your ideas in return. Like defensiveness, listening is often reciprocal: You get what you give.

Lack of Training

Even if we want to listen well, we're often hampered by a lack of skill. As we've already said, listening is a skill much like speaking: Virtually everybody does it, although few people do it well. As you read through this chapter, you'll see that one reason so much poor listening exists is because most people fail to follow the important steps that lead to real understanding.

◆ TYPES OF LISTENING

Although good listening isn't easy, it is possible. An important fact to realize is that there are several different types of listening, and that each one requires a different approach.

Informational Listening

Informational listening is the approach to take when you want to understand another person. As an informational listener, your goal is to make sure you are receiving the same thoughts the other person is trying to convey—not always an easy feat when you consider the forces listed on pages 100–104 that interfere with understanding.

The situations that call for informational listening are endless and varied: following an instructor's comments in class, listening to a friend's account of a night on the town, hearing a description of a new piece of equipment you're thinking about buying, learning about your family history from a relative's tales, swapping ideas in a discussion about religion or politics . . . the list goes on and on. You can become more effective as an informational listener by following several guidelines.

DON'T JUDGE PREMATURELY Most people would agree with the principle that it's essential to understand a speaker's ideas before judging them. Despite this commonsense fact, all of us are guilty of forming snap judgments, evaluating others before hearing them out. This tendency is greatest when the speaker's ideas conflict with our own. Conversations that ought to be exchanges of ideas turn into verbal battles, with the "opponents" trying to ambush one another in order to win a victory. Disagreements aren't the only kind of conversation in which the tendency to judge others is strong: It's also tempting to counter-attack when others criticize you, even when those criticisms might contain valuable truths and when understanding them might lead to a change for the better. Even if there is no criticism or disagreement, we tend to evaluate others based on sketchy first impressions, forming snap

◆ There is no such thing as an uninteresting sub-ject. There are only uninterested people.

G.K. Chesterton

judgments that aren't at all valid. Not all premature judgments are negative. It's also possible to jump to overly favorable conclusions about the quality of a speaker's remarks when we like that person or agree with the ideas being expressed. The lesson contained in these negative examples is clear: Listen first. Make sure you understand. *Then* evaluate.

BE OPPORTUNISTIC   Sooner or later you will find yourself listening to information that is either so unimportant or so badly delivered that you're tempted to tune out. Although making a quick escape from such tedious situations is often the best thing to do, there are times when you can profit from paying close attention to apparently worthless communication. This is especially true when you're trapped in a situation where the only alternatives to attentiveness are pseudolistening or downright rudeness.

As an opportunistic listener you can find *some* value in even the worst situations, if you are willing to invest the effort. Consider how you might listen opportunistically when you find yourself locked in a boring conversation with someone whose ideas are worthless. Rather than torture yourself until escape is possible, you could keep yourself amused—and perhaps learn something

◆ Know how to listen and you will profit even from those who talk badly.

Plutarch

Listening

useful—by listening carefully until you can answer the following (unspoken) questions: "Is there anything useful in what this person is saying?" "What led the speaker to come up with ideas like these?" "What lessons can I learn from this person that will keep me from sounding the same way in other situations?"

You can see for yourself what a difference paraphrasing can make by trying this exercise either in class or with a companion on your own.

a. Find a partner; then move to a place where you can talk comfortably. Designate one person as A and the other as B.

b. Find a subject on which you and your partner apparently disagree— a personal dispute, a philosophical or moral issue, or perhaps a matter of personal taste.

c. A begins by making a statement on the subject. B's job is then to paraphrase the idea back, beginning by saying something like "What I hear you saying is . . ." It is very important that in this step B feeds back only what he or she heard A say without adding any judgment or interpretation. B's job is simply to *understand* here, and doing so in no way should signify agreement or disagreement with A's remarks.

d. A then responds by telling B whether or not the response was accurate. If there were some misunderstanding, A should make the correction, and B should feed back a new understanding of the statement. Continue this process until you're both sure that B understands A's statement.

e. Now it's B's turn to respond to A's statement and for A to help the process of understanding by correcting B.

f. Continue this process until both partners are satisfied that they have explained themselves fully and that they have been understood by the other person.

g. Now discuss the following questions:

(1) As a listener, how accurate was your first understanding of the speaker's statements?

(2) How did your understanding of the speaker's position change after you used paraphrasing?

(3) Did you find that the gap between your position and that of your partner narrowed as a result of your both using paraphrasing?

(4) How did you feel at the end of your conversation? How does this feeling compare to your usual emotional state after discussing controversial issues with others?

(5) How might your life change if you used paraphrasing at home? At work? With friends?

LOOK FOR KEY IDEAS It's easy to lose patience with long-winded speakers who never seem to get to the point—or *have* a point, for that matter. Nonetheless, most people do have a central idea, or what we will call a thesis in Chapter 12. By using your ability to think more quickly than the speaker can talk, you may be able to extract the thesis from the surrounding mass of words you're hearing. If you can't figure out what the speaker is driving at, you can always ask in a tactful way by using the skills of questioning and paraphrasing, which we'll examine now.

ASK QUESTIONS AND PARAPHRASE   Questioning and paraphrasing are forms of verbal feedback, and both are quite different from the one-way passive listening style described earlier in this chapter.

Questioning involves asking for additional information to clarify your idea of the sender's message. If you ask directions to a friend's house, typical questions might be "Is your place an apartment?" or "How long does it take to get there from here?" In more serious situations, questions could include "What's bothering you?" or "Why are you so angry?" or "Why is that so important?" Notice that one key element of these questions is that they request the speaker to elaborate on information already given.

Questioning is often a valuable tool for increasing understanding. Sometimes, however, it won't help you receive a speaker's ideas any more clearly, and it can even lead to further communication breakdown. To see how this can be so, consider our example of asking directions to a friend's home. Suppose the instructions you've received are to "drive about a mile and then turn left at the traffic signal." Now imagine that a few common problems exist in this simple message. First, suppose that your friend's idea of a mile is different from yours: Your mental picture of the distance is actually closer to two miles whereas hers is closer to 300 yards. Next, consider the very likely occurrence that though your friend said "traffic signal," she meant "stop sign"; after all, it's common for us to think one thing and say another. Keeping these problems in

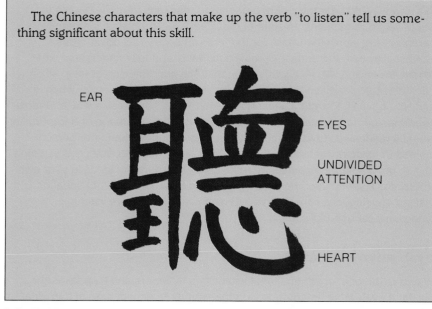

The Chinese characters that make up the verb "to listen" tell us something significant about this skill.

EAR

EYES

UNDIVIDED ATTENTION

HEART

Calligraphy by Angie Au.

Listening

mind, suppose you tried to verify your understanding of the directions by asking, "After I turn at the light, how far should I go?" to which your friend replied that her house is the third from the corner. Clearly, if you parted after this exchange, you would encounter a lot of frustrations before finding the elusive residence.

What was the problem here? It's easy to see that questioning didn't help, for your original ideas of how far to drive and where to turn were mistaken. And contained in such mistakes is the biggest problem with questioning, for such inquiries don't tell you whether you have accurately received the information that has *already* been sent.

Now consider another kind of feedback—one that would tell you whether you understood what had already been said before you asked additional questions. This sort of feedback, termed **paraphrasing,** involves restating in your own words the message you thought the speaker had just sent, without adding anything new. In the example of seeking directions that we've been using, such rephrasing might sound like this: "So you're telling me to drive down to the traffic light by the high school and turn toward the mountains, is that it?" Immediately sensing the problem, your friend could then reply, "Oh no, that's way too far. I meant that you should drive to the four-way stop by the park and turn there. Did I say stop light? I always do that when I mean stop sign!"

Successful paraphrasing depends on the speaker's *restating* the sender's ideas, not parroting them. If you simply repeat the speaker's comments verbatim, you'll sound foolish or hard of hearing, and, just as important, you still might be misunderstanding what's been said.

At first, paraphrasing might seem to have little to recommend it. After all, it's an unfamiliar tool, which means that you'll have to go through a period of awkwardness while learning it. And until you become skillful at responding in this new way, you run the risk of getting odd reactions from the people to whom you're responding. In spite of these very real problems, learning to paraphrase is worth the effort, for it offers some very real advantages.

First, it boosts the odds that you'll accurately and fully understand what others are saying. We've already seen that one-way listening or even asking questions may lead you to think that you've understood a speaker when, in fact, you haven't. Paraphrasing, on the other hand, serves as a way of double-checking your interpretation for accuracy. A second advantage of paraphrasing is that it guides you toward sincerely trying to understand another person instead of using nonlistening styles such as stage hogging, selective listening, and so on. If you force yourself to reflect the other person's ideas in your own words, you'll spend your mental energy trying to understand that speaker instead of using less constructive listening styles: defensive listening, ambushing, or pseudolistening.

Evaluative Listening

Whereas the goal of informational listening is to understand a speaker, the object of **evaluative listening** is to judge—either to accept or reject an idea. Evaluative listening is appropriate when someone is trying to persuade you.

For example, to buy a product, act in a certain way, or accept a belief. You will be most effective as an evaluative listener if you follow several guidelines.

LISTEN FOR INFORMATION BEFORE EVALUATING   The principle of listening for information before evaluating seems almost too obvious to mention, yet all of us are guilty of judging a speaker's ideas before we completely understand them. The tendency to make premature judgments is especially strong when the idea you are hearing conflicts with your own beliefs.

You can avoid the tendency to judge before understanding by following the simple rule of paraphrasing a speaker's ideas before responding to them. The effort required to translate the other person's ideas into your own words will keep you from arguing, and if your interpretation is mistaken, you'll know immediately.

EVALUATE THE SPEAKER'S CREDIBILITY   The acceptability of an idea often depends on its source. If your longtime family friend, the self-made millionaire, invited you to invest your life savings in jojoba fruit futures, you might be grateful for the tip. If your deadbeat brother-in-law made the same offer, you would probably laugh off the suggestion.

Recall three recent instances in which you listened evaluatively. Answer the following questions for each situation:

a. Was this an appropriate time for evaluating, or should you have been listening for information?
b. How did the speaker's competence and impartiality affect the merits of the topic being discussed?
c. What kinds of evidence did the speaker offer? Was the evidence valid?
d. Did the speaker use any emotional appeals? How did you react to them?

Chapter 15 discusses credibility in detail, but two questions provide a quick guideline for deciding whether or not to accept a speaker as an authority:

◆ *Is the speaker competent?* Does the person have the experience or the expertise to qualify as an authority on this subject? Note that someone who is knowledgeable in one area may not be as well qualified to comment on another topic. For instance, your friend who can answer any question about computer programming might be a terrible advisor when the subject turns to romance.

◆ *Is the speaker impartial?* Knowledge alone isn't enough to certify a speaker's ideas as acceptable. People who have a personal stake in the outcome of a topic are more likely to be biased. The unqualified praise a commission-earning salesperson gives a product may be more suspect than the mixed review you get from a user. This doesn't mean you should disregard any comments you hear from an involved party—only that you should consider the possibility of deliberate or unintentional bias.

Listening

EXAMINE THE SPEAKER'S EVIDENCE   Speakers usually offer some kind of support to back up their statements. A car dealer who argues that domestic cars are just as reliable as imports might cite frequency-of-repair statistics from *Consumer Reports* or refer you to satisfied customers, for example; and a professor arguing that students don't work as hard as they used to might tell stories about then and now to back up the thesis.

Chapter 12 describes several types of supporting material that can be used to prove a point: definitions, descriptions, analogies, statistics, and so on. Whatever form the support takes, you can ask two fundamental questions to judge its quality. First, ask whether the evidence is true. Most people won't tell deliberate lies, but they may misquote the facts or even distort them out of enthusiasm—rather like an angler who exaggerates the size of a fish in a desire to make the story more impressive. In addition to making sure the speaker's statements are true, be sure to ask whether enough evidence is given. A small number of examples may not prove a point. For example, one or two bad experiences don't necessarily make it true that "all men (or women) are jerks."

EXAMINE EMOTIONAL APPEALS   Sometimes emotion alone may be enough reason to persuade you. You might lend your friend $20 just for old time's sake even though you don't expect to see the money again soon. In other cases, it's a mistake to let yourself be swayed by emotion when the logic of a point isn't sound. The excitement of fun in an ad or the lure of low monthly payments probably aren't good enough reasons to buy a product you can't afford.

Empathic Listening

We listen both informationally and evaluatively out of self-interest. In **empathic listening,** however, the goal is to help the speaker solve a problem. Sometimes others seek help for personal dilemmas: "I don't know whether to split up or to stay with him." The problem needn't be so profound, however. A friend might be trying to decide what birthday gift to buy or whether to switch jobs.

Although the immediate goal of empathic listening is to help the other person, an additional payoff is that the relationship between speaker and listener improves.[14] For example, couples who communicate in ways that show they understand one another's feelings and ideas are more satisfied with their marriages than couples who express less understanding. The opposite is also true: In marriages where husbands do not give emotional responses to their wives, the stress level grows.

Whatever the issue, there are several ways you can respond to another person's request for help. Perhaps the most common response style is **advising:** recommending a solution to the problem. Although advice can be useful in some instances, it won't always help.

Often your suggestion may not offer the best course to follow, in which case it can even be harmful. There's often a temptation to tell others how you would behave in their place, but it's important to realize that what's right for one person may not be right for another. A related consequence of advising is that it often allows others to avoid responsibility for their decisions. A partner who follows a suggestion of yours that doesn't work out can always pin the blame on you. Finally, often people simply don't want advice: They may not be ready to accept it, needing instead simply to talk out their thoughts and feelings.

Before offering advice, then, you need to be sure that three conditions are present. First, you should be confident that your advice is correct. It's essential to resist the temptation to act like an authority on matters about which you know little. It's equally important to remember that just because a course of action worked for you doesn't guarantee that it will be correct for everybody. Second, you need to be sure that the person seeking your advice is truly ready to accept it. In this way, you can avoid the frustration of making good suggestions, only to find that the person with the problem had another solution in mind all the time. Finally, when offering advice, you should be certain that the receiver won't blame you if the advice doesn't work. You may be offering the suggestions, but the choice and responsibility of following them are up to the other person.

A **judging response** evaluates the sender's thoughts or behaviors in some way. The judgment may be favorable—"That's a good idea" or "You're on the right track now"—or unfavorable—"An attitude like that won't get you anywhere." But, in either case, it implies that the person doing the judging is in some way qualified to pass judgment on the speaker's thoughts or actions.

Sometimes negative judgments are purely critical. How many times have you heard such responses as "Well, you asked for it!" or "I *told* you so!" or "You're just feeling sorry for yourself"? Although comments like these can sometimes serve as a verbal slap that brings problem-holders to their senses, they usually make matters worse.

Peanuts reprinted by permission of UFS, Inc.

In other cases, negative judgments are less critical. These involve what we usually call *constructive criticism,* which is intended to help the problem-holder improve in the future. This is the sort of response given by friends about everything from the choice of clothing to jobs to friends. Another common setting for constructive criticism occurs in school, where instructors evaluate students' work to help them master concepts and skills. But whether it's justified or not, even constructive criticism runs the risk of arousing defensiveness because it may threaten the self-concept of the person at whom it is directed.

Judgments have the best chance of being received when two conditions exist. First, the person with the problem should have requested an evaluation from you. In addition, your judgments should be genuinely constructive and not designed to be disparaging. If you can remember to follow these two guidelines, your judgments will probably be less frequent and better received.

In an **analyzing response,** the listener offers an interpretation to a speaker's message. Analyses like these are probably familiar to you:

"I think what's really bothering you is. . . . "

"She's doing it because. . . . "

"I don't think you really meant that."

"Maybe the problem started when she. . . . "

Interpretations are often effective ways to help people with problems to consider alternative meanings—ways they would have never thought of without your help. Sometimes a clear analysis will make a confusing problem suddenly clear either suggesting a solution or at least providing an understanding of what is occurring.

In other cases, an analysis can create more problems than it solves. There are two problems with analyzing. First, your interpretation may not be correct, in which case the speaker may become even more confused by accepting it. Second, even if your analysis is accurate, telling it to the problem-holder might not be useful. There's a chance that it will arouse defensiveness (for analysis implies superiority and evaluativeness), and even if it doesn't, the person may not be able to understand your view of the problem without working it out personally.

How can you know when it's helpful to offer an analysis? There are several guidelines to follow. First, it's important to offer your interpretation in a tentative way rather than as absolute fact. There's a big difference between saying, "Maybe the reason is . . . " and insisting, "This is the truth." Second, your analysis ought to have a reasonable chance of being correct. We've already said that a wild, unlikely interpretation can leave a person more confused than before. Third, you ought to be sure that the other person will be receptive to your analysis. Even if you're completely accurate, your thoughts won't help if the problem-holder isn't ready to consider what you say. Finally, you should be

Elements of Communication

sure that your motive is truly to help the other person. It's sometimes tempting to offer an analysis to show how brilliant you are or even to make the other person feel bad for not having thought of the right answer in the first place. Needless to say, an analysis offered under these conditions isn't very helpful.

A few pages ago we talked about questioning as one way for you to understand others better. A **questioning response** can also be a way to help others think about their problem and understand it more clearly. For example, questioning can help a problem-holder define vague ideas more precisely. You might respond to a friend with a line of questioning: "You said Greg has been acting 'differently' toward you lately. What has he been doing?" Another example of a question that helps clarify is as follows: "You told your room-mates that you wanted them to be more helpful in keeping the place clean. What would you like them to do?"

Questions can also encourage a problem-holder to examine a situation in more detail by talking either about what happened or about personal feelings, for example, "How did you feel when they turned you down? What did you do then?" This type of questioning is particularly helpful when you are dealing with someone who is quiet or is unwilling under the circumstances to talk about the problem very much.

Although asking questions can definitely be helpful, two dangers can arise from using this style too much or at the wrong times. The first is that your questions may lead the problem-holder on a wild goose chase, away from a solution to the problem. For instance, asking, "When did the problem begin?" might provide some clue about how to solve it—but it could also lead to a long digression that would only confuse matters. As with advice, it's important to be sure you're on the right track before asking questions.

A second danger is that questioning can also be a way of disguising advice or criticism. We've all been questioned by parents, teachers, or other figures who seemed to be trying to trap or indirectly to guide us. In this way, questioning becomes a strategy and often implies that the person doing the asking already has some idea of what direction the discussion should take.

A **supporting response** can take several forms. Sometimes it involves reassuring: "You've got nothing to worry about—I know you'll do a good job." In other cases, support comes through comforting: "Don't worry. We all love you." We can also support people in need by distracting them with humor, kidding, and joking.

Sometimes a person needs encouragement, and in these cases a supporting response can be the best thing. But in many instances this kind of comment isn't helpful at all; in fact, it can even make things worse. Telling a person who is obviously upset that everything is all right or joking about what seems like a serious problem can communicate the idea that you don't think the problem is really worth all the fuss. People might see your comments as a put-down, leaving them feeling worse than before. As with the other styles we've discussed, supporting *can* be helpful . . . but only in certain circumstances.

A final type of helping response involves paraphrasing. This sort of response has several advantages. First, it provides a check on your understanding, allowing you to be sure you are responding to what the speaker is

Listening

actually thinking and not to some misinterpretation. In addition, paraphrasing can be an effective way to show empathy. In order to be truly empathic, however, your response has to include the nonverbal behaviors that show you are really interested. A mechanical rephrasing won't be much help at all. Beyond assuring your understanding and demonstrating empathy, paraphrasing responses can help others sort out and solve problems for themselves.

When you use paraphrasing as a helping tool, your reflection should contain two elements. The first is a restatement of the speaker's *thoughts.* Though it might seem unnecessary to restate an idea the other person has just uttered, your paraphrasing statement can help the speaker take a more objective look at what's been said, and possibly to clarify the idea. Besides a replaying of the speaker's thoughts, it is also important to reflect the often unspoken *emotions* that accompany the verbal message.

The following suggestions will help you become a more effective empathic listener:

USE A VARIETY OF RESPONSE STYLES   Most people rely too heavily on one or two styles of responding. Some are instinctive advisers whereas others reflexively try to offer help by supporting, judging, or analyzing. Although each of these responses has its place, overusing any of them is less effective than choosing the kind of feedback that seems most helpful in a given situation. When you are faced with the chance to help another person, consider which type of communication will do the best job.

LISTEN FOR FEELINGS AS WELL AS THOUGHTS   In most cases, the speaker's feelings are at least as important as the thoughts being expressed. Despite this fact, people often fail to mention their feelings at all. Consider the emotions that accompany each of these statements:

"My boss has been terrible lately, but I'm afraid I'll lose my job if I speak up, and I can't afford that."

"Who does she think she is, talking to me like that? I know that's just her style, but I don't think I can take it any more."

"I really need the vacation, but I can't decide whether to spend my savings or save them for all the expenses I know will come up next year."

By paraphrasing the emotions you recognize in statements like these, you invite the speaker to explore those important feelings in depth. Focusing on just the rational parts of a message often ignores the most fundamental parts of a problem.

AVOID BEING TOO JUDGMENTAL   Although judging responses ("It's your own fault, you know.") may be correct, they rarely help. Most of us receive more judgments than we need, and often having a listener who doesn't evaluate is far more helpful than a lecture.

◆ **SUMMARY**

Even the best message is useless if it goes unreceived or if it is misunderstood. For this reason, listening—the process of giving meaning to an oral message—is a vitally important part of the communication process. We began our look at the subject by identifying and refuting several myths about listening. Our conclusion here was that effective listening is a skill that needs to be developed in order for us to be truly effective in understanding others.

We next took a close look at four steps in the process of listening: hearing, attending, understanding, and remembering. We examined nine types of faulty listening behavior that block understanding, showing the many ways in which we screen out or distort the messages of others. Next we identified several reasons that prevent us from listening effectively even when we want to do so.

The chapter concluded by examining three types of listening. Informational listening is the proper approach to take when the goal is to understand another person's ideas. Information can be best gained with an active approach to listening. This active approach can involve either questioning or paraphrasing—restating the speaker's message in your own words.

Evaluative listening is appropriate when the goal is to judge the quality of an idea. Evaluation will be most successful when the listener ensures correct understanding of a message before passing judgment, when the speaker's credibility is taken into account, when the quality of supporting evidence is examined, and when emotional appeals are separated from logical ones.

The aim of empathic listening is to help the speaker, not the receiver. Various helping responses include advising, judging, analyzing, supporting, and paraphrasing the speaker's thoughts and feelings. Listeners can be most helpful when they use a variety of styles, focus on the emotional dimensions of a message, and avoid being too judgmental.

◆ NOTES

1. Paul T. Rankin, "The Measurement of the Ability to Understand Spoken Language," *Dissertation Abstracts* 12 (1926): 847.
2. L. Barker, R. Edwards, C. Gaines, K. Gladney, and F. Holley, "An Investigation of Proportional Time Spent in Various Communication Activities by College Students," *Journal of Applied Communication Research* 8 (1981): 101–109.
3. See, for example, A. Wolvin and C. Coakley, *Listening*, 3d ed. (Dubuque, Iowa: W.C. Brown, 1988), pp. 59–90 and B. Goss, "Listening as Information Processing," *Communication Quarterly* 30 (Fall 1982): 304.
4. For a complete discussion of the physiology of hearing, see H.A. Newby and G. R. Popleka, *Audiology* (Englewood Cliffs, N.J.: Prentice-Hall, 1985).
5. Jerrold J. Katz and Jerry A. Foder, "The Structure of a Semantic Theory," in Jay F. Rosenberg and Charles Travis (eds.), *Readings in the Philosophy of Language* (Englewood Cliffs, N.J.: Prentice-Hall, 1971).
6. Ralph G. Nichols, "Factors in Listening Comprehension," *Speech Monographs* 15 (1948): 154–163.
7. For a more complete discussion of memory and listening, see Robert N. Bostrom and Carol L. Bryant, "Factors in the Retention of Information Presented Orally: The Role of Short-Term Listening," *Western Journal of Speech Communication* 44 (Spring 1980): 137–145.
8. Nichols, op. cit.
9. Reported by R. Nichols and L. Stevens, "Listening to People," *Harvard Business Review* 35 (September-October 1957): 85–92.
10. W. Winter, A. Ferreira, and N. Bowers, "Decision-Making in Married and Unrelated Couples," *Family Process* 12 (1973): 83–94.
11. Ralph G. Nichols, "Listening Is a Ten-Part Skill," in R. C. Huseman et al. (eds.), *Readings in Interpersonal and Organizational Communication* (Boston: Holbrook Press, 1969), p. 476.
12. David B. Orr, "Time Compressed Speech—A Perspective," *Journal of Communication* 17 (1967): 223.
13. Bert E. Bradley, *Fundamentals of Speech Communication,* 3d ed. (Dubuque, Iowa: W. C. Brown, 1981), pp. 205–206.
14. Research summarized in J. Pearson, *Communication in the Family,* (New York: Harper & Row, 1989), pp. 272–275.

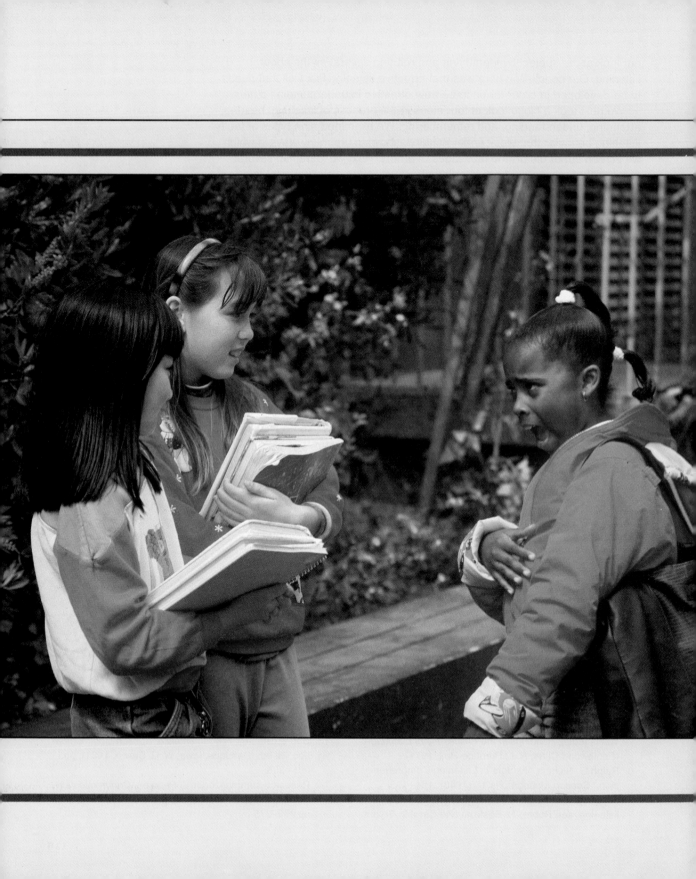

5

After reading this chapter, you should understand the following:

1. Four characteristics of nonverbal communication.

2. Four differences between verbal and nonverbal communication.

3. The six functions nonverbal communication can serve.

4. How the types of nonverbal communication described in this chapter function.

You should be able to do the following:

1. Identify and describe the nonverbal behaviors of yourself or another person in a given situation.

2. Identify nonverbal behaviors that repeat, substitute for, complement, accent, regulate, and contradict verbal messages.

3. Recognize the emotional and relational dimensions of your own nonverbal behavior.

4. Share your interpretation of another person's nonverbal behavior in a tentative manner when such sharing is appropriate.

KEY TERMS

affect blends
chronemics
disfluency
emblems
illustrators
intimate distance
kinesics
manipulators

mixed message
nonverbal communication
paralanguage
personal distance
proxemics
public distance
social distance
territory

Nonverbal Communication

There is often a big gap between what people say and what they feel. An acquaintance says, "I'd like to get together again" in a way that leaves you suspecting the opposite. (But how do you know?) A speaker tries to appear confident but acts in a way that almost screams out, "I'm nervous!" (What tells you this?) You ask a friend what's wrong, and the "nothing" you get in response rings hollow. (Why does it sound untrue?)

Then, of course, there are times when another's message comes through even though there are no words at all. A look of irritation, a smile, a sigh . . . signs like these can say more than a torrent of words.

Sometimes unspoken messages are so obvious that anyone could read them. In other cases, they are subtle, leaving you with a hunch about what's going on but unable to figure out the source of your feeling. And then there are times when you miss an unstated message so completely that the truth comes later as a complete surprise.

All situations like these have one point in common—that the message was sent nonverbally. The goal of this chapter is to introduce you to this world of nonverbal communication. Although you have certainly recognized nonverbal messages before, the following pages should introduce you to a richness of information you have never noticed. And though your experience won't transform you into a mind reader, it will make you a far more accurate observer of others . . . and yourself.

We need to begin our study of nonverbal communication by defining this term. At first this might seem like a simple task. If *non* means "not" and *verbal* means "words," then *nonverbal communication* appears to mean "communication without words." This is a good starting point once we distinguish between *vocal* communication (by mouth) and *verbal* communication (with words). Once this distinction is made, it becomes clear that some nonverbal messages are vocal, and some are not. Likewise, although many verbal messages are vocal, some aren't. Table 5–1 illustrates these differences.

What about languages that don't involve words? Does American Sign Language, for example, qualify as nonverbal communication? Most scholars would say not.[1] Keeping this fact in mind, we arrive at a working definition of **nonverbal communication:** "oral and nonoral messages expressed by other

TABLE 5–1   Types of Communication

	VOCAL COMMUNICATION	NONVOCAL COMMUNICATION
VERBAL COMMUNICATION	Spoken words	Written words
NONVERBAL COMMUNICATION	Tone of voice, sighs, screams, vocal qualities (loudness, pitch, and so on)	Gestures, movement, appearance, facial expression, and so on.

Adapted from John Stewart and Gary D'Angelo, *Together: Communicating Interpersonally,* 2d ed. (Reading, Mass.: Addison-Wesley, 1980), p. 22.

Elements of
Communication

118

than linguistic means." This rules out not only sign languages but written words as well, but it includes messages transmitted by vocal means that don't involve language—sighs, laughs, and other utterances we will discuss soon.

◆ CHARACTERISTICS OF NONVERBAL COMMUNICATION

Our brief definition only hints at the richness of nonverbal messages. You can begin to understand their prevalence by trying a simple experiment. Spend an hour or so around a group of people who are speaking a language you don't understand. (You might find such a group in the foreign students' lounge on campus, in an advanced language class, or in an ethnic neighborhood.) Your goal is to see how much information you can learn about the people you're observing from means other than the verbal messages they transmit. This experiment will reveal several characteristics of nonverbal communication.

Nonverbal Communication Exists

Your observations in the experiment show clearly that even without understanding speech it is possible to get an idea about how others are feeling. You probably noticed that some people were in a hurry whereas others seemed happy, confused, withdrawn, or deep in thought. The point is that without any formal experience you were able to recognize and to some degree interpret messages that other people sent nonverbally. In this chapter, we want to sharpen the skills you already have and to give you a better grasp of the vocabulary of nonverbal language.

One Can't Not Communicate

The pervasiveness of nonverbal communication brings us to its second characteristic. Suppose you were instructed to avoid communicating any messages at all. What would you do? Close your eyes? Withdraw into a ball? Leave the room? You can probably see that even these behaviors communicate messages, suggesting that you are avoiding contact. A moment's thought will show that there is no way to avoid communicating nonverbally.

This impossibility of not communicating is extremely important to understand, for it means that each of us is a kind of transmitter that cannot be shut off. No matter what we do, we give off information about ourselves.

Stop for a moment and examine yourself as you read this. If someone were observing you now, what nonverbal clues would they get about how you are feeling? Are you sitting forward or reclining back? Is your posture tense or relaxed? Are your eyes wide open, or do they keep closing? What does your facial expression communicate? Can you make your face expressionless? Don't people with expressionless faces communicate something?

◆ Writer (to movie producer Sam Goldwyn): Mr. Goldwyn, I'm telling you a sensational story. I'm only asking for your opinion, and you fall asleep.

Goldwyn: Isn't sleeping an opinion?

Nonverbal
Communication

This exercise will both increase your skill in observing nonverbal behavior and show you the dangers of being too sure that you're a perfect reader of body language. You can try the exercise either in or out of class, and the period of time over which you do it is flexible, from a single class period to several days. In any case, begin by choosing a partner, and then follow these directions:

a. For the first period of time (however long you decide to make it), observe the way your partner behaves. Notice how he or she moves; his or her mannerisms, postures, way of speaking; how he or she dresses; and so on. To remember your observations, jot them down. If you're doing this exercise out of class over an extended period of time, there's no need to let your observations interfere with whatever you'd normally be doing: Your only job here is to compile a list of your partner's behaviors. In this step, you should be careful *not* to interpret your partner's actions; just record what you see.

b. At the end of the time period, share what you've seen with your partner. He or she will do the same with you.

c. For the next period of time, your job is not only to observe your partner's behavior but also to *interpret* it. This time in your conference you should tell your partner what you thought his or her actions revealed. For example, if your partner dressed carelessly, did you think this meant he or she overslept, that he or she is losing interest in his or her appearance, or that he or she was trying to be more comfortable? If you noticed him or her yawning frequently, did you think this meant he or she was bored, tired from a late night, or sleepy after a big meal? Don't feel bad if your guesses weren't all correct. Remember that nonverbal clues tend to be ambiguous. You may be surprised how checking out the nonverbal clues you observe can help build a relationship with another person.

Of course, we don't always intend to send nonverbal messages. Consider, for instance, behaviors like blushing, frowning, sweating, or stammering. We rarely try to act in these ways, and often we are unaware of doing so. Nonetheless, others recognize signs like these and make interpretations about us based on their observations.

The fact that you and everyone around you is constantly sending nonverbal clues is important because it means that you have a constant source of information available about yourself and others. If you can tune into these signals, you will be more aware of how those around you are feeling and thinking, and you will be better able to respond to their behavior.

Nonverbal Communication Is Primarily Relational

Nonverbal communication is much better suited to expressing attitudes and feelings than ideas.[2] You can prove this for yourself by imagining how you could express each item on the following list nonverbally:

You're bored.

You are opposed to capital punishment.

You are attracted to another person in the group.

You want to know if you will be tested on this material.

You are nervous about trying this experiment.

The first, third, and fifth items in this list all involve attitudes; you could probably imagine how each could be expressed nonverbally. By contrast, the second and fourth items involve ideas, and they would be quite difficult to convey without using words. The same principle holds in everyday life: Nonverbal behavior offers many cues about the way people feel—often more than we get from their words alone.

Nonverbal Communication Is Ambiguous

Before you get the idea that this book will turn you into a mind reader, it is important to realize that nonverbal communication is often difficult to interpret accurately. To appreciate the ambiguous nature of nonverbal behavior, study the photo on this page. What emotions do you imagine the couple are feeling: grief? anguish? agony? In fact, none of these is even close. The couple has just learned that they won $1 million in the New Jersey state lottery!

Nonverbal behavior is just as ambiguous in everyday life. For example, consider some possible meanings of a partner's silence at the end of an evening together. (Table 5–2 lists some possibilities.) Or suppose a much admired person you have worked with suddenly begins paying much more (or less) attention to you than ever before. What might this mean?

Nonverbal
Communication

TABLE 5-2 Some Meanings of Silence

Agreement	Disagreement ("Silent Treatment")
Thoughtfulness	Ignorance
Revelation (We often say much about the people we are describing by what we choose to omit.)	Secrecy ("If he didn't have something to hide, he'd speak up.")
Warmth (Bind the participants.)	Coldness (Separate the participants.)
Submission	Attack (Not answering a letter—or worse, not answering a comment directed at you.)
Gaining attention	Boredom
Consideration	Inconsideration

Reprinted with permission from Mark L. Knapp, *Interpersonal Communication and Human Relationships* (Boston: Allyn & Bacon, 1984).

While all nonverbal behavior is ambiguous, some emotions are easier to decode accurately than others. In laboratory experiments, subjects are better at identifying positive facial expressions such as happiness, love, surprise, and interest than negative ones like fear, sadness, anger, and disgust.[3] In real life, however, spontaneous nonverbal expressions are so ambiguous that observers are unable to identify the emotions they convey with accuracy any better than blind guessing.[4]

Some people are more skillful than others at accurately decoding nonverbal behavior.[5] Those who are better senders of nonverbal messages also are better receivers. Decoding ability also increases with age and training, although there are still differences in ability owing to personality and occupation. For instance, extroverts are relatively accurate judges of nonverbal behavior whereas dogmatists are not. Interestingly, women seem to be better than men at decoding nonverbal messages. Over 95 percent of the studies examined in one analysis showed that women are more accurate at interpreting nonverbal signals.[6] Despite these differences, even the best nonverbal decoders do not approach 100 percent accuracy.

When you do try to make sense out of ambiguous nonverbal behavior, you need to consider several factors: The *context* in which they occur (e.g., smiling at a joke suggests a different feeling from what is suggested by smiling at another's misfortune); the *history of your relationship* with the sender (friendly, hostile, etc.); *the other's mood* at the time; and *your feelings* (when you're feeling insecure, almost anything can seem like a threat). The important idea is that when you become aware of nonverbal messages, you should think of them not as facts, but as *clues* that need to be checked out.

Elements of Communication

Much Nonverbal Communication Is Culture-Bound

Cultures have different nonverbal languages as well as verbal ones. Fiorello LaGuardia, legendary mayor of New York from 1933 to 1945 was fluent in English, Italian, and Yiddish. Researchers who watched films of his campaign speeches found that they could tell which language he was speaking with the sound turned off by noticing changes in his nonverbal behavior.[7]

The meaning of some gestures varies from one culture to another. The "okay" gesture made by joining thumb and forefinger to form a circle is a cheery affirmation to most Americans, but it has less positive meanings in other parts of the world.[8] In France and Belgium it means "You're worth zero." In Greece and Turkey it is a vulgar sexual invitation, usually meant as an insult. Given this sort of cross-cultural ambiguity, it's easy to imagine how an innocent tourist might wind up in serious trouble.

Less obvious cross-cultural differences can damage relationships without the parties ever recognizing exactly what has gone wrong. Edward Hall points out that whereas Americans are comfortable conducting business at a distance of roughly four feet, people from the Middle East stand much closer.[9] It is easy to visualize the awkward advance and retreat pattern that might occur when two diplomats or businesspeople from these cultures meet. The Middle Easterner would probably keep moving forward to close the gap that feels so wide, whereas the American would continually back away. Both would feel uncomfortable, probably without knowing why.

Like distance, patterns of eye contact vary around the world.[10] A direct gaze is considered appropriate for speakers in Latin America, the Arab world,

◆ Once identified and analyzed, nonverbal communication systems can be taught, like a foreign language. Without this training, we respond to nonverbal communications in terms of our own culture; we read everyone's behavior as if it were our own, and thus we often misunderstand it....

The language of behavior is extremely complex. Most of us are lucky to have under control one subcultural system—the one that reflects our sex, class, generation, and geographic region.

Edward and Mildred Hall

Nonverbal Communication

and southern Europe. On the other hand, Asians, Indians, Pakistanis, and northern Europeans gaze at a listener peripherally or not at all. In either case, deviations from the norm are likely to make a listener uncomfortable.

Even within a culture, various groups can have different nonverbal rules. For example, research in the 1970s revealed that blacks and whites handle conversational turn-taking differently. White listeners (following their own cultural rules) began to speak when black speakers paused with a sustained gaze, whereas the blacks had not actually finished their statements. As long as cultural differences exist, this sort of awkwardness can be decreased when communicators are aware of the different nonverbal rules they bring to a conversation.

Despite differences like these, many nonverbal behaviors are universal. Certain expressions have the same meanings around the world. Smiles and laughter are a universal signal of positive emotions, for example, while the same sour expressions convey displeasure in every culture.[11] Charles Darwin believed that expressions like these are the result of evolution, functioning as survival mechanisms which allowed early humans to convey emotional states before the development of language. The innateness of some facial expressions becomes even more clear when we examine the behavior of children born deaf and blind.[12] Despite a lack of social learning, these children display a broad range of expression. They smile, laugh, and cry in ways virtually identical to normal infants.

While nonverbal expressions like these may be universal, the way they are used varies widely around the world. In some cultures display rules discourage the overt demonstration of feelings like happiness or anger. In other cultures the same feelings are perfectly appropriate. Thus, a Japanese might appear much more controlled and placid than an Arab, when in fact their feelings would be identical.[13]

◆ DIFFERENCES BETWEEN VERBAL AND NONVERBAL COMMUNICATION

The features described in the preceding section suggest some ways in which nonverbal communication differs from the spoken and written word. By examining the key differences between these two forms of communication, you will get a clearer idea of what each type can and can't accomplish.

Single Vs. Multiple Channels

Most verbal messages—words, sentences, and paragraphs—reach us one at a time, rather like pearls on a string. In fact, it's physically impossible for a person to speak more than one word at a time. Unlike the spoken word, however, nonverbal messages don't arrive in such an orderly, sequential manner. Instead, they bombard us simultaneously from a multitude of channels. Consider the everyday act of meeting a stranger for the first time. On a verbal level there's relatively little information exchanged in the clichés that occupy the first few minutes of most conversations ("How's it going . . . " "Great weather we've been having . . . " "What's your major?"). But at the same moment the number of nonverbal messages available to you is overwhelming: the other person's facial expressions, postures, gestures, the clothing he or she wears, the distance he or she stands from you, and so on. In one way, this multichannel onslaught of nonverbal messages is a boon because it provides so many ways of learning about others. In another sense, however, the number of simultaneous messages is a problem, for it's difficult to recognize the overwhelming amount of nonverbal information we receive from others every moment.

Discrete Vs. Continuous

Verbal messages—words, sentences, and paragraphs—form messages with clear beginnings and endings. In this sense, it's possible to say that someone either is or isn't communicating verbally by seeing whether or not he or she is speaking or writing. Unlike the written and spoken word, however, nonverbal communication is continuous and never ending. As we've already said, it's impossible not to communicate nonverbally: The postures, gestures, and other types of messages described in the following pages provide a constant flow of messages. Even the absence of a message (an unanswered letter or an unreturned phone call) is a message. As one communication expert said when referring to nonverbal communication, "Nothing never happens."

Conscious Vs. Unconscious

Whereas we usually think about what we want to say before speaking or writing, most nonverbal messages aren't deliberate. Of course, we do pay attention to some of our nonverbal behavior: smiling when we want to convince others we're happy or making sure our handshakes are firm to show that we're straightforward, decisive people. But there are so many nonverbal channels that it's impossible to think about and control all of them. Thus, our slumping shoulders might contradict our smiles, and our sweating palms might cancel out all the self-confidence of our firm handshakes. The unconscious nature of most nonverbal behavior explains why it offers so many useful cues about how others are feeling.

Clear Vs. Ambiguous

Although verbal communication can be confusing, we have already seen that most nonverbal cues are even more vague. Nonverbal messages aren't completely ambiguous, of course: It's probably accurate to guess that a frown signifies some sort of negative feeling and that a smile indicates a positive emotion. But we often need language to tell us *why* others feel as they do. Is the boss smiling because she likes your idea or because she finds it amusing but completely impractical? Does your instructor's frown indicate confusion with your remarks or disagreement? The best way to find out is to ask for a verbal clarification, not to depend on your reading of the nonverbal cues.

Nonverbal Communication

Although verbal and nonverbal messages differ in many ways, the two forms of communication operate together on most occasions. The following discussion explains the many functions nonverbal communication can serve and shows how nonverbal messages relate to verbal ones.

Repeating

If someone asked you for directions to the nearest drugstore, you could say, "North of here about two blocks" and then repeat your instructions by pointing north. Pointing is an example of what social scientists call **emblems**— deliberate nonverbal behaviors that have precise meanings known to everyone within a cultural group. For example, we all know that a head nod means "yes," a headshake indicates "no," a wave means "hello" or "good-bye," and a hand to the ear means "I can't hear you."

Substituting

Emblems can also replace a verbal message. When a friend asks you what's new, you might shrug your shoulders instead of answering in words. Not all substituting consists of emblems, however. Sometimes substituting responses

◆ **The reality of the other person is not in what he reveals to you, but in what he cannot reveal to you.**

Therefore, if you would understand him, listen not to what he says but rather to what he does not say.

Kahlil Gibran

Elements of Communication

◆ **Whereas it might seem as though the right to go ahead gives one the upper hand, that is only the message level. On the metamessage level, the one who *decides* who goes ahead has the upper hand, regardless of who gets to go. This is why many women do not feel empowered by such privileges as having doors held open for them. The advantage of going first through the door is less salient to them than the disadvantage of being granted the right to walk through a door by someone who is framed, by his magnanimous gesture, as the arbiter of the right-of-way.**

Deborah Tannen

---

are more ambiguous and less intentional. A sigh, smile, or frown may substitute for a verbal answer to your question, "How's it going?" As this example suggests, nonverbal substituting is especially important when people are reluctant to express their feelings in words.

Complementing

Sometimes nonverbal behaviors match the content of a verbal message. Consider, for example, a friend apologizing for forgetting an appointment with you. Your friend's sincerity would be reinforced if the verbal apology were accompanied by the appropriate nonverbal behaviors: the right tone of voice, facial expression, and so on. We often recognize the significance of complementary nonverbal behavior when it is missing. If your friend's apology were delivered with a shrug, a smirk, and a light tone of voice, you probably would doubt its sincerity, no matter how profuse the verbal explanation was.

Much complementing behavior consists of **illustrators**—nonverbal behaviors that accompany and support spoken words. Scratching the head when searching for an idea and snapping your fingers when it occurs are examples of illustrators that complement verbal messages. Research shows that North Americans use illustrators more often when they are emotionally aroused—trying to explain ideas that are difficult to put into words—when they are furious, horrified, very agitated, distressed, or excited.[14]

Accenting

Just as we use italics to highlight an idea in print, we use nonverbal devices to emphasize oral messages. Pointing an accusing finger adds emphasis to criticism (as well as probably creating defensiveness in the receiver). Stressing certain words with the voice ("It was *your* idea!") is another way to add nonverbal accents.

Use your own nonverbal behavior and that of others to provide examples of each function:

a. Repeating	**c.** Complementing	**e.** Regulating
b. Substituting	**d.** Accenting	**f.** Contradicting

Regulating

Nonverbal behaviors can control the flow of verbal communication. For example, parties in a conversation often unconsciously send and receive turn-taking cues.[15] When you are ready to yield the floor, the unstated rule is: Create a rising vocal intonation pattern, then use a falling intonation pattern, or draw out the final syllable of the clause at the end of your statement. Finally, stop speaking. If you want to maintain your turn when another speaker seems ready to cut you off, you can suppress the attempt by taking an audible breath, using a sustained intonation pattern (because rising and falling patterns suggest the end of a statement), and avoiding any pauses in your speech. Other nonverbal clues exist for gaining the floor and for signaling that you do not want to speak.

Contradicting

People often simultaneously express different and even contradictory messages in their verbal and nonverbal behaviors. A common example of this sort of **mixed message** is the experience we've all had of hearing someone with a red face and bulging veins yelling, "Angry? No, *I'm not angry!*"

Usually, however, the contradiction between words and nonverbal clues isn't this obvious. At times we all try to seem different from what we are. There are many reasons for this contradictory behavior: to cover nervousness when giving a speech or in a job interview, to keep someone from worrying about us, or to appear more attractive then we believe we really are.

Even though some of the ways in which people contradict themselves are subtle, mixed messages have a strong impact. Research suggests that when a receiver perceives an inconsistency between verbal and nonverbal messages, the unspoken one carries more weight.[16] Table 5–3 lists situations in which mixed messages are most likely to be obvious.

Explore the significance of nonverbal behavior by violating some cultural rules that govern appropriate communication. *Note:* Be sure your violations aren't so extreme that they generate a harmful reaction. Commit one violation in each of the following areas:

a. Eye contact   **c.** Touch   **e.** Distance
b. Vocal cues   **d.** Clothing   **f.** Territoriality

Report the results of your experiments in class.

◆ TYPES OF NONVERBAL COMMUNICATION

Now that you understand how nonverbal messages operate as a form of communication, we can look at the various forms of nonverbal behavior. The following pages explain how our bodies, artifacts, environments, and the way we use time all send messages.

TABLE 5-3 Leakage of Nonverbal Cues to Deception

DECEPTION CUES ARE MOST LIKELY WHEN THE DECEIVER	DECEPTION CUES ARE LEAST LIKELY WHEN THE DECEIVER
Wants to hide emotions being experienced at the moment.	Wants to hide information unrelated to his or her emotions.
Feels strongly about the information being hidden.	Has no strong feelings about the information being hidden.
Feels apprehensive about the deception.	Feels confident about the deception.
Feels guilty about being deceptive.	Experiences little guilt about the deception.
Gets little enjoyment from being deceptive.	Enjoys the deception.
Needs to construct the message carefully while delivering it.	Knows the deceptive message well and has rehearsed it.

Based on material from "Mistakes When Deceiving" by Paul Ekman, in Thomas A. Sebeok and Robert Rosenthal (eds.), *The Clever Hans Phenomenon: Communication with Horses, Whales, Apes, and People* (New York: New York Academy of Sciences, 1981), pp. 269–278.

Posture and Gesture

Stop reading for a moment and notice how you are sitting. What does your position say nonverbally about how you feel? Are there other people near you now? What messages do you get from their posture and movements? Tune your television to any program, and without turning up the sound, see what messages are communicated by the movements and body position of the people on the screen. These simple experiments illustrate the communicative power of **kinesics,** the study of body movement, gesture, and posture.

Posture is a rich channel for conveying nonverbal information. From time to time postural messages are obvious. If you see a person drag through the door or slump over while sitting in a chair, it's apparent that something significant is going on. But most postural cues are more subtle. For instance, the act of mirroring the posture of another person can have positive consequences. One experiment showed that career counselors who used "posture echoes" to copy the positions of clients were rated as more empathic than those who did not reflect the clients' positions.[17]

Psychologist Albert Mehrabian has found that other postural keys to feelings are tension and relaxation.[18] He says that we take relaxed postures in nonthreatening situations and tighten up when threatened. Based on this observation, he says we can tell a good deal about how others feel simply by watching how tense or loose they seem to be. For example, he suggests that watching tenseness is a way of detecting status differences: The lower-status person is generally the more rigid, tense-appearing one whereas the one with higher status is more relaxed. This is the kind of situation that often happens

◆ **Who's there?...**
Stand, and
unfold yourself.

William Shakespeare
Hamlet

when we picture a "chat" with the boss (or other authority figures), when we sit ramrod straight while the authority figure leans back, relaxed. The same principle applies to social situations, where it is often possible to tell who is uncomfortable by looking at postures. You may see people laughing and talking as if they were perfectly at home, but whose posture almost shouts nervousness. Some people never relax, and their posture shows it.

Sometimes posture communicates vulnerability in situations far more serious than mere social or business settings. One study revealed that rapists sometimes use postural clues to select victims they believe are easy to intimidate.[19] Easy targets are more likely to walk slowly and tentatively, stare at the ground, and move their arms and legs in short, jerky motions.

Sometimes gestures are intentional—emblems like a cheery wave or thumbs up. In other cases, however, gestures are unconscious. Occasionally, an unconscious gesture will consist of an unambiguous emblem, such as a shrug that clearly means "I don't know." Another revealing set of gestures is what the psychiatrist Albert Scheflen calls "preening behaviors"—stroking or combing the hair, glancing in a mirror, and rearranging the clothing. Scheflen suggests that these behaviors signal some sort of interest in the other party: perhaps an unconscious sexual come-on or perhaps a sign of less intimate interest.[20] More often, however, gestures are ambiguous. In addition to illustrators, another group of ambiguous gestures consists of what we usually call fidgeting—movements in which one part of the body grooms, massages, rubs, holds, fidgets, pinches, picks, or otherwise manipulates another body part. Social scientists call these behaviors **manipulators**.[21] Social rules may discourage us from performing most manipulators in public, but people still do so without noticing.

Copr. © 1943 James Thurber. Copr. © 1971 Helen Thurber and Rosemary A. Thurber. From *Men, Women and Dogs*, published by Harcourt Brace Jovanovich.

Research confirms what common sense suggests—that increased use of manipulators is often a sign of discomfort.[22] But not *all* fidgeting signals uneasiness. People also are likely to use manipulators when relaxed. When they let their guard down (either alone or with friends), they will be more likely to fiddle with an earlobe, twirl a strand of hair, or clean their fingernails. Whether or not the fidgeter is hiding something, observers are likely to interpret manipulators as a signal of dishonesty. Because not all fidgeters are liars, it's important not to jump to conclusions about the meaning of manipulations.

Actually, *too few* gestures may be as significant an indicator of mixed messages as *too many.*[23] Lack of gesturing may signal a lack of interest, sadness, boredom, or low enthusiasm. Illustrators also decrease whenever there is caution about speech. For these reasons, a careful nonverbal observer will look for either an increase or a decrease in the usual level of gestures.

Face and Eyes

The face and eyes are probably the most noticed parts of the body, but this doesn't mean that their nonverbal messages are the easiest to read. The face is a tremendously complicated channel of expression for several reasons.

First, it is hard even to describe the number and kinds of expressions we commonly produce with our face and eyes. For example, researchers have found that there are at least eight distinguishable positions of the eyebrows and forehead, eight more of the eyes and lids, and ten for the lower face. When you multiply this complexity by the number of emotions we experience, you can see why it would be almost impossible to compile a dictionary of facial expressions and their corresponding emotions.

Another reason for the difficulty in understanding facial expressions is the speed with which they can change. For example, slow-motion films have been taken that show expressions fleeting across a subject's face in as short a time as a fifth of a second. Also, it seems that different emotions show most clearly in different parts of the face: happiness and surprise in the eyes and lower face, anger in the lower face and brows and forehead, fear and sadness in the eyes, and disgust in the lower face.

Ekman and Friesen have identified six basic emotions that facial expressions reflect—surprise, fear, anger, disgust, happiness, and sadness.[24] Expressions reflecting these feelings seem to be recognizable in and between members of all cultures. Of course, **affect blends**—the combination of two or more expressions showing different emotions—are possible. For instance, it's easy to imagine how someone would look who is fearful and surprised or disgusted and angry.

Research also indicates that people are quite accurate at judging facial expressions of these emotions.[25] Accuracy increases when judges know the "target" or have knowledge of the context in which the expression occurs or when they have seen several samples of the target's expressions.

In spite of the complex way in which the face shows emotions, you can still pick up messages by watching it. One of the easiest ways is to look for expressions that seem to be overdone. Often when people are trying to fool

◆ **Fie, fie upon her! There's language in her eyes, her cheek, her lip. Nay, her foot speaks; her wanton spirits look out at every joint and motive in her body.**

William Shakespeare
Troilus and Cressida

Nonverbal Communication

131

◆ It was terribly dangerous to let your thoughts wander when you were in any public place or within range of a telescreen. The smallest thing could give you away. A nervous tic, an unconscious look of anxiety, a habit of muttering to yourself—anything that carried with it the suggestion of abnormality, of having something to hide. In any case, to wear an improper expression on your face (to look incredulous when a victory was announced, for example) was itself a punishable offense. There was even a word for it in Newspeak: *facecrime,* it was called.

George Orwell
1984

themselves or someone else they will emphasize this mask to a point where it seems too exaggerated to be true. Another way to detect people's feelings is by watching their expression at moments when they aren't likely to be thinking about appearances. Everyone has had the experience of glancing into another car while stopped in a traffic jam or looking around at a sporting event and seeing expressions that the wearer would probably never show in more guarded moments. At other times, it's possible to watch a microexpression as it flashes across a person's face. For just a moment you see a flash of emotion

"Mr. Montague has closed his eyes. That means he likes your idea and will be in touch."

Elements of Communication

◆ **Is there such thing as an honest face? Apparently some people do *look* more honest than others, according to the work of two researchers. George and Naomi Rotter found that raters viewing black and white yearbook photos agreed that some of the subjects appeared honest while others seemed dishonest.**

What characteristics distinguished the seemingly honest subjects from the dishonest ones? The most common feature was facial expression: Honest faces had broad smiles, while most of the dishonest ones had grim expressions. Eye contact was also important, but its meaning depended on the gender of the subject. Men were judged honest if they looked directly into the camera, while women who had a steady gaze were more often rated as dishonest.

While the research helped define what makes people *seem* honest, there has never been any indication that genuinely honest or dishonest people actually do have distinctive traits. Thus, the old warning about not judging a book by its cover still seems true.

Research reported in *Psychology Today* (September 1987), p. 23.

quite different from the one a speaker is trying to convey. Finally, you may be able to spot contradictory expressions on different parts of someone's face: The eyes say one thing, but the expression of the mouth or eyebrows might be sending quite a different message.

The eyes themselves can send several kinds of messages. In our culture, meeting someone's glance with your eyes is usually a sign of involvement whereas looking away signals a desire to avoid contact. This is why solicitors on the street—panhandlers, salespeople, petitioners—try to catch our eye. Once they've managed to establish contact with a glance, it becomes harder for the approached person to draw away. A friend explained how to apply this principle to hitchhiking. "When I'm hitching a ride, I'm always careful to look each driver in the eye as he or she comes toward me. Most of them will try to look somewhere else as they pass, but if I can catch somebody's eye, that person will almost always stop." Most of us remember trying to avoid a question we didn't understand by glancing away from the teacher. At times like these we usually became very interested in our textbooks, fingernails, the clock—anything but the teacher's stare. Of course, the teacher always seemed to know the meaning of this nonverbal behavior and ended up picking on those of us who signaled uncertainty.

Voice

The voice itself is another form of nonverbal communication. Social scientists use the term **paralanguage** to describe nonverbal, vocal messages. You can begin to understand the power of vocal cues by considering how the meaning of a simple sentence can change just by shifting the emphasis from word to word:

Nonverbal Communication

This is a fantastic communication book.
   (Not just any book, but *this* one in particular.)

This is a *fantastic* communication book.
   (This book is superior, exciting.)

This is a fantastic *communication* book.
   (The book is good as far as communication goes; it may not be so great as literature or drama.)

This is a fantastic communication *book.*
   (It's not a play or record; it's a book.)

There are many other ways our voice communicates—through its tone, speed, pitch, volume, number and length of pauses, and **disfluencies** (such as stammering, use of "uh," "um," "er," and so on). All these factors can do a great deal to reinforce or contradict the message our words convey.

Sarcasm is one instance in which both emphasis and tone of voice help change a statement's meaning to the opposite of its verbal message. Experience this yourself with the following three statements. The first time through, say them literally, and then say them sarcastically.

Thanks for waking me up.

I really had a wonderful time on my blind date.

There's nothing I like better than sushi.

Researchers have identified the communicative value of paralanguage through the use of content-free speech—ordinary speech that has been electronically manipulated so that the words are unintelligible, but the paralanguage remains unaffected. (Hearing a foreign language that you do not understand has the same effect.) Subjects who hear content-free speech can consistently recognize the emotion being expressed, as well as identifying its strength.[26]

The impact of paralinguistic cues is strong. In fact, research shows that listeners pay more attention to the vocal messages than to the words that are spoken when asked to determine a speaker's attitudes.[27] Furthermore, when vocal factors contradict a verbal message, listeners judge the speaker's intention from the paralanguage, not from the words themselves.[28]

Vocal changes that contradict spoken words are not easy to conceal. If the speaker is trying to conceal fear or anger, the voice will probably sound higher and louder, and the rate of talk may be faster than normal. Sadness produces the opposite vocal pattern: quieter, lower-pitched speech delivered at a slower rate.[29]

Touch

Besides being the earliest means we have of making contact with others, touching is essential to our healthy development. During the nineteenth and early twentieth centuries many babies died from a disease then called *marasmus,* which, translated from Greek, means "wasting away." In some

◆ In our now more than slightly cockeyed world, there seems to be little provision for someone to get touched without having to go to bed with whomever does the touching. And that's something to think about. We have mixed up simple, healing, warm touching with sexual advances. So much so, that it often seems as if there is no middle way between "Don't you dare touch me!" and "Okay, you touched me, so now we should make love!"

A nation which is able to distinguish the fine points between offensive and defensive pass interference, bogies, birdies, and par, a schuss and a slalom, a technical, a personal, and a player-control foul should certainly be able to make some far more obvious distinctions between various sorts of body contact.

Sidney Simon
Caring, Feeling, Touching

orphanages the mortality rate was quite high, but even children in "progressive" homes, hospitals, and other institutions died regularly from the ailment. When researchers finally tracked down the causes of this disease, they found that many infants suffered from lack of physical contact with parents or nurses rather than poor nutrition, medical care, or other factors. They hadn't been touched enough, and as a result they died. From this knowledge came the practice of "mothering" children in institutions—picking the baby up, carrying it around, and handling it several times each day. At one hospital that began this practice, the death rate for infants fell from between 30 and 35 percent to below 10 percent.[30]

As a child develops, the need for being touched continues. In his book *Touching: The Human Significance of the Skin,* Ashley Montagu describes research that suggests that allergies, eczema, and other health problems are, in part, caused by a person's lack of contact as an infant with his or her mother.[31] Although Montagu says that these problems develop early in life, he also cites cases where adults suffering from conditions as diverse as asthma and schizophrenia have been successfully treated by psychiatric therapy that uses extensive physical contact.

Touch seems to increase a child's mental functioning as well as physical health. L. J. Yarrow has conducted surveys that show that babies who have been given plenty of physical stimulation by their mothers have significantly higher IQs than those receiving less contact.[32]

Touch also plays a large part in how we respond to others and to our environment.[33] For example, touch increases self-disclosure, verbalization of psychiatric patients, and the preference children have for their counselors. Touch also increases compliance. In one study, subjects were approached by a female confederate who requested that they return a dime left in the phone booth from which they had just emerged. When the request was accompanied by a light touch on the subject's arm, the probability that the subject would return the dime increased significantly.[34] In a similar experiment, subjects were asked by a male or female confederate to sign a petition or complete a rating scale. Again, subjects were more likely to cooperate when they were

Nonverbal Communication

touched lightly on the arm. In the rating-scale variation of the study, the results were especially dramatic: 70 percent of those who were touched complied, whereas only 40 percent of the untouched subjects were willing to cooperate (indicating a predisposition not to comply).[35]

An additional power of touch is its on-the-job utility. One study showed that fleeting touches on the hand and shoulder resulted in larger tips for restaurant waiters.[36]

Touch can communicate many messages. Researchers have catalogued twelve different kinds of touches, including "positive," "playful," "control," and "ritualistic."[37] Some types of touch indicate varying degrees of aggression. Others signify types of relationship:[38]

functional/professional (dental examination, haircut)

social/polite (handshake)

friendship/warmth (clap on back, Spanish *abrazo*)

love/intimacy (some caresses, hugs)

sexual arousal (some kisses, strokes)*

You might object to the examples following each of these categories, saying that some nonverbal behaviors occur in several types of relationship. A kiss, for example, can mean anything from a polite but superficial greeting to the most intense arousal. What makes a given touch more or less intense? Researchers have suggested a number of factors:

what part of the body does the touching

what part of the body is touched

how long the touch lasts

how much pressure is used

whether there is movement after contact is made

whether anyone else is present

the situation in which the touch occurs

the relationship between the persons involved

From this list you can see that there is, indeed, a complex language of touch. As nonverbal messages are inherently ambiguous, it's no surprise that this language can often be misunderstood. Is a hug playful or suggestive of stronger feelings? Is a touch on the shoulder a friendly gesture or an attempt at domination? Research suggests the interpretation can depend on a variety of factors, including the sex of the people involved, ethnic background, and marital status, among others.

*Other types of touch can indicate varying degrees of aggression.

Clothing

Besides protecting us from the elements, clothing is a means of nonverbal communication. One writer has suggested that clothing conveys at least ten types of messages to others.[39]

1. economic level
2. educational level
3. trustworthiness
4. social position
5. level of sophistication
6. economic background
7. social background
8. educational background
9. level of success
10. moral character

Research shows that we do make assumptions about people based on their style of clothing. In one study, a male and female were stationed in a hallway so that anyone who wished to go by had to avoid them or pass between them. In one condition, the conversationalists wore "formal daytime dress"; in the other, they wore "casual attire." Passersby behaved differently toward the couple, depending on the style of clothing: They responded positively with the well-dressed couple and negatively when the same people were casually dressed.[40] Similar results in other situations show the influence of clothing. We are more likely to obey people dressed in a high-status manner. Pedestrians were more likely to return lost coins to well-dressed people than to those dressed in low-status clothing.[41] We are also more likely to follow the lead of high-status dressers even when it comes to violating social rules. Eighty-three percent of the pedestrians in one study followed a well-dressed jaywalker who violated a "wait" crossing signal whereas only 48 percent followed a confederate dressed in lower-status clothing.[42]

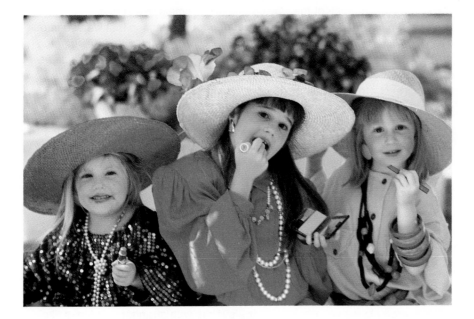

◆ **We may be born naked, but we waste little time correcting the oversight. Almost from the moment we wriggle into the world, we start getting dressed. Conventional wisdom claims that clothing is simply a means of survival, but clearly there's more to it. Whether it's a couple of strategically placed shells or a suit of armor, a G-string or a caribou parka, clothing is a set of signals to all we meet. And though clothes may indeed protect us from the elements, their real job is to protect us from social opprobrium, or to make a statement—to a potential boss, a potential bride, or a very real enemy.**

Banana Republic Catalog

Despite the frequency with which we make them, our clothing-based assumptions aren't always accurate. The stranger wearing wrinkled, ill-fitting old clothes might be a worker on vacation, a normally stylish person on the way to clean a fireplace, or even an eccentric millionaire. As we get to know others better, the importance of clothing shrinks.[43] This fact suggests that clothing is especially important in the early stages of a relationship, when making a positive first impression is necessary in order to encourage others to get to know us better. This advice is equally important in personal situations and in employment interviews. In both cases, your style of dress (and personal grooming) can make all the difference between the chance to progress further and outright rejection.

Distance

Proxemics is the study of the way people and animals use space.

Anthropologist Edward T. Hall has defined four distances that we use in our everyday lives.[44] He says that we choose a particular distance depending on how we feel toward the other person at a given time, the context of the conversation, and our personal goals. (These distance zones describe the behavior of North Americans and don't necessarily apply to members of other cultures.)

INTIMATE DISTANCE The first of Hall's zones is **intimate distance.** It begins with skin contact and ranges out to about eighteen inches. The most obvious context for intimate distance involves interaction with people to whom we're emotionally close—and then mostly in private situations—making love, roughhousing playfully, comforting, and protecting. Intimate distance between individuals also occurs in less intimate circumstances: visiting the doctor or dentist, at the hairdresser's, and during some athletic contests. Allowing someone to move into the intimate zone usually is a sign of trust, an indication that we've willingly lowered our defenses. On the other hand, when someone invades this most personal area without our consent, we usually feel threat-ened. This explains the discomfort that sometimes comes with being forced into crowded places such as buses or elevators with strangers. At times like these the standard behavior in our society is to draw away or tense the muscles and avoid contact. This is a nonverbal way of signaling "I don't like this invasion of personal territory, but the situation has forced it."

In courtship situations, a critical moment usually occurs when one member of a couple first moves into the other's intimate zone. If the partner being approached does not retreat, this usually signals that the relationship is moving into a new stage. On the other hand, if the reaction to the advance is withdrawal to a greater distance, the initiator should get the message that it isn't yet time to get more intimate. We remember from our dating experiences the significance of where on the car seat our companions chose to sit. If they moved close to us, it meant one thing; if they stayed jammed against the opposite door, quite a different message was communicated.

PERSONAL DISTANCE   The second spatial zone, **personal distance,** ranges from eighteen inches at its closest point to four feet at its farthest. Its closer phase is the distance at which most couples stand in public. But if someone of the opposite sex stands this near one partner at a party, the other partner is likely to feel uncomfortable. This "moving in" often is taken to mean that something more than casual conversation is taking place. The far range of personal distance runs from about two and a half to four feet. It's the zone just beyond the other person's reach. As Hall puts it, at this distance we can keep someone "at arm's length." This choice of words suggests the type of communication that goes on at this range: The contacts are still reasonably close, but they're much less personal than the ones that occur a foot or so closer.

Test this for yourself. Start a conversation with someone at a distance of about three feet; then slowly move a foot or so closer. Do you notice a difference? Does the distance affect your conversation?

"Huddleston, I admire your hands-on approach to everything, but get the hell out of my office!"

Drawing by Dana Fradon; © 1986 The New Yorker Magazine, Inc.

Nonverbal Communication

◆ The interrogator should sit fairly close to the subject, and between the two there should be no table, desk, or other piece of furniture. Distance or the presence of an obstruction of any sort constitutes a serious psychological barrier and also affords the subject a certain degree of relief and confidence not otherwise attainable....

As to the psychological validity of the above suggested seating arrangement, reference may be made to the commonplace but yet meaningful expressions such as "getting next" to a person, or the "buttonholing" of a customer by a salesman. These expressions signify that when a person is close to another one physically, he is closer to him psychologically. Anything such as a desk or a table between the interrogator and the subject defeats the purpose and should be avoided.

Inbau and Reid
Criminal Interrogation and Confessions

SOCIAL DISTANCE The third zone is **social distance.** It ranges from four to about twelve feet. Within it are the kinds of communication that usually occur in business situations. Its closer phase, from four to seven feet, is the distance at which conversations usually occur between salespeople and customers and between people who work together. Most people feel uncomfortable when a salesclerk comes as close as three feet whereas four or five feet nonverbally signals, "I'm here to help you, but I don't mean to be too personal or pushy."

We use the far range of social distance—seven to twelve feet—for more formal and impersonal situations. This is the range at which we generally sit from our boss. Sitting at this distance signals a far different and less relaxed type of conversation than if we were to pull a chair around to the boss's side of the desk and sit only three or so feet away.

PUBLIC DISTANCE **Public distance** is Hall's term for the farthest zone, running outward from twelve feet. The closer range of public distance is the one most teachers use in the classroom. In the farther reaches of public space—twenty-five feet and beyond—two-way communication becomes difficult. In some cases it's necessary for speakers to use public distance owing to the size of their audience, but we can assume that anyone who voluntarily chooses to use it when he or she could be closer is not interested in having a dialogue.

Physical invasion isn't the only way people penetrate our spatial bubble; we're just as uncomfortable when someone intrudes on our visual territory. If you've had the unpleasant experience of being stared at, you know this can be just as threatening as having someone get too close. In most situations, however, people respect each other's visual privacy. You can test this the next time you're walking in public. As you approach other people, notice how they shift their glance away from you at a distance of a few paces, almost like a visual dimming of headlights. Generally, strangers maintain eye contact at a

◆ **Status distinctions are sometimes remarkably precise. In many universities, for example, there is an unwritten rule that students must wait 10 minutes for an assistant professor who is late for class, 20 minutes for an associate professor, and 30 minutes for a full professor. Such standards establish comparative worth: I'm permitted to waste my students' time without explanation, but they must not trespass on mine. The higher my rank, the more time I can waste.**

This is peculiar since the students must pay my salary. From a monetary standpoint, they own my time, rather than the other way around. But, along with my professorship, I've been granted control of their grades, which to some degree determines their future. In the end, our rules of waiting make it clear just who's running the show.

Robert Levine

close distance only when they want something—information, assistance, signatures on a petition, recognition, a handout.

Along with eye contact, a variety of other factors interact with physical distance to determine whether or not we feel as if our personal space has been respected or invaded.[45] Some of these factors are age (consider the difference between hugging a three year old and an adult), culture (a kiss in Latin America has different meanings than in North America), task (contact during some kinds of dance has different impact than during conversation), and body position (side-to-side contact in a crowded elevator does not seem like a spatial invasion).

Time

Social scientists use the term **chronemics** to describe the study of how human beings use and structure time. The way we handle time can express both intentional and unintentional messages. Social psychologist Robert Levine describes several ways that time can communicate.[46] For instance, in a culture like ours that values time highly, waiting can be an indicator of status. "Important" people (whose time is supposedly more valuable than others) may be seen by appointment only, while it is acceptable to intrude without notice on lesser beings. To see how this rule operates, consider how natural it is for a boss to drop into a subordinate's office unannounced, while some employees would never intrude into the boss's office without an appointment. A related rule is that low status people must never make more important people wait. It would be a serious mistake to show up late for a job interview, although the interviewer might keep you cooling your heels in the lobby. Important people are often whisked to the head of a restaurant or airport line, while the presumably less exalted are forced to wait their turn.

The use of time depends greatly on culture. In some cultures, punctuality is critically important, while in others it is barely considered. Punctual mainlanders often report welcoming the laid-back Hawaiian approach to time. One

Nonverbal Communication

psychologist discovered the difference between North and South American attitudes when teaching at a university in Brazil.[47] He found that some students arrived halfway through a two-hour class, and that most of them stayed put and kept asking questions when the class was scheduled to end. A half hour after the official end of the period, the professor finally closed off discussion, since there was no indication that the students intended to leave. This flexibility of time is quite different from what is common in most North American colleges and universities!

Even within a culture, rules of time vary. Sometimes the differences are geographic. In New York City, the party invitation may say 9:00, but nobody would think of showing up before 10:30. In Salt Lake City, guests are expected to show up on time, or perhaps even a bit early.[48] Even within the same geographic area, different groups establish their own rules about the use of time. Consider your own experience. In school, some instructors begin and end class punctually, while others are more casual. With some people you feel comfortable talking for hours in person or on the phone, while with others time seems to be precious and not "wasted."

Territoriality

Whereas personal space is the invisible bubble we carry around as an extension of our physical being, **territory** is fixed space. Any geographical area such as a room, house, neighborhood, or country to which we assume some kind of "rights" is our territory. What's interesting about territoriality is that there is no real basis for the assumption of proprietary rights of "owning" some area, but the feeling of "owning" exists nonetheless. Your room in the house is *your room* whether you're there or not (unlike personal space, which is carried around with you), and it's your room because you say it is. Although you could probably make a case for your room's *really being* your room (and not the family's or the mortgage holder's), what about the desk you sit at in each class? You feel the same way about the desk, that it's yours, even though it's certain that the desk is owned by the school and is in no way really yours.

The way people use space can communicate a good deal about power and status relationships. Generally, we grant people with higher status more personal territory and greater privacy.[49] We knock before entering our boss's office whereas a supervisor can usually walk into our work area without hesitating. In traditional schools, professors have offices, dining rooms, and even toilets that are private whereas the students, who are presumably less important, have no such sanctuaries. In the military, greater space and privacy usually come with rank: Privates sleep forty to a barracks, sergeants have their own private rooms, and generals have government-provided houses.

Environment

A large amount of research shows how the design of an environment can shape the kind of communication that takes place in it. In one experiment, researchers found that the attractiveness of a room influenced the happiness

◆ **Campuses are full of conscious and unconscious architectural symbolism. While the colleges at Santa Cruz evoke images of Italian hill towns as they might have been if the peasants had concrete, the administration building is another story. It appears to anticipate the confrontations between students and administration that marked the sixties. At Santa Cruz, administrative offices are located in a two-story building whose rough sloped concrete base with narrow slit windows gives it the look of a feudal shogun's palace. The effect is heightened by the bridge and landscaped moat that one crosses to enter the building. "Four administrators in there could hold off the entire campus," joked one student.**

Sym Van Der Ryn

and energy of people working in it.[50] The experimenters set up three rooms: an "ugly" one, which resembled a janitor's closet in the basement of a campus building; an "average" room, which was a professor's office; and a "beautiful" room, which was furnished with carpeting, drapes, and comfortable furniture. The subjects in the experiment were asked to rate a series of pictures as a way of measuring their energy and feelings of well-being while at work. Results of the experiment showed that while in the ugly room the subjects became tired and bored more quickly and took longer to complete their task. When they moved to the beautiful room, however, they rated the faces they were judging higher; showed a greater desire to work; and expressed feelings of importance, comfort, and enjoyment. The results teach a lesson that isn't surprising: Workers generally feel better and do a better job when they're in an attractive environment.

Many businesspeople show an understanding of how environment can influence communication. Robert Sommer, a leading environmental psychologist, described several such cases in his book *Personal Space: The Behavioral Basis for Design.* He pointed out that dim lighting, subdued noise levels, and comfortable seats encourage people to spend more time in a restaurant or bar.[51] Knowing this, the management can control the amount of customer turnover. If the goal is to run a high-volume business that tries to move people in and out quickly, it's necessary to keep the lights shining brightly and not worry too much about soundproofing. On the other hand, if the goal is to keep customers in the bar or restaurant for a long time, the proper technique is to lower the lighting and use absorbent building materials that will keep down the noise level.

Furniture design can control the amount of time a person spends in an environment too. From this knowledge came the Larsen chair, which was designed for Copenhagen restaurant owners who felt their customers were occupying their seats too long without spending enough money. The chair is constructed to put an uncomfortable pressure on the sitter's back if occupied for more than a few minutes. (We suspect that many people who are careless in buying furniture for their homes get much the same result without trying. One environmental psychologist we know refuses to buy a chair or couch without sitting in it for at least half an hour to test its comfort.)

Nonverbal Communication

In a more therapeutic and less commercial way, physicians have also shaped environments to improve communication. Sommer found that redesigning the convalescent ward of a hospital greatly increased the interaction among patients. In the old design, seats were placed shoulder to shoulder around the edges of the ward. When the chairs were grouped around small tables so that patients faced each other at a comfortable distance, the number of conversations doubled.[52]

The design of an entire building can shape communication among its users. Architects have learned that the way housing projects are designed controls to a great extent the contact neighbors have with each other. People who live in apartments near stairways and mailboxes have many more neighbor contacts than do those living in less heavily traveled parts of the building, and tenants generally have more contacts with immediate neighbors than with people even a few doors away.[53] Architects now use this information to design buildings that either encourage communication or increase privacy, and house hunters can use the same knowledge to choose a home that gives them the neighborhood relationships they want.

So far we have talked about how designing an environment can shape communication, but there is another side to consider. Watching how people use an already existing environment can be a way of telling what kind of relationships they want. For example, Sommer watched students in a college library and found that there's a definite pattern for people who want to study alone. While the library was uncrowded, students almost always chose corner seats at one of the empty rectangular tables.[54] Finally, each table was occupied by one reader. New readers would then choose a seat on the opposite side and far end of an occupied table, thus keeping the maximum distance between themselves and the other readers. One of Sommer's associates tried violating these "rules" by sitting next to, and across from, other female readers when more distant seats were available. She found that the approached women reacted defensively, either by signaling their discomfort through shifts in posture or gesturing or by eventually moving away.

◆ SUMMARY

**Elements of
Communication**

Nonverbal communication consists of messages expressed by nonlinguistic means. Thus, it is inaccurate to say that all wordless expressions are nonverbal or that all spoken statements are totally verbal.

There are several important characteristics of nonverbal communication. First is the simple fact that it exists—that communication occurs even in the absence of language. This leads to the second principle, namely, that it is impossible not to communicate nonverbally; humans constantly send messages about themselves that are available for others to receive. The third principle is that nonverbal communication is ambiguous; that there are many possible interpretations for any behavior. This ambiguity makes it important for the receiver to verify any interpretation before jumping to conclusions about the meaning of a nonverbal message. The fourth principle states that much nonverbal communication is culture-bound. In other words, behaviors that have special meanings in one culture may express different messages in another. Finally, we stated that nonverbal communication serves many functions: repeating, substituting, complementing, accenting, regulating, and contradicting verbal behavior.

We also examined the differences between verbal and nonverbal communication. Whereas verbal messages occupy a single channel and must be received one at a time, many nonverbal messages occur simultaneously in everyday situations. Nonverbal messages are also continuous whereas verbal ones are discrete, having beginnings and endings. Verbal messages are usually intentional whereas nonverbal ones are often expressed unintentionally. Finally, verbal messages are less ambiguous than nonverbal ones, which are almost always open to more than one interpretation.

The remainder of this chapter introduced the many ways humans communicate nonverbally: through posture, gesture, use of the face and eyes, voice, touch, clothing, distance, time, territoriality, and physical environment.

◆ NOTES

1. For a survey of the issues surrounding the definition of nonverbal communication, see M. Hickson III and D.W. Stacks, *NVC: Nonverbal Communication: Studies and Applications,* 2d ed. (Dubuque, Iowa: W. C. Brown, 1989), pp. 5–11.

2. J. Burgeon, D. Buller, J. Hale, and M. de Turck, "Relational Messages Associated with Nonverbal Behaviors," *Human Communication Research* 10 (Spring 1984): 351–378.

3. D. Druckmann, R. M. Rozelle, and J. C. Baxter, *Nonverbal Communication: Survey, Theory, and Research* (Newbury Park, Calif.: Sage, 1982).

4. M. T. Motley and C. T. Camden, "Facial Expression of Emotion: A Comparison of Posed Expressions Versus Spontaneous Expressions in an Interpersonal Communication Setting," *Western Journal of Speech Communication* 52 (Winter 1988): 1–22.

5. See, for example, R. Rosenthal, J. A. Hall, M. R. D. Matteg, P. L. Rogers, and D. Archer, *Sensitivity to Nonverbal Communication: The PONS Test* (Baltimore, Md.: Johns Hopkins University Press, 1979).

6. J. A. Hall, "Gender, Gender Roles, and Nonverbal Communication Skills," in R. Rosenthal (ed.), *Skill in Nonverbal Communication: Individual Differences* (Cambridge, Mass.: Oelgeschlager, Gunn, and Hain, 1979), pp. 32–67.

7. R. Birdwhistell, *Kinesics and Context* (Philadelphia: University of Pennsylvania Press, 1970), Chapter 9.

8. P. Ekman, W. V. Friesen, and J. Baer, "The International Language of Gestures," *Psychology Today* 18 (May 1984): 64–69.

9. E. Hall, *The Hidden Dimension* (Garden City, N.Y.: Anchor Books, 1969).

10. Ibid.

11. S. Weitz, ed. *Nonverbal Communication: Readings with Commentary* (New York: Oxford University Press, 1974).

12. J. Eibl-Eibensfeldt. "Universals and Cultural Differences in Facial Expressions of Emotions," in J. Cole (ed.), *Nebraska Symposium on Motivation* (Lincoln: University of Nebraska Press, 1972).

13. For a comparison of Japanese and Arab nonverbal communication norms, see D. G. Leathers, *Successful Nonverbal Communication* (New York: Macmillan, 1986), pp. 258–261.

14. Hall, op. cit.

15. C. R. Kleinke, "Compliance to Requests Made by Gazing and Touching Experimenters in Field Settings," *Journal of Experimental Social Psychology* 13 (1977): 218–233.

16. For a summary of research on mixed messages and deception, see J. Burgoon, D. Buller, and W. G.

Nonverbal Communication

Woodall, *Nonverbal Communication: The Unspoken Dialogue* (New York: Harper & Row, 1989), pp. 260–288.

17. R. E. Maurer and J. H. Tindall, "Effect of Postural Congruence on Client's Perception of Counselor Empathy," *Journal of Counseling Psychology* 30 (1983): 158–163.

18. Albert Mehrabian, *Silent Messages,* 2d ed. (Belmont, Calif.: Wadsworth, 1981), pp. 47–48.

19. M. B. Myers, D. Templer, and R. Brown, "Coping Ability of Women Who Become Victims of Rape," *Journal of Consulting and Clinical Psychology* 52 (1984): 73–78. See also C. Rubenstein, "Body Language That Speaks to Muggers," *Psychology Today* 20 (August 1980): 20; and J. Meer, "Profile of a Victim," *Psychology Today* 24 (May 1984): 76.

20. A. E. Scheflen, "Quasi-Courting Behavior in Psychotherapy," *Psychiatry* 228 (1965): 245–257.

21. Ekman, *Telling Lies: Clues to Deceit in the Marketplace, Politics, and Marriage* (New York: Norton, 1985), pp. 109–110.

22. Ekman and W. V. Friesen, "Nonverbal Behavior and Psychopathology," in R. J. Friedman and M. N. Katz (eds.), *The Psychology of Depression: Contemporary Theory and Research* (Washington, D. C.: J. Winston, 1974).

23. Ekman, *Telling Lies,* p. 107.

24. Ekman and W. V. Friesen, *Unmasking the Face* (Englewood Cliffs, N.J.: Prentice-Hall, 1975).

25. Ekman, W. V. Friesen, and P. Ellsworth, *Emotion in the Human Face: Guidelines for Research and an Integration of Findings* (Elmsford, N. Y.: Pergamon, 1972).

26. J. A. Starkweather, "Vocal Communication of Personality and Human Feeling," *Journal of Communication* II (1961): 69; and K. R. Scherer, J. Koiwunaki, and R. Rosenthal, "Minimal Cues in the Vocal Communication of Affect: Judging Emotions from Content-Masked Speech," *Journal of Psycholinguistic Speech* I (1972): 269–285. See also F. S. Cox and C. Olney, "Vocalic Communication of Relational Messages," paper delivered at annual meeting of the Speech Communication Association, Denver, 1985.

27. K. L. Burns and E. G. Beier, "Significance of Vocal and Visual Channels for the Decoding of Emotional Meaning," *The Journal of Communication* 23 (1973): 118–130. See also Timothy G. Hegstrom, "Message Impact: What Percentage Is Nonverbal?" *Western Journal of Speech Communication* 43 (1979): 134–143; and E. M. McMahan, "Nonverbal Communication as a Function of Attribution in Impression Formation," *Communication Monographs* 43 (1976): 287–294.

28. A. Mehrabian and M. Weiner, "Decoding of Inconsistent Communications," *Journal of Personality and Social Psychology* 6 (1967): 109–114.

29. Ekman, *Telling Lies,* p. 93.

30. Ashley Montagu, *Touching: The Human Significance of the Skin* (New York: Harper & Row, 1972), p. 93.

31. Ibid., pp. 244–249.

32. L. J. Yarrow, "Research in Dimension of Early Maternal Care," *Merrill-Palmer Quarterly* 9 (1963): 101–122.

33. For a review of research on this subject, see S. Thayer, "Close Encounters," *Psychology Today* 22 (March 1988): 31–36.

34. C. R. Kleinke, "Compliance to Requests Made by Gazing and Touching Experimenters in Field Settings," *Journal of Experimental Social Psychology* 13 (1977): 218–223.

35. F. N. Willis and H. K. Hamm, "The Use of Interpersonal Touch in Securing Compliance," *Journal of Nonverbal Behavior* 5 (1980): 49–55.

36. A. H. Crusco and C. G., Wetzel, "The Midas Touch: Effects of Interpersonal Touch on Restaurant Tipping," *Personality and Social Psychology Bulletin* 10 (1984): 512–517.

37. S. E. Jones and E. Yarbrough, "A Naturalistic Study of the Meanings of Touch," *Communication Monographs* 52 (1985): 221–231.

38. R. Heslin and T. Alper, "Touch: The Bonding Gesture," in J. M. Wiemann and R. P. Harrison (eds.), *Nonverbal Interaction,* (Beverly Hills, Calif.: Sage, 1983).

39. W. Thourlby, *You Are What You Wear* (New York: New American Library, 1978), p. 1.

40. J. H. Fortenberry, J. Maclean, P. Morris, and M. O'Connell, "Mode of Dress as a Perceptual Cue to Deference," *The Journal of Social Psychology* 104 (1978).

41. L. Bickman, "Social Roles and Uniforms: Clothes Make the Person," *Psychology Today* 7 (April 1974): 48–51.

42. M. Lefkowitz, R. R. Blake, and J. S. Mouton, "Status of Actors in Pedestrian Violation of Traffic Signals," *Journal of Abnormal and Social Psychology* 51 (1955): 704–706.

43. T. F. Hoult, "Experimental Measurement of Clothing as a Factor in Some Social Ratings of Selected American Men," *American Sociological Review* 19 (1954): 326–327.

44. E. T. Hall, op. cit., pp. 113–130.

45. Hickson and Stacks, p. 55.

46. R. Levine, "The Pace of Life Across Cultures," in Joseph E. McGrath (ed.), *The Social Psychology of Time,* (Newbury Park, Calif.: Sage, 1988).

47. R. Levine and E. Wolff, "Social Time: The Heartbeat of Culture," *Psychology Today* 19 (March 1985): 28–35. See also R. Levine, "Waiting Is a Power Game," *Psychology Today* 21 (April 1987): 24–33.

48. Burgoon, Buller, and Woodall, p. 148.

49. Mehrabian, op. cit., p. 69.

50. A. H. Maslow and N. L. Mintz, "Effects of Esthetic Surroundings," *Journal of Psychology* 41 (1956): 247–254.

51. Robert Sommer, *Personal Space: The Behavioral Basis of Design* (Englewood Cliffs, N.J.: Spectrum), pp. 122–123.

52. Leon Festinger, S. Schachter, and K. Back, *Social Pressures in Informal Groups: A Study of Human Factors in Housing* (New York: Harper & Row, 1950).

53. Sommer, op. cit., p. 78.

54. Ibid., p. 35.

Nonverbal
Communication

INTERPERSONAL COMMUNICATION

6

Key terms continued on page 152.

After reading this chapter, you should understand the following:

1. The characteristics that distinguish interpersonal relationships from impersonal ones.

2. The role of communication climate in interpersonal relationships.

3. The content and relational dimensions of every message.

4. The role of metacommunication in conveying relational messages.

5. The characteristics of disclosing and nondisclosing communication.

6. The guidelines for appropriate self-disclosure.

7. The characteristics of nonassertive, directly aggressive, passive aggressive, indirect, and assertive messages.

8. The differences between win-lose, lose-lose, and win-win styles of conflict.

You should be able to do the following:

1. Identify the extent to which each of your relationships is interpersonal or impersonal, describe your level of satisfaction with these relationships, and suggest ways to make them more satisfactory.

2. Identify disconfirming messages and replace them with confirming ones, using the Gibb categories of supportive communication.

3. Identify the degree of self-disclosure in your relationships and the functions this disclosing communication serves.

4. Compose disclosing messages that follow the guidelines listed in this chapter.

5. Describe the degree to which you use nonassertive, directly aggressive, passive aggressive, indirect, and assertive messages and choose more satisfying responses as necessary.

6. Apply the win-win approach to resolution of an interpersonal conflict.

KEY TERMS

ambiguous response
assertion
certainty
cliché
communication climate
confirming response
conflict
content message
controlling message
crazymaking
descriptive communication
direct aggression
disconfirming response
empathy
equality
evaluative communication

Gibb categories
"I" language
impersonal communication
impersonal response
impervious response
incongruous response
indirect communication
interpersonal communication
interpersonal relationship
interrupting response

Key terms continued on page 152.

Understanding and Improving Interpersonal Relationships

"Relationship" is one of those words people use a great deal yet have a hard time defining. See if you can explain the term before reading on: It isn't as easy as it might seem.

The dictionary defines a relationship as "the mode in which two or more things stand to one another." This is true enough: You are tall in relation to some people and short in relation to others, and we are more or less wealthy only in comparison to others. But physical and economic relationships don't tell us much that is useful about interpersonal communication.

Interpersonal relationships involve the way people deal with one another *socially.* But what is it about their social interaction that defines a relationship? What makes some relationships "good" and others "bad"? We can answer this question by recalling the three kinds of social needs introduced in Chapter 1: inclusion, control, and affection. When we judge the quality of personal relationships, we are usually describing how well those social needs are being met. Having come this far, we can define the term **interpersonal relationship** as an association in which the parties meet each other's social needs to a greater or lesser degree.

In this chapter we will explore the vitally important topic of interpersonal relationships. We will explore the difference between impersonal and interpersonal communication and identify what makes some interpersonal relationships more rewarding than others. We will look at the subject of self-disclosure, explaining when openness can be helpful and when it can cause harm. Finally, we will examine the role of conflict in relationships, showing how to handle the conflicts that are bound to occur in ways that make relationships stronger and more satisfying.

◆ CHARACTERISTICS OF INTERPERSONAL RELATIONSHIPS

What is interpersonal communication? How does it differ from other types of interaction? When and how are interpersonal messages communicated? Read on and see.

Interpersonal Vs. Impersonal Communication

One way to define interpersonal communication is by looking at how many people are involved and how much access they have to one another. In this sense, a salesclerk and a customer or a police officer ticketing a speeding driver would be examples of interpersonal acts (two-person, face-to-face meetings) whereas a teacher and class or authors such as us and readers like you would not be.

You can probably sense that there's something wrong with this definition. The kind of exchanges that often go on between salespeople and their customers or bureaucrats and the public hardly seem interpersonal . . . or personal in any sense of the word. In fact, after transactions like this, we commonly remark, "I might as well have been talking to a machine." And conversely, some "public" kinds of communication seem quite personal.

**Interpersonal
Communication**

Teachers, religious ministers, and entertainers often establish a personal relationship with their audiences, and we certainly hope this book has at least some personal flavor.

If context doesn't make communication interpersonal, what does? When we talk about interpersonal communication in this book, we're referring to the *quality* of interaction between individuals. In **interpersonal communication** we treat others as individuals whereas in **impersonal communication** we treat them as objects. This definition doesn't mean that all impersonal communication is cruel or that you need to establish a warm relationship with every person you meet. The fact to remember here is that not all two-person interaction is interpersonal.

Make a list of several people who are "close" to you: family members, a roommate, friends, coworkers, and so on. Use the criteria in this chapter to decide where you would place each of these relationships on a spectrum with "interpersonal" at one end and "impersonal" at the other. Now ask yourself the most important question: How satisfied are you with the answers from your list?

Several characteristics make interpersonal relationships qualitatively different from less personal types.[1] As you read about each of them, consider how well they describe your important relationships.

UNIQUENESS   No two interpersonal relationships are alike, and the communication patterns reflect these differences.

The unique quality of interpersonal communication often takes the form of distinctive rules that evolve between the parties. In one relationship you might exchange good-natured insults, while in another you are careful never to offend your partner. Likewise, you might handle conflicts with one friend or family member by expressing disagreements as soon as they arise, whereas the unwritten rule in another relationship is to withhold resentments until they build up, and then clear the air periodically.

Unlike the distinctive quality of interpersonal relationships, impersonal ones are governed by the kind of standardized rules that Miss Manners describes: Say "please" and "thank you." "Shake hands when meeting for the first time." "Be careful about using profanity." Rules like these aren't phony; they are just standard forms to follow until we've created our own interpersonal conventions.

Even language patterns reflect the difference between unique, interpersonal relationships and more common impersonal ones. In less personal relationships we tend to stereotype the other person by using labels: "Anglo," "woman," "liberal," and so on. Such labels may be accurate as far as they go, but they hardly describe everything that is important about the other person. On the other hand, it's almost impossible to use one or two labels to describe someone you know interpersonally. "She's not *just* a police officer," you want to say. Or "Sure, he's against abortions, but there's more. . . ."

IRREPLACEABILITY   Because interpersonal relationships are unique, they can't be replaced. This explains one reason why we usually feel so sad when a close friendship or love affair cools down. We know that no matter how many other relationships fill our lives, none of them will ever be quite like the one that just ended. People in less personal relationships are much easier to replace. Communication with one airline reservations clerk or fast food attendant and another is pretty similar. The same principle applies in situations that *seem* more personal: If all you're looking for in a roommate is someone who will keep the place clean and share expenses, then there are lots of good candidates.

INTERDEPENDENCE   In interpersonal relationships the fate of the parties is connected. You might be able to brush off the anger, affection, excitement, or depression of someone you're not involved with interpersonally, but in an interpersonal relationship the other's life affects you. Sometimes the interdependence that comes with a close relationship is a pleasure, as when you get a lift from a friend's successes. At other times being closely involved is a burden, as when a family member's moodiness makes your life miserable. In either case, interdependence is a fact of life in personal relationships.

DISCLOSURE   Another yardstick of interpersonal relationships is the amount of personal information the parties share with one another. In impersonal relationships we don't reveal much about ourselves, but in interpersonal ones we feel more comfortable sharing our thoughts and feelings. This doesn't mean that all interpersonal relationships are warm and caring, or that all self-disclosure is positive. It's possible to reveal negative, personal information: "I'm really mad at you. . . ."

INTRINSIC REWARDS   In impersonal communication we seek payoffs that have little to do with the people involved. For instance, when you advertise your used car, you deal with potential buyers in order to make a sale, not to make friends. Likewise, most people enroll in a college class to learn the subject matter and get academic credit, not to make friends with the professor. They would be satisfied with any competent instructor. Unlike these examples, communication in interpersonal relationships is its own reward. It doesn't matter *what* you talk about; developing the relationship is what's important.

SCARCITY   The majority of our communication is relatively impersonal. We chat pleasantly with shopkeepers or fellow passengers on the bus or plane; we discuss the weather or current events with most classmates and neighbors; we deal with coworkers and teachers in a polite way—but considering the number of people we communicate with, interpersonal relationships are by far in the minority.

The rarity of interpersonal relationships isn't necessarily unfortunate. Most of us don't have the time or energy to create personal relationships with everyone we encounter. In fact, the scarcity of interpersonal communication contributes to its value. Like precious jewels and one-of-a-kind artwork, interpersonal relationships are special because of their scarcity.

Most relationships aren't completely interpersonal or impersonal. Rather, they fall somewhere between these two extremes. Consider your own communication and you'll find that there is often a personal element in even the most impersonal situations. You might appreciate the unique sense of humor of a grocery checker or spend a few moments sharing private thoughts with the person cutting your hair. And even the most tyrannical, demanding, by-the-book boss might show an occasional flash of humanity.

Just as there's a personal element in many impersonal settings, there is also an impersonal side to our relationships with the people we care most about. There are occasions when we don't want to be personal: when we're distracted, tired, or busy, or just not interested. In fact, interpersonal communication is rather like rich food—it's fine in moderation, but too much can make you uncomfortable.

By now it's clear that there is a place in our lives for both impersonal and interpersonal communication. Each type has its uses. The real challenge, then, is to find the right balance between the two types.

Content and Relational Messages

Virtually every verbal statement contains two kinds of messages. **Content messages,** which focus on the subject being discussed, are the most obvious. The content of such statements as "It's your turn to do the dishes" or "I'm busy Saturday night" is obvious.

Content messages aren't the only kind that are exchanged when two people interact. In addition, most communication—both verbal and nonverbal—conveys **relational messages,** which make statements about how the parties feel toward one another.[2] These relational messages deal with one or more social needs, most often inclusion, control, affection, or respect. Consider the two examples we just mentioned:

◆ Imagine two ways of saying "It's your turn to do the dishes": one that is demanding and another that is matter-of-fact. Notice how the different nonverbal messages make statements about how the sender views control in this part of the relationship. The demanding tone says, in effect, "I have a right to tell you what to do around the house," whereas the matter-of-fact one suggests, "I'm just reminding you of something you might have overlooked."

◆ You can easily visualize two ways to deliver the statement "I'm busy Saturday night": one with little affection and the other with much liking.

The content level of a message is easy to recognize, but relational messages are usually less obvious. Pick three everyday messages you initiate and three you receive within a two-day period. For each, identify

a. The content level of the message.
b. The relational message. If the relational communication is not explicit, describe how it is conveyed.

Notice that in each of these examples the relational dimension of the message was never discussed. In fact, most of the time we aren't conscious of the many relational messages that bombard us every day. Sometimes we are unaware of relational messages because they match our belief about the amount of respect, inclusion, control, and affection that is appropriate. For example, you probably won't be offended if your boss tells you to do a certain job because you agree that supervisors have the right to direct employees. In other cases, however, conflicts arise over relational messages even though content is not disputed. If your boss delivers the order in a condescending, sarcastic, or abusive tone of voice, you probably will be offended. Your complaint wouldn't be with the order itself but with the way it was delivered. "I may work for this company," you might think, "but I'm not a slave or an idiot. I deserve to be treated like a human being."

How are relational messages communicated? As the boss-employee example suggests, they are usually expressed nonverbally. To test this fact for yourself, imagine how you could act while saying, "Can you help me for a minute?" in a way that communicates each of the following relationships:

superiority	aloofness
helplessness	sexual desire
friendliness	irritation

Although nonverbal behaviors are a good source of relational messages, remember that they are ambiguous. The sharp tone you take as a personal insult might be due to fatigue, and the interruption you take as an attempt to ignore your ideas might be a sign of pressure that has nothing to do with you. Before you jump to conclusions about relational clues, it's a good idea to practice the skill of perception checking that you learned in Chapter 2: "When you use that tone of voice to tell me it's my turn to do the dishes, I get the idea you're mad at me. Is that right?" If your interpretation was indeed correct, you can talk about the problem. On the other hand, if you were overreacting, the perception check can prevent a needless fight.

Metacommunication

As the preceding example of perception checking shows, not all relational messages are nonverbal. Social scientists use the term **metacommunication** to describe messages that refer to other messages.[3] In other words, metacommunication is communication about communication. Whenever we discuss a relationship with others, we are metacommunicating: "I wish we could stop arguing so much" or "I appreciate how honest you've been with me." Verbal metacommunication is an essential ingredient in successful relationships. Sooner or later there are times when it becomes necessary to talk about what is going on between you and the other person. The ability to focus on the kinds of issues described in this chapter can be the tool for keeping the relationship on track.

Metacommunication is an important method for solving conflicts in a constructive manner. It provides a way to shift discussion from the content level to relational questions, where the problem often lies. For example, consider the case of a couple bickering because one partner wants to watch television while the other wants to talk. Imagine how much better the chances of a positive outcome would be if they used metacommunication to examine the relational problems that were behind their quarrel: "Look, it's not the TV watching itself that bothers me. It's that I imagine you watch so much because you're mad at me or bored. Are you feeling bad about us?"

Metacommunication isn't just a tool for handling problems. It is also a way to reinforce the good aspects of a relationship: "I really appreciate it when you compliment me about my work in front of the boss." Comments like this serve two functions: First, they let others know that you value their behavior. Second, they boost the odds that the other person will continue the behavior in the future.

Despite the benefits of metacommunication, bringing relational issues out in the open does have its risks. Discussing problems can be interpreted in two ways. On one hand, the other person might see it in a positive light—"Our relationship is working because we can still talk things out." On the other hand, your desire to focus on the relationship might look like a bad omen—"Our relationship isn't working if we have to keep talking it over."[4] Furthermore, metacommunication does involve a certain degree of analysis ("It seems like you're angry at me"), and some people resent being analyzed. These cautions don't mean verbal metacommunication is a bad idea. They do suggest, though, that it's a tool that needs to be used carefully.

◆ COMMUNICATION CLIMATES IN INTERPERSONAL RELATIONSHIPS

The term **communication climate** refers to the emotional tone of a relationship as it is expressed in the messages that the partners send and receive. Just as physical locations have characteristic weather patterns, interpersonal relationships have unique climates, too. You can't measure the interpersonal climate by looking at a thermometer or glancing at the sky, but it's there nonetheless. Every relationship has a feeling, a pervasive mood that colors the interactions of the participants.

A climate doesn't involve specific activities as much as the way people feel about each other as they carry out those activities. Consider two communication classes, for example. Both meet for the same length of time and follow the same syllabus. It's easy to imagine how one of these classes might be a friendly, comfortable place to learn whereas the other could be cold and tense —even hostile. The same principle holds for families, coworkers, and other relationships: Communication climates are a function of the way people feel about one another, not so much the tasks they perform.

Confirming and Disconfirming Climates

What makes some climates positive and others negative? A short but accurate answer is that the *communication climate is determined by the degree to which*

◆ The finest qualities of our nature, like the bloom on fruits, can only be preserved by the most delicate handling, yet we do not treat ourselves nor one another thus tenderly.

Henry David Thoreau

Understanding and Improving Interpersonal Relationships

people see themselves as valued. When we believe others view us as important, we are likely to feel good about our relationship. On the other hand, the relational climate suffers when we think others don't appreciate or care about us.

Messages that show you are valued have been called **confirming responses.**[5] Some kinds of communication are obviously confirming. Sincere *praise* or *compliments* show that you value the recipient. So does *agreeing* with others' opinions. But it isn't necessary to express praise or agreement to send confirming messages. In many cases, simply *acknowledging* the other person can be a confirmation. Stopping to exchange small talk with an acquaintance says, "You're important." So does smiling or waving when you see the other person from a distance. (If you don't believe this, recall how you felt when you were ignored.)

On a more personal level, *listening* attentively to the other person sends a confirming message. Listening is even confirming when you disagree with the speaker. For example, asking sincere questions and using the paraphrasing skills described in Chapter 4 show that you care enough about the other person to listen. When compared to the responses that characterize non-listening (stage hogging, ambushing, pseudolistening, and so on), it's clear that sincerely trying to understand a conversational partner is a sign of respect.

In contrast to confirming communication, messages that deny the value of others have been labeled **disconfirming responses.**[6] These show a lack of regard for the other person either by disputing or ignoring some important part of that person's message. Disagreement can certainly be disconfirming, especially if it goes beyond disputing the other person's ideas and attacks the speaker personally. It may be tough to hear someone say, "I don't think that's a good idea," but a personal attack like "You're crazy" is even more insulting.

However, disagreement is not the most damaging kind of disconfirmation. Far worse are responses that ignore others' ideas—or even their existence. The list of disconfirming responses in Table 6–1 shows several kinds of messages that convey a lack of appreciation. It's easy to see how these sorts of messages can create negative relational climates.

You can probably recognize the communication climate in each of your relationships without much analysis. But answering the following questions will help explain *why* these climates exist. Following these steps may also suggest how to improve negative climates.

a. Identify the communication climate of an important interpersonal relationship. Using weather metaphors (sunny, gloomy, calm) may help.

b. List the confirming or disconfirming communication that created and now maintains this climate. Be sure to identify both verbal and nonverbal messages.

c. Describe what you can do either to maintain the existing climate (if positive) or to change it (if negative). Again, list both verbal and nonverbal behaviors.

How Communication Climates Develop

As soon as two people start to communicate, a relational climate begins to develop. If the messages are confirming, the climate is likely to be a positive one. If they disconfirm one another, the relationship is likely to be hostile, cold, or defensive.

Verbal messages certainly contribute to the tone of a relationship, but many climate-shaping messages are nonverbal. The very act of approaching others is confirming whereas avoiding them can be disconfirming. Smiles or frowns, the presence or absence of eye contact, tone of voice, the use of personal space . . . all these and other cues send messages about how the parties feel toward one another.

Once a climate is formed, it can take on a life of its own and grow in a self-perpetuating spiral. This sort of cycle is most obvious in regressive spirals, when a dispute gets out of hand:[7]

A: *(mildly irritated)* Where were you? I thought we agreed to meet here a half hour ago.

B: *(defensively)* I'm sorry, I got hung up at the library. I don't have as much free time as you do, you know.

A: I wasn't *blaming* you, so don't get so touchy. I do resent what you just said, though. I'm plenty busy. And I've got lots of better things to do than wait around for you!

B: Who's getting touchy? I just made a simple comment. You've sure been defensive lately. What's the matter with you?

Understanding and Improving Interpersonal Relationships

TABLE 6-1   Disconfirming Messages

Disconfirming responses communicate a lack of respect or appreciation. Like their confirming counterparts, these messages can shape the climate of an entire relationship.

Impervious responses ignore the other person's attempt to communicate. Refusing to answer another person in a face-to-face conversation is the most obvious kind of impervious response although not the most common. Failing to return a phone call or write back in answer to a letter are more common impervious responses. So is not responding to a smile or a wave.

Interrupting responses occur when one person begins to speak before the other has finished. They show a lack of concern about what the other person has to say.

A: I'm looking for an outfit I can wear to work and when I travel to…

B: I've got just the thing. It's part wool and part polyester, so it won't wrinkle at all.

A: Actually wrinkling isn't that important. I want something that will work as a business outfit and…

B: We have a terrific blazer that you can dress up or down depending on the accessories you choose.

A: That's not what I was going to say. I want something that will work both here and down south. I have to go to a…

B: Say no more. I know just what you want.

A: Never mind. I think I'll look in some other stores.

Irrelevant responses are unrelated to what the other person has just said.

A: What a day! I thought it would never end. First the car overheated, and I had to call a tow truck, and then the computer broke down at work.

B: Listen, we have to talk about a present for Ann's birthday. The party is on Saturday, and I only have tomorrow to shop for it.

A: I'm really beat. Could we talk about it in a few minutes? I've never seen a day like this one.

B: I just can't figure what would suit Ann. She's got everything…

Tangential responses are conversational "take aways." Instead of ignoring the speaker's remarks completely, they use them as a starting point for a shift to a different topic.

A: I'd like to know for sure whether you want to go skiing during vacation. If we don't decide whether to go soon, it'll be impossible to get reservations anywhere.

B: Yeah. And if I don't pass my botany class, I won't be in the mood to go anywhere. Could you give me some help with this homework?…

Impersonal responses are loaded with clichés and other statements that never truly respond to the speaker.

A: I've been having some personal problems lately, and I'd like to take off work early a couple of afternoons to clear them up.

B: Ah, yes. We all have personal problems. It seems to be a sign of the times.

Ambiguous responses contain messages with more than one meaning, leaving the other party unsure of the responder's position.

A: I'd like to get together with you soon. How about Tuesday?

B: Uh, maybe so.

A: Well, how about it. Can we talk Tuesday?

B: Oh, probably. See you later.

Incongruous responses contain two messages that seem to deny or contradict each other. Often at least one of these messages is nonverbal.

A: Darling, I love you.

B: I love you, too. (giggles)

Fortunately, spirals can work in a progressive direction, too. One confirming behavior leads to a similar response from the other person, which, in turn, leads to further confirmation by the first party.

Spirals—whether positive or negative—rarely go on indefinitely. When a negative spiral gets out of hand, the parties might agree to back off from their disconfirming behavior. "Hold on," one might say. "This is getting us nowhere." At this point, there may be a cooling-off period, or the parties might work together more constructively to solve their problem. If the partners pass the "point of no return," the relationship may end. It is impossible to take back a message once it has been sent, and some exchanges are so lethal that the relationship can't survive them. Positive spirals also have their limit: Even the best relationships go through rocky periods, in which the climate suffers. The accumulated goodwill and communication skill of the partners, however, can

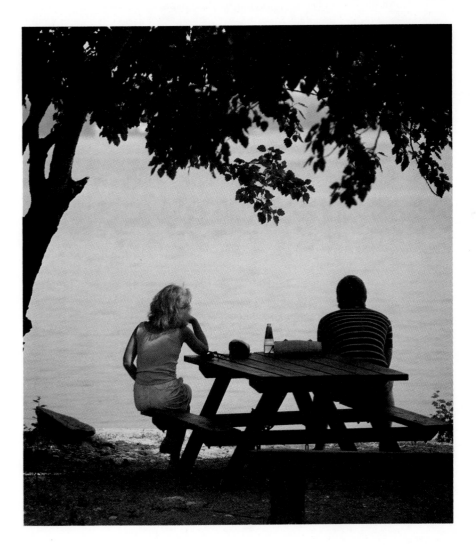

Understanding and Improving Interpersonal Relationships

make these times less frequent and intense. Therefore, most relationships pass through cycles of progression and regression.

Creating Positive Communication Climates

It's easy to see how disconfirming messages can pollute a communication climate. But what are some alternative ways of communicating that encourage positive relationships? The work of Jack Gibb gives a picture of what kinds of messages lead to both positive and negative spirals.[8]

After observing groups for several years, Gibb was able to isolate six types of defense-arousing communication and six contrasting behaviors that seemed to reduce the level of threat and defensiveness. The **Gibb categories** are listed in Table 6–2. Using the supportive types of communication and avoiding the defensive ones will increase the odds of creating and maintaining positive communication climates in your relationships.

EVALUATION VS. DESCRIPTION The first type of defense-provoking behavior Gibb noted was **evaluative communication.** Most people become irritated at judgmental statements, which they are likely to interpret as indicating a lack of regard. Evaluative language has often been described as **"you" language** because most such statements contain an accusatory use of that word. For example,

You don't know what you're talking about.

You're not doing your best.

You smoke too much.

Gibb contrasts evaluative "you" language with **descriptive communication** or **"I" language.** Instead of putting the emphasis on judging another's behavior, the descriptive speaker simply explains the personal effect of the other's action. For instance, instead of saying, "You talk too much," a descriptive communicator would say, "When you don't give me a chance to say what's on my mind, I get frustrated." Notice that statements such as this include an account of the other person's behavior plus an explanation of its effect on the speaker and a description of the speaker's feelings.

TABLE 6–2 The Gibb Categories of Defensive and Supportive Behaviors

DEFENSIVE BEHAVIORS	SUPPORTIVE BEHAVIORS
1. Evaluation	1. Description
2. Control	2. Problem orientation
3. Strategy	3. Spontaneity
4. Neutrality	4. Empathy
5. Superiority	5. Equality
6. Certainty	6. Provisionalism

◆ In interpersonal relationships, I believe first person singular is most appropriate because it places responsibility clearly.

If I say to another person, "I do not like what you did," then no contradiction is possible. No one can correct me because my perception and what I have decided to think about is mine alone. The other person may, however, suggest that I received only a portion of the information, or that I received it unclearly for one reason or another. In such a case, the meaning of the message may be tentative until it can be negotiated. It also is legitimate for me to perceive the message quite differently from the way the other person perceives it.

On the other hand, if I say "You have made me angry," then you may very well contradict me by responding with something such as "No I didn't." In fact, I am eliciting a defensiveness and also inviting "you" to attempt a control of me by your helplessness, suffering, or anger.

Only I am responsible for my behavior. Only I can change what I do. However, when I change my behavior, I may give the other person in the relationship the opportunity to evaluate his behavior and perhaps modify it.

John Narcisco and David Burkett
Declare Yourself

CONTROL VS. PROBLEM ORIENTATION   A second defense-provoking message involves some attempt to control another. A **controlling message** occurs when a sender seems to be imposing a solution on the receiver with little regard for the receiver's needs or interests. The object of controls can range from where to eat dinner or what TV show to watch to whether to remain in a relationship or how to spend a large sum of money. Whatever the situation, people who act in controlling ways create a defensive climate. None of us likes to feel that our ideas are worthless and that nothing we say will change other people's determination to have their way—yet this is precisely the attitude a controller communicates. Whether done with words, gestures, tone of voice, or

Blondie reprinted with special permission of King Features Syndicate, Inc. 1/18/84.

through some other channel; whether control is accomplished through status, insistence on obscure or irrelevant rules, or physical power, the controller generates hostility wherever he or she goes. The unspoken message such behavior communicates is "I know what's best for you, and if you do as I say, we'll get along."

In contrast, in **problem orientation** communicators focus on finding a solution that satisfies both their needs and those of the others involved. The goal here isn't to "win" at the expense of your partner but to work out some arrangement in which everybody feels like a winner. (The last section of this chapter has a great deal to say about "win-win" problem solving as a way to find problem-oriented solutions.)

Approach an important person in your life, and request some help in learning more about yourself. Inform the other person that your discussion will probably take at least an hour, so make sure both of you are prepared to invest this amount of time.

a. Begin by explaining all twelve of the Gibb behaviors to your partner. Be sure to give enough examples so that each category is clearly understood.

b. When your explanation is complete and you've answered all your partner's questions, ask which of the Gibb categories *you use.* Seek specific examples so that you are certain to understand the feedback fully. (As you are requesting an evaluation, be prepared for a little defensiveness on your own part at this point.) Inform your partner that you are interested in discovering both the defense-arousing and the supportive behaviors you use and that you are sincerely interested in receiving a candid answer. (*Note:* if you don't want to hear the truth from your partner, don't try this exercise.)

c. As your partner speaks, record the categories he or she lists in sufficient detail for both of you to be sure that you have understood his comments.

d. When you have finished your list, show it to your partner. Listen to his or her reactions, and make any corrections that are necessary to reflect an accurate understanding of his or her comments. When your list is accurate, have your partner sign it to indicate that you have understood him or her clearly.

e. In a concluding statement, note

◆ How you felt as your partner was describing you.
◆ Whether you agree with the evaluation.
◆ What effect your use of the various Gibb categories has on your relationship with your partner.

STRATEGY VS. SPONTANEITY The third communication behavior that Gibb identified as creating a poor communication climate involves the use of

strategy or manipulation. One of the surest ways to make people defensive is to get caught trying to manipulate them into doing something for you. The fact that you tried to trick them instead of just asking for what you wanted is enough to build mistrust. Nobody likes to be a guinea pig or a sucker, and even well-meant manipulation can cause bad feelings.

Spontaneity is the behavior that contrasts with strategy. Spontaneity simply means expressing yourself honestly. Despite the misleading label Gibb chose for this kind of behavior, spontaneous communication needn't be blurted out as soon as an idea comes to you. You might want to plan the wording of your message carefully so that you can express yourself clearly. The important thing is to be honest. Often spontaneity won't get what you want, but in the long run it's usually better to be candid and perhaps miss out on some small goal than to say all the right things and be a fraud. More than once we've heard people say, "I didn't like what he said, but at least I know he was being honest."

Although it sounds paradoxical at first, spontaneity can be a strategy, too. Sometimes you'll see people using honesty in a calculating way, being just frank enough to win someone's trust or sympathy. This "leveling" is probably the most defense-arousing strategy of all because once we've learned someone is using frankness as a manipulation, there's almost no chance we'll ever trust that person again.

You may be getting the idea that using supportive behaviors such as description, problem orientation, empathy, and so on, is a good way to manipulate others. Before going any further, we want to say loudly and clearly that if you ever act supportively without being sincere in what you're saying, you've misunderstood the idea behind this chapter, and you're running a risk of causing even more defensiveness than before. None of the ideas we present in this book can go into a "bag of tricks" that can be used to control others: If you ever find yourself using them in this way, beware!

NEUTRALITY VS. EMPATHY   Gibb used the term **neutrality** to describe a fourth behavior that arouses defensiveness. Probably a better descriptive word would be *indifference*. A neutral attitude is disconfirming because it communicates a lack of concern for the welfare of another and implies that the other person isn't very important to you. This perceived indifference is likely to promote defensiveness because people do not like to think of themselves as worthless, and they'll protect a self-concept that pictures themselves as worthwhile.

The small child who has urgent things to tell a parent but is met with indifference may be expected to become upset. The physician who seems clinical and detached to his patients may wonder why they look for another doctor.

The poor effects of neutrality become apparent when you consider the hostility that most people have for the large, impersonal organizations with which they have to deal: "They think of me as a number instead of a person"; "I felt as if I were being handled by computers and not human beings." These two common statements reflect reactions to being handled in an indifferent way.

Understanding and Improving Interpersonal Relationships

Gibb has found that **empathy** helps rid communication of the quality of indifference. When people show that they care for the feelings of another, there's little chance that the person's self-concept will be threatened. Empathy means accepting another's feelings, putting yourself in another's place. This doesn't mean you need to agree with that person. By simply letting someone know about your care and respect, you'll be acting in a supportive way. Gibb noted the importance of nonverbal messages in communicating empathy. He found that facial and bodily expressions of concern are often more important to the receiver than the words used.

SUPERIORITY VS. EQUALITY   A fifth behavior creating a defensive climate involves **superiority.** How many interpersonal relationships have you dropped because you couldn't stand the superiority that the other person projected? An individual who communicates superiority arouses feelings of inadequacy in the recipients. We're not particular about the type of superiority presented to us; we just become defensive. Money, power, intellectual ability, physical appearance, and athletic prowess are all areas our culture stresses. Consequently, we often feel a need to express our superiority along these lines.

Individuals who act superior communicate that they don't want to relate on equal terms with others in the relationship. Furthermore, people like this seem to imply that they don't want feedback or need help because it would be coming from someone "inferior." The listener is put on guard because the senders are likely to attempt to reduce the receiver's worth, power, or status to maintain or advance their own superiority.

Perhaps you've had professors who continually reminded their class of their superior intellectual ability and position. Remember how delighted you were when you or a classmate caught one of these superior types in a mistake? Why do you suppose that was so satisfying? Some might argue that this is a good strategy to keep students awake, but in reality much of the student's effort is then directed to defending self-worth rather than pursuing the objectives of the course.

When we detect people communicating superiority, we usually react defensively. We "turn them off," justify ourselves, or argue with them in our minds. Sometimes we choose to change the subject verbally or even walk away. Of course, there is always the counterattack, which includes an attempt to belittle the senders of the superiority message. We'll go to great lengths "to cut them down to size." All these defensive reactions to projected superiority are destructive to an interpersonal climate.

Many times in our lives we are in a relationship with individuals who possess talents greater than ours. But is it necessary for these people to project superiority? Your own experiences will tell you that it isn't. Gibb has found ample evidence that many who have superior skills and talents are capable of projecting feelings of **equality** rather than superiority. Such people communicate that although they may have greater talent in certain areas, they see others as having just as much worth as human beings.

CERTAINTY VS. PROVISIONALISM Have you ever run into people who are positive they're right, who know that theirs is the only or proper way of doing something, who insist that they have all the facts and need no additional information? If you have, you've met individuals who project the defense-arousing behavior Gibb calls **certainty.**

How do you react when you're the target of such certainty? Do you suddenly find your energy directed to proving the dogmatic individual wrong? If you do, you're reacting normally, if not very constructively.

Communicators who regard their own opinions with certainty while disregarding the ideas of others demonstrate a rather clear lack of regard for the thoughts others hold to be important. It's likely the receiver will take the certainty as a personal affront, and react defensively.

In contrast to dogmatic communication is **provisionalism,** in which people may have strong opinions but are willing to acknowledge that they don't have a corner on the truth and will change their stand if another position seems more reasonable.

◆ **Coming out of a meeting they had attended together, the Anglican Archbishop offered the Roman Catholic Cardinal a ride in his limousine. "After all," said the Anglican Archbishop, "we are both engaged in God's work." "Yes," replied the Cardinal, "you in your way and I in His!"**

◆ **SELF-DISCLOSURE IN RELATIONSHIPS**

One way we judge the strength of relationships is by the amount of information we share with others. "We don't have any secrets," some people proudly claim. As you will read in Chapter 7, at least some sharing is important: We find others more attractive when they share certain private information with us. Given the obvious importance of self-disclosure, we need to take a closer look at the subject. Just what is it? When is it desirable? How can it best be done?

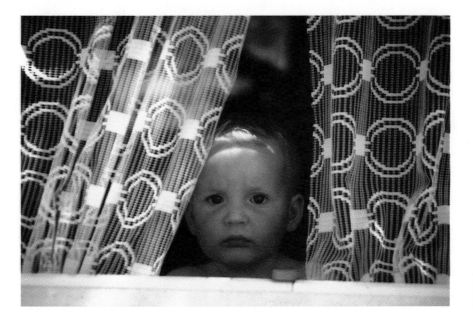

Understanding and Improving Interpersonal Relationships

The best place to begin is with a definition. **Self-disclosure** is the process of deliberately revealing information about oneself that is significant and that would not normally be known by others. Let's take a closer look at some parts of this definition. Self-disclosure must be *deliberate*. If you accidentally mentioned to a friend that you were thinking about quitting a job or proposing marriage, that information would not fit into the category we are examining here. Self-disclosure must also be *significant*. Revealing relatively trivial information—the fact that you like fudge, for example—does not qualify as self-disclosure. The third requirement is that the information being revealed would *not be known by others*. There's nothing noteworthy about telling others that you are depressed or elated if they already know how you're feeling.

Levels of Disclosing and Nondisclosing Communication

Although our definition of self-disclosure is helpful, it doesn't reveal the important fact that not all self-disclosure is equally revealing—that some disclosing messages tell more about us than others.

Social psychologists Irwin Altman and Dalmas Taylor describe two ways in which communication can be more or less disclosing.[9] Their **social penetration** model is pictured in Figure 6–1. The first dimension of self-disclosure in this model involves the *breadth* of information volunteered—the range of subjects being discussed. For example, the breadth of disclosure in your relationship with a fellow worker will expand as you begin revealing information about your life away from the job, as well as on-the-job details. The second dimension of disclosure is the *depth* of the information being volunteered, the shift from relatively nonrevealing messages to more personal ones.

FIGURE 6–1
Social Penetration Model

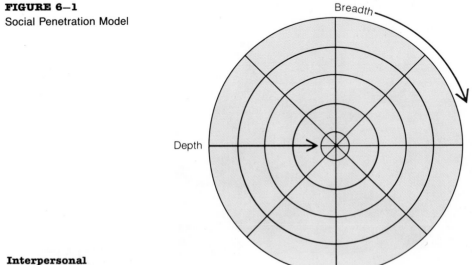

Breadth

Depth

Depending on the breadth and depth of information shared, a relationship can be defined as casual or intimate. In a casual relationship, the breadth may be great, but not the depth. A more intimate relationship is likely to have high depth in at least one area. The most intimate relationships are those in which disclosure is great in both breadth and depth. Altman and Taylor see the development of a relationship as a progression from the periphery of their model to its center, a process that typically occurs over time. Each of your personal relationships probably has a different combination of breadth of subjects and depth of disclosure. Figure 6–2 pictures a student's self-disclosure in one relationship.

Think of a person you would like to know better. Using the levels of self-disclosure in this section, identify the kind of sharing that goes on between you now. Think of two factual statements, two opinions, and two expressions of feeling that you could share as a way of increasing the level of disclosure. Before actually delivering these messages, be sure to read the guidelines on pages 178–180.

What makes the disclosure in some messages deeper than others? One way to measure depth is by how far it goes on two of the dimensions that define self-disclosure. Some revelations are certainly more *significant* than others. Consider the difference between saying "I love my family" and "I love you." Other statements qualify as deep disclosure because they are *private*.

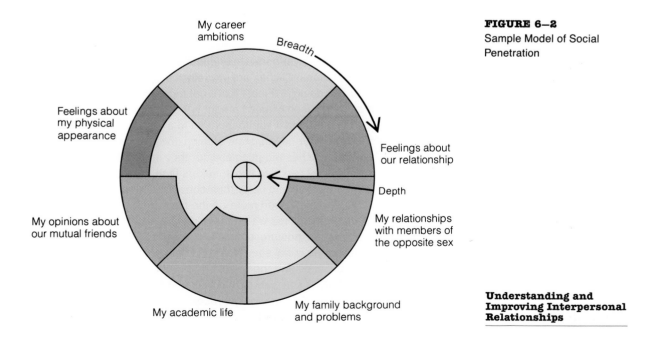

FIGURE 6–2
Sample Model of Social Penetration

FIGURE 6–3
Levels of Self-Disclosure

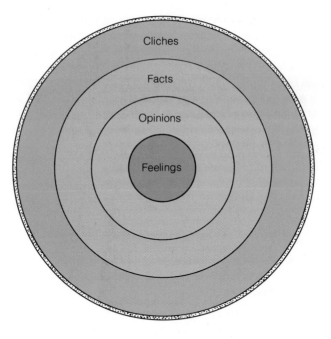

Sharing a secret you've only told a few close friends is certainly an act of self-disclosure, but it's even more revealing to divulge information that you've never told anyone.

Another way to classify the depth of disclosure is to look at the types of information we share. Figure 6–3 pictures a series of four concentric circles. Each circle represents a different type of communication. As a rule, the inner circles are more revealing than the outer ones. An examination of each level will explain their differences.

CLICHÉS The outermost layer consists of **clichés**—ritualized, stock responses to social situations. Clichés are virtually the opposite of self-disclosure: "How are you doing?" "Fine!" "Let's get together soon."

Remarks such as these usually aren't meant to be taken literally; in fact, the other person would be surprised if you responded to a casual "How are you?" with a lengthy speech on your health, state of mind, love life, or finances. Yet it's a mistake to consider clichés meaningless, for they serve several useful functions. For instance, they can give two speakers time to size each other up and decide whether it's desirable to carry their conversation any further. Our first impressions are generally based more on the nonverbal characteristics of the other person than on the words we hear spoken. Things like eye contact, vocal tone, facial expression, posture, and so on can often tell us more about another person than can the initial sentences in a conversation. Given the value of these nonverbal cues and the awkwardness of actually saying, "I want to take a few minutes to look you over before I commit myself to getting acquainted," the exchange of a few stock phrases can be just the thing to get you through this initial period comfortably.

Interpersonal Communication

Clichés can also serve as codes for other messages we don't usually express directly, such as "I want to acknowledge your presence" (for instance, when two acquaintances walk past each other). Additional unstated messages often contained in clichés are "I'm interested in talking if you feel like it" or "Let's keep the conversation light and impersonal; I don't feel like disclosing much about myself right now." Accompanied by a different set of nonverbal cues, a cliché can say, "I don't want to be impolite, but you'd better stay away from me for now." In all these cases, clichés serve as a valuable kind of shorthand that makes it easy to keep the social wheels greased and indicates the potential for further, possibly more profound conversation.

FACTS Moving inward from clichés on our model brings us to the level of volunteering *facts*. Not all factual statements qualify as self-disclosure: They must fit the criteria of being intentional, significant, and not otherwise known:

> "This isn't my first try at college, I dropped out a year ago with terrible grades."

> "I'm practically engaged." (On meeting a stranger while away from home.)

> "That idea that everyone thought was so clever wasn't really mine. I read it in a book last year."

Facts like these can be meaningful in themselves, but they also have a greater significance in a relationship. Disclosing important information suggests a level of trust and commitment to the other person that signals a desire to move the relationship to a new level.

OPINIONS Still more revealing is the level of opinions:

> "I used to think abortion was no big deal, but lately I've changed my mind."

> "I really like Karen."

> "I don't think you're telling me what's on your mind."

Opinions like these usually reveal more about a person than facts alone. If you know where the speaker stands on a subject, you can get a clearer picture of how your relationship might develop. Likewise, every time you offer a personal opinion, you are giving others valuable information about yourself.

FEELINGS The fourth level of self-disclosure—and usually most revealing one—is the realm of feelings. At first glance, feelings might appear to be the same as opinions, but there is a big difference. As we saw, "I don't think you're telling me what's on your mind" is an opinion. Now notice how much more we learn about the speaker by looking at three different feelings that might accompany this statement:

> "I don't think you're telling me what's on your mind, *and I'm suspicious.*"

> "I don't think you're telling me what's on your mind, *and I'm angry.*"

> "I don't think you're telling me what's on your mind, *and I'm hurt.*"

Understanding and Improving Interpersonal Relationships

The difference between these four levels of communication suggests why relationships can be frustrating. One reason has to do with the depth of disclosure, which may not lead to the kind of relationship one or both parties are seeking. Sometimes the communicators might remain exclusively on the level of facts. This might be suitable for a business relationship but wouldn't be very likely in most other circumstances. Even worse, other communicators never get off the level of clichés. And just as a diet of rich foods can become unappealing if carried to excess, the overuse of feelings and opinions can also become disagreeable. In most cases the successful conversation is one in which the participants move from one level to another, depending on the circumstances.

Reasons for Self-Disclosure

Self-disclosure has the potential to improve and expand interpersonal relationships, but it serves other functions as well.[10] As you read each of the following reasons why people reveal themselves, see which apply to you.

CATHARSIS   Sometimes you might disclose information in an effort to "get it off your chest." In a moment of candor you might, for instance, reveal your regrets about having behaved badly in the past.

SELF-CLARIFICATION   Sometimes you can clarify your beliefs, opinions, thoughts, attitudes, and feelings by talking about them with another person. This sort of "talking the problem out" occurs with psychotherapists, but it also goes on with others, all the way from good friends to bartenders or hairdressers.

SELF-VALIDATION   If you disclose information ("I think I did the right thing . . . ") with the hope of seeking the listener's agreement, you are seeking validation of your behavior—confirmation of a belief you hold about yourself. On a deeper level, this sort of self-validating disclosure seeks confirmation of important parts of your self-concept.

RECIPROCITY   A well-documented conclusion from research is that one act of self-disclosure begets another.[11] Thus, in some situations you may choose to disclose information about yourself to encourage another person to do so also.

IMPRESSION FORMATION   In some situations you may choose to reveal yourself to create a particular impression. Dating behavior, particularly on the first few dates, is often aimed at creating a favorable impression. To look good, we sometimes share selected bits of information about ourselves—for example, our accomplishments or goals.

RELATIONSHIP MAINTENANCE AND ENHANCEMENT   Relationships need disclosure to stay healthy and develop. If you don't reveal how you're feeling about your partner, not to mention other parts of your life—the subjects of your interaction become limited and shallow.

SOCIAL CONTROL Revealing personal information may increase your control over the other person, and sometimes over the situation in which you and the other person find yourselves. For example, an employee who tells the boss that another firm has made overtures probably will have an increased chance of getting raises and improvements in working conditions.

MANIPULATION Although most of the preceding reasons might strike you as being manipulative, they often aren't premeditated strategies. There are cases, however, when an act of self-disclosure is calculated in advance to achieve a desired result. Of course, if a disclosure's hidden motive ever becomes clear to the receiver, the results will most likely be quite unlike those intended.

The reasons for disclosing vary from one situation to another, depending on several factors. The strongest influence on why people disclose seems to be how well we know the other person.[12] When the target of disclosure is a friend, the most frequent reason people give for volunteering personal information is relationship maintenance and enhancement. In other words, we disclose to friends in order to strengthen the relationship. The second important reason is self-clarification—to sort out confusion to understand ourselves better.

With strangers, reciprocity becomes the most common reason for disclosing. We offer information about ourselves to strangers to learn more about them, so we can decide whether and how to continue the relationship. The second most important reason is impression formation. In other words, we often reveal information about ourselves to strangers to make ourselves look good. This information, of course, is usually positive—at least in the early stages of a friendship.

The Johari Window Model of Self-Disclosure

One way to look at the important part self-disclosure plays in interpersonal communication is by means of a device called the **Johari Window.**[13] (The window takes its name from the first names of its creators, Joseph Luft and Harry Ingham.) Imagine a frame inside which is everything there is to know about you: your likes and dislikes, your goals, your secrets, your needs—everything. (See Figure 6–4.)

Everything about you

FIGURE 6–4

You can use the Johari Window model to examine the level of self-disclosure in your own relationships.

a. Use the format described in Figure 6–9 to draw two Johari Windows, representing the relationship between you and one other person. Remember to reverse one of the windows so that your open areas and those of the other person face each other.

b. Describe which parts of yourself you keep in the hidden area. Explain your reasons for doing so. Describe the costs or benefits or both of not disclosing these parts of yourself.

c. Look at the blind area of your model. Is this area large or small because of the amount of feedback (much or little) that you get from your partner or because of your willingness to receive the feedback that is offered?

d. Explain whether or not you are satisfied with the results illustrated by your answers. If you are not satisfied, explain what you can do to remedy the problem.

Of course, you aren't aware of everything about yourself. Like most people, you're probably discovering new things about yourself all the time. To represent this, we can divide the frame containing everything about you into two parts: the part you know about and the part you're not aware of, as in Figure 6–5.

We can also divide this frame containing everything about you in another way. In this division one part represents the things about you that others know, and the second part contains the things about you that you keep to yourself. Figure 6–6 represents this view.

When we impose these two divided frames one atop the other, we have a Johari Window. By looking at Figure 6–7 you can see the *everything about you* divided into four parts.

Part 1 represents the information of which both you and the other person are aware. This part is your *open area.* Part 2 represents the *blind area:* information of which you are unaware but the other person knows. You learn about information in the blind area primarily through feedback. Part 3 represents your *hidden area:* information that you know but aren't willing to reveal to others. Items in this hidden area become public primarily through self-disclosure, which is the focus of this chapter. Part 4 represents information that is *unknown* to both you and others. At first, the unknown area seems impossible to verify. After all, if neither you nor others know what it contains, how can you be sure it exists? We can deduce its existence because we are constantly discovering new things about ourselves. It is not unusual to discover, for example, that you have an unrecognized talent, strength, or

FIGURE 6–5   **FIGURE 6–6**   **FIGURE 6–7**

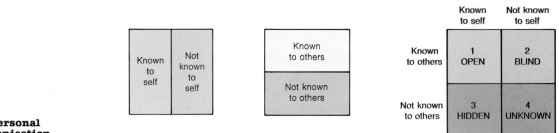

weakness. Items move from the unknown area either directly into the open area when you disclose your insight or through one of the other areas first.

The relative size of each area in our personal Johari Windows changes from time to time, according to our moods, the subject we are discussing, and our relationship with the other person. Despite these changes, most people's overall style of disclosure could be represented by a single Johari Window. Figure 6–8 pictures windows representing four extreme interaction styles.

Style I depicts a person who is neither receptive to feedback nor willing to disclose. This person takes few risks and may appear aloof and uncommunicative. The largest quadrant is the unknown area: Such people have a lot to learn about themselves, as do others. Style II depicts a person who is open to feedback from others but does not voluntarily self-disclose. This person may fear exposure, possibly because of not trusting others. People who fit this pattern may appear highly supportive at first. They want to hear *your* story and appear willing to deny themselves by remaining quiet. Then this first impression fades, and eventually you see them as distrustful and detached. A Johari Window describing such people has a large hidden area.

Style III in Figure 6–8 describes people who discourage feedback from others but disclose freely. Like the people pictured in diagram II, they may distrust others' opinions. They certainly seem self-centered. Their largest quadrant is the blind area: They do not encourage feedback and so fail to learn much about how others view them.

Diagram IV depicts people who are both willing to disclose information about themselves and open to others' ideas. They are trusting enough to seek the opinions of others and disclose their own. In extreme, this communication style can be intimidating and overwhelming because it violates the usual expectations of how nonintimates ought to behave. In moderation, however, this open style provides the best chance for developing highly interpersonal relationships.

Interpersonal communication of any depth is virtually impossible if the individuals involved have little open area. Going a step further, you can see that a relationship is limited by the individual who is less open, that is, who possesses the smaller open area. Figure 6–9 illustrates this situation with Johari Windows. A's window is set up in reverse so that A's and B's open areas are adjacent. Notice that the amount of communication (represented by the

FIGURE 6–8
Four Styles of Disclosure

FIGURE 6-9

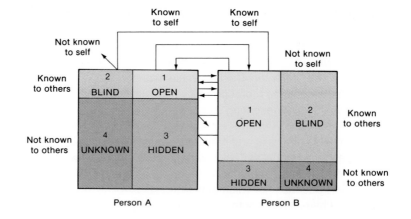

arrows connecting the two open areas) is dictated by the size of the smaller open area of A. The arrows originating from B's open area and being turned aside by A's hidden and blind areas represent unsuccessful attempts to communicate.

You have probably found yourself in situations that resemble Figure 6–9. Perhaps you have felt the frustration of not being able to get to know someone who was too reserved. Perhaps you have blocked another person's attempts to build a relationship with you in the same way. Whether you picture yourself more like Person A or Person B, the fact is that self-disclosure on both sides is necessary for the development of any interpersonal relationship. This chapter will describe just how much self-disclosure is optimal and of what type.

Characteristics of Effective Self-Disclosure

◆ **Hateful to me as are the gates of hell Is he, who hiding one thing in his heart, Utters another.**

Homer
Iliad

The Johari Window suggests several characteristics of self-disclosure.

SELF-DISCLOSURE USUALLY OCCURS IN DYADS   Although it is possible for people to disclose a great deal about themselves in groups, such communication usually occurs in one-to-one settings. Because revealing significant information about yourself involves a certain amount of risk, limiting the disclosure to one person at a time minimizes the chance that your revelations will lead to unhappy consequences.

EFFECTIVE SELF-DISCLOSURE IS USUALLY SYMMETRICAL
Note in Figure 6–9 that the amount of successful, two-way communication (represented by the arrows connecting the two open areas) is dictated by the size of the smaller open area of A. The arrows that are originating from B's open area and being turned aside by A's hidden and blind areas represent unsuccessful attempts to communicate. In situations such as this, it's easy to imagine how B would soon limit the amount of disclosure to match that of A. On the other hand, if A were willing to match the degree of disclosure given by B, the relationship would move to a new level of intimacy. In either case, we

Interpersonal Communication

◆ The personality of man is not an apple that has to be polished, but a banana that has to be peeled. And the reason we remain so far from one another, the reason we neither communicate nor interact in any real way, is that most of us spend our lives in polishing rather than peeling.

Man's lifelong task is simply one, but it is not simple: To remove the discrepancy between his outer self and his inner self, to get rid of the "persona" that divides his authentic self from the world.

This persona is like the peeling on a banana: It is something built up to protect from bruises and injury. It is not the real person, but sometimes (if the fear of injury remains too great) it becomes a lifelong substitute for the person.

The "authentic personality" knows that he is like a banana, and knows that only as he peels himself down to his individuated self can he reach out and make contact with his fellows by what Father Goldbrunner calls "the sheer maturity of his humanity." Only when he himself is detached from his defensive armorings can he then awaken a true response in his dialogue with others.

Most of us, however, think in terms of the apple, not the banana. We spend our lives in shining the surface, in making it rosy and gleaming, in perfecting the "image." But the image is not the apple, which may be wormy and rotten to the taste.

Almost everything in modern life is devoted to the polishing process, and little to the peeling process. It is the surface personality that we work on—the appearance, the clothes, the manners, the geniality. In short, the salesmanship: We are selling the package, not the product.

Sydney J. Harris

---

can expect that most often the degree of disclosure between partners will soon stabilize at a symmetrical level.

EFFECTIVE SELF-DISCLOSURE OCCURS INCREMENTALLY

Although occasions occur in which partners start their relationship by telling everything about themselves to each other, such instances are rare. In most cases, the amount of disclosure increases over time. We begin relationships by revealing relatively little about ourselves; then if our first bits of self-disclosure are well received and bring on similar responses from the other person, we're willing to reveal more. This principle is important to remember. It would usually be a mistake to assume that the way to build a strong relationship would be to reveal the most private details about yourself when first making contact with another person. Unless the circumstances are unique, such baring of your soul would be likely to scare potential partners away rather than bring them closer.

RELATIVELY FEW TRANSACTIONS INVOLVE HIGH LEVELS OF SELF-DISCLOSURE   Just as it's unwise to seek great self-disclosure too soon, it's also unproductive to reveal yourself too much. Except for unique

Understanding and Improving Interpersonal Relationships

settings—such as in therapy—there's usually no need to disclose frequently or steadily.

EFFECTIVE SELF-DISCLOSURE USUALLY OCCURS IN THE CONTEXT OF POSITIVE RELATIONSHIPS   This principle makes sense. We're generally more willing to reveal information about ourselves when we feel accepted by the other person. This doesn't mean that you should avoid making disclosing statements that contain negative messages (for example, "I feel uncomfortable about what happened last night"). Such explanations are likely to be successful if they're designed to be constructive, to help your relationship grow. On the other hand, disclosure that has the effect of attacking the other person ("You sure aren't very bright") is almost guaranteed to be destructive.

Guidelines for Appropriate Self-Disclosure

One fear we've had while writing this chapter is that a few overenthusiastic readers may throw down their books and begin to share every personal detail of their lives with whomever they can find. As you can imagine, this kind of behavior isn't an example of effective interpersonal communication.

No single style of self-disclosure is appropriate for every situation. Let's take a look at some guidelines that can help you recognize how to express yourself in a way that's rewarding for you and the others involved.[14]

IS THE OTHER PERSON IMPORTANT TO YOU?   There are several ways in which someone might be important. Perhaps you have an ongoing relationship deep enough so that sharing significant parts of yourself justifies keeping your present level of togetherness intact. Or perhaps the person to whom you're considering disclosing is someone with whom you've previously related on a less personal level. But now you see a chance to grow closer, and disclosure may be the path toward developing that personal relationship.

IS THE RISK OF DISCLOSING REASONABLE? Take a realistic look at the potential risks of self-disclosure. Even if the probable benefits are great, opening yourself up to almost certain rejection may be asking for trouble. For instance, it might be foolhardy to share your important feelings with someone you know is likely to betray your confidences or ridicule them. On the other hand, knowing that your partner is trustworthy and supportive makes the prospect of speaking out more reasonable. In anticipating risks, be sure that you are realistic. It's sometimes easy to indulge in catastrophic expectations in which you begin to imagine all sorts of disastrous consequences of your opening up when in fact such horrors are quite unlikely to occur.

ARE THE AMOUNT AND TYPE OF DISCLOSURE APPROPRIATE?
A third point to realize is that there are degrees of self-disclosure. Telling others about yourself isn't an all-or-nothing decision you must make. It's possible to share some facts, opinions, or feelings with one person while reserving riskier ones for others. In the same vein, before sharing very important information with someone who does matter to you, you might consider testing reactions by disclosing less personal data.

IS THE DISCLOSURE RELEVANT TO THE SITUATION AT HAND?
Self-disclosure doesn't require long confessions about your past life or current thoughts unrelated to the present. On the contrary, it ought to be directly pertinent to your present situation. It's ludicrous to picture the self-disclosing person as someone who blurts out intimate details of every past experience. Instead, our model is someone who, when the time is appropriate, trusts us enough to share the hidden parts of self that affect our relationship.

Usually, then, the subject of appropriate self-disclosure involves the present, the "here and now" as opposed to "there and then." "How am I feeling now?" "How are we doing now?" These are appropriate topics for sharing personal thoughts and feelings. There are certainly times when it's relevant to bring up the past but only as it relates to what's going on in the present.

IS THE DISCLOSURE RECIPROCATED? There's nothing quite as disconcerting as talking your heart out to someone only to discover that the other person has yet to say anything to you that is half as revealing as what you've been saying. And you think to yourself, "What am I doing?" Unequal self-disclosure creates an imbalanced relationship, one doomed to fall apart.

There are few times when one-way disclosure is acceptable. Most of them involve formal, therapeutic relationships in which a client approaches a trained professional with the goal of resolving a problem. For instance, you wouldn't necessarily expect to hear about a physician's personal ailments during a visit to a medical office. Nonetheless, it's interesting to note that one frequently noted characteristic of effective psychotherapists, counselors, and teachers is a willingness to share their feelings about a relationship with their clients.

Understanding and
Improving Interpersonal
Relationships

WILL THE EFFECT BE CONSTRUCTIVE?   Self-disclosure can be a vicious tool if it's not used carefully. Psychologist George Bach suggests that every person has a psychological "belt line." Below that belt line are areas about which the person is extremely sensitive. Bach says that jabbing at a "below-the-belt" area is a surefire way to disable another person, although usually at great cost to the relationship. It's important to consider the effects of your candor before opening up to others. Comments such as "I've always thought you were pretty unintelligent" or "Last year I made love to your best friend" *may* sometimes resolve old business and thus be constructive, but they also can be devastating—to the listener, to the relationship, and to your self-esteem.

IS THE SELF-DISCLOSURE CLEAR AND UNDERSTANDABLE?
When you express yourself to others, it's important that you share yourself in a way that's intelligible. This means describing the *sources* of your message clearly. For instance, it's far better to describe another's behavior by saying, "When you don't answer my phone calls or drop by to visit anymore . . ." than to complain vaguely, "When you avoid me. . . ."

It's also vital to express your *thoughts* and *feelings* explicitly. "I feel worried because I'm afraid you don't care about me" is more understandable than "I don't like the way things have been going."

◆ RESOLVING INTERPERSONAL CONFLICT

Even the most supportive communication climate won't guarantee complete harmony. Regardless of what we may wish for or dream about, a conflict-free world just doesn't exist. Even the best communicators, the luckiest people, are bound to wind up in situations when their needs don't match the needs of others. Money, time, power, sex, humor, aesthetic taste, as well as a thousand other issues, arise and keep us from living in a state of perpetual agreement.

For many people the inevitability of conflict is a depressing fact. They think that the existence of ongoing conflict means that there's little chance for happy relationships with others. Effective communicators know differently, however. They realize that although it's impossible to *eliminate* conflict, there are ways to *manage* it effectively. And those effective communicators know the subject of this chapter—that managing conflict skillfully can open the door to healthier, stronger, and more satisfying relationships.

The Nature of Conflict

Whatever forms they may take, all interpersonal **conflicts** share certain similarities. Joyce Frost and William Wilmot provide a thorough definition of conflict. They state that conflict is an *expressed struggle between at least two interdependent parties who perceive incompatible goals, scarce rewards, and interference from the other parties in achieving their goals.*[15] Let's look at the various parts of this definition so as to develop a clearer idea of conflicts in people's lives.

EXPRESSED STRUGGLE   Another way to describe this idea is to say that both parties in a conflict know that some disagreement exists. For instance, you may be upset for months because a neighbor's loud stereo keeps you from getting to sleep at night, but no conflict exists between the two of you until the neighbor learns about your problem. Of course, the expressed struggle doesn't have to be verbal. You can show your displeasure with somebody without saying a word. A dirty look, the silent treatment, or avoiding the other person are all ways of expressing yourself. But one way or another both parties must know that a problem exists before they're in conflict.

PERCEIVED INCOMPATIBLE GOALS   All conflicts look as if one party's gain will be another's loss. For instance, consider the neighbor whose stereo keeps you awake at night. Does somebody have to lose? A neighbor who turns down the noise loses the enjoyment of hearing the music at full volume; but if the neighbor keeps the volume up, then you're still awake and unhappy.

But the goals in this situation really aren't completely incompatible—solutions do exist that allow both parties to get what they want. For instance, you could achieve peace and quiet by closing your windows and getting the neighbor to do the same. You might use a pair of earplugs. Or perhaps the neighbor could get a set of earphones and listen to the music at full volume without bothering anyone. If any of these solutions prove workable, then the conflict disappears.

Unfortunately, people often fail to see mutually satisfying answers to their problems. And as long as they *perceive* their goals to be mutually exclusive, then, although the conflict is unnecessary, it is still very real.

PERCEIVED SCARCE REWARDS   Conflicts also exist when people believe there isn't enough of something to go around. The most obvious example of a scarce resource is money—a cause of many conflicts. If a person asks for a raise in pay and the boss would rather keep the money or use it to expand the business, then the two parties are in conflict.

Time is another scarce commodity. As authors and family men, both of us are constantly in the middle of struggles about how to use the limited time we have to spend. Should we work on this book? Visit with our wives? Play with our kids? Enjoy the luxury of being alone? With only twenty-four hours in a day we're bound to wind up in conflicts with our families, editors, students, and friends—all of whom want more of our time than we have available to give.

◆ **Conflict Basic as Hunger?**
Psychologists often find themselves in the position of proving scientifically what people have always known implicitly.

So it is with new data on the value of conflict.

Conflict, a Canadian psychologist reported in *Scientific American*, 215:82, 1966, may be the same sort of driving force as hunger, thirst, sexual appetite and pain. If so, it can be placed among the ranks of those conditions which are most efficient in producing learning, with important implications for education.

All of the basic drives have in common the fact that they arouse the individual physically, sharpen his faculties, motivate him to act and enhance his learning capacity.

Science News

How does your conflict-related communication affect your relationships? You can find out by answering the following questions:

a. Recall five conflicts you've been involved in. The more recent they are, the better, and they should be involvements with people who are relatively important to you.

b. Turn an 8½-by-11-inch sheet of paper horizontally, and divide it into three columns. In the first one describe the nature of each conflict:

Understanding and Improving Interpersonal Relationships

who it involved and what it was about. In the second column describe how you handled the conflict: what you said and how you acted. Use the third column to describe the results of each conflict: how you felt, how the others involved felt, and your satisfaction with the outcome.

c. Based on your findings here, answer the following questions:

(1) Are you happy with the way you've handled your conflicts? Do you come away from them feeling better or worse than before?

(2) Have your conflicts left your relationships stronger or weaker?

(3) Do you recognize any patterns in your conflict style? For example, do you hold your angry feelings inside? Are you sarcastic? Do you lose your temper easily?

(4) If you could, would you like to change the way you deal with your conflicts?

INTERDEPENDENCE   However antagonistic they might feel toward each other, the parties in a conflict are usually dependent on each other. The welfare and satisfaction of one depends on the actions of another. If this weren't true, then even in the face of scarce resources and incompatible goals there would be no need for conflict. Interdependence exists between conflicting nations, social groups, organizations, friends, and lovers. In each case, if the two parties didn't need each other to solve the problem, each would go separate ways. In fact, many conflicts go unresolved because the parties fail to understand their interdependence. One of the first steps toward resolving a conflict is to take the attitude that "we're all in this together."

◆ The history of man is replete with mechanisms and attempts to control aggression. People have tried to pray it away, wish it away, or play it away. More recently they have tried to psychoanalyze it away. But it does not seem to go away.

George Bach and
Herb Goldberg
Creative Aggression

Styles of Expressing Conflict

Table 6–3 describes five ways people can act when their needs are not met. Each one has very different characteristics.

NONASSERTION   Nonassertion is the inability or unwillingness to express thoughts or feelings when necessary. Nonassertive communicators handle conflict in one of two ways. Sometimes they ignore their needs, keeping quiet when things don't go their way. A second nonassertive course of action is to acknowledge that a problem exists and then simply to accept the situation, hoping that it will clear up by itself. In the short run nonassertion usually fails, since problems usually don't clear up by themselves. Despite this fact, nonassertion may be a good choice if it maintains a harmonious relationship—especially with people who have a great deal of power over you. Asserting yourself with a demanding boss or a strict professor may not be worth the risk. In personal relationships the danger of nonassertion is a buildup of resentment toward the other person—often a bigger danger than speaking up.

◆ It is when we all play safe that we create a world of utmost insecurity.

Dag Hammarskjöld

◆ Not everything that is faced can be changed, But nothing can be changed until it is faced.

James Baldwin

TABLE 6–3   Styles of Conflict

	NONASSERTIVE	DIRECTLY AGGRESSIVE	PASSIVE AGGRESSIVE	INDIRECT	ASSERTIVE
APPROACH TO OTHERS	I'm not OK, you're OK.	I'm OK, you're not OK.	I'm OK, you're not OK. (But I'll let you think you are.)	I'm OK, you're not OK or I'm OK, you're not OK.	I'm OK. You're OK
DECISION MAKING	Let others choose	Chooses for others. They know it.	Chooses for others. They don't know it.	Chooses for others. They don't know it.	Chooses for self
SELF-SUFFICIENCY	Low	High or low	Looks high but usually low	High or low	Usually high
BEHAVIOR IN PROBLEM SITUATIONS	Flees; gives in	Outright attack	Concealed attack	Strategic, oblique	Direct confrontation
RESPONSE OF OTHERS	Disrespect, guilt, anger, frustration	Hurt, defensiveness, humiliation	Confusion, frustration, feelings of manipulation	Unknowing compliance or resistance	Mutual respect
SUCCESS PATTERN	Succeeds by luck or charity of others	Beats out others	Wins by manipulation	Gains unwitting compliance of others	Attempts "win-win" solutions

Adapted with permission from Stanlee Phelps and Nancy Austin, *The Assertive Woman* (San Luis Obispo, Calif.: Impact, 1975), p. 11; and Gerald Piaget, American Orthopsychiatric Association, 1975. Further reproduction prohibited.

CATHY   by Cathy Guisewite

DIRECT AGGRESSION   In contrast to nonassertion, **direct aggression** occurs when a person expresses hostility overtly by attacking the other party. The usual consequences of aggressive behaviors are anger and defensiveness or hurt and humiliation, although at times direct aggression may be the only way to get the other person's attention.

PASSIVE AGGRESSION   Communicators who express hostility in an obscure way are engaging in **passive aggression.** In several of his works, psychologist George Bach terms this behavior "crazymaking."[16] **Crazymaking** occurs when people have feelings of resentment, anger, or rage that they are unable or unwilling to express directly. Instead of keeping these feelings to themselves, the crazymakers send aggressive messages in subtle, indirect ways, maintaining a front of kindness. Crazymakers include sarcasm, malicious humor, and deliberately embarrassing the other person. The targets of the crazymaker can leave the victim confused and angry, faced with the unpleasant choice of reacting aggressively or retreating to nurse their hurt feelings. In either case, passive aggression seldom has anything but harmful effects on a relationship.

> Identify your conflict style by describing five recent interpersonal conflicts. (You can use the ones from the preceding activity if you completed it.) For each situation, describe
>
> **a.** Your communication style: nonassertive, directly aggressive, passive aggressive, indirect, or assertive.
> **b.** Your level of satisfaction with the style you used.
> **c.** Responses that would fit the three other styles you did not use (that is, if you behaved nonassertively, describe directly and indirectly aggressive and assertive responses).
>
> Based on the responses you identified here, how effective is your present conflict style? How could you improve it?

Interpersonal Communication

INDIRECT COMMUNICATION   Sometimes we choose to convey messages through **indirect communication,** hinting to others instead of expressing ourselves outright. Indirect communication lacks the hostility of passive-aggressive crazymaking. The goal is simply to convey a message in a roundabout manner.

Sometimes an indirect approach can save face for the other party. If your guests are staying too long, it's probably kinder to yawn and hint about your big day tomorrow than to bluntly ask them to leave. Likewise, if you're not interested in going out with someone who has asked you for a date, it may be more compassionate to claim that you're busy than to say "I'm not interested in seeing you."

At other times we communicate indirectly in order to protect ourselves. You might, for example, test the waters by hinting instead of directly asking the boss for a raise or letting your partner know you could use some affection instead of asking outright. At times like these, an oblique approach may get the message across while softening the blow of a negative response.

The risk of an indirect message is that the other party will misunderstand you or fail to get the message at all. There are also times when the importance of an idea is great enough that hinting lacks the necessary punch. When clarity and directness are your goals, an assertive approach is in order.

ASSERTION   **Assertive** people handle conflicts skillfully by expressing their needs, thoughts, and feelings clearly and directly but without judging others or dictating to them. They have the attitude that most of the time it is possible to resolve problems to everyone's satisfaction. Possessing this attitude and the skills to bring it about doesn't guarantee that assertive communicators will always get what they want, but it does give them the best chance of doing so. An additional benefit of such an approach is that whether or not it satisfies a particular need, it maintains the self-respect of both the assertors and those with whom they interact. As a result, people who manage their conflicts assertively may experience feelings of discomfort while they are working through the problem. They usually feel better about themselves and each other afterward—quite a change from the outcomes of no assertiveness or aggression.

Even though assertion might seem like the best way to approach conflicts, research shows that no single style is always best.[17] Satisfied couples sometimes express their needs to one another assertively, but more often they use other approaches—humor, giving in, and even changing the subject. These findings suggest that relationships seem to work best when assertiveness is used selectively in important conflicts, and when less confrontational approaches are used when problems aren't so important.

Approaches to Conflict Resolution

So far we have looked at the way individuals express (or don't express) conflicts. Now we need to look at the results of these approaches. There are three quite different outcomes of the various interactions among nonassertive, indirectly aggressive, directly aggressive, and assertive communicators. By looking at each of them, you can decide which ones you'll seek when you find yourself facing an interpersonal conflict.

WIN-LOSE Win-lose conflicts are ones in which one party achieves its goal at the expense of the other. People resort to this method of resolving disputes when they perceive a situation as being an "either-or" one: Either I get what I want or you get your way. The most clear-cut examples of win-lose situations are certain games such as baseball or poker in which the rules require a winner and a loser. Some interpersonal issues seem to fit into this win-lose framework: two coworkers seeking a promotion to the same job, for instance, or a couple who disagree on how to spend their limited money.

Power is the distinguishing characteristic in win-lose problem solving, for it is necessary to defeat an opponent to get what you want. The most obvious kind of power is physical. Some parents threaten their children with warnings such as "Stop misbehaving, or I'll send you to your room." Adults who use physical power to deal with each other usually aren't so blunt, but the legal system is the implied threat: "Follow the rules, or we'll lock you up."

Real or implied force isn't the only kind of power used in conflicts. People who rely on authority of many types engage in win-lose methods without ever threatening physical coercion. In most jobs, supervisors have the potential to use authority in the assignment of working hours, job promotions, and desirable or undesirable tasks and, of course, in the power to fire an unsatisfactory employee. Teachers can use the power of grades to coerce students to act in desired ways.

Even the usually admired democratic principle of majority rule is a win-lose method of resolving conflicts. However fair it may be, this system results in one group's getting its way and another group's being unsatisfied.

There are some circumstances when the win-lose method may be necessary as when there are truly scarce resources and where only one party can achieve satisfaction. For instance, if two suitors want to marry the same person, only one can succeed. And to return to an earlier example, it's often true that only one applicant can be hired for a job. But don't be too willing to assume that your conflicts are necessarily win-lose: As you'll soon read, many situations that seem to require a loser can be resolved to everyone's satisfaction.

There is a second kind of situation when win-lose is the best method. Even when cooperation is possible, if the other person insists on trying to defeat you, then the most logical response might be to defend yourself by fighting back. "It takes two to tango," the old cliché goes, and it also often takes two to cooperate.

A final and much less frequent justification for trying to defeat another person occurs when the other party is clearly behaving in a wrong manner and where defeating that person is the only way to stop the wrongful behavior. Few people would deny the importance of restraining a person who is deliberately harming others even if the aggressor's freedom is sacrificed in the process. The danger of forcing wrongdoers to behave themselves is the wide difference in opinion between people about who is wrong and who is right. Given this difference, it would only seem justifiable to coerce others into behaving as we think they should in the most extreme circumstances.

LOSE-LOSE   In **lose-lose problem solving** neither side is satisfied with the outcome. Although the name of this approach is so discouraging that it's hard to imagine how anyone could willingly use the method, in truth lose-lose is a fairly common approach to handling conflicts.

Compromise is the most respectable form of lose-lose conflict resolution. In it all the parties are willing to settle for less than they want because they believe that partial satisfaction is the best result they can hope for.

In his valuable book on conflict resolution, Albert Filley offers an interesting observation about our attitudes toward this method.[18] Why is it, he asks, that if someone says, "I will compromise my values," we view the action unfavorably, yet we talk admiringly about parties in a conflict who compromise to reach a solution? Though compromises may be the best obtainable result in some conflicts, it's important to realize that both people in a dispute can often work together to find much better solutions. In such cases, *compromise* is a negative word.

◆ **Our marriage used to suffer from arguments that were too short. Now we argue long enough to find out what the argument is about.**

Hugh Prather
Notes to Myself

Understanding and Improving Interpersonal Relationships

◆ We struggled together, knowing. We prattled, pretended, fought bitterly, laughed, wept over sad books or old movies, nagged, supported, gave, took, demanded, forgave, resented—hating the ugliness in each other, yet cherishing that which we were.... Will I ever find someone to battle with as we battled, love as we loved, share with as we shared, challenge as we challenged, forgive as we forgave? You used to say that I saved up all of my feelings so that I could spew forth when I got home. The anger I experienced in school I could not vent there. How many times have I heard you chuckle as you remembered the day I would come home from school and share with you all of the feelings I had kept in. "If anyone had been listening they would have thought you were punishing me, striking out at me. I always survived and you always knew that I would still be with you when you were through." There was an honesty about our relationship that may never exist again.

Vian Catrell

Most of us are surrounded by the results of bad compromises. Consider a common example: the conflict between one person's desire to smoke cigarettes and another's need for clean air. The win-lose outcomes on this issue are obvious: Either the smoker abstains or the nonsmoker gets polluted lungs—neither very satisfying. But a compromise in which the smoker only gets to enjoy a rare cigarette or must retreat outdoors and in which the nonsmoker still must inhale some fumes or feel like an ogre is hardly better. Both sides have lost a considerable amount of both comfort and goodwill. Of course, the costs involved in other compromises are even greater. For example, if divorced parents compromise on child care by haggling over custody and then finally grudgingly agree to split the time with their youngsters, it's hard to say that anybody has won.

Compromises aren't the only lose-lose solutions or even the worst ones. There are many instances in which the parties will both strive to be winners, but, as a result of the struggle, both wind up losers. On the international scene, many wars illustrate this sad point. A nation that gains military victory at the cost of thousands of lives, large amounts of resources, and a damaged national consciousness hasn't truly won much. On an interpersonal level the same principle holds true. Most of us have seen battles of pride in which both parties strike out and both suffer. It seems as if there should be a better alternative, and fortunately there often is.

WIN-WIN In **win-win problem solving,** the goal is to find a solution that satisfies the needs of everyone involved. Not only do the partners avoid trying to win at the other's expense, but there's also a belief that by working together it is possible to find a solution in which all parties reach their goals without needing to compromise.

One way to understand how win-win problem solving works is to look at a few examples.

A boss and a group of employees get into a conflict over scheduling. The employees often want to shift the hours they're scheduled to work in order to accommodate personal needs whereas the boss needs to be sure that the operation is fully staffed at all times. After some discussion they arrive at a solution that satisfies everyone: The boss works up a monthly master schedule indicating the hours during which each employee is responsible for being on the job. Employees are free to trade hours among themselves as long as the operation is fully staffed at all times.

A conflict about testing arises in a college class. Owing to sickness or other reasons, certain students need to take exams on a makeup basis. The instructor doesn't want to give these students any advantage over their peers and doesn't want to go through the task of making up a brand-new test for just a few people. After working on the problem together, instructor and students arrive at a win-win solution. The instructor will hand out a list of twenty possible exam questions in advance of the test day. At examination time five of these questions are randomly drawn for the class to answer. Students who take makeups will draw from the same pool of questions at the time of their test. In this way, makeup students are taking a fresh test without the instructor's having to create a new exam.

A newly married husband and wife found themselves arguing frequently over their budget. The wife enjoyed buying impractical but enjoyable items for herself and the house whereas the husband feared that such purchases would ruin their carefully constructed budget. Their solution was to set aside a small amount of money each month for such purchases. The amount was small enough to be affordable yet gave the wife a chance to escape from their Spartan life-style. Additionally, the husband was satisfied with the arrangement because the luxury money was now a budget category by itself, which got rid of the "out-of-control" feeling that came when his wife made unexpected purchases. The plan worked so well that the couple continued to use it, even after their income rose, by increasing the amount devoted to luxuries.

The point here isn't that these solutions are the correct ones for everybody with similar problems: The win-win approach doesn't work that way. Different people might have found other solutions that suited them better. What the win-win method does is give you an approach—a way of creatively finding just the

---

This exercise will help you develop a win-win solution for a problem in your own life.

a. Make a list of the situations in your life where there's a conflict of needs that's creating tension between you and someone else.

b. Analyze what you're doing at present to resolve such conflicts, and describe whether your behavior is meeting with any success.

c. Pick at least one of the problems you just listed, and, together with the other people involved, try to develop a win-win solution by following the steps listed earlier.

d. After following the process described on pages 190–193, share the results of your conference with the class. After you've had time to test your solution, report the progress you've made, and discuss the follow-up conference described on page 193.

Understanding and Improving Interpersonal Relationships

right answer for your unique problem. By using it, you can tailor-make a way of resolving your conflicts that everyone can live with comfortably.

You should understand that the win-win approach doesn't call for compromises in which the participants give up something they really want or need. Sometimes a compromise is the only alternative, but in the method we're talking about you find a solution that satisfies everybody—one in which nobody has to lose.

Win-Win Problem Solving

Of these three styles the win-win approach is clearly the most desirable one in most cases. It is also the hardest one to achieve—for two reasons. First, it requires a noncompetitive attitude and a number of skills that we'll soon discuss. Second, it requires a certain amount of cooperation from the other person, for it's difficult to arrive at a win-win solution with somebody who insists on trying to defeat you.

In spite of these challenges, it is definitely possible to become better at resolving conflicts. In the following pages, we will outline a method to increase your chances of being able to handle your conflicts in a win-win manner, so that both you and others have your needs met. As you learn to use this approach, you should find that more and more of your conflicts wind up with win-win solutions. And even when total satisfaction isn't possible, this method can help by showing you how to solve problems in the most satisfying way possible and also by preventing individual conflict from spoiling your future interactions with the person involved.

The method is patterned after techniques developed by George Bach[19] and Thomas Gordon,[20] and it has proved successful with many people, both young and old, in a variety of settings.

Before we introduce you to this method, there are a few ideas you should keep in mind. This technique is a highly structured activity. While you're learning how to use it, it's important that you follow all the stages carefully. Each step is essential to the success of your encounter, and skipping one or more can lead to misunderstandings that might threaten your meeting and even cause a "dirty fight." After you've practiced the method a number of times and are familiar with it, this style of conflict will become almost second nature to you. You'll then be able to approach your conflicts without the need to follow the step-by-step approach. But for the time being, try to be patient, and trust the value of the following pattern.

As you read the following steps, try to imagine yourself applying them to a problem that's bothering you now.

IDENTIFY YOUR PROBLEM AND UNMET NEEDS Before you speak out, it's important to realize that the problem that is causing conflict is yours. Whether you want to return an unsatisfactory piece of merchandise, complain to a noisy neighbor because your sleep is being disturbed, or request a change in working conditions from your employer, the problem is yours. Why? Because in each case *you* are the person who is dissatisfied. You are the one who has paid for the defective article; the merchant who sold it to you has the use of your good money. You are the one who is losing sleep as a result of your neighbors' activities; they are content to go on as before. You are the one who is unhappy with your working conditions, not your boss.

Realizing that the problem is yours will make a big difference when the time comes to approach your partner. Instead of feeling and acting in an evaluative way, you'll be more likely to share your problem in a descriptive way, which will not only be more accurate but will also reduce the chance of a defensive reaction.

Once you realize that the problem is yours, the next step is to identify the unmet needs that leave you feeling dissatisfied. For instance, in the barking dog incident, your need may be to get some sleep or to study without interruptions. In the case of a friend who teases you in public, your need would probably be to avoid embarrassment.

Sometimes the task of identifying your needs isn't as simple as it first seems. Consider these cases:

> A friend hasn't returned some money you loaned long ago. Your apparent need in this situation might be to get the cash back. But a little thought will probably show that this isn't the only, or even the main, thing you want. Even if you were rolling in money, you'd probably want the loan repaid because of your most important need: *to avoid feeling victimized by your friend's taking advantage of you.*

> Someone you care about who lives in a distant city has failed to respond to several letters. Your apparent need may be to get answers to the questions you've written about, but it's likely that there's another, more fundamental need: *the reassurance that you're still important enough to deserve a response.*

As you'll soon see, the ability to identify your real needs plays a key role in solving interpersonal problems. For now, the point to remember is that before you voice your problem to your partner, you ought to be clear about which of your needs aren't being met.

MAKE A DATE Unconstructive fights often start because the initiator confronts a partner who isn't ready. There are many times when a person isn't in the right frame of mind to face a conflict: perhaps owing to fatigue, being in too much of a hurry to take the necessary time, upset over another problem, or not feeling well. At times like these, it's unfair to "jump" a person without notice and expect to get full attention for your problem. If you do persist, you'll probably have an ugly fight on your hands.

After you have a clear idea of the problem, approach your partner with a request to try to solve it. For example: "Something's been bothering me. Can we talk about it?" If the answer is yes, then you're ready to go further. If it isn't the right time to confront your partner, find a time that's agreeable to both of you.

DESCRIBE YOUR PROBLEM AND NEEDS Your partner can't possibly meet your needs without knowing why you're upset and what you want.

Therefore, it's up to you to describe your problem as specifically as possible. When you do so, it's important to use terms that aren't overly vague or abstract. Recall our discussion of behavioral descriptions in Chapter 3 when clarifying your problem and needs.

CONSIDER YOUR PARTNER'S POINT OF VIEW After stating your problem and describing what you need, it's important to make sure your partner has understood what you've said. As you can remember from our discussion of listening in Chapter 3, there's a good chance—especially in a stressful conflict—that your words will be misinterpreted.

It's usually unrealistic to insist that your partner paraphrase your statement, and fortunately there are more tactful and subtle ways to make sure you've been understood. For instance, you might try saying, "I'm not sure I expressed myself very well just now—maybe you should tell what you heard me say so I can be sure I got it right." In any case, be absolutely sure that your partner understands your whole message before going any further. Legitimate agreements are tough enough, but there's no point in getting upset about a conflict that doesn't even exist.

After you are sure your position is clear, you need to find out what your partner needs to feel satisfied about this issue. There are two reasons why it's important to discover your partner's needs. First, it's fair. The other person has just as much right as you to feel satisfied, and if you expect help in meeting your needs, it's reasonable that you behave in the same way. But in addition to decency, there's another, practical reason for concerning yourself with what the other person wants. Just as an unhappy partner will make it hard for you to become satisfied, a happy one will be more likely to cooperate in letting you reach your goals. Thus, it's in your own self-interest to discover and meet your partner's needs.

You can learn about your partner's needs simply by asking about them: "Now I've told you what I want and why. Tell me what you need to feel OK about this." Once your partner begins to talk, your job is to use the listening skills discussed earlier in this book to make sure you understand.

NEGOTIATE A SOLUTION Now that you and your partner understand each other's needs, the goal becomes finding a way to meet them. This is done by trying to develop as many potential solutions as possible and then evaluating them to decide which one best meets everyone's needs.

Probably the best description of the win-win approach has been written by Thomas Gordon in his book *Parent Effectiveness Training*. The following steps are a modification of his approach.

1. **Identify and Define the Conflict.** We've discussed this process in the preceding pages. It consists of discovering each person's problem and needs, setting the stage for meeting all of them.

2. **Generate a Number of Possible Solutions.** In this step the partners work together to think of as many means as possible to reach their stated ends. The key word here is *quantity:* It's important to generate as many ideas as you can think of without worrying about which ones are good or bad. Write down every thought that comes up, no matter how unworkable; sometimes a farfetched idea will lead to a more workable one.

3. **Evaluate the Alternative Solutions.** This is the time to talk about which solutions will work and which ones won't. It's important for all concerned to be honest about their willingness to accept an idea. If a solution is going to work, everyone involved has to support it.

4. **Decide on the Best Solution.** Now that you've looked at all the alternatives, pick the one that looks best to everyone. It's important to be sure everybody understands the solution and is willing to try it out. Remember, your decision doesn't have to be final, but it should look potentially successful.

FOLLOW UP THE SOLUTION   You can't be sure the solution will work until you try it out. After you've tested it for a while, it's a good idea to set aside some time to talk over how things are going. You may find that you need to make some changes or even rethink the whole problem. The idea is to keep on top of the problem, to keep using creativity to solve it.

Win-win solutions aren't always possible. There will be times when even the best-intentioned people simply won't be able to find a way of meeting all their needs. In cases like this, the process of negotiation has to include some compromising. But even then the preceding steps haven't been wasted. The genuine desire to learn what the other person wants and to try to satisfy those desires will build a climate of goodwill that can help you find the best solution to the present problem and also improve your relationship in the future.

One typical comment people have after trying the preceding method of handling conflicts is "This is a helpful thing sometimes, but it's so rational! Sometimes I'm so uptight I don't care about defensiveness or listening or anything . . . I just want to yell and get it off my chest!"

When you feel like this, it's almost impossible to be rational. At times like these, probably the most therapeutic thing to do is to get your feelings off your chest in what Bach calls a "Vesuvius"—an uncontrolled, spontaneous explosion. A Vesuvius can be a terrific way of blowing off steam, and after you do so, it's often much easier to figure out a rational solution to your problem.

So we encourage you to have a Vesuvius with the following qualifications: Be sure your partner understands what you're doing and realizes that whatever you say doesn't call for a response. He or she should let you rant and rave for as long as you want without getting defensive or "tying in." Then, when your eruption subsides, you can take steps to work through whatever still troubles you.

Understanding and Improving Interpersonal Relationships

An interpersonal relationship is an association in which two or more people meet one another's social needs to a greater or lesser degree. Communication in relationships consists of both content and relational messages. Explicit relational messages are termed metacommunication.

This chapter explored several factors that help make interpersonal communication satisfying or unsatisfying. It defined communication climate as the emotional tone of a relationship as it is expressed in the message exchanged. The chapter examined factors that contribute to positive and negative climates, showing that the underlying factor that shapes climate is the degree to which a person feels valued by others. The chapter looked at research on the causes and reduction of defensiveness, a major problem in interpersonal relationships.

Self-disclosure is the process of deliberately revealing significant information about oneself that would not normally be known. This chapter introduced several models to illustrate the breadth, depth, and exchange of disclosing messages. It also discussed the various reasons people disclose personal information. Self-disclosure is not always desirable: The chapter listed several guidelines to help determine when it is and is not appropriate.

The final section of the chapter dealt with the matter of interpersonal conflict. We began by asserting that conflict is natural and inevitable, pointing out that when it is handled skillfully, it can be a means of improving relationships. We looked at several styles of conflict that individuals take, then examined three interpersonal approaches to resolving a conflict. We examined one of these approaches, the win-win orientation, in some detail, showing that it is often a possible and realistic method of resolving disputes.

◆ **NOTES**

1. For further discussion of the characteristics of impersonal and interpersonal communication, see Arthur P. Bochner, "The Functions of Human Communication in Interpersonal Bonding," in C. C. Arnold and J. W. Bowers (eds.), *Handbook of Rhetorical and Communication Theory* (Boston: Allyn and Bacon, 1984), p. 550; S. Trenholm and A. Jensen, *Interpersonal Communication* (Belmont, Calif.: Wadsworth, 1987), p. 37; J. Stewart and G. D'Angelo, *Together: Communicating Interpersonally,* 3d ed. (New York: Random House, 1988), p. 5.

2. See P. Watzlawick, J. H. Beavin, D. D. Jackson, *Pragmatics of Human Communication* (New York: Norton, 1967); and W. J. Lederer and D. D. Jackson, *The Mirages of Marriage* (New York: Norton, 1968).

3. See C. M. Rossiter, Jr, "Instruction in Metacommunication," *Central States Speech Journal* 25 (1974): 36–42;

and W. W. Wilmot, "Metacommunication: A Re-examination and Extension," in *Communication Yearbook* 4 (New Brunswick, N.J.: Transaction Books, 1980).

4. D. Tannen, *That's Not What I Meant! How Conversational Style Makes or Breaks Your Relations with Others* (New York: Morrow, 1986), p. 190.

5. E. Sieburg, "Confirming and Disconfirming Communication in an Organizational Setting," in J. Owen, P. Page, and G. Zimmerman (eds.), *Communication in Organizations* (St. Paul, Minn.: West, 1976), pp. 129–149.

6. Ibid.

7. W. Wilmot, *Dyadic Communication,* 3d ed. (New York: Random House, 1987), p. 150.

8. J. Gibb, "Defensive Communication," *Journal of Communication* II (September 1961): 141–148. See also W. F. Eadie, "Defensive Communication Revisited: A

Critical Examination of Gibb's Theory," *Southern Speech Communication Journal* 47 (1982): 163–177.

9. I. Altman and D. A. Taylor, *Social Penetration: The Development of Interpersonal Relationships* (New York: Holt, Rinehart and Winston, 1973).

10. Adapted from V. J. Derlega and J. Grezlak, "Appropriateness of Self-Disclosure," in G. J. Chelune (ed.), *Self-Disclosure* (San Francisco, Calif.: Jossey-Bass, 1979).

11. See V. J. Derlega and A. L. Chaikin, *Sharing Intimacy: What We Reveal to Others and Why* (Englewood Cliffs, N.J.: Prentice-Hall, 1975).

12. L. B. Rosenfeld and W. L. Kendrick, "Choosing to Be Open: Subjective Reasons for Self-Disclosing," *Western Journal of Speech Communication* 48 (Fall 1984): 326–343.

13. J. Luft, *Of Human Interaction* (Palo Alto, Calif.: National Press, 1969).

14. Summarized in J. Pearson, *Communication in the Family* (New York: Harper & Row, 1989), pp. 252–257.

15. J. L. Hocker and W. W. Wilmot, *Interpersonal Conflict,* 2d ed. (Dubuque, Iowa: W. C. Brown, 1985), pp. 22–29.

16. George R. Bach and Herb Goldberg, *Creative Aggression* (Garden City, N.Y.: Doubleday, 1974).

17. Pearson, pp. 319–320.

18. Albert C. Filley, *Interpersonal Conflict Resolution* (Glenview, Ill.: Scott, Foresman, 1975), p. 23.

19. George Bach and Yetta Bernhard, *Aggression Lab: The Fair Fight Training Manual* (Dubuque, Iowa: Kendall-Hunt, 1971).

20. Thomas Gordon, *Parent Effectiveness Training* (New York: New American Library, 1975), pp. 263–264.

Understanding and Improving Interpersonal Relationships

7

After reading this chapter, you should understand the following:

1. The various forms families can take.

2. How family communication is systemic in nature.

3. The functions served by family communication.

4. The types of communication networks that can operate in families.

5. The characteristics of effective family communication introduced in this chapter.

6. The factors that contribute to the formation and growth of friendships.

7. The relationship between gender and friendship.

KEY TERMS

all-channel network
blended family
chain network
communal family
expressive
 communication
extended family
family
gatekeeper
homeostasis

instrumental
 communication
open system
single-parent family
 system
two-parent biological
 family
wheel network
Y network

You should be able to do the following:

1. Describe how systemic variables (interdependence, wholeness, patterns and self-regulation, and openness to the environment) influence communication in a family you have observed.

2. Describe the ways in which communication in a family you have observed affects the members' everyday behavior, shapes their identity, and provides social support.

3. Describe the communication networks in a family you have observed.

4. Describe the explicit and implicit rules that govern communication in a specific family.

5. Rate the degree to which a specific family follows the characteristics for effective communication described in this chapter.

6. Evaluate the number and quality of your friendships in terms of reciprocity, similarity, availability, and disclosure.

7. Identify the degree to which your friendships are affected by gender.

Communication with Family and Friends

No one would argue that liking and loving are two keys to happiness, but few people realize that a strong social network may make the difference between sickness and health—or even life and death. According to research gathered by the California Department of Mental Health, people who have strong relationships with others, whether friends or family, tend to live longer and suffer from fewer diseases.[1] Consider a few sobering facts:

◆ People who lack strong relationships have two to three times the risk of early death, regardless of whether they smoke, drink alcoholic beverages, or exercise regularly.

◆ Terminal cancer strikes socially isolated people more often than those who have close personal relationships.

◆ Divorced, separated, and widowed people are five to ten times more likely to need mental hospitalization than their married counterparts.

◆ Pregnant women under stress and without supportive relationships have three times more complications than pregnant women who suffer from the same stress but have strong social support.

Figures like these make it clear that relationships with friends and family are important. And of course, communication is what keeps those relationships strong and healthy. In this chapter we will look at the role of communication with the friends and relations who play such a vital role on our lives. We will discuss what kinds of communication occur, and how to make that interaction more effective and satisfying.

◆ COMMUNICATION IN THE FAMILY

Our first, and arguably our most important communication of a lifetime begins with our family of origin. Interaction with others in the early years provides models and sets patterns that can shape relationships for the remainder of our lives. As adults, most of us acquire families of our own, and with the arrival of children we have the opportunity to teach lessons to the next generation. Because the family is such a vital arena for communication, we will spend the first part of our chapter looking at that setting.

Types of Families

What image comes to mind when you hear the word "family"? You might recall the people you grew up with, or perhaps everyone related to you by kinship: cousins, aunts and uncles, grandparents, and so on. Maybe you visualize an idealized or troubled family from films, books, or television. Before defining the notion of family, let's consider all the forms families can take in today's society.[2]

A **two-parent biological family** is the traditional image for most people. It consists of a husband and wife and children from the union of their marriage. While it is not obsolete, the traditional family is becoming less and less

◆ In the 1950's and early 1960's, television almost always portrayed a family as a married couple and their children. "Leave It to Beaver" gave us Ward, June, Wally, and "The Beaver." Ricky, Lucy, and Little Ricky frolicked through "I Love Lucy." And, of course, the Anderson household gained familial strength from the axiom that gave the show its title, "Father Knows Best." Times have changed, and so has the media definition of the family. Two men share an apartment on "The Odd Couple." "Eight Is Enough" and "The Brady Bunch" depict families combined after the death of a spouse. "Diff'rent Strokes" and "Webster" portray interracial families. And "Love, Sidney" has given us a glimpse of a young career woman raising her illegitimate child while living with a homosexual—clearly a family structure that would have shocked Ozzie and Harriet!

Steven Beebe and John Masterson

common. The number of **single-parent families,** consisting of either a father or mother and one or more children is growing. In 1985 the U.S. Census Bureau reported that 26 percent of all families had only one parent—an increase of 18 percent in only five years.[3] Most commonly, single-parent families result from a divorce, although death and desertion can produce the same result. A growing number of single-parent families involve a mother who never married, caring for children who were conceived either intentionally or accidentally.

The number of **blended families** is also increasing. These consist of two adults and children who may not have come from the union of their marriage. Many blended families follow the "Brady Bunch" model, resulting from the remarriage of adults who brought the children from their previous relationships. Other blends involve adopted or foster children.

An **extended family** is a collection of blood relatives, other than or in addition to parents and their children, united as a family unit. Many extended families are cross-generational, involving grandparents, parents, and children. In some cases, parents may be missing from the extended family. In other situations aunts or uncles, brothers or sisters can be members of the family group. Despite the nostalgic idea that extended families were common before our fast-paced industrial society developed, there has never been a time when three-generation households were common.[4] Unlike today, when grandparents might not choose to live with younger generations (or vice versa), before the 1900's an early death prevented this as an option.

Finally, **communal families** are groups of people who are unrelated by blood but who share a commitment to each other, live together, and consider themselves to be a family. Some communal families define themselves formally: kibbutzim in Israel and religious communities are examples. Other communal families evolve informally from friendships or common commitments. The key to identifying a communal family is that members think of themselves as part of a family unit.

After considering all these categories, you can see why defining the term **family** isn't as easy as it might seem. Perhaps the most useful definition is

Communication with Family and Friends

"a group of people with a past history, a present reality, and a future expectation of interconnected transactional relationships."[5] This definition includes all of the family types we have considered here. It includes groups that are bound together by blood relationships, legal contracts, and by nonformal but nonetheless strong ties.

Families as Systems

No matter what its form, every family is a **system**—a group of people who interact with one another to form a whole greater than the sum of its parts. Your own experience will show you the systemic nature of families. Members probably seem quite different when you consider them alone or as they relate to people outside the family. But when the family interacts, there is a sense of identity—of connectedness—that is different from anything else. Several characteristics make every family a system.

INTERDEPENDENCE   For better or worse, the members of a family are connected together so that each person is affected by the behavior of the others. If one person is happy, the other members will probably benefit too. Likewise, if another is having problems, everyone else in the family system will probably suffer in some way. To test the interdependent nature of families out for yourself, consider the effects on each member of your family when one member

> is especially energetic and healthy (or ill)
>
> falls in (or out of) love
>
> suffers a job advance (or setback)
>
> does well (poorly) in school

Describe how your family of origin was a system. Discuss how it exhibited the following properties:

a. interdependence
b. wholeness
c. patterns
d. self-regulation

Communication, of course, is the web that connects families together. It can be the tool that improves the quality of interaction, and it can also be the means for causing problems. But for better or worse, family members can't easily be separated. Even if you physically remove yourself from other family members, memories and habits developed over the years connect you to them.

WHOLENESS   The principle of wholeness means that it is impossible to understand a family by looking at just a few of its members. To understand how and why a family functions, you have to look at it as a single unit. In this sense, a family is like an athletic team. The team doesn't win or lose only because of the talents of its members. How those members interact will also determine its quality of play. If the people work together smoothly, the team may succeed, even though none of the individuals may be outstanding athletes. On the other hand, if the members don't get along, then they may do poorly, even though several of the members are superstars.

The principle of wholeness explains why most family therapists will insist on examining the entire family system before treating the "identified patient"—the member who has the most obvious problem. This approach often reveals that a child's wild behavior or one parent's dissatisfactions arise from the way that person is affected by other members.

PATTERNS AND SELF-REGULATION   Just like a climate or an eco-system, family systems have rather predictable patterns of behavior. The pattern may vary from one family to another. In some families the pattern is one of outward serenity and calm, while in others there is almost constant turbulence. Still other families follow an intermittent pattern of calm punctuated by upheavals. Patterns can involve a variety of areas: how open or nondisclosing members may be, how they will handle conflicts, who will make decisions, and who will act maturely or immaturely.

Whatever patterns a family develops, there is a tendency to maintain **homeostasis**—a kind of equilibrium that keeps the family following its standards of behavior. The metaphor that best describes the drive for homeostasis is a thermostat. Whenever things deviate too much from the norm, one or more members will act in ways that get the family back on track. If things get too serious in a family where the pattern is taking matters lightly, someone is likely to make a joke. If the norm is to handle issues emotionally, someone is likely to have an outburst after a period of calm. As this last example suggests, homeostasis isn't always peaceful. In some families, hostility, and even cruelty is the normal state of affairs. In this sort of environment, members may find themselves repeating destructive patterns without knowing why, even though these ways of behaving cause pain.

OPENNESS   Families are **open system** that are influenced by the environment in which they operate. Despite the drive for homeostasis, outside influences can change the way a system operates. Economic forces are a powerful influence that have changed many family systems from traditional ones in which there was a single breadwinner (usually the father) and a single homemaker (usually the mother) into ones where both partners take work outside the home. The changes that follow from two incomes go far beyond the jobs themselves. Consider, for example, the issue of control. If a former homemaker—unsalaried, of course—now contributes to the family's financial well-being, then she may want to play a greater role in deciding how the money is spent. Likewise, if the other partner is playing a greater role in caring for children, then he might insist on a greater hand in deciding on their activities, education, friends, and so on. This sort of change in roles and rights can lead to an altered system.

As you read these words, think of the forces outside your family that have led to changes in your family system. In addition to economic factors, consider changes in the people with whom the family communicates, and the social standards of the community, where the family lives.

Functions of Family Communication

Communication within families takes many forms and deals with many subjects: everything from negotiating who will wash the dishes or do the shopping to judging the quality of whom a child (or a parent) may be dating to sharing memories of past birthdays or vacations. Sometimes the communication is pleasant and sometimes it is tedious or painful. Sometimes messages take written form ("At the library. Back before dinner."). Sometimes members communicate over the phone, and sometimes face to face. No matter what the content or context, family communication serves several functions.

> Describe how communication in your family of origin or your current family has served the following functions:
>
> **a.** shaping your identity
> **b.** providing social support
> **c.** affecting your everyday functioning

CONVENIENCE   A great deal of family communication deals with the pragmatics of everyday life. Who will drive to and from the soccer game? What does everyone need from the market? Can anyone help solve an algebra problem for tonight's homework assignment?

Communicating efficiently can make family members' lives much easier and happier. In many cases members can help one another, thanks to their complementary skills. One person may have a gift for style, and can be a fashion consultant. Another can be an academic problem solver or career consultant. One may be a terrific chef or offer advice for the lovelorn. On an even more practical level, families can be a convenient source of everything from chauffeur service to baby sitting.

This sort of mutual support will only work if the family members have good enough communication skills to manage the logistics of everyday life. If members are too busy to help one another or don't care enough to do so, then life together is likely to become more difficult instead of easier.

IDENTITY   As you read in Chapter 2, the self-concept shapes the way each of us views ourselves and others. Because we spend so much of our time in the family, especially during our first years of life, the interactions there shape the self more than any other factor (see Table 7–1). These influences can be either positive or negative. In healthy families, children grow up taking for granted that they are lovable, capable people. By contrast, in troubled families youngsters often view themselves as incompetent, unlovable, and even a cause of the family's problems. As a child grows older, the number of significant others from outside the family increases. Friends, teachers, coaches, and others begin to play a greater role in shaping the youngster's sense of self. By adolescence, the importance of reference groups outside the home is strong.

TABLE 7–1   Some Elements of the Self-Concept Shaped by Communication within the Family

aesthetic taste	helpfulness	physical attractiveness
artistic talent	intelligence	problem-solving ability
athletic ability	leadership ability	sense of humor
compassion	likability	social savvy
courage	personal worth	verbal ability

Despite this fact, parents still have a strong influence upon their children's self-concept, especially in certain areas. Messages about ability ("You'll never get into college with grades like these"), friends ("Alicia and Matt seem like good kids") and most of all about the teen's place in the family ("Why are you so moody these days?") still make an impression.

The ability of children to influence their parents' sense of self can be just as strong as the other way around. For most mothers and fathers, the role of "parent" is central to a sense of self. And more than anyone else's, children's messages suggest an answer to the question "Am I a good parent?" In other large and small ways, children influence their parents' self-concepts. Are they grateful or unappreciative? Do they see parents as "cool" or backward, enjoyable or a "drag"? When they leave home for a life on their own, do children make an effort to keep in touch? Messages like these can shape the self-esteem and satisfaction of mothers and fathers more than children may ever know.

Parent-child messages aren't the only form of communication that shapes the self-concept of family members. The way couples interact influences their feelings of competence and self-worth. Communication between siblings determines self-esteem. Messages exchanged with relatives and other family members create a sense of belonging or isolation. In summary, the way we view ourselves comes in great measure from the way we communicate in the family.

SOCIAL SUPPORT   Family systems aren't guaranteed to be supportive. In fact, you could use the information up to this point in the chapter to describe how a family could act in an extremely nonsupportive manner. There certainly

Lazlo Daffodil Blintz

Kilgore Trout is writing a story now about a time when our Government understands that it isn't taking care of the people because it's too clumsy and slow. It wants to help people, but it can't get anywhere in time. So the President happens to visit Nigeria, where extended families have been the style since the beginning of time. He is impressed, and properly so. Huge families take care of their own sick and old, of any relative in trouble. They do it right away and at no cost to the government. So the President of the United States comes home and he announces that the trouble with the country is that nobody has enough relatives within shooting distance. Nobody can just yell for help. Everybody has to fill out forms. So the President is going to have the computers of the Social Security Administration assign everybody thousands of relatives.

You have to throw out whatever middle name you have and substitute whatever name the computers give you—names of Greek gods, colors, chemical elements, flowers, animals. The story begins with a political refugee coming to America, and he not only has to swear allegiance to the country and all that, he also has to accept a new middle name from the computers. They give him the middle name Daffodil. His name becomes Laszlo Daffodil Blintz. He has 20,000 relatives all over the country with the same Government Issue middle name. He gets a Daffodil family directory, a subscription to the Daffodil family's monthly magazine. There would be lots of ads in there for jobs, things to buy, things to sell.

And there would be ads and articles in the family monthly about crooks or deadbeats in the family. The joy of it would be that nobody would feel alone and anybody who needed seven dollars until next Tuesday or a baby sitter for an hour or a trip to the hospital could get it. Whenever I'm alone in a motel in a big city, I look up Vonneguts and Liebers in the telephone book, and there never are any. Lieber was my mother's maiden name. But if I were a Daffodil or a Chipmunk or a Chromium, there would be plenty of numbers to call.

Kurt Vonnegut

---

are unhappy, hostile families that are quite interdependent and that have a strong sense of identity with destructive patterns of behavior. But at their best, family systems offer support and intimacy to their members. Families can be a kind of safe harbor, where members can count on receiving nourishment and rest that isn't available anywhere else.

Families offer support in a variety of ways.[6] Attachment is certainly one: Friends may come and go, but we will always belong to families. At their best, family relationships provide a feeling of belonging that can't be shaken by life's setbacks. The family may not always approve of what we do, but for better or worse, we know we belong. On a more fundamental level, families often provide support in the face of physical illness, and often they provide assistance in meeting our material needs. Another way families provide support is by providing a sense of intimacy. There are three kinds of intimacy: physical, emotional, and intellectual. Few relationships are intimate in every respect,

Communication with Family and Friends

which explains why family members can be "close" in so many different ways. For some, intimacy may come from hugs, kisses, and even playful wrestling. For others, it can come from sharing ideas and feelings. Whatever form it takes, the chance to be intimate without risk is one way that communication in families provides a form of social support that is rare in other relationships.

> What rules govern communication within your current family or family of origin? Describe rules in the following areas:
>
> **a.** everyday activities
> **b.** standards of intimacy
> **c.** control and power
> **d.** specialized roles of members

Rules of Family Communication

Like other relationships, families develop rules to govern their communication. Some rules are explicit:

◆ If you don't do the chores, you don't get your allowance.

◆ If you're going to be more than a half hour late, phone home so the others don't worry about you.

◆ Be sure and write down phone messages for other family members.

◆ If the gas gauge reads "empty," fill up the tank before bringing the car home.

◆ Don't make plans for Sunday nights. That's time for the family to spend together.

◆ Daniel gets to watch "Sesame Street" from 5:00 to 6:00 P.M.

Most rules, however, are unstated—though they are usually understood quite well:

◆ Don't talk back to Dad unless he's in a very silly mood.

◆ When Mother is hassled, don't discuss school problems.

◆ Tell the truth at all times unless it involves a happy surprise.

◆ Do not fight except with Mom about your appearance.

◆ Don't talk about the family's money with anyone except a parent.

◆ Do not discuss sex, but act as if it were an acceptable topic for discussion.

◆ Don't mention Sally's boyfriend except in a very noncommittal way.

◆ Kiss Mom when coming and going. Kiss Dad at night. Don't kiss sisters.

◆ Grandpa's cancer is not discussed.

◆ Mother's pregnancy at marriage is not admitted.[7]

As these examples suggest, rules fall into a number of categories. Some govern activities: who is responsible for chores, what activities are acceptable at what times, and so on. Others describe standards of intimacy and autonomy: how to express affection, what topics are and are not acceptable to discuss, how much time people should spend together, and so on. Some govern control: how decisions are made in areas like finances, leisure time, and so on.

Family communication rules serve several functions. First, they create bonds that create a sense of family identity. Even apparently destructive rules serve this purpose, as this reminiscence shows:

> I don't know whether to laugh or cry when I think about our family holidays. Thanksgiving, Christmas, Fourth of July, they're all the same. Everyone starts out sincerely glad to see one another. But after a few hours the same pattern begins. My grandmother starts criticizing each of us: my dad and mom for not visiting her more, my cousins for looking so "unhealthy," my brother for not having a good job, and me for not having a husband yet! My dad rolls his eyes, and my mom starts defending everybody. My grandfather makes lame jokes to change the subject, and all the kids start thinking about how we can get away as soon as possible. But in spite of this crazy scene, it's hard to imagine spending the holidays any other way.

One of the reasons why even apparently unpleasant family rules and customs have merit is because they make life predictable. Communication theorists have identified the need to reduce uncertainty as a major function of relationships, and family rules serve this purpose extremely well.[8] The world is a confusing place, and families provide a kind of stability that makes life predictable, if exasperating.

Along with unique patterns, family communication is governed by cultural rules.[9] Issues as basic as the definition of *family* are often rooted in culture and ethnicity. For example, the dominant white Anglo-Saxon Protestant (WASP) definition focuses on the intact nuclear family, while blacks expand their definition to include a network of kin and community. Italians and Latin Americans traditionally think in terms of tightly knit three- or four-generation families, often including godparents and old friends. Traditional Chinese include all ancestors and descendants in their definition.[10] In the same way, the social expectations of family members vary from one culture to another. Cultural patterns do play a role in communication rules. As a group, WASPs may be concerned about expressing emotionality, Italians worry about family disloyalty, and Puerto Ricans are especially concerned about not receiving respect from their children.[11] Of course, there are exceptions to these generalizations and stereotyping can be dangerous, but the fact remains that culture influences the way families communicate.

Patterns of Family Communication

Like all groups, families have distinctive patterns of communication. These patterns can be viewed from several perspectives.[12]

TO WHOM DO YOU SPEAK?   If families always stayed together in a group and shared every piece of information with one another, their communication would flow through what communication researchers have called an **all-channel network** (see Figure 7–1). But this pattern isn't the only communica-

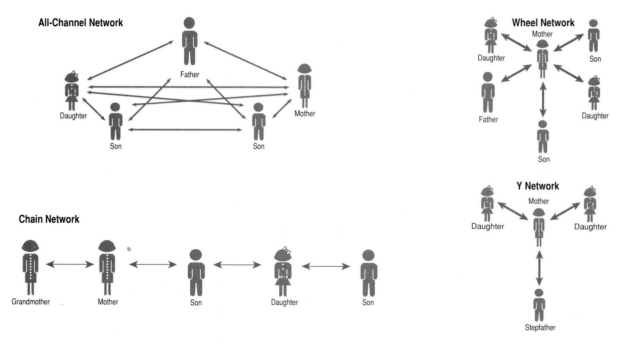

Father

Daughter

Son

Son

Mother

Wheel Network

Mother

Daughter

Son

Father

Daughter

Son

Chain Network

Grandmother

Mother

Son

Daughter

Son

Y Network

Mother

Daughter

Daughter

Stepfather

Figure 7–1
Family Communication
Networks

tion pattern, or even the most common one. Some messages follow a **chain network,** moving sequentially from one member to another. Chains are sometimes a matter of necessity, especially in busy families where members rarely are all together at the same time. Another communication pattern is the **wheel network,** in which one person channels messages to all the other members. Like chains, wheel networks are sometimes a practical choice, especially if one member is available to communicate with others all or most of the time. In traditional families, for example, the mother may spend most of her time around the home and is the only person who can dependably have face-to-face communication with her husband, the children, and other relatives. Sometimes families use wheel networks to communicate about difficult topics. In situations like this, the central member can serve as a mediator or facilitator who manages messages as they flow between others.

Describe the types of communication networks used in a family you have experienced. Is one type of network used in all situations, or does the network structure vary according to the type of information being communicated?

A fourth pattern of communication is the **Y network,** in which messages are channeled through one person to one or more other members. A Y network often operates when one member filters, interprets, or otherwise manages the messages from another in order to keep the family running smoothly. Y networks are especially common in blended families, where the biological parent often delivers messages to his or her children after talking matters over with the other partner.

The success of wheel and Y networks depends heavily on the skill of the **gatekeeper**—the person through whom information flows. If he or she is a skilled communicator, these mediated messages may help the family function effectively. But if the gatekeeper consciously or unconsciously distorts messages to suit personal goals or play members off against one another, then the family is likely to suffer.

The all-channel, chain, wheel, and Y networks, aren't the only possible patterns. In some cases, one or more members may be left out of a network completely. For example, a husband and wife might not discuss financial problems with their younger children, or all the females in a family might discuss common interests in an all-channel manner that excludes the males. Patterns also can vary from one topic to another. The Y network might be appropriate when a parent discusses sexual issues with children of the same gender, while an all-channel forum may be the best way to handle issues that affect everyone.

WHAT CAN YOU TALK ABOUT? The nature of communication can vary from one family to another. As we have already seen, rules in most families govern what topics are acceptable and which ones are taboo. Common out-of-bounds topics may include finances, sexual practices, and the personal problems of some members. Even certain words that are not used in one family may be used commonly in another.

Another way to analyze the content of family messages is in terms of their functional, practical nature, which social scientists have described as **instrumental communication** versus their emotional, feeling content, which has been labeled **expressive communication.** In some families almost all communication is instrumental, while in others a far larger percentage of expressive messages are exchanged. Even the degree of emotional expressiveness is also usually governed by unspoken, unwritten rules. In what ways is it acceptable to convey anger? Affection? Sadness? In many families expressive rules vary according to different combinations of family members. Siblings might express anger loudly and openly, while parents handle their issues more calmly in private. A father might lavish expressions of love on his daughter, both verbally and through hugs and kisses, but feel awkward expressing the same feelings toward his son. These sorts of patterns usually evolve without deliberate planning, and families need to consider whether they lead to satisfaction or whether they need changing.

WHEN AND WHERE CAN YOU SPEAK? The patterns governing how much members can speak to one another vary radically from one family to another. In one household privacy may be valued highly. Each member might have his or her own territory, and others are only allowed to interrupt after receiving permission. Members of other families are more accessible to one another, and communication is more frequent. More specific rules can also apply: Sunday evenings are for family dinner, so don't make personal plans. Don't bother people when they're doing their homework. It's okay to ask Mom for help any time, but don't bother Dad unless he's obviously not busy. Nobody should interrupt the speaker around the dinner table.

Communication with Family and Friends

Some Characteristics of Effective Family Communication

By now it should be clear that there is no single model of the effective family. Despite the wide range of family circumstances and diverse ways of communicating, there are some elements that characterize effective communication in all types of family systems.[13]

ROLE FLEXIBILITY One characteristic that distinguishes healthy, satisfied families from poorly functioning ones is the ability to handle roles flexibly, and to renegotiate them as the need arises.[14] Rules need to change as families develop over time. The kinds of parental control that are appropriate for young children don't work as well during adolescence. Likewise, as teens become adults, they need to act differently and be treated differently by other family members. Failure to make these changes can lead to problems:

> My brother Paul just turned 26, but my parents still treat him like he's ten years younger. He quit college three years ago but they still "help him out," which as near as I can figure means they pay for his rent, car, medical insurance, and most of his food and clothes. I know they wish he'd take care of himself, and I think Paul feels bad about being so dependent too. But they don't face the problem. They keep talking about how things will change as soon as Paul gets a good job, which never happens.

Age isn't the only factor that can lead to role changes. The start or ending of a new job can require a shift in family behavior. A new set of interests or friendships can also require changes. Whatever the shift, effective families monitor their communication to make sure it suits their present circumstances.

SHARED POWER Successful families aren't necessarily democracies in which each person has an equal vote, but there is recognition that each member can and should have influence over the family's welfare. Since families are interdependent systems in which every member influences all the others, recognition that power is shared is really an acknowledgement of reality. An unhappy infant, a resentful teenager, or a morose grandparent all can drag down the spirits of other members, so effective families find ways of letting each member freely exert at least some control on the system. There are countless ways to assert control. By choosing the radio station or volume, deciding whether or not to join the family on an outing, changing the topic of conversation around the dinner table, or picking a dating partner, members have a sense of controlling their own destiny.

Evaluate the degree to which your family follows the characteristics for effective communication described in this section. Provide specific examples to support your evaluations.

a. How flexible are members about their roles?
b. Are members willing to share power?
c. Do members view one another in a favorable light?
d. Do members communicate positive regard for one another?

Consensus is not the only way to share power. Paradoxically, satisfaction can even come when families agree to disagree by handling conflicts in ways that seem counterproductive: arguing, withdrawing, and so on. The key to success seems to be a shared definition of how the relationship should be handled.[15] Thus, one satisfied family may communicate in ways that would shock others. The key to satisfaction seems to be finding a way to manage power and conflict that meets the needs of all members.

POSITIVE REGARD FOR OTHER FAMILY MEMBERS Family members who view one another favorably are more satisfied than those who see other members in a critical light. This fact isn't especially surprising. It is interesting, however, to learn that satisfied members often *distort* their perceptions of one another in order to arrive at charitable interpretations.[16] If one person acts grumpy or hostile, other members of a satisfied family might choose the most favorable interpretation to explain the behavior by saying "he's probably had a tough time at work" or "she's just having an off day" instead of reacting critically. Likewise, the unpleasant behavior of an infant—or even an adolescent—could be chalked up to a developmental stage instead of being viewed as the sign of a difficult person.

CONFIRMING COMMUNICATION Viewing others positively is important, but communicating that level of appreciation is a separate ingredient in successful families. Research shows that satisfied families send confirming, reinforcing messages more often than do unsatisfied ones.[17] Recall from Chapter 6 that agreeing with others is one type of confirming communication, but it isn't the only way to show that you value them. Simply acknowledging their concerns is another measure of regard, which explains why listening can be a powerful way to be supportive.

It is easy to see the value of positive regard. If one member responds positively to others, they in turn are more likely to view that person positively. Communication then becomes reciprocally reinforcing, leading to an upward spiral in satisfaction with the relationship.[18]

◆ COMMUNICATION IN FRIENDSHIPS

Friendship has been called "the most holy bond of society." Life without friends would be empty, and so friendship is worthy of a close look in a book about human communication.

What Makes a Friend?

Unlike other relationships, the key element in forming friendships is choice. While we are born into families and hired into most jobs, we choose our friends. What leads us to want some people as friends and have little interest in others, and what makes others want to be friends with us? Social scientists

TABLE 7—2 Ingredients of Friendship

What qualities do we value in a friend? The percentages in this table represent the number of people who said that the particular quality was "important" or "very important." Notice the important role communication plays in friendships.

Keeps confidences	89%	Similar education	17%
Loyalty	88%	About my age	10%
Warmth, affection	82%	Physical attractiveness	9%
Supportiveness	76%	Job accomplishments	8%
Frankness	75%	Similar income	4%
Sense of humor	74%	Similar occupation	3%

Mary Brown, "Ingredients of Friendship," *Psychology Today* (October 1979).

have collected an impressive body of research on interpersonal attraction, and it suggests several factors that affect the formation and growth of friendships.[19] (See Table 7—2.)

RECIPROCITY   The single most important determinant of whether we like others is whether they like us.[20] Numerous studies reinforce this fact. In one, researchers gathered groups of college students who were complete strangers.[21] Before the groups met for the first time, the experimenters gave each student a list of names of others whom they said would like him or her very much, based on psychological tests. In truth, the lists were generated at random. When the groups were first assembled, the students did indeed express a desire to spend time with the people whom they thought liked them. These partners were then paired off for a series of meetings and data about liking was collected after the third and sixth sessions. As the partners got to know one another, the bogus nature of the experiment became clear. Students learned through interaction whether or not their partner really did like them, and as they gained this knowledge their liking for one another was based on more accurate information about the degree of reciprocal liking.

Make a list of your close friends. Describe the degree to which each of the following factors affect the strength of each friendship:

a. reciprocity   **c.** availability
b. similarity   **d.** disclosure

If these factors have changed over time for a particular relationship, has the strength of the friendship changed as well?

It's no mystery why reciprocal liking reinforces friendships. People who approve of us bolster our feelings of self-esteem. This approval is rewarding in its own right, and it can also confirm a self-concept that says, "I'm a likable person." The degree to which we like ourselves influences whom we seek out as friends. "Needy" people—those with low self-esteem—welcome friendships with just about anyone who seems to like them. In fact, insecure people will often seek out less attractive people in order to minimize the chances of being rejected. By contrast, communicators with greater self-esteem are more selective about whom they approach.[22]

Liking others is an important condition for friendship, but others have to *know* that we care about them to give the relationship appeal. One way to demonstrate this concern is by the amount of time we choose to spend with them, which suggests one reason why friendships can weaken when people become too busy to spend time with one another. In addition to the *quantity* of time spent together, its *quality* is another dimension of caring. The kinds of acknowledgement and agreement described in Chapter 6 are tangible signs that we matter to others, and knowing that we are important leads to feelings of friendship.

SIMILARITY Another important ingredient in friendship is similarity. There are two ways in which we can be similar to others: in our attitudes and in our activities. Intuition suggests that similar attitudes would form a stronger bond than activities. It sounds comforting to know that a friend likes the things you like, shares the same values, and may even be of the same race, economic class, or educational standing. For married couples, this sort of similarity is important.[23] For friends, however, it is more rewarding to be liked by someone whose attitudes are different than ours.[24] In other words, if others like you *in spite* of your different opinions, you are likely to believe that they appreciate you for yourself, not for your attitudes.

"What'll it be, handsome?"

Communication with Family and Friends

If shared attitudes aren't a key factor in forming friendships, what is? Research shows that shared activities are a more common basis of the relationship. The importance of shared activities was revealed by a study that showed friendships can be identified more accurately by what people *do* than by what they think or feel.[25] In fact, the attitudes of friends were no closer than those of complete strangers. Doing things together seemed to be the glue that bound the relationship. Members of a softball team or computer hackers' group might consider themselves good friends, even though they have completely different views about politics, religion, and almost everything else. Of course, shared activities by themselves are no guarantee of friendships. We grow closer to some fellow workers or teammates than to others. But we can say that shared activities are an important ingredient of friendship.

AVAILABILITY   Extensive research confirms the fact that we are more likely to create and maintain bonds with people we see frequently.[26] Students tend to develop stronger friendships with other students who live nearby or with whom they share classes. Even small distances make a difference. Students are more likely to strike up friendships with people who sit adjacent to them than those who sit a few chairs distant. The same principle holds for people in a wide range of positions ranging from airplane crews to department store clerks: There is a tendency to form friendships with people who are immediately at hand more than with those who work a few feet away. This doesn't mean long distance friendships are impossible. Telephone calls, letters, and occasional visits can keep friends in touch and nourish the relationship enough to give it life. But all other things being equal, friendships are stronger when they don't have to battle distance.

Proximity alone isn't a guarantee of friendship. In fact, familiarity can sometimes breed contempt. Evidence to support this fact comes from police blotters as well as university laboratories. Thieves often prey on nearby victims, even though there is a risk of being recognized by their victims. Most aggravated assaults occur within the family or between close neighbors. Within the law, the same principle holds: You are likely to develop strong personal feelings of either like or dislike toward others you encounter frequently.

DISCLOSURE   A commonsense model of friendship includes a high degree of self-disclosure. Ralph Waldo Emerson captured this view when he said "A friend is a person with whom I may be sincere. Before him I may think aloud." Research supports the notion that there is a relationship between self-disclosure and closeness among friends. In one study, deeper friendships were characterized by an exchange of more personal information, while more superficial relationships were related to physical proximity.[27]

Sharing important information can help build friendships in several ways. Sometimes the basis of this attraction comes from learning ways that you and the other person are similar, either in experiences ("I broke off an engagement myself") or in attitudes ("I feel nervous with strangers too"). Self-disclosure also increases liking because it indicates regard. Sharing private information is also a form of respect and trust, revealing that we are important enough to hear some of a friend's most private thoughts.

Not all disclosure supports friendships. One key to satisfaction is reciprocity: getting back an amount and kind of information equivalent to that which you have revealed.[28] Another important ingredient in successful self-disclosure is timing. It's probably unwise to talk about your problems when a friend is having troubles of her own or to bring up your pet peeves at her birthday party. The information you reveal ought to be appropriate for the setting and stage of the relationship. Chapter 6 lists guidelines for effective self-disclosure that are important in all relationships, including friendships.

Even in communication between friends, total honesty isn't the norm when difficult subjects arise. Research shows that roughly a third of the messages communicators share are "white lies" that hide the truth in order to save one of the parties' embarrassment.[29] Even when they don't lie, friends often use equivocal language to avoid sharing a hurtful truth. For example, suppose a friend asks what you think about his or her new hairstyle. You might think it looks terrible; but at the same time you know that there's no way the haircut can be undone. So, to spare your friend, you say something equivocal, such as "It's right in fashion" or "It's really unusual!" This sort of ambiguous response is a common and useful strategy "when it would be unkind to be honest, but dishonest to be kind."[30] To summarize: Honesty is certainly important in a relationship, but this does not mean that you have to reveal everything to the other person. A more realistic guideline is to be honest about matters relevant to your friendship while maintaining a concern for the other person's self-esteem and right to privacy.

Gender and Friendship

Social scientists have discovered that friendship has different properties for men and women. Think about it yourself: Do you have the same number of male and female friends? Do you appreciate them in the same way? Do you talk about the same subjects with men and women? If you are like most people, the answer to these questions will most often be "no."

Even in early childhood, differences between same-sex friendships are different for boys and girls.[31] Boys are more likely to form play groups that are competitive in nature, while girls' play is more often cooperative. Thus, patterns for traditional sex roles are set. In friendship surveys focusing on preteen play, men recall being highly responsive to the sex-role opinions of other boys, while girls are less susceptible to pressures of conforming to stereotyped sex roles. The worst label for most boys is "sissy," while being called a "tomboy" is less common and less hurtful in an era of coeducational soccer and unisex clothing.

As adults, same-sex friendships of men and women differ. Men report having more of these relationships, while women describe their same-sex friendships as being more intimate. Women are more than three times as likely to have an intimate confidante.[32] In general, the topics men and women discuss in same-sex friendships differ. As some writers have put it, women are

Communication with Family and Friends

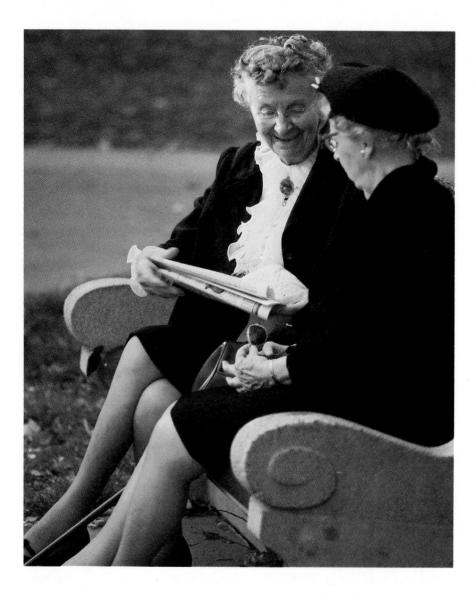

more likely to talk about who they are, while men traditionally talk about what they do.[33] Women's conversations focus more on relational, personal, and family matters and involve a greater sharing of emotions, while men are more likely to talk about less personal topics such as current events, sports, money, and music.[34]

When problems arise, the response in same-sex friendships also varies by gender. Women friends are more likely to listen noncritically and offer mutual support. If a man finds that his friend is unhappy, a more common response is to change the subject. This is not necessarily a sign of being unconcerned. Rather, it reflects both a form of respect for the other's privacy and a strategy of diverting the attention of the troubled friend.[35]

So far, we have been talking about same-sex friendships. But what about mixed-sex friendships? Surveys reveal that the number of friendships between men and women is less common than those between members of the same sex. In one study, respondents reported having only about 60 percent as many close friends of the opposite sex as compared with same-sex friendships.[36] Neither men nor women find mixed-sex friendships as comfortable or easy to establish as relationships with members of the same sex. Roughly 40 percent did not even express a desire to have friends of the opposite sex.[37] One problem with these relationships is the issue of sex. A majority of respondents confess that sexual dynamics intrude into the friendship, often creating problems for one or both people: "Too tempting," they say. "Looking for trouble," "bound to evolve into something sexual," "won't work" are similar reactions. The potential for sexual complications is especially great when at least one of the friends is married.

> Describe the similarities and/or differences between communication in your same-sex and opposite-sex friendships. To what degree does gender play a role in the number, strength, and quality of these relationships?

Given these pressures, it's not surprising that roughly 70 percent of the people surveyed report that the nature of opposite friendships is different than same-sex friendships. The most frequent differences cited were the ability to communicate openly about personal topics with same-sex friends, different interests and activities, and the issue of sex which we have already discussed.[38]

Despite the pressures working against mixed-sex friendships, the figures show that these relationships *are* possible. Because they are less common, male-female friendships are especially precious. Rather than writing them off as hopeless, a smarter approach is to treasure them when they do occur. Most people who do have close friends of the opposite sex are conscious of not allowing sexual or romantic interest to jeopardize the relationship, and they proceed slowly or back away from it if it happens.

◆ SUMMARY

The social support offered by family and friends not only makes life more pleasant, but it also has a significant effect on physical health. Families in the late twentieth century take many forms: two-parent biological, single-parent, blended, extended, and communal. No matter its form, every family is a system, characterized by interdependence, wholeness, patterns and self-regulation, and openness to the environment. Through communication, families serve several functions. Some are practical, while others shape the identity of members and provide social support.

Communication with Family and Friends

Every family's behavior is governed by a set of rules; some are explicit, but most are unstated. These rules can either improve or harm the quality of the members' relationships. Communication among family members usually follows discernible patterns, which govern who speaks with whom, what subjects are discussed, and when and where communication takes place. Although there is no single set of rules that will result in good family relationships, several characteristics do describe most effective families: role flexibility, shared power, positive regard for family members, and confirming communication.

Friendships can provide many of the same kinds of support as families, but their voluntary nature means that they are shaped by different factors. Reciprocity is the most important ingredient in friendship formation. Shared activities also play an important role. Proximity is often necessary to keep friendships strong, although they can be maintained over time and distance with effort. Disclosure of personal information characterizes many friendships, although few friends are completely open and honest with one another.

Same-sex friendships differ in some significant ways for men and women. Male friendships more commonly revolve around shared activities, while female relationships have a higher degree of expressiveness and intimacy. Though possible, mixed-sex friendships are less common, partly due to the complicating factor of sexual attraction.

◆ **NOTES**

1. California Department of Mental Health, *Friends Can Be Good Medicine* (Sacramento: California State Department of Mental Health, 1981).
2. K. M. Galvin and B. J. Brommel, *Family Communication: Cohesion and Change,* 2d ed. (Glenview, Ill.: Scott, Foresman, 1986), pp. 3–4.
3. Reported in J. C. Pearson, *Communication in the Family: Seeking Satisfaction in Changing Times* (New York: Harper & Row, 1989), p. 111.
4. T. K. Hareven, "American Families in Transition: Historical Perspectives on Change" in F. Walsh (ed.), *Normal Family Process* (New York: Guilford Press, 1982), p. 448.
5. C. H. Kramer, *Becoming a Family Therapist* (New York: Human Sciences Press, 1980), p. 43.
6. For a research summary of familial social support, see L. L. Eggert, "Support in Family Ties: Stress, Coping, and Adaptation," in T. L. Albrecht and M. B. Adelman (eds.), *Communicating Social Support* (Newbury Park, Calif.: Sage, 1987), pp. 80–104.
7. Galvin and Brommel, p. 56.
8. See C. J. Berger and J. J. Bradac, *Language and Social Knowledge: Uncertainty in Interpersonal Relations* (London: Edward Arnold, 1982).
9. See, for example, M. McGoldrick, "Normal Families: An Ethnic Perspective" in F. Walsh (ed.) *Normal Family Process* (New York: Guilford Press, 1982), pp. 399–424 and M. McGoldrick, J. K. Pearce, and J. Giordano, *Ethnicity and Family Therapy* (New York: Guilford Press, 1982).
10. I. Goldenberg and H. Goldenberg, *Family Therapy: An Overview* (Monterey, Calif.: Brooks-Cole, 1985), p. 25.
11. M. McGoldrick, "Ethnicity and Family Therapy: An Overview" in M. McGoldrick, J. K. Pearce, and J. Giordano (eds.), *Ethnicity and Family Therapy* (New York: Guilford Press, 1982).
12. J. Pearson, *Family Communication: Seeking Satisfaction in Changing Times* (New York: Harper & Row, 1989), pp. 50–71.
13. For a detailed discussion of communication patterns contributing to family satisfaction, see Pearson 1989, chapters 10–13 and W. R. Beavers, "Healthy, Midrange, and Severely Dysfunctional Families" in F. Walsh (ed.), *Normal Family Process* (New York: Guilford Press, 1982), pp. 45–66.
14. See, for example, S. Ting-Toomey, "An Analysis of Verbal Communication Patterns in High and Low Marital Adjustment Groups," *Human Communication*

Research 9 (1983): 306–319, and J. M. Gottman, *Marital Interaction: Experimental Investigations* (New York: Academic Press, 1979).

15. M. A. Fitzpatrick and P. G. Best, "Dyadic Adjustment in Traditional, Independent, and Separate Relationships: A Validation Study," *Communication Monographs* 46 (1979): 167–178 and J. M. Gottman, *Marital Interaction: Experimental Investigations* (New York: Academic Press, 1979), pp. 9–10.

16. S. R. H. Beach and I. Arias, "Assessment of Perceptual Discrepancy: Utility of the Primary Communication Inventory," *Family Process* 22 (1983): 309–316.

17. J. P. Vincent, L. Friedman, J. Nugent, and L. Messerley, "Demand Characteristics in the Observation of Marital Interaction," *Journal of Consulting and Clinical Psychology* 47 (1979): 557–567.

18. W. Wilmot, *Dyadic Communication,* 3d ed. (New York: Random House, 1987): pp. 148–150.

19. For summaries of research on interpersonal attraction, see M. S. Poole, J. P. Folger, and D. E. Hewes, "Analyzing Interpersonal Attraction," in M. E. Roloff and G. R. Miller (eds.), *Interpersonal Process: New Directions in Communication Research* (Newbury Park, Calif.: Sage, 1987), D. E. Hamachek, *Encounters with Others: Interpersonal Relationships and You* (New York: Holt, Rinehart and Winston, 1982), and E. Berscheid-Walster, *Interpersonal Attraction,* 2d ed. (Reading, Mass.: Addison-Wesley, 1979), pp. 29–33, and M. James and L. M. Savary, *The Heart of Friendship* (New York: Harper & Row, 1976).

20. E. Aronson, *The Social Animal,* 4th ed. (New York: W. H. Freeman, 1984), p. 302.

21. C. W. Backman and P. F. Secord, "The Effect of Perceived Liking on Interpersonal Attraction," *Human Relations* 12 (1959): 379–384.

22. Aronson, 303–304.

23. D. M. Buss, "Human Mate Selection," *American Scientist* 73 (January–February 1985): 47–51.

24. E. E. Jones, L. Bell, and A. Aronson, "The Reciprocation of Attraction from Similar and Dissimilar Others: A Study in Person Perception and Evaluation," in *Experimental Social Psychology* (New York: Holt, Rinehart and Winston, 1971), pp. 142–183.

25. C. Werner and P. Parmelee, "Similarity of Activity, Preferences Among Friends: Those Who Play Together Stay Together," *Social Psychology Quarterly* 42 (1979): 62–66.

26. Berscheid-Walster, pp. 29–33.

27. Z. Rubin and S. Shenker, "Friendship, Proximity, and Self-Disclosure," *Journal of Personality* 46 (1978): 1–22.

28. V. J. Derlega, M. Wilson, and A. L. Chaikin, "Friendship and Disclosure Reciprocity," *Journal of Personality and Social Psychology* 34 (1976): 578–582.

29. R. E. Turner, C. Edgely, and G. Olmstead, "Information Control in Conversation: Honesty Is Not Always the Best Policy," *Kansas Journal of Sociology* 11 (1975): 69–89.

30. J. Bavelas, "Situations That Lead to Disqualification," *Human Communication Research* 9 (1983): 130–145.

31. J. D. Block, *Friendship* (New York: Macmillan, 1980), p. 79.

32. E. J. Aries and F. L. Johnson, "Close Friendship in Adulthood: Conversational Content Between Same-Sex Friends," *Sex Roles* 9 (1983): 1183–1196.

33. L. P. Steward, P. J. Cooper, and S. A. Friedley, *Communication Between the Sexes: Sex Differences and Sex-Role Stereotypes* (Scottsdale, Ariz.: Gorsuch Scarisbrick, 1986), p. 100.

34. A. Haas and M. A. Sherman, "Reported Topics of Conversation Among Same-Sex Adults," *Communication Quarterly* 30 (1982): 332–342. See also M. A. Sherman and A. Haas, "Man to Man, Woman to Woman," *Psychology Today* (June 1984): 72–73.

35. W. S. Howell, *The Empathic Communicator* (Belmont, Calif.: Wadsworth, 1982).

36. W. N. Shellen and C. M. Cole, "Friendly Relations: Same and Opposite Sex Friendships Among the Married and Unmarried," paper presented at the Western Speech Communication Association, Denver, 1982.

37. Block, p. 100.

38. Shellen and Cole, p. 15.

Communication with
Family and Friends

COMMUNICATION IN GROUPS

8

After reading this chapter, you should understand the following:

1. The characteristics that distinguish groups from other collections of people.
2. The types of goals that operate in groups.
3. The various types of groups.
4. The characteristics of groups described in this chapter.
5. The advantages and disadvantages of the decision-making methods introduced in this chapter.

You should be able to do the following:

1. Identify the groups you presently belong to and those you are likely to join in the future.
2. List the personal and group goals in groups you observe or belong to.
3. Identify the norms, roles, and interaction patterns in groups you observe or belong to.
4. Choose the most effective decision-making method for a group task.

KEY TERMS

consensus
dysfunctional role
functional role
group
group goals
growth group
hidden agenda
individual goals
learning group
norms

problem-solving group
procedural norms
roles
rules
social goals
social group
social norms
social roles
sociogram
task norms
task-related goals
task roles

The Nature of Groups

How important are groups?

You can answer this question for yourself by trying a simple experiment. Start by thinking of all the groups you belong to now and have belonged to in the past: the family you grew up with, the classes you have attended, the teams you have played on, the many social groups you have been a member of.... The list is a long one. Now, one by one, imagine that you had never belonged to each of these groups. Start with the less important ones, and the results aren't too dramatic; but very soon you will begin to see that a great deal of the information you have learned, the benefits you have gained . . . even your very identity have all come from group membership.

This doesn't mean that every group experience is a good one. Some are vaguely unrewarding, rather like eating food that has no taste and gives no nourishment. And others are downright miserable. Sometimes it is easy to see why a group succeeds or fails, but in other cases matters aren't so clear.

This chapter will help you understand better the nature of group communication. It will start by explaining just what a group is—for not every collection of people qualifies. It will go on to examine the reasons people form groups and then look at several different types of groups. Finally, it will conclude by looking at some common characteristics all groups share.

◆ WHAT IS A GROUP?

Imagine that you are taking a test on group communication. Which of the following would you identify as groups?

> a crowd of onlookers gawking at a burning building
>
> several passengers at an airline ticket counter discussing their hopes to find space on a crowded flight
>
> an army battalion

As all these situations seem to involve groups, your experience as a canny test taker probably tells you that a commonsense answer will get you in trouble here—and you're right. When social scientists talk about groups, they use the word in a special way that excludes each of the preceding examples.

What are we talking about when we use the term *group*? For our purposes a **group** consists of a *small collection of people who interact with each other, usually face to face, over time in order to reach goals.* A closer examination of this definition will show why none of the collections of people described in the preceding quiz qualify as groups.

Interaction

Without interaction, a collection of people isn't a group. Consider, for example, the onlookers at a fire. Though they all occupy the same area at a given time, they have virtually nothing to do with each other. Of course, if they should begin interacting—working together to give first aid or to rescue victims, for example—the situation would change. This requirement of interaction highlights the difference between true groups and collections of individuals who merely *coact*—simultaneously engaging in a similar activity without communicating with one another. For example, students who passively listen to a lecture don't technically constitute a group until they begin to exchange messages with each other and their instructor. (This explains why some students feel isolated even though they spend so much time on a crowded campus. Despite being surrounded by others, they really don't belong to any groups.)

As you read in Chapters 3 and 5, there are two types of interaction that go on in any communication setting. The most obvious type is verbal, in which group members exchange words either orally or in writing. But people needn't talk to each other in order to communicate as a group: Nonverbal channels can do the job, too. We can see how by thinking again about a hypothetical

THE FAR SIDE　　　By GARY LARSON

©1987 Universal Press Syndicate　　7-15

"And so you just threw everything together?... Mathews, a posse is something you have to organize."

The Nature of Groups

classroom. Imagine that the course is in its tenth week and the instructor has been lecturing nonstop for the entire time. During the first few meetings there was very little interaction of any kind: Students were too busy scribbling notes and wondering how they would survive the course with grade-point averages and sanity intact. But as they became more used to the class, the students began to share their feelings with each other. Now there's a great amount of eye rolling and groaning as the assignments are poured on, and the students exchange resigned sighs as they hear the same tired jokes for the second and third time. Thus, even though there's no verbal exchange of sentiments, the class has become a group—interestingly, in this sense a group that doesn't include the professor.

Time

A collection of people who interact for a short while don't qualify as a group. As you'll soon read, groups that work together for any length of time begin to take on characteristics that aren't present in temporary aggregations. For example, certain standards of acceptable behavior begin to evolve, and the way individuals feel about each other begins to affect their behavior toward the group's task and toward each other. According to this criterion, onlookers at a fire might have trouble qualifying as a group even if they briefly cooperated with one another to help out in the emergency. The element of time clearly excludes temporary gatherings such as the passengers gathered around the airline ticket counter. Situations like this simply don't follow many of the principles you'll be reading about in the next two chapters.

Size

Our definition of groups included the word *small.* Most experts in the field set the lower limit of group size at three members. This decision isn't arbitrary, for there are some significant differences between two- and three-person communication. For example, the only way two people can resolve a conflict is either to change one another's minds, give in, or compromise; in a larger group, however, there's a possibility of members' forming alliances either to put increased pressure on dissenting members or to outvote them.[1]

There is less agreement about when a group stops being small. Though no expert would call a 500-member army battalion a group in our sense of the word (it would be labeled an organization), most experts are reluctant to set an arbitrary upper limit. Probably the best description of smallness is the ability for each member to be able to know and react to every other member. It's sufficient to say that our focus in these pages will be on collections of people ranging in size from three to between seven and twenty.

Goals

Group membership isn't always voluntary, as draftees and prison inmates will testify. But whether or not people choose to join groups, they usually hope to achieve one or more goals. At first the goal-related nature of group membership seems simple and obvious. In truth, however, there are several types of goals, which we will now examine.

◆ GOALS OF GROUPS AND THEIR MEMBERS

We can talk about two types of goals when we examine groups. The first category involves **individual goals**—the motives of individual members—whereas the second involves **group goals**—the outcome the group seeks to accomplish.

Individual Goals

TASK-RELATED GOALS   The most obvious reason individuals join groups is to accomplish **task-related goals**—to get a job done. Some people join study groups, for example, in order to improve their knowledge. Others belong to religious groups as a way of improving the quality of their lives and those of others. (There may be additional reasons for going to school and church, as we will soon see.)

Sometimes a member's task-related goals will have little to do with a group's stated purpose. Many merchants, for example, join service clubs such as Kiwanis, Rotary, or Lions primarily because doing so is good for business. The fact that these groups help achieve worthy goals such as helping the blind or disabled is fine, of course, but for many people it is not the prime motive for belonging.

SOCIAL GOALS   What about groups with no specifically defined purpose? Consider, for instance, gatherings of regulars at the beach on sunny weekends or a group of friends who eat lunch together several times a week. Collections such as these meet the other criteria for being groups: They interact, meet over time, and have the right number of members. But what are the members' reasons for belonging? In our examples here, the goals can't be sunbathing or eating because these activities could be carried out alone. The answer to our question introduces **social goals,** the second type of group goals. In many cases, people join together in order to get the inclusion, control, and affection we mentioned in Chapter 1.

We join many, if not most, groups in order to accomplish both task and social goals. School becomes a place both to learn important information and to meet desirable friends. Our work becomes a means of putting food on the table and getting recognition for being competent. The value of making a distinction between task and social goals comes from recognizing that the latter are usually important but often not stated or even recognized by group members. Thus, asking yourself whether social goals are being met can be one way of identifying and overcoming blocks to group effectiveness.

The Nature of Groups

Think about two groups to which you belong.

a. What are your task-related goals in each?

b. What are your social goals?

c. Are your personal goals compatible or incompatible with those of other members?

d. Are they compatible or incompatible with the group goals?

e. What effect does the compatibility or incompatibility of goals have on the effectiveness of the group?

Group Goals

So far we have discussed the forces that motivate individual group members. In addition to these individual motives, there also exist group goals. For example, athletic teams exist to compete with each other, and academic classes strive to transmit knowledge.

Sometimes there is a close relationship between group and individual goals. In athletic teams the group goal is to win whereas individual members' goals include helping the group succeed. If you think about it for a moment, however, you'll see that the individual members have other goals as well: improving their physical ability, having a good time, overcoming the personal challenges of competition, and often gaining the social benefits that come from being an athlete. The difference between individual and group goals is even more pronounced when the two are incompatible. Consider, for instance, the case of an athletic team that has one player more interested in being a "star" (satisfying personal needs for recognition) than in helping the team win. Or recall classes you have known in which a lack of student enthusiasm made the personal goal of many students—getting by with the smallest possible amount of work—hardly consistent with the stated group goal of conveying information. Sometimes the gap between individual and group goals is public whereas in other cases an individual's goal becomes a **hidden agenda.** In either case, this discrepancy can be dangerous for the well-being of the group and needs to be dealt with. We'll have more to say about this subject in Chapter 10.

◆ TYPES OF GROUPS

So far we have seen that there are a variety of goals that groups fulfill. Another way of examining groups is to look at some of the functions they serve.

Learning Groups

When the term **learning group** comes up, most people think first about school. Although academic settings certainly qualify as learning groups, they aren't the only ones. Members of a scuba-diving class, friends who form a Bible

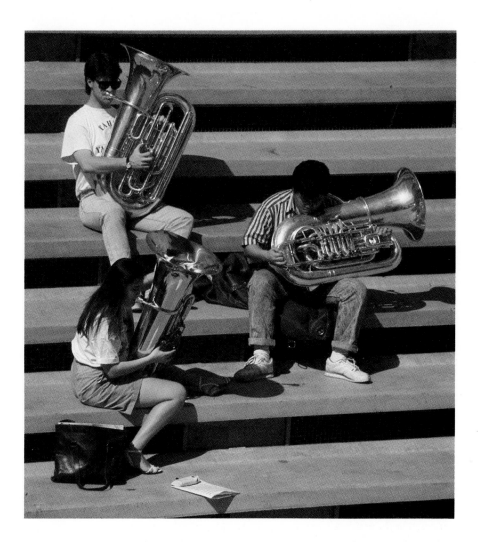

study group, and members of a League of Women Voters chapter all belong to learning groups. Whatever the setting or subject, the purpose of learning groups is to increase the knowledge or skill of each member.

Learning groups take a variety of formats. Most familiar is the lecture, in which one or more speakers dispense information to several listeners. Learning also takes place in two-way exchanges of information, when each member is both a contributor and receiver of knowledge. Sometimes the learning becomes more active, as when skiers or aspiring musicians develop their skill by practicing it.

Growth Groups

Unlike learning groups, in which the subject matter is external to the members, **growth groups** focus on teaching the members more about themselves.

Consciousness-raising groups, marriage encounter workshops, counseling, and group therapy are all types of growth groups. These are unlike most other types of groups in that there is no real collective goal: The entire purpose of the group is to help the members identify and deal with their personal concerns.

Problem-solving Groups

Problem-solving groups work together to resolve a mutual concern. Sometimes the concern involves the group itself, as when a family decides how to handle household chores or when coworkers meet to coordinate vacation schedules. In other instances, the problem is external to the group. For instance, neighbors who organize themselves to prevent burglaries or club members who plan a fund-raising drive are focusing on external problems.

Problem-solving groups can take part in many activities: One type is gathering information, as when several students compile a report for a class assignment. At other times, a group makes policy—a club's deciding whether or not to admit the public to its meetings being an example. Some groups make individual decisions; an interview committee that decides which candidate to hire is fulfilling this function.

Social Groups

We have already mentioned that some groups serve strictly to satisfy the social needs of their participants. Some **social groups** are organized whereas others are informal. In either case, the inclusion, control, and affection that such groups provide are reason enough for belonging.

◆ CHARACTERISTICS OF GROUPS

Whatever their function, all groups have certain characteristics in common. Understanding these characteristics is a first step to behaving more effectively in your own groups.

Rules and Norms

Many groups have formal **rules**—explicit, officially stated guidelines that govern what the group is supposed to do and how the members should behave. In a classroom, these rules include how absences will be treated, whether papers must be typed or may be handwritten, and so on. Alongside the official rules, an equally powerful set of standards also operate, often without ever being discussed. Sociologists call these unstated rules **norms.** Norms are shared values, beliefs, behaviors, and procedures that govern a group's operation. For instance, you probably won't find a description of what

Communication in Groups

◆ A fighter pilot soon found he wanted to associate only with other fighter pilots. Who else could understand the nature of the little proposition (right stuff/death) they were all dealing with? And what other subject could compare with it? It was riveting! To talk about it in so many words was forbidden, of course. The very words *death, danger, bravery, fear* were not to be uttered except in the occasional specific instance or for ironic effect. Nevertheless, the subject could be adumbrated in *code* or *by example*... They diced that righteous stuff up into little bits, bowed ironically to it, stumbled blindfolded around it, groped, lurched, belched, staggered, bawled, sang, roared, and feinted at it with self-deprecating humor. Nevertheless!—they never mentioned it by name.

Tom Wolfe
The Right Stuff

jokes are and aren't acceptable in the bylaws of any groups you belong to, yet you can almost certainly describe the unstated code if you think about it. Is sexual humor acceptable? How much, and what types? What about religious jokes? How much kidding of other members is proper? Matters such as these vary from one group to another, according to the norms of each one.

There are three categories of group norms: social, procedural, and task.[2] **Social norms** govern the relationship of members to each other. How honest and direct will members be with one another? What emotions will and won't be expressed, and in what ways? Matters such as these are handled by the establishment of social norms, usually implicit ones. **Procedural norms** outline how the group should operate. Will the group make decisions by accepting the vote of the majority, or will the members keep talking until consensus is reached? Will one person run meetings, or will discussion be leaderless? **Task norms** focus on how the job itself should be handled. Will the group keep working on a problem until everyone agrees that its product is the best one possible, or will members settle for an adequate, if imperfect, solution? The answer to this question results in a task-related norm. All groups have social norms whereas problem-solving, learning, and growth groups also have procedural and task norms.

Table 8–1 lists some of the norms most people bring to a task-oriented group's first meeting. It is important to realize that cultural norms such as these are *idealized* and that a group's actual norms emerge as its members spend time together. Consider the matter of punctuality, for example. A cultural norm in our society is that meetings should begin at the scheduled time, yet some groups soon generate the usually unstated agreement that the real business won't commence until ten or so minutes later. On a more serious level, one cultural norm is that other people should be treated politely and with respect, but in some groups failure to listen, sarcasm, and even outright hostility make the principle of civility a sham.

The Nature of Groups

TABLE 8–1 Expected Norms for a Discussion Group's First Meeting

SOCIAL	PROCEDURAL	TASK
Do	**Do**	**Do**
—serve refreshments	—introduce people	—criticize ideas, not people
—dress casually	—plan to participate	—support the best idea
—use first names	—establish goals	—commit yourself to group
—discuss uncontroversial	—build agenda	solutions
subjects	—hold routine meetings one	—share in the work load
—tell humorous jokes	hour in length	—say so if you disagree
—tell political jokes (they will be	—have someone in charge	—ask questions about group
tolerated)	—sit face-to-face	ideas
—tell trend or one-line jokes		
—tell cultural truisms	**Don't**	**Don't**
	—leave meetings without cause	—push your idea on the group
Don't	—monopolize conversation	—support ideas just because of
—smoke (perhaps)	—stand up and speak in small-	people who presented them
—swear	group meetings (generally)	—be verbally violent if you
—arrive late	—demand to lead	disagree with ideas
—be absent without apology	—refuse to speak when	—consider your ideas as the
—tell sexist, racist, ethnic, agist,	addressed	only ones of merit
or religious jokes		

You can understand the nature of norms by thinking of one specific group to which you belong as you answer the following questions.

a. What explicit rules govern your group's behavior? How were they announced?

b. What implicit norms are in operation? What is the evidence of their existence?

c. Use the examples from the preceding steps plus others to identify two social norms, two procedural norms, and two task norms.

It is important to understand a group's norms. Following them is one way to gain acceptance into the group, and sometimes recognizing norms that cause problems can be a way to help the group operate more effectively. For instance, in some groups a norm is to discourage new ideas by criticism, sarcasm, or indifference. Pointing this out to members might be a way to change the unwritten rules, and thereby improve the group's work.

If norms are rarely stated, how is it possible to identify them? There are two sets of clues that can help you pin down norms. First, look for behaviors that occur often.[3] For instance, notice what time meetings begin. Observe the amount of work members are willing to contribute to the group. See what kinds

Communication in Groups

◆ "What are we? Humans? Or animals? Or savages? What's grownups going to think? Going off—hunting pigs—letting fires out—and now!"

A shadow fronted him tempestuously.

"You shut up, you fat slug!"

There was a moment's struggle and the glimmering conch jigged up and down. Ralph leapt to his feet.

"Jack! Jack! You haven't got the conch! Let him speak."

Jack's face swam near him.

"And you shut up! Who are you, anyway? Sitting there telling people what to do. You can't hunt, you can't sing—"

"I'm chief. I was chosen."

"Why should choosing make any difference? Just giving orders that don't make any sense—"

"Piggy's got the conch."

"That's right—favor Piggy as you always do—"

"Jack!"

Jack's voice sounded in bitter mimicry.

"Jack! Jack!"

"The rules!" shouted Ralph. "You're breaking the rules!"

"Who cares?"

Ralph summoned his wits.

"Because the rules are the only thing we've got!"

William Golding
Lord of the Flies

---

of humor are and aren't used. Habitual behaviors like these suggest the unspoken rules that the group lives by. Another way to identify norms is to look for clues that members are being punished for violating them. Most punishments are subtle, of course: pained expressions from other members when a speaker talks too much, no laughter following an inappropriate joke, and so on.

Roles

Where norms define acceptable group standards, **roles** refer to the patterns of behavior expected of individual members. Just like norms, some roles are formally recognized. These explicit roles usually come with a label, such as "professor," "chairperson," or "student." Other roles are informal; they are very real although group members may not acknowledge—or even consciously realize—their existence. For instance, you can probably think of many informal groups in which some members are clearly leaders and others followers although these positions have never been discussed.

Formal titles don't describe all the roles that operate in groups. Social scientists have found that there are certain **functional roles** that also must be filled if task-related groups are to get a job done (see Table 8–2). These

The Nature of Groups

TABLE 8—2 Functional Roles of Group Members

TASK ROLES	TYPICAL BEHAVIORS	EXAMPLES
1. Initiator/contributor	Contributes ideas and suggestions; proposes solutions and decisions; proposes new ideas or states old ones in a novel fashion.	"How about taking a different approach to this chore. Suppose we…"
2. Information seeker	Asks for clarification of comments in terms of their factual adequacy; asks for information or facts relevant to the problem; suggests information is needed before making decisions.	"Do you think the others will go for this?" "How much would the plan cost us?" "Does anybody know if those dates are available?"
3. Information giver	Offers facts or generalizations that may relate to the group's task.	"I bet Chris would know the answer to that." "*Newsweek* ran an article on that a couple of months ago. It said.."
4. Opinion seeker	Asks for clarification of opinions made by other members of the group and asks how people in the group feel.	"Does anyone else have an idea of this?" "That's an interesting idea, Ruth. How long would it take to get started?"
5. Opinion giver	States beliefs or opinions having to do with suggestions made; indicates what the group's attitude should be.	"I think we ought to go with the second plan. It fits the conditions we face in the Concord plant best…"
6. Elaborator/clarifier	Elaborates ideas and other contributions; offers rationales for suggestions; tries to deduce how an idea or suggestion would work if adopted by the group.	"If we followed Lee's suggestion, each of us would need to make three calls." "Let's see…at 35 cents per brochure, the total cost would be $525.00."
7. Coordinator	Clarifies the relationships among information, opinions, and ideas or suggests an integration of the information, opinions, and ideas of subgroups.	"John, you seem most concerned with potential problems. Mary sounds confident that they can all be solved. Why don't you list the problems one at a time, John, and Mary can respond to each one."
8. Diagnostician	Indicates what the problems are.	"But you're missing the main thing, I think. The problem is that we can't afford…"
9. Orienter/summarizer	Summarizes what has taken place; points out departures from agreed-on goals; tries to bring the group back to the central issues; raises questions about the direction in which the group is heading.	"Let's take stock of where we are. Helen and John take the position that we should act now. Bill says, 'Wait.' Rusty isn't sure. Can we set that aside for a moment and come back to it after we…"

(continued on next page)

TABLE 8–2 Functional Roles of Group Members (*continued*)

TASK ROLES	TYPICAL BEHAVIORS	EXAMPLES
10. Energizer	Prods the group to action.	"Come on, guys. We've been wasting time. Let's get down to business."
11. Procedure developer	Handles routine tasks such as seating arrangements, obtaining equipment, and handing out pertinent papers.	"I'll volunteer to see that the forms are printed and distributed." "I'd be happy to check on which of those dates are free."
12. Secretary	Keeps notes on the group's progress.	"Just for the record, I'll put these decisions in a memo and get copies to everyone in the group."
13. Evaluator/critic	Constructively analyzes group's accomplishments according to some set of standards; checks to see that consensus has been reached.	"Look, we said we only had two weeks, and this proposal will take at least three. Does that mean that it's out of the running, or do we need to change our original guidelines?"

SOCIAL/MAINTENANCE ROLES	TYPICAL BEHAVIORS	EXAMPLES
1. Supporter/encourager	Praises, agrees with, and accepts the contributions of others; offers warmth, solidarity, and recognition.	"I really like that idea, John." "Priscilla's suggestion sounds good to me. Could we discuss it further?"
2. Harmonizer	Reconciles disagreements; mediates differences; reduces tensions by giving group members a chance to explore their differences.	"I don't think you two are as far apart as you think. Henry, are you saying ____? Benson, you seem to be saying ____. Is that what you mean?"
3. Tension reliever	Jokes or in some other way reduces the formality of the situation; relaxes the group members.	"Let's take a break…maybe have a drink." "You're a tough cookie, Bob. I'm glad you're on our side!"
4. Conciliator	Offers new options when his or her own ideas are involved in a conflict; disciplines to admit errors so as to maintain group cohesion.	"Looks like our solution is halfway between you and me, John. Can we look at the middle ground?"
5. Gatekeeper	Keeps communication channels open; encourages and facilitates interaction from those members who are usually silent.	"Susan, you haven't said anything about this yet. I know you've been studying the problem. What do you think about ____?"
6. Feeling expresser	Makes explicit the feelings, moods, and relationships in the group; shares own feelings with others.	"I'm really glad we cleared things up today." "I'm just about worn out. Could we call it a day and start fresh tomorrow?"
7. Follower	Goes along with the movement of the group passively, accepting the ideas of others sometimes serving as an audience.	"I agree. Yes, I see what you mean. If that's what the group wants to do, I'll go along…"

(continued on next page)

TABLE 8-2 **Functional Roles of Group Members** (*continued*)

DYSFUNCTIONAL ROLES	TYPICAL BEHAVIORS	EXAMPLES
1. Blocker	Interferes with progress by rejecting ideas or taking a negative stand on any and all issues; refuses to cooperate.	"Wait a minute! That's not right! That idea is absurd." "You can talk all day, but my mind is made up."
2. Aggressor	Struggles for status by deflating the status of others; boasts; criticizes.	"Wow, that's really swell! You turkeys have botched things again." "Your constant bickering is responsible for this mess. Let me tell you how you ought to do it."
3. Deserter	Withdraws in some way; remains indifferent, aloof, sometimes formal; daydreams; wanders from the subject; engages in irrelevant side conversations.	"I suppose that's all right...I really don't care."
4. Dominator	Interrupts and embarks on long monologues; is authoritative; tries to monopolize the group's time.	"Bill, you're just off base. What we should do is this. First..."
5. Recognition seeker	Attempts to gain attention in an exaggerated manner; usually boasts about past accomplishments; relates irrelevant personal experiences, usually in an attempt to gain sympathy.	"That reminds me of a guy I used to know..." "Let me tell you how I handled old Marris..."
6. Playboy	Displays a lack of involvement in the group through inappropriate humor, horseplay, or cynicism.	"Why try to convince these guys? Let's just get the mob to snuff them out." "Hey, Carla, wanna be my roommate at the sales conference?"

Adapted from Gerald L. Wilson and Michael S. Hanna, *Groups in Context: Leadership and Participation in Decision-Making Groups.* © Random House, Inc., 1986, pp. 144–146.

functional roles are not formally assigned to members. In fact, they are rarely even recognized as existing. Many of the roles may be filled by more than one member, and some of them may be filled by different people at different times. The important fact is that, at crucial times, each of the functional roles must be filled by someone.

The list of functional roles in Table 8–2 is a valuable tool because it can serve as a checklist you can use to diagnose why a group is or isn't working effectively. Notice that the roles fall into two categories, task and maintenance. **Task roles** help the group accomplish its goals, and **social roles** (also called "maintenance roles") keep the relationships among the members running smoothly. Table 8–2 also lists several **dysfunctional roles** that prevent a group from working effectively.

Communication in Groups

Figure 8–1 shows that task and social functions are related. The social relationship among members influences how well the job at hand is managed, and conversely the task influences the way members feel about one another. What is the optimal balance between task and social functions? According to Robert Bales, one of the earliest and most influential researchers in the area, the ideal ratio is 2–1, with task-related behavior dominating.[4] This balance allows the group to get its work done, while at the same time taking care of the personal needs and concerns of the members.

ROLE EMERGENCE   We said earlier that most group members aren't aware of the existence of functional roles. You will rarely find members saying things like "You ask most of the questions, I'll give opinions, and she can be the summarizer." Yet it's fairly obvious that over time certain members do begin to fulfill specific functions. How does this process occur?

There are two answers to this question. One factor in role differentiation is certainly the personal characteristics of each member. Some people, for example, seem to be more critical than others and thus feel comfortable as diagnosers and evaluators. Others are particularly aware of personality dynamics and find it easy to get along with other members, which makes them good harmonizers and interpersonal problem solvers.

Think of a group to which you belong.

a. What functional roles do you fill in that group?
b. Are those roles similar or different in other groups to which you belong?
c. Are there any roles that are going unfilled in your group? How does this absence affect the group's functioning?

FIGURE 8–1
Relationship of task and social/maintenance dimensions of member behaviors

Amount of social or relational impact

Primarily social

High impact on both

Little or no impact

Primarily task

Amount of impact on group task achievement

● Specific act or behavior

In addition to the personal skills and traits of individual members, the idiosyncrasies of each particular group shape the roles that each member takes. In other words, each of us plays a different role in different groups. For example, a normally nonassertive person might act as a starter or direction giver in a group where no one else was performing that necessary task. In some cases, this assumption of uncharacteristic roles isn't voluntary: Members informally assign functions to members who wouldn't otherwise have taken them. This kind of role assignment shows up in movies, where the hapless passenger or the untrained but courageous flight attendant saves the plane after an accident wipes out the pilot. In more humdrum but common situations, you've probably heard people assigning roles by saying things like "You know something about that, what do you think?"—a clear invitation to become an information or opinion giver.

ROLE-RELATED PROBLEMS Groups can suffer from at least two role-related problems. The first occurs when one or more important functional roles go unfilled. The most common example of this happens in groups where there is no information giver to provide some vital knowledge. A more subtle (but equally dangerous) role vacuum occurs when maintenance functions aren't filled. If nobody relieves interpersonal tensions, gives praise, or solves inter-personal problems at critical times, a group will have a hard time accomplish-ing its task. There are other cases when the problem isn't an *absence* of candidates to fill certain roles, but an *overabundance* of them. This situation can lead to unstated competition between members, which gets in the way of group effectiveness. You have probably seen groups in which two people both want to be the tension-relieving comedian. In such cases, the problem arises when the members in question become more concerned with getting laughs than with getting the group's job done.

Patterns of Interaction

In Chapter 1 we said that communication involves the flow of information between and among people. It almost goes without saying that this exchange needs to be complete and efficient for the communicators to reach their goals. In interpersonal and public speaking settings, information exchange is relatively uncomplicated, taking basically two routes: either between the two individuals in an interpersonal dyad or between speaker and audience in a public speaking situation.* In groups, however, things aren't so simple. The mathematical formula that identifies the number of possible interactions between individuals is

$$\frac{N\,(N\,-\,1)}{2}$$

*Actually, this is a slight oversimplification. In public-speaking situations, members of an audience also exchange messages with one another with their laughter, restless movements, and so on. It's still fair to say, however, that the exchange of information is basically two-way.

Communication in
Groups

where N equals the number of members in a group.[5] Thus, in even a relatively small five-member group, there are ten possible combinations of two-person conversations and a vastly greater number of potential multiperson interactions. Besides the sheer quantity of information exchange, the more complex structure of groups affects the flow of information in other ways, too.

Construct a sociogram picturing the interaction pattern in a group you have observed for a five-minute period. Based on your observations, decide whether the participation pattern contributes to or detracts from the group's task behavior. Also determine how well the interaction pattern promotes smooth social functioning.

A look at Figure 8–2 (usually called a **sociogram**) will suggest the number and complexity of interactions that can occur in a group. Arrows connecting members indicate remarks shared between them. Two-headed arrows represent two-way conversations, while single-headed arrows indicate remarks which did not arouse a response. Arrows directed to the center of the circle indicate remarks made to the group as a whole. A network analysis of this sort can reveal both the amount of participation by each member and the recipients of every member's remarks. As such, it provides a graphic look at who seems to be making the most significant contributions (at least in terms of their quantity), as well as who is not contributing.

In the group pictured in Figure 8–2, person E appears only to be connected to the group through a relationship with person A; E never addressed any other members, nor did they address E. Also notice that Person A is the most active and best-connected member. A addressed remarks to the group as a

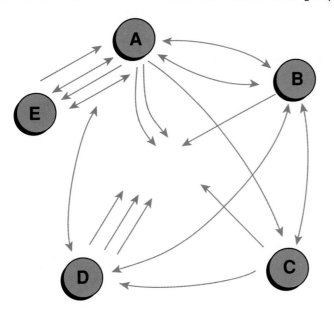

FIGURE 8–2
Sociogram representing patterns of interaction in a five-person group.

The Nature of Groups

whole and to every other member, and was the object of remarks from three individuals as well.

Sociograms don't tell the whole story, since they do not indicate the quality of the messages being exchanged. Nonetheless, they are a useful tool in diagnosing group communication.

Physical arrangement influences communication in groups. It's obviously easier to interact with someone you can see well. Lack of visibility isn't a serious problem in dyadic settings, but it can be troublesome in groups. For example, group members seated in a circle are more likely to talk with persons across from them than with those on either side.[6] Different things happen when members are seated in rectangular arrangements. Research with twelve-person juries showed that those sitting at either end of such tables participated more in discussions and were viewed by other members as having more influence on the decision-making process.[7] Rectangular seating patterns have other consequences as well. Research conducted on six-person groups seated at rectangular tables showed that as distance between two persons increased, other members perceived them as being less friendly, less talkative, and less acquainted with each other.[8]

Decision-Making Methods

Another way to classify groups is according to the approach they use to make decisions. There are several methods a group can use to decide matters. We'll look at each of them now, examining their advantages and disadvantages.[9]

AUTHORITY RULE WITHOUT DISCUSSION Authority rule without discussion is the method most often used by autocratic leaders (see Chapter 10). Though it sounds dictatorial, there are times when such an approach has its advantages. First, the method is quick: There are some cases when there simply isn't time for a group to decide what to do. The method is also perfectly acceptable with routine matters that don't require discussion in order to gain approval. When overused, however, this approach causes problems. As Chapter 10 will show, much of the time group decisions are of higher quality and gain more support from members than those made by an individual. Thus, failure to consult with members can lead to a decrease of effectiveness even when the leader's decision is a reasonable one.

EXPERT OPINION Sometimes one group member will be defined as an expert and, as such, will be given the power to make decisions. This method can work well when that person's judgment is truly superior. For example, if a group of friends are backpacking in the wilderness and one becomes injured, it would probably be foolish to argue with the advice of a doctor in the group. In most cases, however, matters aren't so simple. Who is the expert? There is often disagreement on this question. Sometimes a member might think he or she is the best qualified to make a decision, but others will disagree. In a case like this, the group probably won't support that person's advice, even if it is sound.

AUTHORITY RULE AFTER DISCUSSION   The method of authority rule after discussion is less autocratic than the preceding two, for it at least takes into consideration the opinions of more than one person. Thus, the unilateral decisions of an open-minded authority gain some of the increases in quality and commitment that come from group interaction while also enjoying the quickness that comes from avoiding extensive discussion. This approach has its disadvantages, however. Often other group members will be tempted to tell the leader what they think he or she wants to hear, and in other cases they will compete to impress the decision maker.

MAJORITY CONTROL   A naive belief of many people (perhaps coming from overzealous high school civics teachers) is that the democratic method of majority rule is always superior. This method does have its advantages in cases where the support of all members isn't necessary, but in more important matters it is risky. Remember that even if a 51 percent majority of the members favor a plan, 49 percent might still oppose it—hardly sweeping support for any decision that needs the support of all members in order to work.

MINORITY CONTROL   Sometimes a few members of a group will decide matters. This approach works well with noncritical questions that would waste the whole group's time. In the form of a committee, a minority of members also can study an issue in greater detail than can the entire group. When an issue is so important that it needs the support of everyone, it's best at least to have the committee report its findings for the approval of all members.

The Nature of Groups

CONSENSUS Consensus occurs when all members of a group support a decision. The advantages of consensus are obvious: Full participation can increase the quality of the decision as well as the commitment of members to support it. Consensus is especially important in decisions on critical or complex matters; in such cases, methods using less input can diminish the quality of or enthusiasm for a decision. Despite its advantages, consensus also has its drawbacks. It takes a great deal of time, which makes it unsuitable for emergencies. In addition, it is often very frustrating: Emotions can run high on important matters, and patience in the face of such pressures is difficult. Because of the need to deal with these emotional pressures, consensus calls for more communication skill than do other decision-making approaches. As with many things in life, consensus has high rewards, which come at a proportionately high cost.

Which of these methods is best? There's no single answer. The most effective method in a given situation depends on the circumstances: the amount of time available, the importance of the decision, the abilities of the group's leader, and the members' attitudes toward that person. The best approach might be to use the preceding descriptions of each method as guidelines in deciding which method to use in a particular situation.

Describe the methods of decision making used in family, classroom, and on-the-job groups to which you have belonged. Then answer the following questions for each group:

a. Does the group use the same decision-making method in all circumstances, or does it use different methods at different times?
b. After reading the advantages and disadvantages of each method, do you think the methods used by each group are appropriate? If not, what methods would be better? Why?

◆ SUMMARY

Groups play an important role in many areas of our lives—families, education, on the job, and in friendships, to name a few. Groups possess several characteristics that distinguish them from other communication contexts. They involve interaction over time among a small number of participants with the purpose of achieving one or more goals. Groups have their own goals, as do individual members. Member goals fall into two categories: task-related and social. Sometimes individual and group goals are compatible, and sometimes they conflict.

Groups can be put into several classifications—learning, growth, problem-solving, and social. All these types of groups share certain characteristics: the existence of group norms, individual roles for members, patterns of interaction that are shaped by the group's structure, and the choice of one or more ways of reaching decisions.

Communication in Groups

1. F. Williams, *The New Communications,* 2d ed. (Belmont, Calif.: Wadsworth, 1989), pp. 164–165. See also W. Wilmot, *Dyadic Communication,* 3d ed. (New York: Random House, 1967), pp. 21–29.

2. John F. Cragan and David W. Wright, *Communication in Small Group Discussions: A Case Study Approach,* 2d ed. (St. Paul, Minn.: West Publishing, 1986), p. 16.

3. S. B. Shimanoff, "Coordinating Group Interaction via Communication Rules," in R. S. Cathcart and L. A. Samovar (eds.), *Small Group Communication: A Reader*, 4th ed. (Dubuque, Iowa: W. C. Brown, 1984), p. 36.

4. R. F. Bales and F. L. Strodbeck, "Phases in Group Problem Solving," *Journal of Abnormal and Social Psychology* 46 (1951): 485–495.

5. E. M. Rogers, *Diffusion of Innovations,* 3d ed. (New York: Free Press, 1983), p. 294.

6. B. Steinzor, "The Spatial Factor in Face-to-Face Discussion Groups," *Journal of Abnormal and Social Psychology* 45 (1950): 552–555.

7. F. L. Strodtbeck and L. H. Hook, "The Social Dimensions of a Twelve Man Jury Table," *Sociometry* 24 (1961): 397–415.

8. N. F. Russo, "Connotations of Seating Arrangements," *Cornell Journal of Social Relations* 2.

9. Adapted from David W. Johnson and Frank P. Johnson, *Joining Together: Group Theory and Group Skills* (Englewood Cliffs, N.J.: Prentice-Hall, 1975), pp. 80–81.

The Nature of Groups

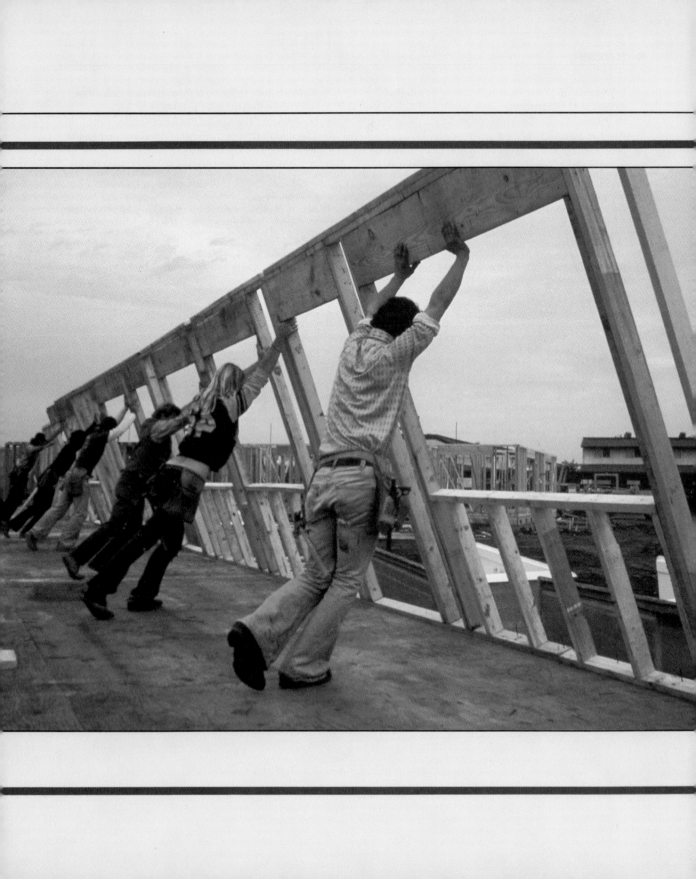

9

After reading this chapter, you should understand the following:

1. The advantages of solving problems in groups.
2. The characteristics of several common discussion formats.
3. The six basic problem-solving steps in the rational problem-solving method.
4. The developmental stages in a problem-solving group.
5. The factors that contribute to group cohesiveness.
6. The factors that contribute to balanced participation in groups.
7. The differences between a "leader" and "leadership."
8. The various types of power in groups.
9. The various approaches to studying leadership.
10. The dangers in group discussion outlined in this chapter.

You should be able to do the following:

1. Use the problem-solving steps outlined in this chapter in a group task.
2. Suggest ways to build the cohesiveness and participation in a group.
3. Analyze the sources of leadership and power in a group.
4. Suggest the most effective leadership approach for a specific group task.
5. Identify the obstacles to effective functioning of a specific group and suggest more effective ways of communicating.

KEY TERMS

authoritarian leadership style
brainstorming
coercive power
cohesiveness
conflict stage
democratic leadership style
emergence stage
expert power
force field analysis
forum
information power
laissez-faire leadership style
leader
leadership
legitimate power
managerial grid
nominal leader
orientation stage
panel discussion
parliamentary procedure
participative decision making
probative question
referent power
reinforcement stage
reward power
situational leadership
symposium
trait theories of leadership

Solving Problems in Groups

Chapter 8 described various types of groups—learning, growth, social, and problem-solving. Of all these, problem-solving groups have been studied most intensively by social scientists. Once we understand the nature of problem-solving, the reason becomes clear. *Problems,* as we define them here, don't refer only to situations where something is wrong. Perhaps *meeting challenges* and *performing tasks* are better terms. Once you recognize this, you can see that problem-solving not only occupies a major part of our working life but plays an important role in other areas as well. At one time or another, all groups need to solve problems.

There are two sets of communication skills that any group must possess in order to come up with successful solutions. The first has to do with the group task itself: how to analyze the problem, choose the best solution, and make it work. A second area involves building and maintaining good relationships: making sure, first, that members feel good about each other and, second, that they enjoy the experience of working together.

This chapter will focus on both the task and relational aspects of problem-solving groups. In addition, it will explore the nature of leadership, defining that important term and suggesting how groups can be led most effectively. Finally, it will list several common problems task-oriented groups can encounter and describe how to overcome them.

◆ PROBLEM-SOLVING IN GROUPS: WHEN AND WHY

To many people, groups are to communication what Muzak is to music or Twinkies are to food—a joke. The snide remark, "A camel is a horse designed by a committee" reflects this attitude as does this ditty:

> Search all your parks in all your cities . . .
> You'll find no statues to committees![1]

This unflattering reputation is at least partly justified. Most of us would wind up with a handsome sum if we had a dollar for every hour wasted in groups. On the other hand, it's unfair to view all groups as bad, especially when this accusation implies that other types of communication are by nature superior. After all, we also have wasted time listening to boring lectures, reading worthless books, and making trivial conversation.

So what's the truth? Is group problem-solving a waste of effort, or is it the best way to manage a task? As with most matters, the truth falls somewhere between these two extremes. Groups do have their shortcomings, which we will discuss in a few pages. But extensive research has shown that when these shortcomings can be avoided, groups are clearly the most effective way to handle many tasks.

Advantages of Group Problem-Solving

Research over fifty years that has compared problem-solving by groups and by individuals shows that, in most cases, groups can produce more solutions to a problem than individuals working alone . . . and that the solutions will be of higher quality.[2] Groups have proved superior at a wide range of tasks—everything from assembling jigsaw puzzles to solving complex reasoning problems. There are several reasons why groups are effective.[3]

RESOURCES For many tasks, groups possess a greater collection of resources than do most individuals. Sometimes the resources are physical. For example, three or four people can put up a tent or dig a ditch better than a lone person. But on other problems the pooled resources lead to *qualitatively* better solutions. Think, for instance, about times when you have studied with other students for a test, and you will remember how much better the group was at preparing for all the questions that might be asked and at developing answers to them. (This, of course, assumes that the study group members cared enough about the exam to have studied for it before the group meeting.) Groups not only have more resources than individuals; through interaction among the members they also are better able to mobilize them. Talking about an upcoming test with others can jog your memory about items you might not have thought of if you had been working alone.

ACCURACY Another benefit of group work is the increased likelihood of catching errors. At one time or another, we all make stupid mistakes, like the man who built a boat in his basement and then wasn't able to get it out the door. Working in a group increases the chance that foolish errors like this won't slip by. Sometimes, of course, errors aren't so obvious, which makes groups even more valuable as an error-checking mechanism. Another side to the error-detecting story is the risk that group members will support each other in

Solving Problems in Groups

Another meeting! One after another without coming up with a proposal that would fly.

This one took place in early September and (not surprisingly) only a few people showed up—12, to be precise. And so they talked for some days and finally came up with a plan for still another meeting, eight months hence. It was hoped this would offer sufficient time to generate interest in the matter.

They also moved the location. It was not that the September site had been unpleasant—on the contrary, the facilities were quite good—but variety in meeting places might induce more individuals to attend.

Of the 74 invitees, 55 showed up. But they didn't all come at once. They were supposed to convene on Monday, May 14, but it wasn't until Friday, May 25, that enough were present to conduct business. They decided to work diligently from that day on until they finished their proposal. They even agreed to put a lid on their deliberations.

They were a relatively young group; the average age was 42. The youngest was 30 and the oldest 82 and prone to nod during long meetings. Although some were lackluster in ability, most were able and would later move to high executive positions.

They were together for 116 days, taking off only Sundays and 12 other days. And you might have guessed it: During a very hot summer they were without air conditioning. In addition to the formal sessions of the entire group, much of their work was done in committee and after hours.

The formal sessions sometimes got out of hand. One faction had come with a proposal that was almost the reverse of an outline offered by another group. The advocates of each seemed unwilling to bend, and by the end of June tempers were flaring so much that the oldest participant suggested beginning each session with an invocation.

By early June, they got wind of a way out of their impasse: Adopt a portion of each plan. By compromising, they might be better able to sell their product to a broad market. Yet even this task of drawing the line between two extremes was not easy, and so some decided to go home or back to their offices. It simply was not worth the effort.

Even among those who remained there was still criticism of the final proposal. It was much too short, some argued—only 4,000 words. Four months of work and only 4,000 words! It was scarcely enough to fill a few sheets of paper. But 39 of them felt it was the best they could come up with. It was good enough to sign, which they did on the 17th day of September, 1787.

And they called their proposal the Constitution of the United States.

Thomas V. DiBacco

a bad idea. We'll discuss this problem when we focus on conformity later in this chapter.

COMMITMENT   Besides coming up with superior solutions, groups also generate higher commitment to carrying them out. Members are most likely to accept solutions they have helped create, and they will work harder to carry out those actions. This fact has led to the principle of **participative decision making,** in which the people who will live with a plan help make it. This is an especially important principle for those in authority such as supervisors, teachers, and parents. As professors, we have seen the difference between the sullen compliance of students who have been forced to accept a policy with which they disagree and the much more willing cooperation of classes who have helped develop it. Though the benefits of participative decision making are great, we need to insert a qualification here: There are times when an autocratic approach of imposing a decision without discussion is most effective. We will discuss this question of when to be democratic and when to be directive in the section on leadership later in this chapter.

When to Use Groups for Problem-Solving

Despite their advantages, groups aren't always the best way to solve a problem. Many jobs can be tackled more quickly and easily—even more efficiently by one or more people working independently. Answering the following questions will help you decide when to solve a problem using a group, and when to tackle it alone.[4]

IS THE JOB BEYOND THE CAPACITY OF ONE PERSON?   Some jobs are simply too big for one person to manage. They may call for more *information* than a single person possesses or can gather. For example, a group of friends planning a large New Year's party will probably have a better event if they pool their ideas than if one person tries to think of everything. Some jobs also require more *time and energy* than one person can spare. Putting on the New Year's party could involve a variety of tasks: inviting the guests, hiring a band, finding a place large enough to hold the party, buying food and drinks, and so on. It's both unrealistic and unfair to expect one or two people to do all this work.

ARE INDIVIDUALS' TASKS INTERDEPENDENT?   Remember that a group is more than a collection of individuals working side by side. The best tasks for groups are ones where the individuals can help one another in some way. Think of a group of disgruntled renters considering how to protest unfair landlords. In order to get anywhere, they realize that they have to assign areas of responsibility to each member: researching the law, seeking additional members, publicizing their complaints, and so on. It's easy to see that these jobs are all interdependent: Getting new members, for example, will require publicity; and publicizing complaints will involve showing how the renters' legal rights are being violated.

Even when everyone is working on the same job, there can be interdependence if different members fulfill the various functional roles described in Chapter 8. Some people might be better at task-related roles like information giving, diagnosing, and summarizing. Others might contribute by filling social roles such as harmonizing, supporting, or relieving tension. People working independently simply don't have the breadth of resources to fill all these functions.

Solving Problems in Groups

IS THERE MORE THAN ONE DECISION OR SOLUTION?   Groups are best suited to tackling problems without a single cut-and-dried answer: What's the best way to boost membership in a campus organization? How can funds be raised for a charity? What topic should the group choose for a class project? Gaining the perspectives of every member boosts the odds of finding high quality answers to questions like these.

By contrast, a problem with only one solution won't take full advantage of a group's talents. For example, phoning merchants to get price quotes or looking up a series of books in the library don't require much creative thinking. Jobs like these can be handled by one or two people working alone. Of course, it may take a group meeting to decide how to divide the work to get the job done most efficiently.

IS THERE POTENTIAL FOR DISAGREEMENT?   Tackling a problem as a group is essential if you need the support of everyone involved. Consider a group of friends planning a vacation trip. Letting one or two people choose the destination, schedule, and budget would be asking for trouble, since their decisions would almost certainly disappoint at least some of the people who weren't consulted. It would be far smarter to involve everyone in the most important decisions, even if doing so took more time. Once the key decisions were settled, it might be fine to delegate relatively minor issues to one or two people.

Which of the following tasks would best be managed in a group?

a. Collecting and editing a list of films illustrating communication principles.

b. Deciding what the group will eat for lunch at a one-day meeting.

c. Choosing the topic for a class project.

d. Finding which of six companies had the lowest auto insurance rates.

e. Designing a survey to measure community attitudes toward a subsidy for local artists.

◆ TYPES OF PROBLEM-SOLVING FORMATS

Groups meet to solve problems in a variety of settings and for a wide range of reasons. The formats they use are also varied. Some groups meet before an audience to address a problem. The onlookers may be involved in, and affected by, the topic under discussion like the citizens who attend a typical city council meeting or voters who attend a candidate's debate. In other cases, the audience members are simply interested spectators, as occurs in televised discussions such as "Meet the Press" and "Face the Nation."

Most problem-solving meetings do not occur before an audience. The members meet privately because it is most efficient for a small number of decision makers to tackle the problem facing a larger group or because their discussions are confidential or because there is no interest in the problem beyond the people present.

Problem-solving meetings can follow a variety of formats. A session that uses **parliamentary procedure** observes specific rules about how topics may be discussed and decisions made. The standard reference book for parliamentary procedure is the revised edition of *Robert's Rules of Order.* Although the parliamentary rules may seem stilted and cumbersome, when well used, they do keep a discussion on track and protect the rights of the minority against domination by the majority.

Another common problem-solving format is the **panel discussion,** in which the participants talk over the topic informally, much as they would in an ordinary conversation. A leader (called a "moderator" in public discussions) may help the discussion along by encouraging the comments of some members, cutting off overly talkative ones, and seeking consensus when the time comes for making a decision.

In a **symposium** the participants divide the topic in a manner that allows each member to deliver in-depth information without interruption. Although this format lends itself to good explanations of each person's decision, the one-person-at-a-time nature of a symposium won't lead to a group decision. The contributions of the members must be followed by the give-and-take of an open discussion.

A **forum** allows nonmembers to add their opinions to the group's deliberations before the group makes a decision. This approach is commonly used by public agencies to encourage the participation of citizens in the decisions that affect them.

◆ STAGES IN PROBLEM-SOLVING

Groups may have the *potential* to solve problems effectively, but they don't always live up to this promise. What makes some groups succeed and others fail? Researchers have spent much of the twentieth century asking this question. Two useful answers have emerged from their work.

Rational Problem-Solving Approaches

Research shows that, to a great degree, a group's effectiveness is determined by whether or not it approaches the problem rationally and systematically. Just as a poor blueprint or a shaky foundation can weaken a house, groups can fail by skipping one or more of the necessary steps in solving a problem.

As early as 1910, John Dewey introduced his famous "reflective thinking" method as a systematic method for solving problems.[5] Since then, other experts have suggested modifications of Dewey's approach. Some emphasize answering key questions whereas others seek "ideal solutions" that meet the needs of all members. Research comparing various methods has clearly shown that, although no single approach is best for all situations, *some* structured procedure produces better results than "no pattern" discussions.[6]

Solving Problems in Groups

The following problem-solving model contains the elements common to most structured approaches developed in the last 80 years:

1. Identify the problem
   a. What are the group's goals?
   b. What are individual members' goals?
2. Analyze the problem
   a. Word the problem as a probative question
   b. Gather relevant information
   c. Identify impelling and restraining forces
3. Develop alternative solutions
   a. Avoid criticism at this stage
   b. Encourage "freewheeling" ideas
   c. Develop a large number of ideas
   d. Combine two or more individual ideas
4. Evaluate the solutions by asking which solution
   a. Will best produce the desired changes
   b. Is most achievable
   c. Contains the fewest serious disadvantages
5. Implement the plan
   a. Identify specific tasks
   b. Determine necessary resources
   c. Define individual responsibilities
   d. Provide for emergencies
6. Follow up on the solution
   a. Meet to evaluate progress
   b. Revise approach as necessary

IDENTIFY THE PROBLEM   Sometimes a group's problem is easy to identify. The crew of a sinking ship, for example, doesn't need to conduct a discussion to understand that its goal is to avoid drowning or being eaten by a large fish.

There are many times, however, when the problems facing a group aren't so clear. As an example, think of an athletic team stuck deep in last place well into the season. At first the problem seems obvious: an inability to win any games. But a closer look at the situation might show that there are other unmet goals—and thus other problems. For instance, individual members may have goals that aren't tied directly to winning: making friends, receiving acknowledgment as good athletes . . . not to mention the simple goal of having fun—of playing in the recreational sense of the word. You can probably see that if the coach or team members took a simplistic view of the situation, looking only at the team's win-lose record, analyzing player errors, training methods, and so on, some important problems would probably go overlooked. In this situation, the team's performance could probably be best improved by working on the basic problems—the frustration of the players about having their personal needs met. What's the moral here? That *the way to start understanding a group's problem is to identify the concerns of each member.*

What about groups that don't have problems? Several friends planning a surprise birthday party or a family deciding where to go for its vacation don't seem to be in the dire straits of a losing athletic team: They simply want to have fun. In cases like these, it may be helpful to substitute the word *challenge* for the more gloomy term *problem*. However we express it, the same principle applies to all task-oriented groups: The best place to start work is to identify what each member seeks as a result of belonging to the group.

ANALYZE THE PROBLEM   Once you have identified the general nature of the challenge facing the group, you are ready to look at the problem in more detail. There are several steps you can follow to accomplish this important job.

Word the Problem as a Probative Question[7]   If you have ever seen a formal debate, you know that the issue under discussion is worded as a proposition: "The United States should reduce its foreign aid expenditures," for example. Many problem-solving groups define their task in much the same way. "We ought to spend our vacation in the mountains," suggests one family member. The problem with phrasing problems as propositions is that such wording invites people to take sides. Though this approach is fine for formal debates (which are contests rather like football or card games), premature side-taking creates unnecessary conflict in most problem-solving groups.

A far better approach is to state the problem as a question. Note that this should be a **probative question**—an open one that encourages exploratory thinking. Asking, "Should we vacation in the mountains or at the beach?" still forces members to choose sides. A far better approach involves asking a question to help define the general goals that came out during the problem-identification stage: "What do we want our vacation to accomplish?" (that is, "relaxation," "adventure," "low cost," and so on).

Notice that this question is truly exploratory. It encourages the family members to work cooperatively, not forcing them to make a choice and then defend it. This absence of an either-or situation boosts the odds that members will listen openly to one another rather than listening selectively in defense of their own positions. There is even a chance that the cooperative, exploratory climate that comes from wording the question probatively will help the family

"B.C." reprinted by permission of Johnny Hart and Creators Syndicate.

arrive at consensus about where to vacation, eliminating the need to discuss the matter any further.

Gather Relevant Information   Groups often need to know important facts before they can make decisions or even understand the problem. We remember one group of students who determined to do well on a class presentation. One of their goals, then, was "to get an A grade." They knew that, to do so, they would have to present a topic that interested both the instructor and the students in the audience. Their first job, then, was to do a bit of background research to find out what subjects would be well received. They interviewed the instructor, asking what topics had been successes and failures in previous semesters. They tested some possible subjects on a few classmates and noted their reactions. From this research they were able to modify their original probative question—"How can we choose and develop a topic that will earn us an A grade?"—into a more specific one—"How can we choose and develop a topic that contains humor, action, and lots of information (to demonstrate our research skills to the instructor) and that contains practical information that will either improve the audience's social life, academic standing, or financial condition?"

Identify Impelling and Restraining Forces   Once members understand what they are seeking, the next step is to see what forces stand between the group and its goals. One useful tool for this approach is the **force field analysis**—a list of the forces that help and hinder the group.[8] By returning to our earlier example of the troubled team, we can see how the force field operates. Suppose the group defined its problem-question as "How can we (a) have more fun and (b) grow closer as friends?"

One restraining force in area (a) was clearly the team's losing record. But, more interestingly, discussion revealed that another damper on enjoyment came from the coach's obsession with winning and his infectiously gloomy behavior when the team failed. The main blocking force in area (b) proved to be the lack of socializing between team members in nongame situations. The helping forces in the first area included the sense of humor possessed by several members and the confession by most players that winning wasn't nearly as important to them as everyone had suspected. The helping force in the area of friendship was the desire of all team members to become better friends. In addition, the fact that members shared many interests was an important plus.

It's important to realize that most problems have many impelling and constraining forces, all of which need to be identified during this stage. This may call for another round of research. Once the force field is laid out, the group is ready to move on to the next step—namely, deciding how to strengthen the impelling forces and weaken the constraining ones.

DEVELOP ALTERNATIVE SOLUTIONS   Once the group has set up a list of criteria for success, its next job is to consider a number of ways to reach its

Communication in Groups

"Frank and Ernest" reprinted by permission of NEA, Inc.

goal. During this development phase, creativity is essential. The goal is to generate a number of approaches, not to choose just one. The biggest danger here is the tendency of members to defend their own idea and criticize others'. This kind of behavior leads to two problems. First, evaluative criticism almost guarantees a defensive reaction from members whose ideas have been attacked. A second consequence is the stifling of creativity. People who have just heard an idea rebuked—however politely—will find it hard even to think of more alternatives, let alone share them openly and risk possible criticism.

Probably the best-known method for encouraging creativity and avoiding the dangers just described is the process of **brainstorming.**[9] There are four important rules connected with this approach:

1. **Criticism Is Forbidden.** As we have already said, nothing will stop the flow of ideas more quickly than negative evaluation.
2. **"Freewheeling" Is Encouraged.** Sometimes even the most outlandish ideas prove workable, and even an impractical suggestion might trigger a workable idea.
3. **Quantity Is Sought.** The more ideas generated, the better the chance of coming up with a good one.
4. **Combination and Improvement Are Desirable.** Members are encouraged to "piggyback," by modifying ideas already suggested, and to combine previous suggestions.

EVALUATE POSSIBLE SOLUTIONS   Once it has listed possible solutions, the group can evaluate the usefulness of each. One good way of identifying the most workable solutions is to ask three questions.[10]

1. **Will This Proposal Produce the Desired Changes?** One way to find out is to see whether it successfully overcomes the restraining forces in your force field analysis.
2. **Can the Proposal Be Implemented by the Group?** Can the members strengthen impelling forces and weaken constraining ones? Can they influence others to do so? If not, the plan isn't a good one.
3. **Does the Proposal Contain Any Serious Disadvantages?** Sometimes the cost of achieving a goal is too great. For example, one way to

Solving Problems in Groups

◆ **Creativity Killers in Group Discussion**

Nothing squelches creativity like criticism. Although evaluating ideas is an important part of problem-solving, judging suggestions too early can discourage members from sharing potentially valuable ideas. Here is a list of creativity-stopping statements that people should avoid making in the development phase of group work.

"That's ridiculous."

"It'll never work."

"You're wrong."

"What a crazy idea!"

"We tried it before and it didn't work."

"It's too expensive."

"There's no point in talking about it."

"It's never been done like that."

"We could look like fools."

"It's too big a job."

"We could never do that."

"It's too risky."

"You don't know what you're talking about."

---

raise money for a group is to rob a bank. Although this plan might be workable, it raises more problems than it solves.

IMPLEMENT THE PLAN   Everyone who makes New Year's resolutions knows the difference between making a decision and carrying it out. There are several important steps in developing and implementing a plan of action.[11]

Identify Specific Tasks to be Accomplished   What needs to be done? Even a relatively simple job usually involves several steps. Now is the time to anticipate all the tasks facing the group. Remember everything now, and you will avoid a last-minute rush later.

Determine Necessary Resources   Identify the equipment, material, and other resources the group will need in order to get the job done.

Define Individual Responsibilities   Who will do what? Do all members know their jobs? The safest plan here is to put everyone's duties in writing, including due date. This might sound compulsive, but experience shows that it increases the chance of having jobs done on time.

Provide for Emergencies   Murphy's Law states, "Whatever can go wrong, will." Anyone experienced in group work knows the truth of this statement. People forget or welsh on their obligations, get sick, or quit. Machinery breaks down. (One corollary of Murphy's Law is "the copying machine will be out of order whenever it's most needed.") Whenever possible, you ought to develop contingency plans to cover foreseeable problems. Probably the single best suggestion we can give here is to plan on having all work done well ahead of the deadline, knowing that, even with last minute problems, your time cushion will allow you to finish on time.

FOLLOW UP ON THE SOLUTION   Even the best plans usually require some modifications once they're put into practice. You can improve the group's effectiveness and minimize disappointment by following two steps.

Meet Periodically to Evaluate Progress   Follow-up meetings should be part of virtually every good plan. The best time to schedule these meetings is as you put the group's plan to work. At that time, a good leader or member will suggest: "Let's get together in a week (or a few days or a month, depending on the nature of the task). We can see how things are going and take care of any problems."

Revise the Group's Approach as Necessary   These follow-up meetings will often go beyond simply congratulating everyone for coming up with a good solution. Problems are bound to arise, and these periodic meetings, in which the key players are present, are the place to solve them.

Although these steps provide a useful outline for solving problems, they are most valuable as a general set of guidelines and not as a precise formula that every group should follow. As Table 9–1 suggests, certain parts of the model may need emphasis depending on the nature of the specific problem; the general approach will give virtually any group a useful way to consider and solve a problem.

TABLE 9–1   Adapting Problem-Solving Methods to Special Circumstances

CHARACTERISTIC	EMPHASIZE
Members have strong feelings about the problem.	Consider allowing a period of emotional ventilation before systematic problem-solving.
Task difficulty is high.	Follow structure of problem-solving method carefully.
Many possible solutions.	Emphasize brainstorming.
High level of member acceptance required.	Carefully define needs of all members, and seek solutions that satisfy all needs.
High level of technical quality required.	Emphasize evaluation of ideas; consider inviting outside experts.

Adapted from John Brilhart, *Effective Group Discussion,* 5th ed. (Dubuque, Iowa: W. C. Brown, 1986), p. 310.

Solving Problems in Groups

Despite its advantages the rational, systematic problem-solving approach isn't perfect. It suffers from several drawbacks.[12] First, it is artificial. You will rarely find a group—even one that is trained in communication skills—willing to follow the steps in an orderly, sequential way. Some members are likely to balk at doing the necessary research. At least one member is almost certain to push solutions before the problem has been defined. Likewise, pure brainstorming sessions are rare: The tendency to criticize ideas is just too strong to squelch in most groups. Rational problem-solving may look terrific in principle, but it is often ignored in practice.

A second flaw in the rational approach is that it requires complete knowledge and anticipation of the consequences that will follow from each choice—an impossible feat. For example, a group planning an outdoor fund-raising concert on a Saturday in September might thoroughly research the talent, the site, and the potential size of the audience but fail to discover that another, more popular program is scheduled for the same date. Or even worse, the band might cancel or it might rain. Even the most systematic plans don't always work.

Finally, a truly rational approach requires a choice from all the possible alternatives. In reality, even creative groups only consider a few options. The old computer saying, "Garbage in, garbage out" applies here: If the group doesn't possess creative talent, a rational and systematic approach to solving problems won't do much good.

Despite these drawbacks, the rational approach does increase the odds that a group can solve problems successfully. Following the guidelines—even imperfectly—will help members analyze the problem, come up with solutions, and carry them out better than they could probably do without a plan.

Developmental Stages in Problem-Solving Groups

When it comes to solving problems in groups, research shows that the shortest distance to a solution isn't always a straight line. Communication scholar Aubrey Fisher analyzed tape recordings of problem-solving groups and discovered that successful groups seem to follow a four-stage process when arriving at a decision.[13] As you read about his findings, visualize how they apply to problem-solving groups in your experience.

In the **orientation stage,** members approach the problem and one another tentatively. In some groups people may not know one another well, and even in ones where they are well acquainted they may not know one another's position on the issue at hand. For these reasons, people are reluctant to take a stand during the orientation phase. Rather than stating their own position clearly and unambiguously, they test out possible ideas cautiously and rather politely. There is little disagreement. This cautiousness doesn't mean that members agree with one another; rather, they are sizing up the situation before asserting themselves. The orientation stage can be viewed as a calm before the storm.

Once members understand the problem and become acquainted, a successful group enters the **conflict stage.** During this phase, members take strong positions and defend them against those who oppose their viewpoint.

Coalitions are likely to form, and the discussion may become polarized. The conflict needn't be personal: It can focus on the issues at hand while preserving the members' respect for one another. Even when the climate does grow contentious, conflict seems to be a necessary stage in group development. The give and take of discussion tests the quality of ideas, and weaker ones may suffer a well-deserved death here.

After a period of conflict, effective groups move to an **emergence stage.** One idea might emerge as the best one, or the group might combine the best parts of several plans into a new solution. As they approach consensus, members back off from their dogmatic positions. Statements become more tentative again: "I guess that's a pretty good idea," "I can see why you think that way."

Finally, an effective group reaches the **reinforcement stage.** At this point members not only accept the group's decision; they endorse it. Whereas participants used evidence to back up differing positions in the conflict state, now they find evidence that will support the decision. Even if members disagree with the outcome, they do not voice their concerns. There is an unspoken drive toward consensus and harmony.

Ongoing groups can expect to move through this four-step process with each new issue, so that their interaction takes on a cyclic pattern (see Figure 9–1). In fact, a group that deals with several issues at once might find itself in a different stage for each problem.

What is the significance of Fisher's findings? They tell us that, like children growing toward adulthood, groups can expect to pass through phases.

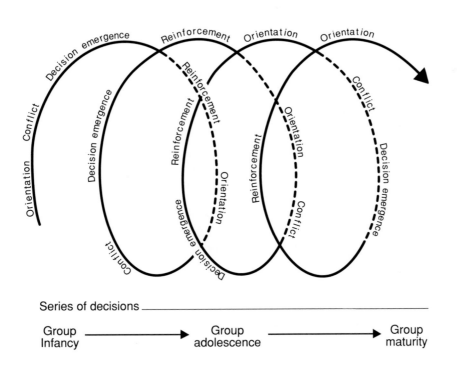

FIGURE 9–1
Cyclical stages in an ongoing problem-solving group. From John K. Brilhart and Gloria J. Galanes, *Effective Group Discussion*, 6th ed. (Dubuque, Iowa: W. C. Brown, 1989), p. 167.

Series of decisions

Group Infancy → Group adolescence → Group maturity

Solving Problems in Groups

Knowing that these phases are natural and predictable can be reassuring. It can help curb your impatience when the group is feeling its way through an orientation stage. It can also help you feel less threatened when the inevitable and necessary conflicts take place. Understanding the nature of emergence and reinforcement can help you know when it is time to stop arguing and seek consensus.

◆ MAINTAINING POSITIVE RELATIONSHIPS

The task-related advice in the preceding pages will be little help if the members of a group don't get along. We therefore need to look at some ways to maintain good relationships among members. Many of the principles described earlier in this book apply here. Because these principles are so important, we will review them here.

Basic Skills

Probably the most important ingredient in good personal relationships is mutual respect, and the best way to demonstrate respect for the other person is to *listen* carefully. A more natural tendency, of course, is to assume you understand the other members' positions and to interrupt or ignore them. Even if you are right, however, these reactions can create a residue of ill feelings. On the other hand, careful listening can at least improve the communication climate . . . and it may even teach you something.

Groups are bound to disagree sooner or later. When they do, the win-win problem-solving methods outlined in Chapter 6 boost the odds of solving the immediate issue in the most constructive way. As you read in Chapter 8, taking votes and letting the majority rule can often leave a sizable minority whose unhappiness can haunt the group's future work. Consensus is harder to reach in the short term but far more beneficial in the long run.

Building Cohesiveness

Cohesiveness can be defined as the totality of forces that cause members to feel themselves part of a group and make them want to remain in that group. You might think of cohesiveness as the glue that bonds individuals together, giving them a collective sense of identity.

Highly cohesive groups communicate differently than less cohesive ones. Members spend more time interacting, and there are more expressions of positive feelings for one another. They report more satisfaction with the group and its work. In addition, cohesive groups have greater control over the behavior of their members.[14] With characteristics like these, it's no surprise that highly cohesive groups have the potential to be productive. But cohesiveness is no guarantee of success: If the group is united in supporting *unproductive* norms, they will feel close but won't get the job done. For example, consider a group of employees who have a boss they think is incompetent and unfair.

They might grow quite cohesive in their opposition to the perceived tyranny, spending hours after (or during) work swapping complaints. They might even organize protests, work slowdowns, grievances to their union, or mass resignations. All these responses would boost cohesiveness, but they would not necessarily make the company more successful nor help the employees.

The goal, then, is to boost cohesiveness in a way that also helps get the job done. There are eight factors that can bring about these goals.[15]

> Recall two groups to which you have belonged: one with a low level of cohesiveness and one highly cohesive one. Use the factors listed on pages 261–262 to analyze what contributed to the level of commitment of each group. How could matters be improved in the low-cohesiveness group?

SHARED OR COMPATIBLE GOALS   People draw closer when they share a similar aim or when their goals can be mutually satisfied. For example, members of a conservation group might have little in common until a part of the countryside they all value is threatened by development. Some members might value the land because of its beauty; others, because it provides a place to hunt or fish; and still others, because the nearby scenery increases the value of their property; but as long as their goals are compatible, this collection of individuals will find that a bond exists that draws them together.

PROGRESS TOWARD THESE GOALS   While a group is making progress, members feel highly cohesive; when progress stops, cohesiveness decreases. All other things being equal, members of an athletic team feel closest when the team is winning. During extended losing streaks, it is likely that players will feel less positive about the team and less willing to identify themselves as members of the group.

SHARED NORMS AND VALUES   Although successful groups will tolerate and even thrive on some differences in members' attitudes and behavior, wide variation in the group's definition of what actions or beliefs are proper will reduce cohesiveness. If enough members hold different ideas of what behavior is acceptable, the group is likely to break up. Disagreements over values or norms can fall into many areas, such as humor, finance, degree of candor, and proportion of time allotted to work and play.

LACK OF PERCEIVED THREAT BETWEEN MEMBERS   Cohesive group members see no threat to their status, dignity, and material or emotional well-being. When such interpersonal threats do occur, they can be very destructive. Often competition arises within groups, and as a result members feel threatened. Sometimes there is a struggle over who will be nominal leader. At other times, members view others as wanting to take over a functional role (problem solver, information giver, and so on), either through competition or criticism. Sometimes the threat is real, and sometimes it's only imagined, but in

Solving Problems in Groups

either case the group must neutralize it or face the consequences of reduced cohesiveness.

INTERDEPENDENCE OF MEMBERS   Groups become cohesive when their needs can be satisfied only with the help of other members. When a job can be done just as well by one person alone, the need for membership decreases. This factor explains the reason for food cooperatives, neighborhood yard sales, and community political campaigns. All these activities enable the participants to reach their goal more successfully than if they acted alone.

THREAT FROM OUTSIDE THE GROUP   When members perceive a threat to the group's existence or image (groups have self-concepts, just as individuals do), they grow closer together. Almost everyone knows of a family whose members seem to fight constantly among themselves—until an outsider criticizes one of them. At this point, the internal bickering stops, and for the moment the group unites against its common enemy. The same principle works on a larger scale when nations often bind up their internal differences in the face of external aggression.

MUTUAL PERCEIVED ATTRACTIVENESS AND FRIENDSHIP   The factor of mutual attraction and friendship is somewhat circular because friendship and mutual attraction often are a result of the points just listed, yet groups often do become close simply because members like each other.

SHARED GROUP EXPERIENCES   When members have been through some unusual or trying experience, they draw together. This explains why soldiers who have been in combat together often feel close and stay in touch for years after; it also accounts for the ordeal of fraternity pledging and other initiations. Many societies have rituals that all members share, thus increasing the group's cohesiveness.

It's important to realize that the eight factors just described interact with one another, often in contradictory ways. For instance, members of many groups are good friends who have been through thick and thin together (cohesiveness builders), but they find themselves less dependent on each other than before and now struggle over playing certain roles. In cases like this, cohesiveness can be figured as the net sum of all attracting and dividing forces.

Encouraging Participation

In most groups, there is an unequal amount of participation from member to member. Though it probably isn't desirable to have every person speak equally on every subject, neither is it good to have one or more members keep almost totally quiet. There are two reasons why: First, the group could probably benefit from hearing the additional information; second, having wallflowers in a group can become nerve-racking both for the quiet ones themselves and for the contributors. How, then, can participation be encouraged?

KEEP THE GROUP SMALL   Common sense suggests that as a group grows larger, there is less time for each member to speak. But, just as important, the imbalance between talkers and nontalkers grows with membership.[16] In small groups of three or four members, participation is roughly equal; but once the size increases to between five and eight, there's a dramatic gap between the contributions of members. Therefore, one simple way to increase participation is to keep the group small whenever the task permits.

SOLICIT CONTRIBUTIONS FROM QUIET MEMBERS   Sometimes contributions from quiet members can be obtained by simply asking for a member's input, ideally using open questions to guarantee a complete response: "What can you suggest to improve that idea, Gus?" In other cases, the nominal leader can assign quiet members certain tasks that will ensure their participation, such as reporting to the group on research.

REINFORCE CONTRIBUTIONS   When a quiet member does make a contribution, it is especially important for others in the group to acknowledge it. Acknowledgment can be direct: "Thanks for suggesting that, Lisa." Another way to reinforce a comment is to refer to it later in the discussion: "That ties in with what Will said a while ago about . . . "

Think of one low-level participator in a group you have observed. Using the guidelines on pages 263–264, suggest how the quiet member's contributions could be increased.

Of course, there's a danger of becoming a phony, being overly complimentary. Gushing undeserved praise at shy people will probably discourage them

Solving Problems in Groups

from contributing again, so be sure to keep your reinforcements sincere and not effusive.

When we first read over these suggestions for encouraging participation, they sounded so obvious that we almost tossed them in the trash basket. But before doing so, we took a look at groups we belong to and realized that following these three simple steps really does draw out quiet speakers. So we encourage you not to discount these obvious but effective suggestions.

◆ LEADERSHIP IN GROUPS

For most of us, leadership ranks not far below motherhood in the hierarchy of values. "What are you, a leader or a follower?" we're asked, and we know which position is the better one. On the job, for instance, leadership means promotion. Even in the earliest grades of school, we knew who the leaders were, and we admired them. What is leadership all about?

Leadership and Leaders: A Matter of Power

Most people use the terms *leader* and *leadership* interchangeably when, in fact, there is a big difference between these two concepts. Some leaders don't exert leadership, and much leadership doesn't come from leaders . . . or at least people we identify by that term. Let us explain.

We can begin by defining **leadership** as *the ability to influence the behavior of others in a group.* And how are people influenced? By some sort of power. Power comes in several forms.[17]

LEGITIMATE POWER   The ability to influence others through legitimate power comes from the position one holds—supervisor, parent, professor, and so on. In many situations, this sort of power comes from the title alone: We follow the directions of police officers in traffic because we figure they know what they're doing. At other times, however, a person's title isn't the prime motivation.

COERCIVE POWER   Sometimes we do what the boss tells us, not out of any respect for the wisdom of the decision but because the consequences of not obeying would be unpleasant. Economic hardship, social disapproval, unpleasant work, even physical punishment . . . all are coercive forces that can shape behavior.

REWARD POWER   The ability to reward is the reverse side of coercive power. Like punishments, rewards can be social, material, or physical.

EXPERT POWER   Sometimes we are influenced by people because of what they know or can do. For example, when a medical emergency occurs, most group members would gladly let a doctor, nurse, or paramedic call the shots (no pun intended) because of that person's obvious knowledge.

"I was just going to say 'Well, I don't make the rules.' But, of course, I do make the rules."
Drawing by Ziegler; © 1988 The New Yorker Magazine, Inc.

REFERENT POWER   We might regard referent power as social power because we are talking about the influence that comes from the members' respect, attraction, or liking for someone in the group.

INFORMATION POWER   Sometimes a member's knowledge of otherwise obscure facts can make a big difference in how the group operates. If you're working on a group project for one of your classes, the experiences of a fellow student who has taken another class from your instructor can give you important clues about how to approach the topic. This example shows the difference between expert power ("I can use an on-line computer data base to search for that information") and information power ("This professor is a fanatic about spelling and formatting mistakes"). Both technical expertise and insider information are important, but they can be possessed by different members.

Logic suggests that if leadership is the power to influence others, then the **leader** is someone who exerts that influence. But a look at the discussion you have just read shows that matters aren't this simple. For instance, there are some times when the **nominal leader**—the person who is designated by title to direct the group's functioning—really has very little influence on a group. We remember those happy days of junior high school when a certain substitute teacher took control (and we use that term loosely) of one civics class. She may have reigned, but she certainly didn't rule. Instead, a band of rowdy

Solving Problems in
Groups

students, headed by two ringleaders with great referent power, ran the show: telling jokes, falling out of chairs, and finally escaping from the room through open windows. In the end, the dean's coercive power was the only way to put down the rebellion.

The lesson in this story of teenage mayhem is that some nominal leaders don't really lead and that some superficially powerless members are, in fact, the real movers and shakers of the group. One way to analyze the influence of a nominal leader is to identify that person's true power in the group by applying the six dimensions we just discussed. If the nominal leader scores high in most of these categories, we can say that he or she is a "strong leader." If the power is spread throughout the group, however, that leader's influence isn't as great.

Don't conclude from this that highly visible, powerful, centralized leadership is the best way to get a job done. There are many cases in which shared leadership is very effective. One mark of many effective leaders is their ability to enlist subtly the powerful support—by reward, coercive, expert, and referent methods—of other members to back a policy. Even leaders who want to take a highly influential and visible role can't do everything. Recall our discussion of functional roles in Chapter 8, and you'll realize that no single person can possibly perform every task necessary to have the group achieve its goal. We will have more to say about the pros and cons of directive, centralized leadership in a few pages, when we discuss autocratic and democratic styles of designated leaders.

> Think of two effective leaders you have known. How would you describe the style of each one: autocratic, democratic, or laissez-faire? Task- or relationship-oriented? Imagine that the two leaders were transferred, so that each one was directing the other's group. Would the same approach work equally well in each situation? Why or why not?

What Makes Leaders Effective?

Because the position of nominal leader is such an important one in our society, the next few pages will describe the factors that contribute to leader effectiveness.

TRAIT ANALYSIS   Over 2,000 years ago Aristotle proclaimed, "From the hour of their birth some are marked out for subjugation, and others for command."[18] This is a radical expression of the "great man" (or "great woman") view of leadership. Social scientists began their studies of leader effectiveness by conducting literally hundreds of studies that compared leaders with nonleaders. The results of all this research were mixed. Yet a number of distinguishing characteristics did emerge in several categories:[19]

Physical Appearance   As a rule, leaders tend to be slightly taller, heavier, and physically more attractive than others. They also seem to possess greater athletic ability and stamina.

Sociability   The category of sociability involves behaviors related to maintaining personal relationships within the group. For example, leaders talk more often and more fluently and are regarded as more popular, cooperative, and socially skillful.

Goal Facilitation   Leaders have skills that help groups perform their tasks. They are somewhat more intelligent, possess more task-relevant information, and are more dependable than other members.

Desire for Leadership   Leaders *want* that role and act in ways that will help them get it. They exercise initiative, are persistent, and express their beliefs assertively.

Despite these general findings, the research on **trait theories of leadership** is of only limited practical value: Later research has shown that many other factors are important in determining leader success, and not everyone who possesses these traits becomes a leader. We'll now examine this body of knowledge.

LEADERSHIP STYLE   Some leaders have an **authoritarian leadership style,** using **legitimate, coercive,** and **reward power** to dictate what will happen in a group. Others use a more **democratic leadership style,** inviting other members to share in decision making. In a third style, called the **laissez-faire leadership style,** the leader gives up the power to dictate, transforming the group into a leaderless collection of equals. Early research suggested that the democratic style produced the highest-quality results,[20] but later experiments showed that matters weren't so simple. For instance, groups with autocratic leaders proved more productive under stressful conditions, but democratically led groups did better when the situation was nonstressful.[21]

Some researchers have focused on leadership style from a different perspective. Robert R. Blake and Jane S. Mouton developed an approach based on the relationship between the designated leader's concern with the task and with the relationships among members.[22] Their **Managerial Grid**® consists of a two-dimensional model pictured in Figure 9–2. The horizontal axis measures the leader's concern for production. This involves a focus on accomplishing the organizational task, with efficiency being the main concern. The vertical axis measures the leader's concern for people's feelings and ideas. Blake and Mouton suggest that the most effective leader is the one who adopts a 9,9 style—showing high concern for both task and relationships.

CONTEMPORARY APPROACHES   Most contemporary scholars are convinced that the best style of leadership varies from one set of circumstances to another. In an effort to pin down what approach works best in a given type of situation, psychologist Fred Fiedler attempted to find out when a task-oriented approach was most effective and when a more relationship-oriented style produced the best results.[23] From his research, Fiedler developed a **situa-**

Solving Problems in Groups

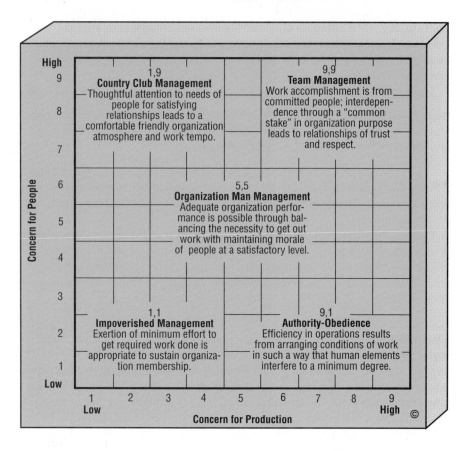

FIGURE 9–2

Source: Blake, Robert R., and Mouton, Jane Srygley. *The Managerial Grid III: The Key to Leadership Excellence.* Houston: Gulf Publishing Company, Copyright © 1985, page 12. Reproduced by permission.

Communication in Groups

tional theory of **leadership.** Although the complete theory is too complex to describe here, its general conclusion is that a leader's style should change with the circumstances. A task-oriented approach works best when conditions are either highly favorable (good leader-member relations, strong leader power, and clear task structure) or highly unfavorable (poor leader-member relations, weak leader power, and an ambiguous task) whereas a more relationship-oriented style is appropriate in moderately favorable or moderately unfavorable conditions.

More recently, Paul Hersey and Kenneth Blanchard have suggested that a leader's focus on task or relational issues should vary according to the maturity of the group being led (see Figure 9–3).[24] Maturity isn't a function of age in the life-cycle model; rather, it involves the members' level of motivation, willingness to take responsibility, and the amount of knowledge and experience they have in a given situation.[25] For example, a new, inexperienced group would need more task-related direction, while a more experienced one might require more social support and less instruction about how to do the job. A well seasoned team could probably handle the job well without much supervision at all. Since a group's maturity level changes from one job to another, Hersey and Blanchard suggest that the best way to lead should vary as well.

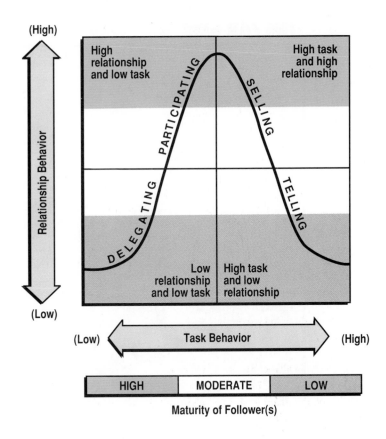

FIGURE 9–3
Hersey and Blanchard's leadership model. (Reprinted by permission of Paul Hersey, Center for Leadership Studies. All rights reserved.)

◆ DANGERS IN GROUP DISCUSSION

Even groups with the best of intentions often find themselves unable to reach satisfying decisions. At other times, they make decisions that later prove to be wrong. Though there's no foolproof method of guaranteeing high-quality group work, there are several dangers to avoid.

Absence of Critical Information

Many groups are so anxious to make decisions that they do so without having important information. We know of one group that scheduled a fund-raising party without enough forethought and later found that their event had to compete with a championship football game. A bit of checking could have prevented much disappointment and earned the group more sorely needed funds.

Domination by a Minority

We have already said that participation in most groups is unequal. Besides leaving quieter members feeling hurt and unenthusiastic, domination by the

Solving Problems in Groups

THE FAR SIDE — By GARY LARSON

"As if we all knew where we're going."

vocal few can reduce a group's ability to solve a problem effectively. Research shows that the proposal receiving the largest number of favorable comments is usually the one chosen even if it isn't the best one.[26] Furthermore, ideas of high-status members (who aren't always talkers) are given more consideration than those of lower-status people.[27] The moral to this story? Don't assume that quantity of speech or the status of the speaker automatically defines the quality of an idea: Instead, seek out and seriously consider the ideas of quieter members.

Pressure to Conform

There's a strong tendency for group members to go along with the crowd, which often results in bad decisions. A classic study by Solomon Asch illustrated this point.[28] College students were shown three lines of different lengths and asked to identify which of them matched with a fourth line. Although the correct answer was obvious, the experiment was a setup: Asch had instructed all but one member of the experimental groups to vote for the wrong line. As a result, fully one-third of the uninformed subjects ignored their own good judgment and voted with the majority. If simple tasks like this one generate such conformity, it is easy to see that following the (sometimes mistaken) crowd is even more likely in the much more complex and ambiguous

◆ When we look a little closer, we see an inconsistency in the way our society seems to feel about conformity (team playing) and nonconformity (deviance). For example, one of the great best-sellers of the 1950s was a book by John F. Kennedy called *Profiles in Courage,* wherein the author praised several politicians for their courage in resisting great pressure and refusing to conform. To put it another way, Kennedy was praising people who refused to be good team players, people who refused to vote or act as their parties or constituents expected them to. Although their actions earned Kennedy's praise long after the deeds were done, the immediate reactions of their colleagues were generally far from positive. The nonconformist may be praised by historians or idolized in films or literature long after the fact of his nonconformity, but he's usually not held in high esteem, at the time, by those people to whose demands he refuses to conform.

Elliot Aronson
The Social Animal

tasks that most groups face. It's interesting to note that pressures toward conformity are strongest when group members have low confidence in their ability to solve a problem and are highly attracted to the group and when the conforming majority is relatively large.[29]

Premature Decision Making

Probably because uncertainty is not a happy state, many groups become emotionally attached to an alternative early in the decision-making process.[30] Such attachment leads members to ignore other ideas that might prove to be better. This tendency explains why the brainstorming process described on page 255 should be considered without criticism during early stages of discussion.

Confusing Disagreement with Dislike

Many group members see criticism of their ideas as a personal attack. This often leads them either to withdraw from the discussion or to lash back at the personality or proposal of the original critic. Hard as it sometimes is, it's important to distinguish disagreement from dislike.[31]

◆ SUMMARY

Despite the bad reputation of groups in some quarters, research shows that they are often the most effective setting for problem-solving. They command greater resources, both quantitatively and qualitatively, than either single individuals or a collection of persons working in isolation; their work can result in greater accuracy; and the participative nature of the solutions they produce generates greater commitment from members.

Solving Problems in Groups

Groups aren't always the best forum for solving problems. They should be used when the problem is beyond the capacity of one person to solve, when tasks are interdependent, when there is more than one desired solution or decision, and when the agreement of all members is essential.

Groups use a wide variety of discussion formats when solving problems. Some use parliamentary procedure to govern decision-making procedures. Others use moderated panel discussions, symposia, or forums. The best format depends on the nature of the problem and the characteristics of the group.

Groups stand the best chance of developing effective solutions to problems if they begin their work by identifying the problem, avoiding the mistake of failing to recognize hidden needs of individual members. Their next step is to analyze the problem, including identification of forces both favoring and blocking progress. Only at this point should the group begin to develop possible solutions, taking care not to stifle creativity by evaluating any of them prematurely. During the implementation phase of the solution, the group should monitor the situation carefully and make any necessary changes in its plan.

Most groups can expect to move through several stages as they solve a problem. The first of these stages is orientation, during which the members sound each other out. The conflict stage is characterized by partisanship and open debate over the merits of contending ideas. In the emergence stage, the group begins to move toward choosing a single solution. In the reinforcement stage members endorse the group's decision.

Groups that pay attention only to the task dimension of their interaction risk strains in the relationships among members. Many of these interpersonal problems can be avoided by using the skills described in Chapter 6 as well as by following the guidelines in this chapter for building group cohesiveness and encouraging participation.

Many naïve observers of groups confuse the concepts of leader and leadership. We defined leadership as the ability to influence the behavior of other members through the use of one or more types of power—legitimate, coercive, reward, expert, or referent. We saw that many nominal leaders share their power with other members. Leadership has been examined from many perspectives—trait analysis, leadership style, and situational variables.

◆ NOTES

1. Cal Downs, David M. Berg, and Wil A. Linkugel, *The Organizational Communicator* (New York: Harper & Row, 1977), p. 127.
2. Marvin E. Shaw, *Group Dynamics: The Psychology of Small Group Behavior,* 3d ed. (New York: McGraw-Hill, 1981), pp. 61–64.
3. Ibid., p. 391.
4. R. B. Adler, *Communicating at Work: Principles and Practices for Business and the Professions,* 3d ed. (New York: Random House, 1989), pp. 219–221.
5. John Dewey, *How We Think* (New York: Heath, 1910).
6. See R. Y. Hirokawa, "Group Communication and Problem-Solving Effectiveness: An Investigation of Group Phases," *Human Communication Research* 9

(1983): 291–305; Edward R. Marby and Richard E. Barnes, *The Dynamics of Small Group Communication* (Englewood Cliffs, N.J.: Prentice-Hall, 1980), p. 78; Norman R. F. Maier and Robert A. Maier, "An Experimental Test of the Effects of 'Developmental' vs. 'Free' Discussions on the Quality of Group Decisions," *Journal of Applied Psychology* 41 (1957): 320–323; and Ovid L. Bayless, "An Alternative Model for Problem-Solving Discussion," *Journal of Communication* 17 (1967): 188–197.

7. Adapted from David Potter and Martin P. Andersen, *Discussion in Small Groups: A Guide to Effective Practice* (Belmont, Calif.: Wadsworth, 1976), pp. 20–22.

8. Kurt Lewin, *Field Theory in Social Science* (New York: Harper & Row, 1951), pp. 30–59.

9. Alex Osborn, *Applied Imagination* (New York: Scribner's, 1959).

10. Bobby R. Patton and Kim Giffin, *Problem-Solving Group Interaction* (New York: Harper & Row, 1973), pp. 167–168.

11. Ibid, adapted from pp. 182–185.

12. P. K. Tompkins, *Communication as Action* (Belmont, Calif.: Wadsworth, 1982), p. 147. See also R. M. Dawes, *Rational Choice in an Uncertain World* (San Diego, Calif.: Harcourt Brace Jovanovich, 1988).

13. B. A. Fisher, "Decision Emergence: Phases in Group Decision Making," *Speech Monographs* 37 (1970): 53–66.

14. H. L. Nixon II, *The Small Group* (Englewood Cliffs, N.J.: Prentice-Hall, 1979), pp. 74–76.

15. Adapted from Ernest G. Bormann, *Discussion and Group Methods: Theory and Practice,* 2d ed. (New York: Harper & Row, 1975), pp. 141–171.

16. R. F. Bales, F. L. Strodtbeck, T. M. Mills, and M. E. Roseborough, "Channels of Communication in Small Groups," *American Sociological Review* 16 (1951): 461–468.

17. John R. French and Bertram Raven, "The Basis of Social Power," in Dorwin Cartwright and Alvin Zander (eds.), *Group Dynamics* (New York: Harper & Row, 1968), p. 565.

18. Aristotle, *Politics* (New York: Oxford University Press, 1958), Book 7.

19. John F. Cragan and David W. Wright, *Communication in Small Group Discussions: A Case Study Approach* (St. Paul, Minn.: West Publishing, 1980), p. 74.

20. Kurt Lewin, R. Lippitt, and R. K. White, "Patterns of Aggressive Behavior in Experimentally Created Social Climates," *Journal of Social Psychology* 10 (1939): 271–299.

21. L. L. Rosenbaum and W. B. Rosenbaum, "Morale and Productivity Consequences of Group Leadership Style, Stress, and Type of Task," *Journal of Applied Psychology* 55 (1985): 343–358.

22. Robert R. Blake and Jane S. Mouton, *The Managerial Grid III* (Houston: Gulf Publishing, 1964).

23. Fred E. Fiedler, *A Theory of Leadership Effectiveness* (New York: McGraw-Hill, 1967).

24. P. Hersey and K. Blanchard, *Management of Organizational Behavior,* 4th ed. (Englewood Cliffs, N.J.: Prentice-Hall, 1982).

25. P. Hersey and K. Blanchard, "So You Want to Know Your Leadership Style?" *Training and Development Journal* (February 1974): 22–37.

26. L. Richard Hoffman and Norman R. F. Maier, "Valence in the Adoption of Solutions by Problem-Solving Groups: Concept, Method, and Results," *Journal of Abnormal and Social Psychology* 69 (1964): 264–271.

27. E. P. Torrence, "Some Consequences of Power Differences on Decision Making in Permanent and Temporary Three-Man Groups," *Research Studies,* Washington State College 22 (1954): 130–140.

28. Solomon E. Asch, "Effects of Group Pressure upon the Modification and Distortion of Judgments," in H. Guetzkow (ed.), *Groups, Leadership and Men* (Pittsburgh: Carnegie Press, 1951), pp. 177–190.

29. Shaw, op. cit., p. 398.

30. Hoffman and Maier, op. cit.

31. Patton and Giffin, op. cit., p. 158.

10

After reading this chapter, you should understand the following:

1. The frequency and importance of communication in your career.

2. The common types of on-the-job interviews.

3. The characteristics that define interviewing and distinguish it from other types of conversations.

4. The responsibilities of both interviewer and interviewee during the opening, body, and closing stages of an interview.

5. The steps to take as an applicant when preparing for and participating in employment, informational, and performance appraisal interviews.

6. The characteristics of upward, downward, and horizontal communication in formal organizational networks.

7. The characteristics of informal communication networks.

You should be able to do the following:

1. Identify the kinds of on-the-job communication that are important to your career success.

2. Follow the guidelines in this chapter when participating in employment, informational, and performance appraisal interviews.

3. Describe the types of upward, downward, and horizontal communication in an organization and suggest ways each could be improved.

4. Define a personal goal within an organization, choose the best audience to deal with, and select the best channel to deliver your message.

KEY TERMS

communication network
closed question
direct question
downward
  communication
employment interview
factual question
flowchart
formal communication
  network
horizontal
  communication
hypothetical question
indirect question

informal communication
  network
informational interview
interview
opinion question
open question
organization chart
performance appraisal
  interview
primary question
probe
secondary question
upward communication

Communicating on the Job

The amount of time most people spend on the job is staggering. Consider the arithmetic: With time off for vacations and holidays, you will probably work about forty-eight weeks per year. If you assume an eight-hour work day—a conservative estimate in many fields—over a forty-year career you will spend *over 76,000 hours* on the job. Even if you dedicate part of your life to home-making, traveling, or some other pursuit, it is almost certain that sooner or later you will find yourself working in a traditional job.

Even if you never hold a job yourself, you will certainly communicate with people representing organizations: the electric or phone company, school, the Internal Revenue Service, libraries, hospitals, traffic courts, and of course commercial stores. Like it or not, job-related communication is a fact of twentieth-century life.

Many of the skills you have already learned in *Understanding Human Communication* will help you communicate more effectively on the job. The information in Chapters 8 and 9 will help boost teamwork in working groups, as well as making your meetings more productive. The interpersonal skills outlined in Chapter 6 can serve you well in building a positive communication climate at work, as well as improving your negotiating skills. The advice in Chapters 11–15 will prove helpful when you have to give presentations to an audience.

This chapter will introduce more skills that will help you be more successful on the job. We will look at the kind of interviews that will help you get the job you want, as well as those you will use after you are hired. We will examine the kinds of communication networks you will use to communicate in the course of your career. Finally, we will offer a number of guidelines for improving your communication in every part of your working life.

◆ THE IMPORTANCE OF COMMUNICATION ON THE JOB

Communication in the workplace is worth studying for two reasons. First, it is frequent; and second, the quality of communication often determines whether your career will be a success or a failure.

Communication Is Frequent

Whatever the job, people communicate. Research shows that in most jobs people spend more time exchanging messages than in any other activity— between 50 and 90 percent, according to most studies.[1] The amount of time spent communicating increases along with responsibility: First-line managers may spend 60 percent of their working hours communicating. For higher level executives, the figure is even greater—70 to 80 percent or more.

Communication isn't only common in people-oriented jobs like sales or personnel; it is also necessary in fields that seem to deal more with things. An engineer, for example, has to communicate with designers and production staff to get a job done. Researchers work with associates in the lab. Artisans have to deal with customers and suppliers. Accountants meet with clients, staff, and government personnel. As Table 10–1 shows, communication on the job is the rule, not the exception.

Dealing with organizations as an outsider is, of course, almost totally a matter of communication. You must communicate effectively to show the credit card company that your bill is wrong, to convince the emergency room clerk that your medical problem can't wait, or to persuade the service manager that your car problem is indeed covered by the warranty.

Conduct an informational interview of someone whose job interests you. Cover the following areas:

a. What types of communication occur in this job?
b. What percentage of time on the job is spent communicating?
c. What role does communication play in the success of this job?
d. What are the requirements for an entry level job in this field?

Communicating
on the Job

TABLE 10—1   Types of On-the-Job Communication

Interviews

   Employment (career exploration, hiring, placement, orientation, exit)
   Information-gathering (survey, research, investigation, journalistic)
   Information-giving (orientations, instructions)
   Problem-solving/goal-setting (performance appraisal, grievance)

Personal and group activities

   Negotiating
   Promoting a point of view
   Building rapport
   Exchanging information

Presentations

   Briefings
   Reports
   Training
   Proposals
   Motivational speeches
   Goodwill speeches

Communication Is Important

On-the-job communication is not only frequent, it is also a vitally important ingredient in a successful career. College alumni recognize this fact. Graduates in every field who were surveyed one, seven, and ten years after leaving school all identified communication as critical for job success. In fact, the majority of graduates ranked communication as more important than the major subject they studied.[2]

Employers also recognize the importance of communication skills. When 170 well-known firms were asked to list the most common reasons they did not hire applicants, the most frequent replies were "poor communication skills" and "inability to communicate."[3] When employers are asked what they look for when hiring new people, the emphasis on communication skills is almost unanimous. Consider a few examples:

Walt Disney Co.: "Communication skills, particularly when it comes to motivating workers and conveying ideas and concepts, are very important."

Hughes Aircraft Co.: "... We also want to see strong written and oral communication skills and an ability to interact effectively with people."

Fleur Corp.: "We are looking for strong communication skills."

First Interstate Bank: "We look for people with good interpersonal skills."

Southern California Gas Co.: "We also want to see strong written and oral communication skills and an ability to interact effectively with people."[4]

Once on the job, communication is just as important. In one survey, business executives in over fifty of America's largest corporations unanimously agreed that communication skills had played a part in their advancement. Two-thirds believed that the ability to communicate well played a major role in their success.[5] In another survey, subscribers to the *Harvard Business Review* rated the ability to communicate as more important in gaining promotions than ambition, education, and the capacity for hard work.[6]

◆ INTERVIEWING ON THE JOB

For most people, interviewing is the gateway to getting a job. But employment isn't the only kind of interviewing you can expect during a career. Medical personnel collect histories. Market researchers conduct surveys. Journalists interview constantly when researching an article. Managers review their subordinates' performance. Along with these specialties, almost everyone interviews to investigate products and services and to get the information it takes to solve problems.

Characteristics of Interviews

When handled well, an interview resembles a good conversation in many ways. Talk flows freely, information is exchanged, and the parties feel good about one another. Despite these similarities, interviews do differ in some ways from other conversations. First, interviews are always *purposeful:* At least one, and sometimes both parties have specific reasons for arranging the session. Interviews—at least good ones—also have *structure.* Conversations can be aimless affairs in which neither person knows or cares when the exchange will end or exactly what topics will be covered. A good interview, in contrast, has a clear agenda. Another difference between interviews and casual conversations involves *control.* Whereas conversations don't require any guidance from one of the parties, an interviewer should always act in ways that keep the exchange moving toward the preset purpose. A final difference involves *balance.* Though most conversations involve roughly the same amount of input from each person, authorities on interviewing suggest that participation ought to be in the 70 to 30 percent ratio, with the interviewee doing most of the talking.[7]

> Construct a job description for an entry level position in a field that you have been exploring. Exchange lists with a partner and develop and conduct employment interviews with each other for these positions.

Communicating on the Job

With this information in mind, we can define an **interview** as a structured form of oral communication involving two parties, at least one of whom communicates in ways designed to achieve a preconceived purpose.

Stages of an Interview

No matter what the setting or purpose, an effective interview ought to have three distinct parts.

OPENING This beginning stage serves two important functions. Most important, it establishes the tone of the relationship between interviewer and subject: formal or informal, relaxed or tense, serious or humorous. Just as the first stages of a date or party will generally shape what comes later, the success or failure of an interview is often determined before the first question is asked. Besides setting the tone, a good introduction will also give the interviewee a preview (or reminder) of the interviewer's goals and what subjects will be covered.

The usual format for an opening begins with some sort of greeting, which includes any introductions that are necessary. A period of informal con-

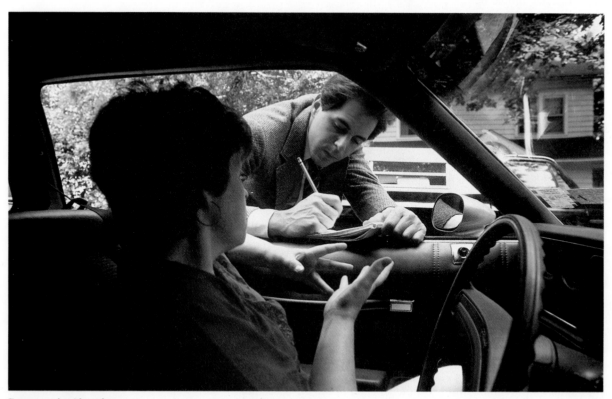

Communication in Groups

versation sometimes follows, in which the interviewer and subject talk about subjects of mutual interest not necessarily related to the interview topic. This period gives both people a chance to get settled and acquainted before getting down to business. This greeting stage may sound artificial—which it often is. But there's no need to discuss obviously trivial subjects or act phony here: The idea is to establish some common ground sincerely between interviewer and subject.

In the final stage of the opening, the interviewer should preview topics of discussion and brief the subject on plans for proceeding: "I appreciate your coming in today. I expect our talk will take about forty-five minutes. I'd like to start by learning a little more about your background, both in school and in other jobs. Then we'll talk about what attracted you to our company, and where you see yourself headed if you do come to work with us. And I'll be sure we have time to answer any questions you have for us at the end."

BODY During the body of the interview, the person asking the questions is responsible for several areas. The first is controlling and focusing the conversation. The interviewer's job is to make sure all the important content areas are covered. It's easy to get off on a tangent and discover too late that the available time is up.

As an interviewee, you can make the best impression by giving complete and detailed answers to the questions you are asked. Put yourself in the interviewer's shoes, and be as specific and helpful as you would want others to be for you. Be sure you keep your answers focused on the subject of questions. It is often a good idea to ask the questioner whether your answer gives the information he or she was seeking. Finally, be sure to correct any misunderstandings. If an interviewer misinterprets your ideas, be sure to correct the mistaken impression.

More than any other factor, the quality of the questions and the way they are asked will determine the success or failure of an interview. Truly good questions rarely come spontaneously, even to the best of interviewers. When you are responsible for conducting an interview, you should plan your questions before the interview itself. As an interviewee, you should be able to anticipate the content of many questions, even if you can't predict their precise wording.

Questions come in several forms, each of which has its own use:

Factual Vs. Opinion Questions Some questions involve matters of fact: What's the difference between an integrated amplifier and a preamplifier?" or "Do you have any management experience?" These can be called **factual questions.** In other cases an interviewer will ask **opinion questions:** "What occupations do you think will offer the best chances for advancement in the next few years?" or "How do you think I should go about apologizing?" When planning for an interview, you should think about whether it is more appropriate to explore questions of fact or opinion.

In some cases a question can be approached either factually or subjectively. For example, imagine that you are interviewing two fellow workers, trying to resolve a conflict between them. Notice the difference between asking "Where do you think the problem lies?" (a broad, subjective question that invites disagreement between the disputants) and "What are some of the things bothering each of you?" (a factual question that doesn't call for the parties to read each other's minds). Each type of question has its place. The key is to determine which sort of information is most useful and then to ask questions that will uncover it.

Open Vs. Closed Questions   You have almost certainly had the frustrating experience of trying to draw out an uncommunicative partner:

You: "How've you been?"
Other: "Fine."
You: "Up to anything new lately?"
Other: "Nope. Same old stuff."
You: "You look good. Have you been getting a lot of exercise?"
Other: "Not really."

Although the respondent here could have certainly done better at holding up the other end of the conversation, much of the problem grew out of the type of questions being asked. All of them were *closed:* questions that could be answered in a word or two. Though some talkative subjects will freely amplify on a closed question, less outgoing ones will give you the briefest response possible. The best way to encourage interviewees to talk up is by asking **open questions,** which require the subject to answer in detail:

"If you had the chance to start your career over again, what things would you do differently?"

"What were some of the things you liked best about New York?"

"Start at the beginning and tell me just what happened."

It will take time and thought to develop a list of open questions to cover all your content areas, but your effort will be rewarded in several ways. First, you will almost certainly have enough lengthy responses to fill the allotted time, soothing a common fear of inexperienced interviewers. Your open questions, inviting comment as they do, will also make your subject feel more comfortable. Furthermore, the way in which your subject chooses to answer your open questions will tell you more about him or her than you could probably learn by only asking more restrictive **closed questions,** which can be answered in a few words.

Closed questions aren't all bad: For one thing they're easy for many subjects to answer, and you can ask many of them in a short period of time. Also, closed questions are appropriate for some subjects. For example, you wouldn't want long-winded replies to questions such as "What's the cost of part #1234?" or "What is your social security number?" As an interviewer, you should decide what type of information you need and then choose the combination of open and closed questions that will get it for you.

Direct Vs. Indirect Questions   Most of the time the best way to get information is to ask a **direct question:**

"Have you had any experience in this kind of work?"
"How much were you planning to spend for a new coat?"
"What kinds of things are you looking for in an apartment?"

There are times, however, when a subject won't be able to answer a direct question. At one time or another, most of us have been so confused that we've answered the question "What don't you understand?" by replying in exasperation, "Everything!" In other cases, you've heard yourself or someone else sincerely answer the question "Do you understand?" in the affirmative, only to find out later that this wasn't true.

There are also times when a subject might be *able* to answer a question sincerely but isn't *willing* to do so. This sort of situation usually occurs when a candid answer would be embarrassing or risky. For instance, when interviewing a prospective tenant, you'd be naïve to ask, "Do you always pay your share of the rent on time?" because a truly shifty person would probably answer yes.

At times like these it's wise to seek information by using **indirect questions,** which do not directly request the information you are seeking. You could ask potential tenants whether their share of the rent money would be coming from current work (then check to see if they're employed) or from savings. In the same way, instead of asking, "Are you creative?" a prospective employer might present a job applicant with a typical situation, looking for an innovative solution.

Primary Vs. Secondary Questions   Sometimes you will need to ask only an initial **primary question** to get the fact or opinion you need in a given content area. But more often you will need to follow up your first question with others to give you all the information you need. These follow-up **probes** are called **secondary questions.**

Primary Question: "In your opinion who are the best people for me to ask about careers in the computer field?"

Secondary Questions: "How could I meet them?" "Do you think they'd be willing to help?" "How could each one help me?"

Sometimes an interviewer can follow up with secondary responses that aren't really questions. Simple probes often uncover useful information.

Interviewer: "What features are you looking for in a phone system?"
Respondent: "Flexibility is the most important thing for us."
Interviewer: "Flexibility?"
Respondent: "Yes. We want to be able to add new phone lines in the future without having to replace the whole system."

Even silence or a well timed nod of the head can trigger a good response:

Manager: "How would you rate yourself in your first month on the job?"
Employee: "Oh, not bad."
Manager: "Uh huh." (pauses)
Employee: "I've learned a lot about the inventory system, but I'm having a hard time remembering the names of all our important customers."

Communicating on the Job

Hypothetical Questions   Sometimes an interviewer will ask the respondent to answer a "what-if" type of question. For example:

> "Suppose you were promoted to supervisor and you had to criticize the work of a friend who now reports to you. How would you handle the situation?"

> "If you were in my position, how would you do the job?"

> "Imagine you were a first-time customer. What would you think of our service?"

These **hypothetical questions** ask the respondent to respond to an imaginary situation. They are a useful way of indirectly getting an interviewee to volunteer attitudes or beliefs. An employee might not volunteer gripes to the boss, but would be willing to answer the question "If you were in charge here, what's the most important thing you would change?" Hypothetical questions are also a good way of learning how employment candidates would handle common situations.

CLOSING   In many ways, the closing is similar to the opening. Instead of previewing, however, the conclusion is a time for reviewing what's occurred during the interview. This helps ensure that the interviewer has correctly understood any points that might be unclear and has gotten the general tone of the subject matter correctly.

The closing is also a time to establish the future of the relationship between interviewer and subject: to decide if any future meetings are necessary, possibly to set a date for them. Finally, it's usually good to conclude the interview with an exchange of sincere pleasantries. Table 10–2 summarizes the points to remember when planning, conducting, and evaluating an interview.

Employment Interviewing

For most people the short time spent facing a potential employer is the most important interview of a lifetime. Getting the right job depends on making a good impression on the person or people who can hire you, and the **employment interview** is usually the place where this decision is made.

Most people naively believe that employment interviews reveal the best qualified candidate, and that the person who has the best qualifications will get the job. Although this principle might be fair and logical, research shows that employment interviews are not good predictors of career success. Interviewers are easily biased, by their own mood and by irrelevant characteristics of applicants.[8] In reality, *the person who knows the most about getting hired* usually gets the desired position. Though job-getting skills are no substitute for qualifications once the actual work begins, they are necessary if you are going to be hired in the first place. The following guidelines will help your communication in interviews give you the best chance of getting the job you deserve.

CONDUCT BACKGROUND RESEARCH   Your first step should be to explore the types of work and specific organizations where you'd like to work. This phase involves looking into all those areas that have interested you in the past. Through library research, reading magazine and newspaper articles, taking classes, and simply fantasizing, find out as much as possible about jobs that might interest you. The result of your research should be a list of organizations and people who can tell you more about your chosen field and help you make contacts.

TABLE 10—2   Checklist for Evaluating Interviews

Opening
- ☐ Sincere, appropriate pleasantries exchanged to help both parties feel comfortable
- ☐ Proper tone established (formal vs. informal, serious vs. casual)
- ☐ Interviewer previews subject and approach

Body
- ☐ Interviewer's nonverbal behavior reflects interest and lack of threat to subject
- ☐ Interviewer asks enough questions to cover all content areas established in advance
- ☐ Interviewer uses probes to explore client's responses (repetition, amplification, paraphrasing, silence)
- ☐ Interviewee gives clear, detailed answers
- ☐ Interviewee keeps on subject
- ☐ Interviewee corrects any misunderstandings of interviewer
- ☐ Interviewee achieves own goals

Closing
- ☐ Interviewer reviews results of interview
- ☐ Future relationship between interviewer and interviewee established
- ☐ Sincere pleasantries exchanged

At this point arrange to meet the people on the list you have just developed. These meetings are *not* employment interviews in which you are asking for a job. Rather, they serve three purposes. First, they are a way to learn more about the fields and companies that interest you. Second, they help you make contacts that might later lead to a job offer. Finally, they can give you leads about other people you can contact for help in your job search. These background interviews are information-gathering in nature, so you should read the section of this chapter that deals with this subject before beginning this step.

MAKING A GOOD FIRST IMPRESSION   First impressions can make or break an interview. Research shows that many interviewers form their opinions about candidates within the first four minutes of conversation.[9] Physical attractiveness is a major influence on how applicants are rated, so it makes sense to do everything possible to look your best. The basic rules apply, no matter what the job or company: Be well-groomed, and neatly dressed. The proper style of clothing can vary from one type of job or organization to another, but when in doubt it's best to dress formally and conservatively. It's unlikely an employer will think less of you for being overdressed, but looking too casual can be taken as a sign that you don't take the job or the interview seriously.

FOLLOW THE INTERVIEWER'S LEAD   Let the interviewer set the emotional tone of the session. If he or she is informal, you can loosen up, be yourself; but if the approach is formal and proper, you should act the same way. A great deal depends on the personal chemistry between interviewer and candidate, so try to match the interviewer's style without becoming phony. If the tone of the interview doesn't fit well with you, this may be a signal that you won't feel comfortable with this organization. It may be smart to see whether the interviewer's approach represents the whole company, either by asking for a tour or speaking with other employees on your own. This desire to learn about the company shows that you are a thinking person who takes the job seriously, so your curiosity isn't likely to offend the interviewer.

RESPOND TO THE EMPLOYER'S NEEDS   Though you may need a job to repay your student loan or finance your new Porsche, these concerns won't impress a potential employer. Companies hire an employee to satisfy *their* needs. Your approach in an interview, then, should be to show your potential employer how your skills match up with the company's concerns. Here's where your background research will pay off: If you've spent time learning about your potential employer, you'll be in a good position to talk about that company's concerns and how you can satisfy them.

RECOGNIZE AND RESPOND TO HIDDEN QUESTIONS   As you read earlier in this chapter, some questions are indirect. For example, the question "Where do you see yourself five years from now?" most likely means "How ambitious are you? How well do your plans fit with this company's goals? How realistic are you?" In the same way, when an interviewer asks, "Why did you leave your last job?" the real questions are probably "Are you competent? Can you get along with others?"

BE HONEST   Whatever else an employer may be seeking, honesty is a key job requirement. If an interviewer finds that you've misrepresented yourself by lying or exaggerating about even one answer, everything else you say will be suspect. Emphasize your strengths, and downplay your weak areas, of course, but always be honest.

KEEP YOUR ANSWERS BRIEF   It's easy to rattle on in an interview, either out of enthusiasm, a desire to show off your knowledge, or nervousness; but in most cases long answers are not a good idea. The interviewer probably has lots of ground to cover, and long-winded answers won't help this task. A good rule of thumb is to keep your responses under two minutes.

HAVE YOUR OWN QUESTIONS ANSWERED   Any good employer will recognize that you have your own concerns about the job. After you've answered the interviewer's questions, you should be prepared to ask a few of your own. See Table 10–3 for some suggestions.

"Yes, I'm sure you are, but unfortunately this place is already crawling with 'swell guys.'"

Drawing by Woodman; © 1981 The New Yorker Magazine, Inc.

FOLLOW UP AFTER THE INTERVIEW   Follow up your meeting with a note of thanks to the interviewer. Most candidates don't take this step, which will make your response especially impressive. Express your appreciation for

TABLE 10-3 Common Job Interview Questions

Questions from the employer

What makes you think you're qualified to work for this company? (How can you help us?)

What have you been doing since your last job?

Why are you interested in this company? This job?

What do you want in your career?

What would you do if...(hypothetical situation)

Where do you see yourself in five years?

Tell me about your experience.

What did you like (not like) about your last job?

What's your greatest strength (limitation) for this job?

Questions for the employer

Will you describe the duties of the job for me, please?

Will you tell me where this job fits within the organization?

What characteristics do you most hope to find in people for this kind of assignment?

Can you tell me about the prospects for advancement beyond this level?

What is the biggest problem facing your staff now? How have past and current employees had trouble solving this problem?

What have been the best results produced by people in this job?

What are the primary results you would like to see me produce?

Can you describe the ideal candidate for this job? Then we can see how closely I fit your requirements.

the chance to get acquainted with the company, and let the interviewer know that the session left you excited about the chance of becoming associated with it.

Informational Interviewing

Although you might not label them as such, you can expect to take part in a great many information-gathering interviews during your career. Whenever you are seeking facts or opinions, you are conducting an **informational interview:** investigating an offer of goods or services, seeking advice about how to do your job better, collecting facts as part of an investigation, or conducting a survey of employees or customers. The following suggestions will help you do a good job.

PREPARE FOR THE INTERVIEW Sometimes a period of research can pay dividends when the actual interview begins. Suppose, for instance, that you have decided to buy a new computer. Before you go shopping it would be

TABLE 10—4 Common Interviewer Complaints About Job Applicants

1. Is caught lying.
2. Shows lack of interest in the interview, merely shopping around.
3. Has a belligerent attitude, is rude or impolite.
4. Lacks sincerity.
5. Is evasive concerning information about himself or herself.
6. Is concerned only about salary.
7. Is unable to concentrate.
8. Displays a lack of initiative.
9. Is indecisive.
10. Has an arrogant attitude.
11. Has a persecuted attitude.
12. Tries to use pull to get a job.
13. Has dirty hands or face.
14. Is cynical.
15. Is intolerant and has strong prejudices.
16. Is late for the interview.
17. Has a limp-fish handshake.
18. Is unable to express himself clearly.
19. Shows lack of planning for career.
20. Has not done research into history and products of the company.
21. Wants to start in an executive position.
22. Lacks maturity.
23. Has low moral standards.
24. Presents extreme appearance.
25. Oversells case.

Based on Charles S. Goetzinger, Jr., "An Analysis of Irritating Factors in Initial Employment Interviews of Male College Graduates," unpublished doctoral dissertation, Purdue University, 1954. Cited in Charles J. Stewart and William B. Cash, Jr., *Interviewing: Principles and Practices,* 2d ed. (Dubuque, Iowa: W. C. Brown, 1978).

smart to become knowledgeable about the various types of systems available. What are the differences between MS-DOS, OS/2, and Macintosh operating systems, for example? Does your work need to be compatible with computers already used by others? What software programs would best suit your needs, and what kind of system do they operate on? If you have answers to questions like these, your questions to dealers will be much more effective, and your chances of getting the best product will be greatest.

**Communicating
on the Job**

CHOOSE THE RIGHT INTERVIEWEE Sometimes the most obvious subject for an information interview isn't the best person to answer your questions—or at least not the only person you should ask. Consider our example of shopping for a computer. It's certainly necessary to interview sales representatives from the companies you're considering, but you might also get useful information from people who use that kind of equipment. Likewise, if you are trying to figure out why employee turnover is too high, be sure to consider all the people who might be able to offer useful information: employees who have already left the company, those who haven't quit, managers in your company, people in similar businesses that don't suffer from the problem, and professors or other experts in the field. Sometimes knowing *whom* to ask is just as important as knowing *what* to ask.

CHECK YOUR UNDERSTANDING After reading Chapter 4 you know that much listening is inaccurate. Keeping this fact in mind, you will find it a good idea to check your understanding of important ideas with the interviewee. Sometimes the consequences of misunderstanding are fairly small: a botched recipe (was it a tablespoon or a cup of vinegar?) or getting lost (were you supposed to turn right or left?). In other cases, however, misunderstandings can be more serious. The fact that you thought you understood an instructor's explanation won't change your low grade on a final exam, and the Internal Revenue Service won't forgive your tax penalties because you thought the local agent said something that turned out to be something else. Whenever there's a chance of misinterpretation, it's a good idea to use the active listening skills you learned earlier in this book.

Performance Appraisal Interviewing

Performance appraisals are a fixture in most organizations, once the number of employees grows beyond a handful. Their purpose is to acknowledge good performance, identify any areas where problems exist, resolve problems, improve productivity, and help develop the employee's talents.

At its best, the appraisal process is a valuable tool for helping employees feel better about work and for helping the organization. But in practice things often work out differently. More often than not, appraisal interviews result in lower productivity and greater apathy among employees.[10]

Performance appraisals have the greatest chance of success when the interviewer takes a supportive, constructive approach. This means acknowledging good work as well as pointing out problem areas. It is also helpful to set specific goals for improvement to aim for during the next evaluation period. The information in Chapter 3 on behavioral goals applies here. The interviewer needs to follow the descriptive approach described in Chapter 6, instead of using an excess of evaluative "you" language. Finally, it is essential for the interviewer to be a good listener who sincerely tries to understand the respondent's point of view. The surest way to get most employees to change is to involve them in the review process. Top-down, "I talk, you listen" approaches rarely work.[11]

As an interviewee, you can do plenty to make performance appraisals more successful, even with a superior who doesn't follow the advice in the preceding paragraph. Remember that criticism of your work in one area doesn't mean you are no good as a person, or even in other areas in which you interact with the interviewer. Approach the interview with a sincere desire to do better. View the interview as a chance to start improving your performance. This attitude will impress the interviewer and will help you grow.

When faced with vague descriptions of your behavior ("You're doing well" or "You're not keeping up"), ask the interviewer for specific examples. The goal here isn't to be argumentative, but to understand exactly what the interviewer is talking about. Finally, do your best to avoid acting defensively by counter-attacking or withdrawing. Though reactions like these are understandable, they probably won't make you feel any better and are likely to lower your stature in the interviewer's eyes.

◆ COMMUNICATION NETWORKS

Communication networks are systems of stable person-to-person relationships through which information flows in an organization.[12] The easiest way to visualize networks is to imagine that a line is drawn between two people in an organization every time they communicate. The patterns that emerge after enough time would characterize the communication networks. There are two types of networks that operate within an organization: formal and informal.

Formal Networks

Formal communication networks are management's idea of who ought to work with whom to accomplish the organization's mission. Formal networks that lay out lines of authority are described in **organization charts** like the one in Figure 10–1. Organization charts describe some, but not all kinds of formal communication networks. An organizational chart doesn't include interaction among people from different departments or among members of the organization and the public. To outline all the formal communication involved in getting a job done, one must construct a **flowchart.** The flowchart in Figure 10–2 illustrates some of the communication that occurs as a textbook is developed.

Notice that the information described in Figure 10–2 doesn't flow only from superiors to subordinates. In fact, information within an organization can pass in three directions: downward, upward, and horizontally.

DOWNWARD COMMUNICATION   Downward communication occurs when a superior sends a message to one or more subordinates. The most obvious type of downward communication is *job instructions,* but there are other types of downward messages that are equally important.

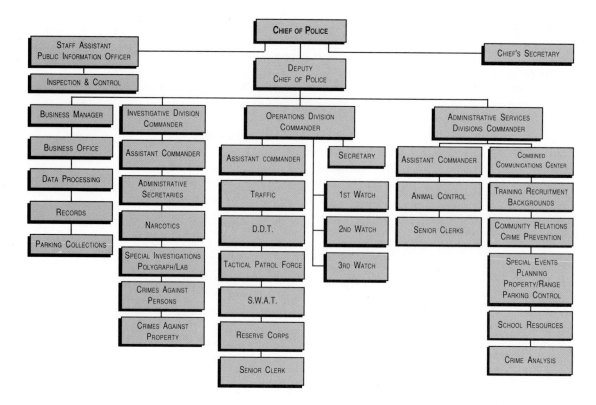

FIGURE 10–1
Organization Chart

A second type of downward communication involves *job rationale:* explanations of why a task needs to be performed. An office manager might offer job rationale by explaining the reason behind an apparently useless order: "I know it seems foolish both to type up a repair order and to phone it in, but we've found that a phone call gets the custodians out here much faster. It's definitely worth the few extra minutes."

Downward communication can also deal with *procedures and practices.* Information about rules and regulations falls into this category. For example, the boss might send out a memo stating the company's policy on a personal use of the copying machine, and a sales manager might announce that his or her approval is required for all deals over a certain amount.

A fourth type of downward communication conveys *feedback* from the top down. This feedback can be praise ("You really handled that job well") or constructive criticism ("We could have made the deadline if you'd sent the contracts by Express Mail"). Sometimes, of course, criticism isn't constructive at all: "That was a stupid thing to do. One more stunt like that and you're finished!"

Communication in Groups

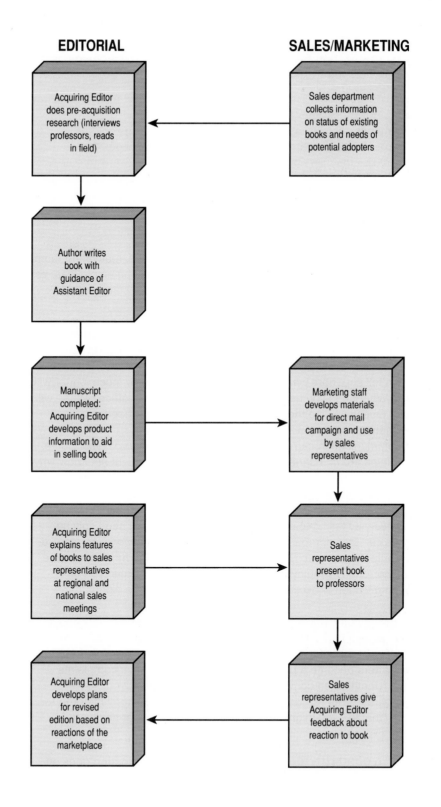

EDITORIAL

Acquiring Editor does pre-acquisition research (interviews professors, reads in field)

Author writes book with guidance of Assistant Editor

Manuscript completed: Acquiring Editor develops product information to aid in selling book

Acquiring Editor explains features of books to sales representatives at regional and national sales meetings

Acquiring Editor develops plans for revised edition based on reactions of the marketplace

SALES/MARKETING

Sales department collects information on status of existing books and needs of potential adopters

Marketing staff develops materials for direct mail campaign and use by sales representatives

Sales representatives present book to professors

Sales representatives give Acquiring Editor feedback about reaction to book

FIGURE 10–2
Simplified Flow Chart: Editorial, sales, and marketing interface at Holt, Rinehart and Winston.

Communicating on the Job

Using an organization from your own experience, describe the types of communication you initiate and receive:

a. Downward (job instructions, job rationale, policies and procedures, feedback, and indoctrination).
b. Upward (what subordinates are doing, unsolved work problems, suggestions for improvement, how subordinates feel about themselves and the job).
c. Horizontal (task coordination, problem-solving, sharing information, resolving conflict, building rapport).

How could each type of communication be improved?

Finally, some downward messages *indoctrinate* employees, motivating them to perform better. Sales meetings are often aimed at motivating employees, as are some performance appraisal interviews and "state of the company" speeches by top management.

UPWARD COMMUNICATION   As its name suggests, **upward communication** occurs when subordinates send messages to their superiors. Upward communication can convey four types of information.[13]

First, it can tell superiors *what subordinates are doing.* How much longer will the job take? Where can you be reached when you leave the office? When will you be back? Questions like these may be obvious, but they need to be answered if management is to know what is going on.

Upward communication can also deal with *unsolved work problems.* Some of these problems are mundane, though important. A boss might not know why last week's sales figures are so hard to get (too many people using one computer terminal) unless somebody tells him. Some bosses discourage this sort of communication, either actively by lashing out at the bearers of bad news or passively by failing to invite reports on problems that need solving.

Employees can also approach their superiors with *suggestions for improvement.* How could we get more repeat business? How can the turnaround time on a job be shortened? Employees who are willing to initiate this type of upward communication show that they have potential to move higher in the organization.

Finally, upward communication can describe *how subordinates feel about themselves and the job.* If you want more responsibility or are interested in learning a different part of the business, it is probably wise to let your superiors know. Matters become a bit more delicate when you have complaints about the job. Unmitigated complaining usually isn't well received, so it's important to phrase your message positively. Instead of saying, "I'm bored" or "I can't stand Charlie," you might say, "I'd like to tackle a bigger challenge" or "I'd like to get experience working with other people."

HORIZONTAL COMMUNICATION   **Horizontal communication** goes on among members who are not connected vertically on an organizational chart.

Some horizontal exchanges occur among people who work closely together in the same group. Other horizontal messages flow from one part of the organization to another—between departments, for example. In either case, horizontal messages can serve several functions.[14]

First, they can improve *task coordination*. "When can we meet to talk about those new electronic typewriters?" you might ask a purchasing agent. "Let's work out a vacation schedule that keeps both our departments covered," a fellow worker might suggest to you.

Other horizontal messages involve *problem-solving*. Quality control personnel might meet with assembly line supervisors before work to figure out how mistakes can be cut on a new procedure. Likewise, an office manager might ask the maintenance staff how the fresh air circulation can be improved in the work area.

*"Season's greetings from Slug Wassleman, on forklift twenty-seven,
Container Division, Fulton, New York, plant."*

Drawing by H. Martin; © 1981 The New Yorker Magazine, Inc.

**Communicating
on the Job**

A third type of horizontal communication involves *sharing information*. The change-of-shift briefings common in nursing and police operations are primarily information-sharing sessions, as are meetings in which a sales staff explains customer needs to designers.

Horizontal communication also can focus on *conflict resolution*. Some conflicts are personal. One employee might be offended by another's ethnic jokes, for example. Other disputes focus on job-related issues, such as who was responsible for losing a major account or whether women are being excluded from top management positions.

A final type of horizontal communication can *build rapport*. You might have lunch or play tennis with someone in another department, knowing that a good relationship between your divisions will help work run more smoothly.

Informal Networks

Not all communication in organizations follows formal channels. Consider these examples:

◆ You overhear the personnel officers talking about a new job opening. You mention the opening to a fellow worker, who asks for and gets reassigned to the new position before the opening is formally announced.

◆ Your running partner is assistant to the boss. She tells you that the boss was grumbling about the way salary expenses have gotten out of hand. You decide to postpone your request for a raise.

◆ At the annual Christmas party, you mention to the data-processing manager that you've been having trouble understanding the weekly progress report printouts. As a result of your conversation, the format of the reports is reorganized in a clearer format.

Informal communication networks are patterns of interaction that have little or nothing to do with organizational flowcharts. (See Figure 10–3.) Informal networks arise for a number of reasons, including proximity, similar interests, and personal friendships.

Whatever their basis, informal networks can be a useful way to send and receive information. One advantage of informal networks is their speed. Because they are based on personal relationships, informal messages usually travel much more quickly than more formal ones that must follow official channels. In one organization, for example, 46 percent of the management staff heard about one member's newborn child within thirteen hours after the birth.[15]

The off-the-record nature of informal messages allows them to convey information that simply can't be sent officially. A friend who might tell you over a cup of coffee that Jones is a two-faced liar certainly wouldn't put the message into a memo. Likewise, your supervisor might relay management's announcement that use of the copying machine is absolutely forbidden and yet make it clear from his or her tone of voice that he or she thinks the rule is too strict.

Informal networks often are described as "grapevine" communication, a term that has connotations of an inaccurate rumor mill. How reliable is grape-

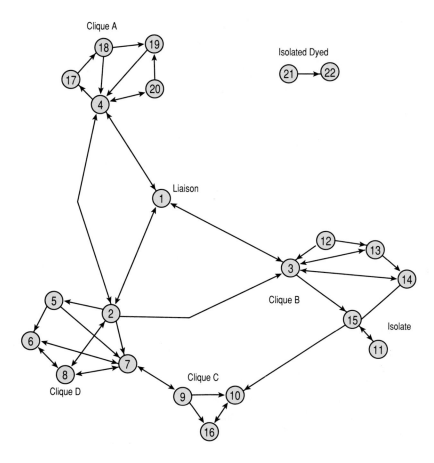

Clique A

18 → 19

17

4

20

Isolated Dyed

21 → 22

Liaison

1

12 → 13

3

14

Clique B

5

2

15

Isolate

6

11

7

8

Clique D

Clique C

9 → 10

16

FIGURE 10–3
Informal Communication Net-
work. From *Communication in
Organizations* by Everett M.
Rogers and Rehka Agarwala-
Rogers. Copyright © 1976 by
The Free Press, a division
of Macmillan Publishing
Co., Inc.

vine information? Surprisingly, research shows that its accuracy is quite high—
between 80 and 90 percent, according to many studies.[16] Not all grapevine
information is equally reliable: Noncontroversial information is more likely to be
transmitted accurately than is more sensational news. Also, accuracy
decreases as the number of people passing along a message grows. (This is
also true for formal messages that travel through a long chain of senders and
receivers.)

What informal networks do you belong to in organizations? Who are
the other members? What types of information does each network
carry? How reliable is it? How can you use these networks to your
advantage?

Choose a personal goal you have as a member of an organization.

a. Define the results you seek in realistic, specific terms.
b. Identify the best audience or audiences to approach.
c. Describe the best channel or channels to convey your message.
d. Construct the message you could send.

**Communicating
on the Job**

Whether you are communicating in interviews, meetings, presentations, negotiations, or in ordinary day-to-day conversations, there are several principles that can help you get the results you are seeking.

The communication challenges that occur on the job are frequent and varied. Consider a few examples:

◆ After hammering out a work schedule with a boss or colleague, the other person begins to ask for a "few changes" that will make life much less convenient for you. You are starting to feel victimized, and you vow not to give up what you need.

◆ You have an idea of how some computer programming methods you learned in school might improve the efficiency of the company you have just joined. You know, however, that the president of the company is an old-fashioned operator who mistrusts new "gadgets," as he calls them. Despite this attitude, you want to promote the new idea.

◆ Two months ago your boss assured you that your work would be rewarded. Yesterday you found that the assistant manager's position you were hoping for went to an outsider. You are angry and disappointed.

Your success in situations like these depends partly on the skills introduced elsewhere in this book: the ability to handle yourself well in an interview, to work in a group, to participate in meetings, and to express your ideas in a presentation. In addition to these contextual skills, however, there are some general principles that apply to every type of organizational communication.

Define Your Goal

People communicate to get results, but they don't always know exactly what results they are seeking. Consider the earlier example of the promotion you didn't receive: Would your goal be to persuade the manager to reconsider and give you the position you believe you are entitled to? Would you hope to get the next opening? To receive a raise, regardless of a promotion? To hear where you stand with the boss?

As these examples show, most opportunities for communicating on the job can have several goals. Before you speak or write, you need to define yours by answering two questions. First, *decide exactly what you want to happen.* Be sure to state your goal in terms of the results you are seeking. Don't say, "I want to complain about how badly I've been treated." After all, you don't even need an audience to do this! Instead, say, "I want to know for certain whether my boss appreciates my work, and to be sure I will be promoted within the next year." It's also important to *make sure your goal is realistic.* It is probably unrealistic to expect that your boss will give you a job that has already been promised to someone else. It is also unlikely that a skeptical customer will be converted to your product in one presentation. Your goal, then, ought to be one that has a chance of success. You might, for instance, aim to get your boss to

Communication in Groups

agree that you are, indeed, entitled to a promotion and that you deserve a raise in the meantime.

Choose the Best Audience

Suppose you work in a computer store and see opportunities to sell low-priced systems for students to use. You could aim your message at several audiences: teachers, principals, or school boards might support purchasing equipment for use at school, and parents and students could be persuaded to buy machines for home. Which audience is best? The answer will depend on many factors such as the financial situation of each group, the reputation of you and your company with each kind of recipient, the degree to which each group recognizes the value of computers, and so on.

Almost every message has several potential audiences. Communicating with each one requires a different approach and is likely to get different results. Within an organization, protocol usually requires you to clear any ideas or problems with your immediate superior, and most of the time this is a good idea. There are instances, however, when your boss will be too hostile, busy, uninterested, or stupid to appreciate your ideas. There are still ways to deliver a message to the outside world without going over your boss's head. You can mention it in a meeting where others are present: "I've had some ideas on cost cutting that might work for other departments, and I can share them if you're interested. . . ." You can put the idea in a memo to your boss and send copies to others. You can discuss the idea with people not in your chain of command as long as the subject is related to their work: "You guys in purchasing are always telling us to keep costs down. I heard about a new software program that might be able to save us some money. . . ."

Communicating on the Job

Choose the Best Channel

How you deliver a message can be as important as what you say. You have several communication channels available when sending business messages: face-to-face conversations, telephone, and writing. As Table 10–5 shows, there are separate varieties within each of these channels. Choosing one channel over another shouldn't be a casual decision. Each method of delivery has advantages and disadvantages, which we will now consider.

ORAL COMMUNICATION The biggest advantage of oral communication— both face-to-face and by telephone—is its *speed.* Once you have made contact with your receiver, the message is conveyed instantly. This speed is especially valuable when time is of the essence. Should a customer's check be approved? Are the parts you desperately need available? An oral response can answer questions like these in a timely manner.

A second advantage of oral communication is the *instant feedback* it provides. Do your listeners have any questions? Did you forget to say anything? A conversation can let you know. Nonverbal reactions are just as revealing as the words your receiver speaks. Does the other person look bored? Do your remarks get enthusiastic nods and smiles or frowns and head shaking? You can even get valuable feedback in telephone conversations from the speaker's tone of voice.

Finally, oral communication gives you *control* of the situation—far more than you have with written messages. Your receivers might briefly scan the letter you worked so hard on and toss it aside. Even worse, they might not read it at all. In a conversation, however, the audience has at least to pretend to pay attention; and if you use the speaking skills outlined in Chapters 11 to 15, your message ought to be clear and effective enough to be well received.

TABLE 10–5 Communication Channels in Organizations

Face-to-face
    Two-person
    Group
    Speaker-to-audience

Telephone
    Personal contact
    Through intermediary (secretary, coworker, etc.)
    Recording device (answering machine, voice mail)

Written
    Personal letter or memo (handwritten or typed)
    Duplicated letter (copies to several recipients)
    Printed publication (newsletter, mass mailing, etc.)
    Mailgram, telegram
    Electronic mail (via computer network)

WRITTEN COMMUNICATION   Written communication also has advantages. First, it is *permanent.* Most members of organizations file all correspondence, which means a record of your message exists. Listeners might forget three of the five reasons outlined in your oral presentation, but with a written document they have a record of your ideas.

Written records also *prevent distortion* of your ideas. As you read in Chapter 4, listeners routinely filter comments through their own experiences and prejudices. A letter or memo can guarantee that what you say is what they will receive. Then, if someone makes an unfair accusation, a record of your message is available: "Sure I told you about the problem. Here's a copy of my March 15 memo to you."

Written messages also have the advantage of being most easily *planned in advance.* You can take all the time you want to shape their content and tone. You can test out several versions on sample audiences to predict the response of your real audience, and you can make modifications until you get the desired result. In contrast, oral messages are more difficult to plan. You can rehearse a presentation, but one unforseen question from a listener can throw your whole plan off track. A personal conversation is even harder to plan because you can only guess at what the other person will say.

WHICH METHOD IS BEST?   There is no single answer to this question. As Table 10–6 shows, some messages are most effective when delivered orally whereas others ought to be committed to paper. Oral communication is usually advisable when your message needs to be personal. It also works best with ideas that have a strong need for visual support: demonstrations, charts, slides, and so on. Oral communication also is usually best when you need immediate feedback—either an answer from the other party or assurance that your message has been understood.

Written communication is the best choice when you want your message to be more formal. It is also better than oral channels when you must choose your

TABLE 10–6   Oral Vs. Written Communication

ORAL COMMUNICATION	WRITTEN COMMUNICATION
More personal	More formal
Effective for relatively simple ideas	Effective for relatively complex ideas
Provides immediate feedback	Feedback delayed or nonexistent
Off-the-record	Formal record exists
Effective for messages with visual or hands-on elements	Less effective for visual or hands-on messages
Effective when seeking immediate, emotional response (motivation, sales, and so on)	Effective when seeking delayed, thoughtful response

Communicating on the Job

words carefully. Written messages are also better when you are communicating complicated ideas. Finally, written messages are best for any message when you want a record to exist.

Sometimes it is wise to send a message in both oral and written forms. You might write a note of thanks to a potential employer (adding an impressive document to your application file) and then phone to express your appreciation personally. You could express a complaint in person to a merchant and follow it up with a letter (with a copy to the Better Business Bureau).

◆ SUMMARY

Job-related communication is a fact of life for almost everyone. Within organizations, most employees spend more time communicating than in any other activity, and the amount of communication increases with the responsibility of a job. College alumni and employers agree that the ability to communicate well is an essential ingredient for a successful career. Even people who do not work in organizations must communicate with them.

Interviews are one common type of job-related communication. They are structured conversations between two parties, at least one of which has a preconceived purpose. Interviews—at least effective ones—are characterized by three stages: an opening, in which the tone is established and the information to be covered is previewed; a body, in which the subject matter of the discussion is covered in detail, and a closing that reviews what has been accomplished and the future of the relationship established. The chapter described several points that characterize effective employment, information-gathering, and performance-appraisal interviews.

Communication networks carry the flow of information within an organization. Formal networks convey information upward, downward, and horizontally. Informal networks are patterns of interaction that are not represented on organization charts. Despite their bad reputation, they can be a useful way to send and receive information.

Three strategies can result in more successful communication. The first is to define your goal before expressing yourself. Choosing the best audience is another way to achieve the desired results. Finally, using the most effective communication channel can make the difference between a message being received well or poorly.

Communication in Groups

1. For documentation of the importance of communication on the job, see R. B. Adler, *Communicating at Work: Principles and Practices for Business and the Professions* (New York: McGraw-Hill, 1989), pp. 4–8.

2. A. S. Bisconti and L. C. Solmon, *College Education on the Job—The Recent Graduates' Viewpoint* (Bethlehem, Pa.: The College Placement Council Foundation, 1976), p. 43.

3. F. S. Endicott, "The Endicott Report: Trends in the Employment of College and University Graduates in Business and Industry 1980" (Evanston, Ill.: Placement Center, Northwestern University, 1979).

4. "What Employers Are Looking For," *Los Angeles Times,* September 17, 1989, p. 5.

5. J. C. Bennett, "The Communication Needs of Business Executives," *Journal of Business Communication* 9 (1971): 5–12.

6. G. W. Bowman, "What Helps or Harms Promotability?" *Harvard Business Review* (January–February 1964): 14.

7. Charles J. Stewart and William B. Cash, Jr., *Interviewing: Principles and Practices,* 3d ed. (Dubuque, Iowa: W. C. Brown, 1982), p. 10.

8. R. D. Avery and J. E. Campion, "The Employment Interview: A Summary and Review of Recent Research," *Personnel Psychology* 35 (1982): 284–288.

9. Avery and Campion, pp. 290 and 303. See also S. Forsythe, M. F. Drake, and C. Cox, "Influence of Applicant's Dress on Interviewer's Selection Decisions," *Journal of Applied Psychology* 70 (1985): 374–

378; H. Carl, "Nonverbal Communication During the Employment Interview," *ABCA Bulletin* (December 1980): 14–18.

10. See, for example, K. Loraine, "How Effective Are Work Evaluations?" *Supervision* 45 (1983): 7–8, 13 and M. Zippo and M. Miller, "Performance Appraisal: Current Practices and Techniques," *Personnel* 61 (1984): 57–59.

11. See R. N. F. Maier, *The Appraisal Interview: Objectives, Methods, and Skills* (New York: Wiley 1958).

12. P. Monge, J. A. Edwards, and K. K. Kirste, "The Determinants of Communication and Communication Structure in Large Organizations: A Review of Research," in B. D. Rubin (ed.), *Communication Yearbook 2* (New Brunswick, N.J.: Transaction Books, 1978). For further information on the subject, see P. R. Monge, "The Network Level of Analysis," in C. R. Berger, S. H. Chafee (eds.), *Handbook of Communication Science* (Newbury Park, Calif.: Sage, 1987): pp. 239–269.

13. D. Katz and R. Kahn, *The Social Psychology of Organizations,* 2d ed. (New York: Wiley, 1978), p. 245.

14. Adapted from G. Goldhaber, *Organizational Communication,* 3d ed. (Dubuque, Iowa: Wm. C. Brown, 1983), p. 162.

15. Keith Davis, "Management Communication and the Grapevine," *Harvard Business Review* (September–October 1953): 43–49.

16. Keith Davis, *Human Behavior at Work* (New York: McGraw-Hill, 1972).

**Communicating
on the Job**

PUBLIC COMMUNICATION

11

After reading this chapter, you should understand the following:

1. The importance of defining a clear speech purpose.

2. The difference between a general and a specific speech purpose.

3. The necessity of analyzing a speaking situation.

4. The importance of audience analysis.

You should be able to do the following:

1. Choose an effective topic.

2. Formulate a purpose statement that will help you develop that topic.

3. Analyze the three components of a speaking situation.

4. Perform an audience analysis.

5. Gather information on the topic from a variety of sources.

KEY TERMS

attitude
audience analysis
belief
demographics
general purpose
on-line data base

purpose statement
specific purpose
survey research
thesis statement
value

Choosing and Developing a Topic

In the early 1980's, Candy Lightner's thirteen-year-old daughter Cari was killed by a hit-and-run driver. The driver who killed her was drunk at the time of the accident, and he had a long list of drunk driving violations. In fact, he had been out on bail for only two days following an earlier hit-and-run offense. The police told Candy Lightner that, because of the state's lenient drunk driving laws, the man who killed her daughter would probably never go to jail.

"I was so angry," Lightner said later, "that I wanted to kill. But I decided to do something constructive instead." What she did was to establish Mothers Against Drunk Driving (MADD), an organization dedicated to finding solutions to the drunk driving problem.

Before she founded MADD, Candy Lightner had never spoken in public—in fact, like many people, the thought of public speaking terrified her. But she soon discovered that speechmaking was going to be necessary to keep her organization alive. The people with the power to make a difference, such as her governor and state legislators, simply would not pay attention to her unless she had popular support.

Lightner decided that her first speech would be a press conference, held at the state capital, publicizing MADD and its aims. She had to prepare carefully for it, and fight back a bad case of jitters, but it was a successful speech.[1] The press took notice, and MADD began to gather support.

Lightner's speech marked the beginning of what was to become a nation-wide movement with a long list of accomplishments. California adopted the nation's strictest laws against drunk driving. Legislation against drunk driving was also introduced in most of the other states. A federal blue-ribbon commission was formed and charged with finding solutions to the nationwide problem. Several large corporations decided to provide free taxi service after

Public Communication

Unaccustomed As I Am . . .

. . . I am, God help me, about to do it for the fifth time. My hands I know will be wet and my mouth dry. There will even be an actual bumping inside my chest as I scrape back my chair and walk unsteadily to the podium. "Thank you very much" (gulp . . . weak smile), "and good evening, ladies and gentlemen."

My horror of stages, speeches, spotlights and footlights is old stuff. I am a born spectator. My natural habitat is the audience. I know my place and it is not in the spotlight. It is back up there in the snug anonymous dark. . . .

I first emerged from the wings in a walnut shell towed by two mice. It was a fourth-grade production of *Thumbelina,* and my mortifying costume was a leaf. Merciful obscurity closed in after that until the time came to make a speech at my eighth-grade graduation. By then I was burdened with 20 pounds of overweight, a mouthful of braces and a broken leg. The event was so traumatic that for the next 20 years I stayed resolutely off the stage, refusing to take part in school plays, team athletics, dance contests or campus politics. I even got my college diploma by mail. Though my wedding took place in the relative privacy of my parents' living room, I would have preferred the even greater anonymity of city hall.

For years I refused all invitations to participate in panel discussions, disk-jockey interviews, political rallies, awards ceremonies or tree plantings. I never asked questions from the floor at lectures or volunteered to help the magician in the nightclub. At raffles, half of me hoped I didn't have the lucky number.

The carrot that finally coaxed me out of the wings was of all things a journalism award. No acceptance speech, they said, no award. O vanity, vanity! I said I'd be there.

But there was something more to it than that. I really started speaking for the same reason that I stopped smoking. I was ashamed of myself. It was time to grow up. But the older one gets, it seems, the harder that is to do.

As my D-day approached, I retreated. Friends had rallied round with all sorts of advice, mostly contradictory. Don't be afraid to write it out. Read it. Memorize it. Put it on cards. Speak it off the cuff. Start funny. Start dull—an early joke lets them off the hook of curiosity. Turn from side to side so they can all see you. Find one nice face in the audience and tell it all to him. Get a new dress. Get a little drunk.

By the afternoon of the speech, trying to follow all this advice at once, I sat stupefied with terror in my room in the hotel where the banquet was to be held. My new gown hung on the back of the door, flowers and telegrams began to arrive. Were they condolences? Had I already died? . . . I barely remember going downstairs to the hotel ballroom, or the dais, or the dinner, or anything at all until I felt my wet palms gripping the smooth sides of the lectern, and heard my own weird, oddly magnified voice rumble out over the crowd.

I was most unprepared for my own total unpreparedness: I didn't know where to look, where to put my hands, where to pitch my voice, when to pause, when to smile. To be *that* unknowing rarely happens to an adult; it gave me a giddy feeling; nothing to do but push on.

After a few moments I heard faint laughter. I was not quite conscious of it at first, but then it came again a bit stronger, until I was sure I heard it, and then as I was reading I began to wait for it, and to make spaces in sentences for it, to enjoy it, and finally to play with the words and with the audience, to swoop and glide and describe arabesques with all the nutty abandon of Donald Duck on ice skates.

Success. Triumph. Waves of applause. The night came to a kind of crescendo Andy Hardy finish that I have never been able to recapture. In the next three speeches I was nearly as scared as the first time, but not nearly as good. But I am going to try it again. I am getting to know the ropes.

Shana Alexander

parties at which alcohol was served. "Safe-ride" programs were established in which teenagers provided rides home for other teenagers who had had too much to drink. The National Restaurant Association made a recommendation to its members that they train bartenders in how to handle drinkers who want to drive. A movie was even made by CBS about Lightner and her accomplishments.

Public speaking enabled Candy Lightner to take a personal stand against a social problem that had been around for so long that people had just learned to accept it. When she first started speaking out, she told one interviewer, "The public doesn't perceive drunk driving as a crime, yet more people are killed each year in this manner than they are by handguns. Drunk driving is the only socially acceptable form of homicide." Today, if you ask Lightner what MADD's main accomplishment is, she'll tell you, "The biggest accomplishment is that public attitude is changing. That's the bottom line."

Most of us realize that the ability to speak well in public is a benefit in both business and in our personal lives. And yet most of us, like Candy Lightner, view the prospect of standing before an audience with the same enthusiasm we have for a trip to the dentist or the tax auditor. In fact, giving a speech seems to be one of the most anxiety-producing things we can do: *The Book of Lists* claims that Americans fear public speaking more than they do insects, heights, accidents, and even death.[2]

Despite the discomfort that speech giving causes, sooner or later most of us will need to talk to an audience of some kind: while giving a class report, as part of our jobs, or as part of a community action group. And even in less "speech-like" situations, we often need the same skills good speakers possess: the ability to talk with confidence, to organize ideas in a clear way, and to make those ideas interesting and persuasive.

Attaining a mastery of public speaking is at least partially a matter of practice. But practice doesn't always make perfect; without a careful analysis of what you are practicing, practice has a tendency to make old public speaking habits permanent rather than perfect. This final section of this book will provide you with some tools to analyze your performance as a public speaker.

♦ CHOOSING A TOPIC

Often the difference between a successful and an unsuccessful speech is the choice of topic. Your topic should be familiar enough for your audience to understand, yet be innovative enough to hold their attention. This chapter will discuss a number of approaches to choosing and developing the right topic. The following guidelines will help you pick a topic that is appropriate for you, your audience, and your assignment.

Look for a Topic Early

Public Communication

The best student speakers usually choose a topic as soon as possible after a speech is assigned by their instructor, and then they stick with it. One reason

There is no such thing as an uninteresting subject. There are only uninterested people.

G. K. Chesterton

TABLE 11—1 Checklist for Choosing a Topic

Review:	Discuss current events:	Think about:
newspapers	international	activities
magazines	national	hobbies
books	local	special interests
	family	
	personal	

to look for a topic early is so that you will have plenty of time to complete the speech and practice it. Adequate practice time is essential to effective speechmaking. And yet the reasons for choosing a topic early run even deeper than that. Ideas seem to come automatically to speakers who have a topic in mind; things they read or observe or talk about that might have otherwise been meaningless suddenly relate to their topic, providing material or inspiration for sources of material.[3] The earlier you decide on a topic, the more of these happy coincidences you can take advantage of.

Choose a Topic That Interests You

Your topic must be interesting to your audience, and the best way to accomplish that is to find a topic that is interesting to *you*. Your interest in a topic will also improve your ability to create the speech, and it will increase your confidence when it comes time to present it.

Sometimes it's difficult to pinpoint *what* your interests are—especially when you are being pressed to come up with a speech topic. If that happens to you, you might want to review your favorite newspapers, magazines and books, discuss current events with family and friends, or just contemplate your interests in solitude. The checklist in Table 11—1 could be used as a guide.

Choose a Topic You Know Something About

The main problem for most people is realizing how *much* they know. It is a mistake to think that you have nothing new to say; your experiences, your thoughts, and your investigation of a topic will be, by definition, unique.

One student who felt he had no unique knowledge came up with the following list after reviewing his interests:

1. Cars: driving them, different types, safety features, and problems.
2. Learning English as a second language: from his experiences as both a student and a tutor.
3. Dealing with adoption (he was adopted).
4. Different forms of discrimination: age, sex, racial, and student discrimination, to be specific.
5. Religion: He was deeply involved with his own and very interested in others.

With these preliminary guidelines out of the way, we can turn to the next step in choosing and developing your topic: defining your purpose.

All Communication Is Purposeful

No one gives a speech—or expresses *any* kind of message—without having a reason to do so. This is easy to see in those messages that ask for something: "Pass the salt" or "How about a movie this Friday?" or "Excuse me. That's my foot you're standing on." But even in subtler messages, the speaker always has a purpose—to evoke a response from the listener.

Sometimes purposes are misunderstood or confused by the speaker. This causes wasted time both in the preparation and in the presentation of the speech. It is essential, therefore, that the speaker keep in mind a clear purpose.

The first step in understanding your purpose is to formulate a clear and precise purpose statement. This requires an understanding of both *general purpose* and *specific purpose*.

General Purpose

Most students, when asked *why* they are giving a speech in a college class, will quickly cite course requirements. But you have to analyze your motives more deeply than that to develop a complete speech purpose. Even if you are only giving your speech for the grade, you still have to affect your audience in some way to earn that grade.

If your motive for speaking is to learn effective speech techniques (as we hope it is), you still have to influence your audience to accomplish your goal because that is what effective speaking is all about.

When we say you have to influence your audience, we mean you have to *change* them in some way. If you think about all the possible ways you could change an audience, you'll realize that they all boil down to three options, which happen to be the three basic **general purposes** for speaking:

1. **To Entertain:** To relax your audience by providing them with a pleasant listening experience.
2. **To Inform:** To enlighten your audience by teaching them something.
3. **To Persuade:** To move your audience toward a new attitude or behavior.

A brief scrutiny of these purposes will reveal that no speech could ever have *only* one purpose. These purposes are interrelated because a speech designed for one purpose will almost always accomplish a little of the other purposes; even a speech designed purely to entertain might change audience attitudes or teach that audience something new. In fact, these purposes are *cumulative* in the sense that, to inform an audience, you have to make your remarks entertaining enough to hold their interest—at least long enough to convince them your topic is worth learning about. And you certainly have to inform an audience (about your arguments) in order to persuade them.

Deciding your general purpose is like choosing the "right" answer on one of those multiple-choice tests in which *all* the answers are right to a certain degree, but *one* answer is more right than the others. Thus, we say that any speech is *primarily* designed for one of these purposes. A clear understanding of your general purpose gets you on the right track for choosing and developing a topic. Understanding your **specific purpose** will keep you on that track.

Specific Purpose

Whereas your general purpose is only a one-word label, your *specific* goal is expressed in the form of a **purpose statement**—a complete sentence that describes exactly what you want your speech to accomplish. The purpose statement usually isn't used word for word in the actual speech; its purpose is to keep you focused as you plan your speech.

There are three criteria for a good purpose statement.[4]

1. **A Purpose Statement Must Describe the Result You Are Seeking.** As we mentioned earlier, all communication seeks some response from a receiver. This receiver orientation should be reflected in your purpose statement. For example, if you were giving an informative talk on gourmet cooking, this would be an inadequate purpose statement:

   "My purpose is to tell my audience about gourmet cooking."

   As that statement is worded, your purpose is "to tell" an audience something, which means that the speech could be successful even if no one listens. Your purpose statement should refer to the response you want from your audience: It should tell what the audience members will know or be able to do after listening to your speech. Thus, the purpose statement above could be improved this way:

   "After listening to my speech, my audience will know more about gourmet cooking."

   That's an improvement because you now have stated what you expect from your audience. But this purpose statement could still be improved through the judicious application of a second criterion:

2. **A Purpose Statement Must Be Specific.** To be effective, a purpose statement should be worded specifically, with enough details so that you would be able to measure or test your audience, after your speech, to see if you had achieved your purpose. In the example given earlier, simply "knowing about gourmet cooking" is too vague; you need something more specific, such as:

   "After listening to my speech, my audience will be able to cook *coq au vin* at home."

   At least now you've limited your purpose to a single dish rather than the entire world of gourmet cooking. This is an improvement, but it can still be made better by applying a third criterion:

3. **A Purpose Statement Must Be Realistic.** You must be able to accomplish your purpose as stated. Some speakers insist on formulating purpose statements such as "My purpose is to convince my audience to make federal budget deficits illegal." Unfortunately, unless your audience happens

Choosing and Developing a Topic

to be a joint session of Congress, it won't have the power to change United States fiscal policy. But any audience can write their congressional represen-tative or sign a petition. Similarly, an audience will not "learn how to play championship tennis" or "understand the dangers of business regulation" in one sitting. You must aim for an audience response that is possible to accomplish. In your gourmet cooking speech, it would be impossible for you to be sure that each of your audience members will actually be able to cook a meal. You might have no idea, for example, if they all have access to a kitchen. So a better purpose statement for this speech might sound something like this:

"After listening to my speech my audience will be able to list the five steps for preparing *cog au vin* at home."

This purpose statement is audience-oriented, precise, and attainable. It also suggests an organizational pattern for the speech ("the five steps").

Consider the following sets of purpose statements:

Less Effective	More Effective
To tell my audience about day-care centers. (not result-oriented)	After listening to my speech, my audience will be able to identify the three basic types of day-care cen-ters.
After listening to my speech, my audience will understand solar power. (not realistic)	After listening to my speech, my audience will understand how solar power can be used at home, in business, and in government. (Once again, this type of purpose state-ment can be particularly effective because it shows you what your main points will be.)
After listening to my speech, my audience will know about drunken driving. (not specific)	After listening to my speech, my audience members will think twice before driving a car after having had more than two drinks.

Write a specific purpose statement for each of the following speeches:

a. An after dinner speech at an awards banquet in which you will honor a team that has a winning, but not championship, record. (You pick the team.)

b. A classroom speech in which you explain how to do something. (Once again, you choose the topic: rebuilding an engine, cooking a favorite dish, playing a guitar, or whatever.)

c. A campaign speech in which you support the candidate of your choice.

Answer the following questions about each of your purpose statements: Is the purpose audience-oriented? Is it precise? Is it attainable?

Turn each of the following purpose statements into a statement that expresses a possible thesis:

a. At the end of my speech the audience members will be willing to sign my petition requesting our congressional representative to support a balanced federal budget.

b. After listening to my speech, the audience members will be able to list five advantages of recycling.

c. During my speech on the trials and tribulations of sailing, the audience members will show their interest by paying attention and their amusement by occasionally laughing.

◆ THE THESIS STATEMENT

So far we have discussed how to select a topic, how partially to focus that topic through its general purpose, and how to focus it further through its specific purpose. Your next step in the focusing process is to formulate your thesis statement. The **thesis statement** tells you what the central idea of your speech is. It tells you the one idea that you want your audience to remember after they have forgotten everything else you had to say. The thesis statement for your *coq au vin* speech might be worded like this:

—Cooking *coq au vin* is a simple, five-step process that can start you on the road to "gourmet cooking."

Unlike your purpose statement, your thesis statement is often spoken directly to your audience. The thesis statement contains more information than the purpose statement, and it is usually formulated later in the speechmaking process, after you have done some research on your topic. The progression from topic to central idea is, therefore, another focusing process as you can see in the following examples:

Topic: Why must an injured horse be destroyed?

General Purpose: To inform

Specific Purpose: After listening to my speech, my audience will understand why certain types of equine injuries cannot be healed. They will not criticize people who put horses to sleep for good reasons.

Thesis Statement: If a horse cannot recover, it is more humane to destroy it than to let it suffer a slow, agonizing death.

Topic: The Bottle Bill

General Purpose: To persuade

Specific Purpose: After listening to my speech, at least half my audience members will sign my petition to the governor supporting a state bottle bill.

Thesis Statement: Returnable-container laws reduce litter, create new employment, and save resources.

Choosing and Developing a Topic

Imagine that Congress has just passed a law requiring that all young people—male and female, without exception—perform two years of required national service immediately after high school (or at the age of eighteen, for those who don't finish high school). This period of national service could be spent in the military, park service, or any government agency. Pay would be at the subsistence level, below minimum wage. The exercise proceeds as follows:

a. Decide whether you will support or oppose this law.
b. Write a purpose statement for a speech in support of your position.
c. Draw up a list of points you might like to make in the speech.
d. With the help of this list, select your thesis and main points.

Once again, this thesis statement evolved after research. This thesis statement is particularly useful because it reveals the three main points of the speech. Another example:

Topic: Saving Water

General Purpose: To persuade

Specific Purpose: After listening to my speech, audience members will use less water in their daily activities.

Thesis Statement: Conserving water is a relatively simple process that will save us from much greater inconveniences in the future.

◆ ANALYZING THE SPEAKING SITUATION

A good speech purpose should be attainable, but it's impossible to know just what you can expect to attain—or the best way to go about attaining it—without analyzing the speaking situation.

There are three components to analyze in any speaking situation: the speaker, the audience, and the occasion. To be successful, every choice you make in putting together your speech—your choice of purpose, topic, and all the material you use to develop your speech—must be appropriate to all three of these components.

You, the Speaker: Self-Analysis

"Above all else," Polonius urged Laertes, in Hamlet, "to thine ownself be true." This is good advice to follow in speech preparation. Don't become so involved in finding a "correct" topic or material that you lose yourself.

One student, after reviewing his personal experience, decided to give a speech that related to his experience as a summer law clerk. He began his speech this way:

At the conclusion of his adventures, Ivanhoe fights an evil knight in that ancient ritual of trial by combat. Ivanhoe, of course, wins the battle, and justice is served. Two summers ago when I took a job as a law clerk in a firm, I was under the impression that this ancient practice of trial by combat had ended centuries ago. But has it?

Today, in our country, we have what is known as an adversarial system of justice. According to legal historian Stuart Nagel, our current adversary system is the direct descendant of trial by combat started in 11th Century England. Nagel characterizes the adversary system as two sides which "combat" one another, each trying desperately to win their case.

But when I worked within our legal system, I did not get that same sense of justice as Sir Walter Scott produced in his novel, *Ivanhoe*. Instead, I saw a legal system that has become too adversarial—a system more concerned with winning the combat than with justice.[5]

Thus, this student's examination of his personal experience became the jumping-off point for an examination of our legal system. Later in his speech, he again called on his personal experience for evidence:

The crimes associated with expert witness testimony became real to me when I worked as a law clerk. The firm I worked for is what is called a plaintiffs' firm. We sent all of our injured clients to a particular doctor who very consistently issued medical reports which said something to the effect of, "This woman will never be able to work again." But, on the opposing side you had your defense firms, and they always had their doctors too who in the same cases would examine the same clients and issue medical reports which said, "This woman should have reported back to work months ago."[6]

Self-analysis is largely a matter of staying in touch with three factors you have already considered: your own purpose, feelings, and unique knowledge and interests.

PURPOSE   We already discussed one step in self-analysis when we considered your purpose as a speaker. The first question to ask yourself when planning a speech (or any other act of communication) is, "What do I want to accomplish?" Having answered this question, you should check every decision that follows to be sure it contributes to your goal.

YOUR FEELINGS   After your purpose has been clarified, a second kind of self-analysis involves your feelings about yourself in the specific speaking situation. As we discussed in Chapter 2, the perceptions of both the speaker and the listener can greatly alter the outcome of any act of communication. Your perception of yourself as a speaker will influence you along every step of the speech-preparation process. If you have a negative self-concept or if you feel negative about the topic, those feelings will show through in the final product. You will be just a little "off" in terms of the topic you've selected, the information you've gathered, the way you present that information, and in every other aspect of your speech. Therefore it's important to look at yourself objectively and to choose a purpose, topic, and material about which you can feel confident and enthusiastic. If you really don't care about gourmet cooking,

◆ **A New York couple decided to spend their vacation in Baltimore, where they were born and raised. En route, they visited the battlefield at Gettysburg, Pennsylvania. The guide who showed them around waxed eloquent about Northern strategy and Northern heroism. They thanked him, paid the usual fee, and happened to drop the remark that they must be getting home to Baltimore before dark.**

The guide's face dropped. "Gosh, from your license plates I took you for New York folks. I should have given you the Southern lecture—matter of fact, I like it better myself."

Jacob Braude

---

the barter economy, consumer credit, or any other subject, then that's not an appropriate topic for you as a speaker—no matter how potentially interesting that topic is to your audience.

YOUR UNIQUE KNOWLEDGE AND INTERESTS A third step in your self-analysis involves recognizing and building on your uniqueness as a person. Though you are obviously similar in many ways to your audience, there are also many respects in which you are different. You can capitalize on this uniqueness by offering the audience something new—your knowledge, your experiences, or perhaps your opinions. Analyze yourself from the point of view of how you are different from your audience. This will give you insight into what you have to offer them. For example, if you have been the object of discrimination or if you know someone who has, then you have an area of uniqueness to talk about.

At the same time, this third step in your self-analysis will help you keep your message close to the listeners' interests and backgrounds; if you know where you're different from them, you'll know where you have to explain things in depth and add human-interest touches to keep from losing their attention. This brings us to our second step in analyzing the situation: your analysis of the audience.

The Listeners: Audience Analysis

When you choose a gift, it's important to consider the person who will receive it; what would be an ideal present for one person could be a disaster for another. In the same way, you need to think about your audience—especially in terms of their interests—when planning a speech. Because the audience's reaction determines the success or failure of a speech we say that public speaking is "audience-oriented." In essence, this means that the more you know about your audience, the more successful your speech will be.

Audience adaptation is something that we have a tendency to do naturally. Research suggests, for example, that in everyday conversations what we say to children and the elderly is simpler, more redundant, and less complex than what we say to other adults.[7] Your speeches will tend to be successful if you extend this principle of audience adaptation to your prepared remarks to a group of listeners.

There are several factors to consider in **audience analysis.**

AUDIENCE TYPE   There are at least three types of audience you are likely to encounter—we could call these types "passersby," "captives," and "volunteers." Each type suggests different audience interests.[8]

"Passersby," as the name implies, are people who aren't much interested—at least not in advance—in what you have to say. A crowd milling around the student union or a shopping mall would fit into this category. With this type of audience, your first concern is to make them aware of you as a speaker either by interesting them in the topic or in you as a speaker. You might have to pick a really sensational topic or begin developing your topic by using some kind of device or gimmick to get their attention, such as the loud costumes or wild theatrics street speakers often rely on.

"Captives" are audience members who have gathered for some reason besides the joy of hearing you speak. Students in a required class often begin as a type of "captive" audience. So do military formations, mandatory work meetings, and other "required" gatherings. With captives you don't have to worry about devices and gimmicks to make them aware of you as a speaker; you do, however, have to use material that will get them interested and keep them interested in what you have to say.

"Volunteers" are audience members who have gathered together because of a common interest. Students in elective courses, especially those with long waiting lists, would fit into this category. So would gatherings of most clubs, social organizations, and "action" groups. Even with an audience of volunteers,

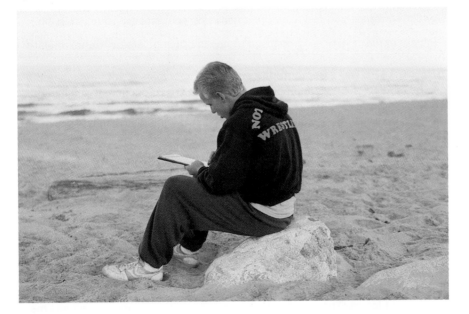

◆ **Think before thou speakest.**

Cervantes
Don Quixote

Choosing and Developing a Topic

you still have to maintain the listeners' interest; you never lose that responsibility. But when the audience is informed and involved, as volunteers tend to be, you can treat your topic in greater depth without worrying about *losing* their interest.

Most college speech classes are a mixture of captives and volunteers, which means that you don't have to sensationalize your topic or use gimmicks, but you do have to maintain interest and provide depth.

AUDIENCE PURPOSE   Just as you have a purpose for speaking, the audience members have a purpose for gathering. Sometimes virtually all members of your audience will have the same, obvious goal. Expectant parents at a natural childbirth class are all seeking a healthy, relatively painless delivery, and people attending an investment seminar are looking for ways to increase their net worth.

There are other times, however, when audience purpose can't be so easily defined. In some instances, different listeners will have different goals, some of which might not be apparent to the speaker. Consider a church congregation, for example. Whereas some members might listen to a sermon with the hope of applying religious principles to their lives, others might be interested in being entertained or in appearing pious. In the same way, the listeners in your speech class probably have a variety of motives for attending; becoming aware of as many of these motives as possible will help you predict what will interest them.

For practice in choosing topics through self-analysis, list the following:

a. Three topics you feel are *inappropriate* for you as a speaker, and for your class as an audience.
b. Three topics you feel are *appropriate* for you, and for your class.

Briefly explain *why* each of these topics is appropriate or inappropriate.

DEMOGRAPHICS   **Demographics** are characteristics of your audience that can be labeled, such as number of people, age, sex, group membership, and so on. Demographic characteristics might affect your speech planning in a number of ways.[9] For example:

1. **Number of People.** Topic appropriateness varies with the size of an audience. With a small group you can be less formal and more intimate— you can, for example, talk more about your own inner feelings and personal experiences. If you gave a speech before five people as impersonally as if they were a standing-room-only crowd in a lecture hall, they would probably find you stuffy. On the other hand, if you talked to 300 people about your unhappy childhood, you'd probably make them uncomfortable. Also, the larger your audience, the broader the range of interests and knowledge; with a small audience, you can choose a more specific topic.

2. **Gender.** Traditionally, men and women have tended to be interested in different topics. These differences are becoming less pronounced as time

goes on because men and women are becoming conscious of sexual stereotypes and are rebelling against them. Still, the differences in interest that prevail are of concern to a speaker in choosing and developing a topic. There are still more men than women interested in automotive engineering and more women than men interested in cooking. The guideline here might be: *Do not exclude or offend any portion of your audience on the basis of sex.* Every speech teacher has a horror story about a student getting up in front of a class composed primarily, but not entirely, of men and speaking on a subject such as "Picking up Chicks." The women, once they realize that the speech is not about methods of handling poultry, are invariably offended. And most of the men will feel the same way.

As with any of these demographic characteristics, the point is to *analyze,* not *stereotype* your audience. This will enable you to adapt your idea (rather than throwing it away) according to who is in your audience. The speaker who wants to speak to a mixed audience on how man meets woman, or vice versa, may still do so; the topic of the speech, however, should be "meeting people." That way it can be treated in a manner that would be appropriate for both men and women. This is true of topics like "weight lifting" (which could be changed to "body conditioning") and "home economics" (which could be changed to "survival for singles").

3. **Age.** In many areas younger people and older people have different interests. Topics such as social security, child rearing, and school success are all influenced by the age of the audience. These differences run relatively deep; Aristotle observed long ago that young people "have strong passions," that "their lives are spent not in memory but in expectation," and that they have high ideals because "they have not been humbled by life or learned its necessary limitations." Older people, on the other hand, tend to have more practical interests.

4. **Group Membership.** Organizations to which the audience members belong provide more clues to audience interests. By examining the groups to which they belong, you can surmise an audience's political leanings (Young Republicans or Young Democrats), religious beliefs (CYO or Hillel), or occupation (Bartenders Union or Speech Communication Association). Group membership is often an important consideration in college classes. Consider the difference between "typical" college day classes and "typical" college night classes. At many colleges the evening students are generally older and tend to belong to civic groups, church clubs, and the local chamber of commerce. Daytime students tend to belong to sororities and fraternities, sports clubs, and social-action groups.

For practice in analyzing speech situations, carry out the following exercise with your classmates:

a. Prepare, in advance, three index cards: one with a possible topic for a speech, one with a possible audience, and one with a possible occasion.

◆ **Length Versus Depth**

The speaker steps up on the podium
To give his speech of praise or odium,
And as he lays his papers out
And ranges them with care about
And thinks, "My speech is for the ages,"
His hearers try to count the pages.

Richard Armour

Choosing and Developing a Topic

b. Form groups of three members each, and place your cards face down, with one member's "audience" matched with a second member's "topic" and a third member's "occasion," and so on.

c. Turn the cards over. For each set, decide which characteristics of the audience, topic, and occasion would most likely affect the way the speech was developed.

d. Compare notes with the other groups to see who had the most unlikely matchup, as well as the best analysis.

A sample set of cards might look like this:

Topic: Morals on campus.

Audience: The auxiliary for the local ambulance squad. All members are between the ages of thirty-five and fifty, and all married to members of the volunteer ambulance squad.

Occasion: Annual awards banquet, at which you're about to receive an award for special achievement in your topic area.

These four demographic characteristics are important examples, but the list goes on and on. Other demographic characteristics include ethnic background, religion, educational level, economic status, and occupation; demographics that might be important in a college class include hometown, year in school, and major subject. A student at North Dakota State University adapted her speech on adult illiteracy to her college audience by beginning it like this:

College campuses are saturated with Greek-named sorority and fraternity houses. If you're unaccustomed to Kappa, Rho, or Delta, these letters are as meaningless as a blank piece of paper. Or picture yourself in downtown Tokyo trying to translate the written squiggles on a billboard into common words like "restaurant" or "bus stop." Fortunately, most of us don't have these problems in everyday life. But there are individuals who must interpret the written English language in much the same way.[10]

Here is how another student adapted her speech on "Learning to Communicate" to an audience of speech majors:

With backgrounds in speech, we can be the solution to this problem. It's actually very simple. Since we possess the skills that the children need to learn, we can instruct them in the basics of oral communication. This solution involves no tricky legislation or money, just a little time. . . . [11]

As these examples show, audience consideration doesn't stop with prior analysis. You should use your understanding of your audience to include audience references within your speech. In short, any demographic characteristic of the audience that you can identify should be used as part of your audience analysis.

A final factor to consider in audience analysis concerns their attitudes, beliefs, and values.

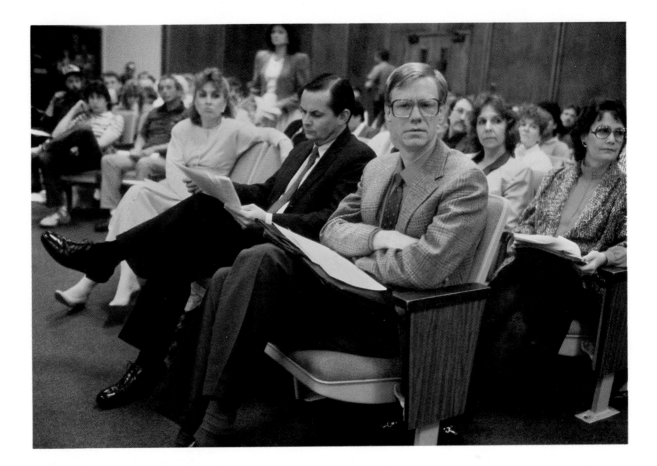

ATTITUDES, BELIEFS, AND VALUES   An audience's feelings about you, your subject, and your intentions for them are central issues in audience analysis. One way to approach these questions is through a consideration of attitudes, beliefs, and values. These characteristics are structured in human consciousness like layers of an onion. They are all closely interrelated, but attitudes lie closest to the surface whereas beliefs and values underlie them. An **attitude** is a predisposition to respond to something in a favorable or unfavorable way. A **belief** is an underlying conviction about the truth of something, which is often based on cultural training. A **value** is a deeply rooted belief about a concept's inherent worth or worthiness. An audience might hold the value that "freedom is a good thing," for example, which will be expressed in a belief such as "people should be free to choose their political leaders," which, in turn, will lead to the attitude that "voting is an important right and responsibility for all citizens." This, in short, leads to a predisposition to vote— in other words, a positive attitude toward voting.

In diagram form, attitudes, beliefs, and values might appear as shown in Figure 11–1.

◆ **You must look into people, as well as at them.**

Lord Chesterfield

Choosing and Developing a Topic

FIGURE 11–1
Structure of Values, Beliefs,
and Attitudes

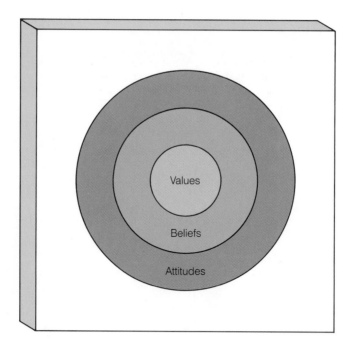

One publication recently polled a group of philosophers, historians, and other observers of the American character, and came up with five values we seem to share:[12]

1. Citizenship: Americans believe, at least subconsciously, that informed participation in government is the key to democracy. The power of this value is revealed in everything from our willingness to vote or serve on juries to our insistence on "knowing everything" about political scandals.
2. Work Ethic: For Americans, work isn't just a way to make money, it's a virtue—something we believe makes us better people.
3. Tolerance: The acceptance of a wide variety of views and traditions is America's oldest value. It is the reason the Pilgrims arrived on the *Mayflower* and the reason Soviet Jews come to our shores today. We pride ourselves on remaining a "melting pot" for the whole world.
4. Justice for All: Americans believe in the importance of a fair and effective legal system. We believe that the guilty should be punished and the innocent should go free.
5. Individualism: Americans believe people should be able to do what they want, to "be themselves," to fail or succeed through their own efforts.

Experts in audience analysis, such as professional speechwriters, often try to concentrate on values. As one team of researchers pointed out, "Values have the advantage of being comparatively small in number, and, owing to their abstract nature, are more likely to be shared by large numbers of people.[13]

President George Bush recognized this characteristic of values when he said in his inaugural address,

> We are not the sum of our possessions...We cannot hope only to leave our children a bigger car, a bigger bank account. We must hope to give them a sense of what it means to be a loyal friend, a loving parent, a citizen who leaves his home, his neighborhood and town better than he found it.[14]

President Bush knew that he could appeal to deeply felt values in his audience. These values exist within people of many differing political beliefs.

You can often make an inference about audience attitudes by recognizing beliefs and values they are likely to hold. For example, a group of religious fundamentalists might hold the value of "obeying God's word." This might lead to the belief—based on their interpretation of the Bible—that women are not meant to perform the same functions in society as men. This, in turn, might lead to the attitude that women ought not to pursue careers as fire fighters, police officers, or construction workers.

You can also make a judgment about one attitude your audience members hold based on your knowledge of other attitudes they hold. If your audience is made up of undergraduates who have a positive attitude toward liberation movements, it is a good bet they also have a positive attitude toward civil rights and ecology. If they have a negative attitude toward collegiate sports, they probably also have a negative attitude toward fraternities and sororities. This should not only suggest some appropriate topics for each audience, but it should also suggest ways that those topics could be developed.

The Occasion

The third phase in analyzing a speaking situation focuses on the occasion. The "occasion" of a speech is determined by the circumstances surrounding it. Three of these circumstances are time, place, and audience expectations.

TIME Your speech occupies a space in time that is surrounded by other events. For example, other speeches might be presented before or after yours, or comments might be made that set a certain tone or mood. There are also external events (such as elections, the start of a new semester, or even the weather) that color the occasion in one way or the other. The date on which you give your speech might have some historical significance. If that historical significance relates in some way to your topic, you can use it to help build audience interest.

The time *available* for your speech is also an essential consideration. You should choose a topic that is broad enough to say something worthwhile but brief enough to fit your time limits. "Wealth," for example, might be an inherently interesting topic to some college students, but it would be difficult to cover such a broad topic in a ten-minute speech and still say anything significant. But a topic like "How to Make Extra Money in Your Spare Time" could conceivably be covered in ten minutes in enough depth to make it worthwhile. All speeches have time limitations, whether they are explicitly stated or not. If you are invited to say a few words and you present a few volumes, you won't be invited back.

◆ **Of the three elements in speechmaking— speaker, subject, and person addressed—it is the last one, the hearer, that determines the speech's end and object.**

Aristotle

Choosing and Developing a Topic

Sample Analysis of A Speaking Situation

Audience: Sons of Italy Club

Situation: Acceptance speech for scholarship award.

Purposes
1. The audience will know that I'm grateful for receiving the scholarship.
2. The audience will realize that I'm not the stereotyped bookworm that scholarship recipients are usually viewed as.
3. The audience will think that they've given the scholarship to the right person.

When I began planning the speech, I couldn't decide if I wanted to do it in Italian or English. I was considering Italian because of the nature of the club and because I thought it would impress the audience if I used that language: They might think "She's a good Italian" and "She's bright." In the end I decided to speak in English. Even though most of the audience would understand my Italian, there were a few important people who didn't speak it.

My audience consisted of mostly middle-aged and older people. There were about 150 to 200 of them. Among the special guests were the mayor and some club representatives from out of town. I knew that I had to sound sincere and yet be organized enough to show that I had a "good head on my shoulders." On the other hand, I didn't want to give the audience the impression that I was superstudious and did nothing but study. For this reason, I began the speech by acknowledging the audience's feelings of boredom after sitting through forty minutes of other speeches. I thought this would show that I was one of them. I acknowledged this feeling because from past experiences with this particular audience I know that they are more interested in the festivities and dancing following dinner than with any ceremonies.

Also to get away from the bookworm stereotype, I dressed in a very sophisticated (yet not too sexy—I'm a "nice Italian girl"!) manner, in a black midcalf dress.

My entire speech supported the idea that I was honored to receive the scholarship by describing my sincere feelings of enthusiasm. I also threw in a few Italian phrases for authenticity and concluded the speech by encouraging everyone to have a great time that evening.

The speech was a big success. I was very sincere and emotional while giving it, so the audience knew it was coming from my heart. My happiness showed in my smile. I felt comfortable looking at the audience a lot because I had practiced the speech well and because I knew they were behind me. Because of my nervousness and excitement my voice was quivery, but I think even this helped my purpose although I didn't plan it that way.

The reception I received from the audience was tremendous, which made me feel good because it made me realize that I had accomplished my purposes.

PLACE Your speech also occupies a physical space. The beauty or squalor of your surroundings or the noise or stuffiness of the room should all be taken into consideration. These physical surroundings can be referred to in your speech if appropriate. If you were talking about world poverty, for example, you could compare your surroundings to those that might be found in a poorer country.

AUDIENCE EXPECTATION Finally, your speech is surrounded by audience expectations. A speech presented in a college class, for example, is usually expected to reflect a high level of thought and intelligence. This doesn't necessarily mean that it has to be boring or humorless; wit and humor are, after all, indicative of intelligence. But it does mean that you have to put a little more effort into your presentation than if you were discussing the same subject with friends over coffee.

When you are considering the occasion of your speech, as well as when you are considering your audience and yourself as a speaker, it pays to remember that every occasion is unique. Although there are obvious differences between the occasion of a college class, a church sermon, and a bachelor party "roast," there are also many subtle differences that will apply only to the circumstances of each unique event. A sample analysis of a speaking situation can be found on p. 326.

◆ GATHERING INFORMATION

This discussion about planning a speech purpose and analyzing the speech situation makes it apparent that it takes time, interest, and knowledge to develop a topic well. Much of the knowledge you present in your speech will be based on your own thoughts and experience. Setting aside a block of time to reflect on your own ideas is essential. However, you will also need to gather information from outside sources.

There are three types of information you need for a speech. We've already discussed the first category, which is information dealing with the speaking situation (you, the audience, and the occasion). In addition, you also need information about the *ideas* you use and *facts* to substantiate and help develop your ideas. By this time, of course, you are familiar with library research as a form of gathering information. Sometimes, however, speakers overlook some of the less obvious resources of the library; more often they also overlook interviewing, personal observation, and survey research as equally effective methods of gathering information. We will review all these methods here and perhaps provide a new perspective on one or more of them.

Library Research

Libraries, like people, tend to be unique. It's important to get to know your own library, to see what kind of special collections and services it offers, and just to find out where everything is. There are, however, a few resources that are common to most libraries, including the card catalog, reference works, periodicals, and nonprint materials.

THE CARD CATALOG   The card catalog is an ancient and noble information-storing device. Today many card catalogs are computerized or stored on microfilm. Whatever its form, the card catalog is your key to all the books in the library, filed according to subject, author, and title, so that you can look under general topics as well as for specific books and authors.

◆ A library is a sacred place. For four thousand years, humanity has gone through dreadful horrors, dreadful turmoils, varied glories. How do we distill the past? How do we retain the memories? Libraries.

Vartan Gregorian

Choosing and
Developing a Topic

This exercise will give you practice in gathering information.

a. Choose a current expression with a derivation that you are interested in but unsure about. For example, you might choose a term such as *bogus, bodacious,* or *retro.*

b. Once you have decided on an expression, try to find out as much as you can about its derivation. Use the library, conduct an interview or two, do a survey, and observe the context in which your chosen expression is used around your campus and among your friends and acquaintances.

REFERENCE WORKS   Reference works will also be listed in the card catalog, but it would be a better idea to spend some time wandering through the reference room yourself. There are wonders there that could turn you into a trivia expert for life. There are encyclopedias galore, even specialized ones such as *The Encyclopedia of Social Sciences* and *The Encyclopedia of American History;* there are statistical compilations such as *The World Almanac, Facts on File,* and *The Guinness Book of World Records;* you can find out *Who's Who in America* or even *Who Was Who.* You can collect a lot of facts in a short time in the reference room. Reference works are good for uncovering basic information, definitions, descriptions, and sources for further investigation.

PERIODICALS   Magazines, journals, and newspapers are good resources for finding recently published material on interesting topics. Indexes such as

The Readers' Guide to Periodical Literature will enable you to find popular magazine articles on just about any subject. Specialized indexes such as *The Education Index* and *Psychological Abstracts* can be used to find articles in specific fields, and newspaper indexes such as *The New York Times Index* can be used to find microfilmed newspaper articles. Periodicals are a good source of high-interest, up-to-date information on your topic.

NONPRINT MATERIALS   Most libraries are also treasuries of nonprint and audiovisual materials. Films, records, tapes, and videotapes can be used not only as research tools but as aids during your presentation. Your library probably has an orientation program that will acquaint you with what it has to offer in the way of nonprint materials.

ON-LINE DATA BASES   A growing number of libraries have access to **on-line data bases.** These are computerized collections of information that can be searched via telephone link. One popular collection of data bases is Dialog Information Retrieval Service. Dialog contains over 80,000,000 records from news services, magazines, scholarly journals, conference papers, books, and other sources. Other popular databases include Infotrac Academic Index, which covers popular journals for the last few years, and the *New York Times* for the most recent six months; Infotrac National Newspapers Index, which covers the *Christian Science Monitor, Los Angeles Times, New York Times, Wall Street Journal,* and the *Washington Post;* and ERIC. Many libraries also have computerized card catalogs. With a conscientious search strategy, you can locate scores of citations on your topic in just a few minutes rather than spending hours or weeks looking manually. Once you have located the items you want, it is possible to read abstracts or even entire articles on the screen of the library's computer terminal—or print out a list of citations for further review. For example, if you were searching for statistics about AIDS in the Fall of 1989, you would have fed "AIDS statistics" into Infotrac and received the following printout:

```
                                           Academic Index
AIDS PATIENTS
  -statistics
  AIDS in a deficit year: more plans than money. (column) by
Bruce Lambert ii 16 col in. v138 The New York Times  April 23  89
sec 4  pE24 (N) pE24 (L) col )

  AIDS is still on rise in U.S., but the rate of growth is
slower. (National Pages) 7 col in.  v138 The New York Times
April 15  89  p8 (N) p28 (L)  col 4

  How to block a killer's path; new infections are down among
gays but up in the drug culture. (includes a related article on 5
other sexually transmitted diseases) (Special Report: good and
bad news about AIDS) (obituary) by John Langone ii  v133  Time
Jan 30  89  p89 (3) 48C0 625  42Y2259
```

◆ **The mind of the orator grows and expands with the subject. Without ample materials no splendid oration was ever yet produced.**

Tacitus, A.D. 80

Choosing and Developing a Topic

AIDS toll underestimated in IV drug users, by Kathy
Hackelmann v134 Science News Nov 12 88 p311 (1)
47E0008

The AIDS numbers racket: chapter 37. by Michael Humento v40
National Review Oct 14 88 p45 (2)
46K0258

Global grip of AIDS. (meeting of international AIDS experts)
il v104 U.S. News & World Report Feb 8 88 p8 (1)
43C1159 3652964

How widespread is AIDS? (AIDS: everything you must know.) by
Elizabeth M. Whelan il v116 USA Today Oct 87 p7 (2)
4101376

AIDS and women; nonwhites face the biggest risk. v129 Time
April 27 87 p34 (10) 38H5/45

Q. and A. on AIDS. by Michael Stone il v20 New York March 23
87 p34 (10) 38H5/45

The bind that ties all nations. (AIDS is pandemic) by Avery
Comarow il v102 U.S. News & World Report Jan 12 87 p64 (1)
37C0561

AIDS goes from bad to worse. (spread of AIDS is forecast) il
v100 U.S. News & World Report June 23 88 p8 (1)
34J2703

LIBRARIANS If you have explored all the sources mentioned in the
preceding section and you still can't find exactly what you need, seek out a
librarian. Today's librarians are trained in special search techniques, and their
familiarity with the resources of their library is exhaustive. Of course, part of
the effectiveness of your interaction with the librarian will depend on your
communication skills: your ability to ask clear, specific questions; to be direct
but polite; and to listen effectively. This is also true in other forms of
information-gathering interviews.

Interviewing

As we discussed in Chapter 8, the information-gathering interview is an
especially valuable form of research on a college campus because so many
experts of every stripe run loose there. The interview allows you to view your
topic from an expert's perspective, to take advantage of that expert's years of
experience, research, and thought. You can use an interview to collect facts
and to stimulate your own thinking. Often the interview will save you hours of
library research and allow you to present ideas that you could not have

uncovered any other way. And because the interview is a face-to-face interaction with an expert, many ideas that otherwise would be unclear can become more understandable.

Personal Observation

Personal *experience* is one of the basic ingredients of any speech, but unsupported personal *opinions* can be detrimental. As a method of gathering information, personal observation gives some extra weight to your personal opinion. For example, if you were suggesting to an audience that the TV sets in your student union should be removed, you might say this:

> I think people would interact more here if the televisions were removed from the student union.

But all you have there is personal opinion, which could be based on anything, including a purely emotional hatred of television or of college students. The use of personal observation, however, might allow you to say this:

> Last Wednesday I spent 7:00 to 10:00 P.M. in the lounge of the student union. Only three times during the evening did anyone attempt to start a conversation. Two of those attempts were met with a request for silence in deference to the television.

If you wanted to prove your point further, you could go one step beyond and observe the same situation under different circumstances:

> This Wednesday I received permission to remove the television from the student union. During those same hours, 7:00 to 10:00 P.M., I observed the following behavior in that lounge, this time without television:
>
> 1. Thirty conversations were begun.
> 2. Twenty-four of these conversations continued, in depth, for more than ten minutes.
> 3. Seven groups of students decided on alternative entertainment for the evening, including table games, singing, dancing, and going to the library.
> 4. Four new male-female acquaintances were made, one of which resulted in a TV date for the following Wednesday night.

Personal observation is used to collect information about human beings. Because your job as a public speaker is communicating with human beings and because human beings love information about themselves, observing their behavior firsthand can be an extremely valuable form of investigation. Survey research is also valuable in this respect.

Survey Research

One advantage of handing out a survey to your audience (a week or so before your speech) is that it gives you up-to-date answers concerning "the way things are" for a specific audience. Consider the following ideas, either of which might be presented in a speech on giving children a right to divorce their parents:

◆ I've been vaguely aware that what I'm searching for in some loony, unfathomable manner, are not the answers, but The Answers. Somewhere, sprinkled out amongst the best minds of the century, are clues. And someone's tongue is bound to slip.

Digby Diehl
Supertalk

A survey conducted in 1980 suggests that five out of ten college students are in favor of greater civil rights for children. (library-type data)

According to a survey I conducted last week, 90 percent of the students in this class are in favor of greater civil rights for children. And yet the same proportion—nine out of ten—are undecided about granting children the right to divorce their parents. (survey-type data)

That second statement would probably be of more immediate interest to an audience of students. That is one advantage of conducting your own survey. Another advantage is that it is one of the best ways to find out about your audience: It is in fact *the* best way to collect the demographic data mentioned earlier. The one disadvantage of conducting your own survey is that, if it is used as evidence, it might not have as much credibility as published evidence found in the library. But, all in all, the advantages seem to outweigh the disadvantages of **survey research** in public speaking.

No matter how you gather your information, remember that it is the *quality* rather than the quantity of the research that is most important. The key is to determine carefully what type of research will answer the questions you need to have answered. Sometimes only one type of research will be necessary; at other times every type mentioned here will have to be used.

◆ SAMPLE SPEECH

The following speech was given by Kevin Smith, a student at William Jewell College in Missouri. He was coached by Gina Lane, and presented the speech at the 1988 Interstate Oratorical Association Annual Contest, which was held in Oregon. Kevin didn't win the contest, but he does provide us with an excellent example of a well chosen topic and a speech that sticks to its purpose. Notice also, as you read his speech, the effectiveness of his research and his audience analysis.

Kevin's general purpose was "to persuade." His specific purpose could be stated as follows:

After listening to my speech, the members of my audience will consider becoming involved with the illiteracy problem—either as volunteer tutors, or as casual advocates.

His thesis statement:

Illiteracy is an extremely serious problem that we could all help solve.

The Shadow People[15]   KEVIN SMITH

1. It is dark in the cave. Those who live there—the Shadow People, as Plato called them—see each other, but in the murk and gloom, see no eyes, no smiles, only ghostly outlines. In the darkness of the cave, the Shadow People think that is the way everything looks—just shadows.

2. The impenetrable darkness of this cave is the darkness of illiteracy. The Shadow People are like adult illiterates everywhere, often unable to do more than grope from a meaningless job to the unemployment line, where they will be not only a burden to taxpayers, but menace to their own self-respect.

3. Those of us who believe acquiring knowledge is ennobling, and providing knowledge is noble, recognize well the importance of illiteracy. Unfortunately, despite that recognition, the ranks of the Shadow People have grown to outrageous proportions, requiring our immediate action. As a volunteer literacy tutor, I've had the opportunity to see firsthand the darkness of the cave. But, I've also seen how that cave can be illuminated through our efforts. So, in examining the subject of adult illiteracy, let's find out how dark the cave is, then let's see how we can carry a lamp of literacy into the cavern.

4. Any debater who has ever had trouble reading their partner's flowsheet will have no trouble believing illiteracy knows no boundaries. In truth, the darkness of illiteracy has fallen across millions of lives. The Department of Education estimates that the number of adult illiterates at near 25 million people. But, Harvard English professor and adult literacy activist Jeanne Chall estimates the number of illiterates at up to 78 million. Whatever the correct estimate is, at least one in eight Americans, a greater number than the population of Canada, is illiterate.

5. But, the problem goes beyond mere widespread reading problems. In 1984, two researchers at the University of Texas investigated how many adults lack the skill to manage and survive as a result of their inability to read and write. Their Adult Performance Level study found that 14% could not fill out a check that would clear a bank. Thirteen percent could not address an envelope well enough to guarantee it would reach its destination. And, 28% were unable to calculate the change they should get back after paying at a check-out stand with a twenty dollar bill. According to the researchers, if the Adult Performance Level is right, 35% of our adult population is unequipped to carry out most basic tasks.

6. This losing battle to cope has many casualties. According to Ben Craig, President of a Charlotte, North Carolina bank that has donated $50,000 to adult literacy programs, "The drain of illiterates on the economy and our tax dollars can be measured by their numbers in social welfare programs, in our prisons, in our juvenile delinquency programs and in our unemployment lines."

**Choosing and
Developing a Topic**

According to the Department of Health and Human Services, $6 billion goes to adult illiterates unable to perform tasks required for employment. According to a 1985 Department of Education study, 42% of adult illiterates had no earnings the previous year, and required public aid.

7. But, for society, the unlettered will be at best a burden, at worst a menace. Almost 60% of our nation's prison population is unable to read. It is estimated that $6.6 billion is spent annually on the imprisonment of illiterate convicted felons for whom crimes against us seem the only road.

8. The examples of the damage of illiteracy are numerous. Senator George McGovern reported to the U. S. Senate that one illiterate Navy recruit recently caused $250,000 in damage—a quarter of a million dollars damage—because he could not read the repair manual. The sad irony of the event was emphasized by McGovern's words: "He tried, but failed to follow the illustrations." We have to wonder how many similarly disabled people are staffing hospitals, airport maintenance hangars and nuclear reactors, no longer endangering only costly equipment, but our lives, as well.

9. Illiteracy takes a personal toll, as well. It consigns countless souls to lives of wordless isolation. Michael Harrington, author of *The Other America,* writes, "Whatever the precise calibrations, it is obvious that these statistics represent an enormous, an unconscionable amount of human suffering. They should be read with a sense of outrage."

10. One soul in Plato's modern cave is particularly poignant. *Time* magazine recently reported that one illiterate mother gave her infant son two harmless looking pink tablets, thinking they were antacid. A few minutes later, the child was dead. The tablets weren't Pepto-Bismol, as she had thought. They were chlorine tablets used to purify campground dishwashing water. Another mother signed what she thought was a simple school field trip permission form, only to discover that she had relegated her daughter to a home for the mentally retarded.

11. Perhaps nothing could better describe the day-to-day plight of the Shadow People than the words of a Vermont cow farmer: "I was alone without my wife's guidance when it come to readin'. In order to find out what's goin' on, you've got to read. When you're on the farm with cows they don't ask you no questions. But when you're out in public, you got to know it all. And if you don't read, you can't."

12. This farmer and others like him in factories, in garages, in offices across the country are living in darkness, never fully managing the obstacles they find in the cave. They may have been victims of a poor reading program, or passed along in school without ever having to show they could read, or perhaps they weren't motivated to learn during their school years. Whatever the reason,

millions of illiterates want to learn today. Yet, according to Barbara Holmes, Senior Policy Analyst for the Education Commission for the state, fewer than 10% of those who need help are receiving any. But, we have the opportunity to change all that. What can we do to illuminate the cave?

13. First, we who call communication our specialty, must communicate to others—government, business people, civic leaders—the tragedy of adult illiteracy. We must encourage them to support adult literacy programs, whether through federal, state and local programs, or through business or charity groups. Such programs won't be cheap, but when compared to what Patricia Weir, President of Encyclopedia Britannica, Incorporated calls the $225 billion annual cost for illiteracy, they are a steal. It is important, too, that we teach adults as adults. We should realize what the Moonlight Schools of Kentucky knew 80 years ago, when they ran adult literacy programs using books about farming, family care and their adult-life problems. We should be wary, though, of those who, despite the obvious darkness of the cave, would try to snuff out our lamp. Jeff Riggenbach wrote in a March *USA Today* column, "The moral of the story is quite simple: The furor over illiteracy has been exaggerated by self-serving interests. We would do well to ignore it." As part of our effort to bring light to the cave, we must be prepared to fight such apathy. We can all help as tutors, too. Several national programs exist that offer training for tutors. In the program with which I am involved, I have had the opportunity to help those like the grandmother who simply wanted to be able to read to her granddaughter and the middle-aged man who had to learn to read to keep his job. If you would like to help, most public libraries can help you connect with adults who need help.

14. With each person we tell about the costs of adult illiteracy, we increase the chances that one more person will become involved in the fight against illiteracy. When we get involved with tutoring, we are assuring that at least one more person is no longer stumbling in the darkness.

15. It is dark in the cave. We are drawn to it. We can hear the Shadow People in the dimness within. We can only imagine the chaos inside. Let us pick up the lamp. Let us pierce the darkness of the cave. Let us bring the light of literacy to the Shadow People.

Comments on Speech

Through his research, Kevin has dug up an intriguing metaphor based on classical literature (paragraphs 1, 2, 10, 15), as well as current information culled from books, periodicals, and interviews (4–13). He has adapted to his specific audience: the speech tournament judges and participants who sit before him would be very familiar with a flowsheet (4), which is a chart that debaters use to keep track of arguments. Later (13), he appeals to this audience as a group of communication experts. He also makes use of his personal experience, first as the basis of his topic choice, and later (3, 13) as supporting material for his ideas. We'll have more to say about supporting material in the next chapter.

Choosing and Developing a Topic

This chapter dealt with your first tasks in preparing a public speech: choosing and developing a topic.

Some guidelines for choosing a topic include these: Look for a topic early and stick with it, choose a topic you find interesting, and choose a topic you know something about to begin with.

One of your tasks is to understand your purpose so that you can stick to it as your prepare your speech. General purposes include entertaining, informing, and persuading. Specific purposes are expressed in the form of purpose statements, which must be audience-oriented, precise, and attainable.

Your next step is to formulate a thesis statement, which tells what the central idea of your speech is.

Another early task is to analyze the three components of the speaking situation—yourself, the audience, and the occasion. When analyzing yourself, you should consider your feelings about your topic and your unique knowledge and interests, as well as your purpose. When analyzing your audience, you should consider the audience type (passersby, captives, volunteers), purpose, demographics, attitudes, beliefs, and values. When analyzing the occasion, you should consider the time (and date) your speech will take place, the time available, the location, and audience expectations.

Although much of your speech will be based on personal reflection about your own ideas and experiences, it is usually necessary to gather some information from outside sources. Techniques for doing so include interpersonal research (such as interviewing), personal observation, and surveys, as well as library research.

Throughout all these preliminary tasks you will be organizing information. This process will be discussed in the next chapter.

◆ NOTES

1. A complete analysis of the steps Candy Lightner followed in preparing and presenting her first speech is provided in George Rodman, *Public Speaking,* 3d ed. (New York: CBS College Publishing, 1986), pp. 5–17.

2. David Wallechinsky, Irving Wallace, and Amy Wallace, *The Book of Lists* (New York: William Morrow, 1977), p. 469.

3. Those interested in further reading on the topic of stimulating creativity about speech topics, or any task, will want to read the following: "Take a Break and Incubate," *Prevention* 39 (September 1987): 75–78; "The Creativity Doctors," *Health* (April 1989): 61–63 (see especially "How to Mind-Map" on p. 62; and Richard L. Weaver, "Second Wind: Capitalizing on Your Full Creative Potential," *Vital Speeches of the Day,* February 1, 1987, pp. 235–238 (an inspirational speech from one of the acknowledged masters of the field).

4. Leon Fletcher, *How to Design and Deliver a Speech,* 4th ed. (New York: Harper & Row, 1990).

5. David G. Levasseur, "Justice and the Balance," *Winning Orations, 1988* (Interstate Oratorical Association, 1988).

6. Ibid.

7. Gwen Asburn and Alice Gordon, "Features of Simplified Register in Speech to Elderly Conversationalists," *International Journal of Psycholinguistics* 8:3 (1981): 7–31.

8. Different theorists mention different audience "types." See, for example, H. L. Hollingsworth, *The Psychology*

of the Audience (New York: American Book, 1935), pp. 19–32.

9. An example of how demographics such as race, age, and union membership affect an audience's perception of messages can be found in Carl H. Botan and Lawrence R. Frey, "Do Workers Trust Labor Unions and Their Messages?" *Communication Monographs* 50 (September 1983): 233–244.

10. Joan Braaten, "It's English," *Winning Orations, 1984* (Interstate Oratorical Association, 1984), p. 64.

11. Marcie Groover, "Learning to Communicate: The Importance of Speech Education in Public Schools," *Winning Orations, 1984,* p. 9.

12. Leah Eskin, "Five American Values," *Scholastic Update,* February 26, 1988, pp. 6–9.

13. Randall K. Stutman and Sara E. Newell, "Beliefs Versus Values: Salient Beliefs in Designing a Persuasive Message," *Western Journal of Speech Communication* 48:4 (Fall 1984): 364. For an example of how values are used in the analysis of political speeches, see Steve Goldzwig, "James Watt's Subversion of Values: An Analysis of Rhetorical Failure," *Southern Speech Communication Journal* 4 (Summer 1985): 305–326. According to Goldzwig, Watt "violated the sacred values and shibboleths of the American Dream."

14. The transcript of President Bush's Inaugural Address can be found in the *New York Times* of January 22, 1989.

15. Kevin Smith, "The Shadow People," *Winning Orations, 1988,* p. 68.

Choosing and Developing a Topic

12

After reading this chapter, you should understand the following:

1. The importance of clear speech organization.

2. The basic structure of a speech.

3. The steps involved in organizing the body of a speech.

4. The importance of effective introductions, conclusions, and transitions.

5. The functions and types of supporting material.

You should be able to do the following:

1. Construct an effective speech outline, using the organizing principles described in this chapter.

2. Develop an effective introduction, conclusion, and transitions.

3. Choose verbal supporting material for a speech to make your points clear, interesting, memorable, and convincing.

4. Choose appropriate visual aids for a presentation.

KEY TERMS

analogy
anecdote
bar charts
basic speech structure
cause-effect patterns
climax patterns
column chart
conclusion (of a speech)
diagram
example
formal outline
hypothetical example
introduction (of a speech)
line chart
model

number chart
pictograph
pie chart
problem-solution pattern
quantification
space pattern
statistics
testimony
time pattern
topic pattern
transition
visual aid
word chart
working outline

Organization and Support

Knowing what you want to say and *communicating* that knowledge aren't the same thing. It's frustrating to know you aren't expressing your thoughts clearly, and it's equally unpleasant to know another speaker has something worth saying, yet be unable to figure out just what it is.

In the following pages, you will learn methods of organizing your thoughts in a way that others can follow. Clarity isn't the only benefit of good organization: Structuring a message effectively will help you refine and clarify your own ideas and then present them in a way that is comprehensible and persuasive.

◆ STRUCTURING THE SPEECH

◆ **If you have an important point to make, don't try to be subtle or clever. Use a pile driver. Hit the point once. Then come back and hit it again. Then hit it a third time—a tremendous whack.**

Winston Churchill

A good speech is like a good building: Both grow from a careful plan. In Chapter 11 you began this planning by analyzing your audience, formulating a purpose, and conducting research. Now you will learn how to apply the information you developed there.

Types of Outlines

An outline is the framework on which your speech is built. It contains your main ideas and shows how they relate to one another and your thesis. Virtually every speech outline ought to follow the basic structure outlined in Figure 12–1.

This **basic speech structure** demonstrates the old aphorism for speakers: "Tell what you're going to say, say it, and then tell what you said." Although this structure sounds redundant, the research on listening cited in Chapter 4 demonstrates that receivers forget most of what they hear. The clear, repetitive nature of the basic speech structure reduces the potential for memory loss, because audiences have a tendency to listen more carefully during the beginning and ending of a speech.[1] Outlines come in all shapes and sizes, but they can generally be classified in one of three categories.

WORKING OUTLINES   **Working,** or "scratch," **outlines** are construction tools used in building your speech. Unlike a formal outline, a working outline is a constantly changing, personal device. You begin organizing your speech material from a rough working outline; then, as your ideas solidify, your outline changes accordingly.

A working outline is for your eyes only. No one else need understand it, so you can use whatever symbols and personal shorthand you find functional. In fact, your working outline will probably become pretty messy by the time you are ready to create a formal outline for others to see.

FORMAL OUTLINES   The outline seen in Figure 12–2 is a **formal outline.** It uses a consistent format and set of symbols to identify the structure of ideas.

A formal outline serves several purposes. In simplified form, it can be used as a visual aid (on a poster board, for example, or distributed as a handout). It can serve as a record of a speech that was delivered. Many organizations send outlines to members who miss meetings at which presentations were

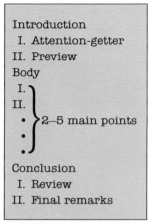

FIGURE 12–1
Basic Speech Structure

FIGURE 12–2
Speech Outline

Topic: "The Causes of Modern Illness"
Purpose: After listening to my speech, my audience members will be able to list at least three ways to avoid typical modern illness.
Thesis: The three main causes of modern illness are poor diet, pollution, and stress, all of which can be controlled to some extent by each of us.
Title: "Are You Committing Nutritional Suicide?"

Introduction
  I. Do you ever feel like this?
     Quotation: Adelle Davis on exhaustion.
 II. You *can* make yourself feel better. (Preview main points)
Body
  I. Modern people often suffer from poor diets.
     A. Too many convenience foods can cause malnutrition.
     B. Too many chemical preservatives can cause toxic reactions.
     C. Irregularly scheduled meals can cause gastric disorders.
        Internal summary: What to do about it.
        Transition: Diet is only one form of "pollution."
 II. Modern people are subjected to more pollution than ever before.
     A. Air pollution contributes to respiratory diseases.
        Statistics: Bergsman
     B. Water pollution contributes to digestive diseases.
     C. Noise pollution contributes to nervous disorders.
        Internal summary: What to do about it.
        Transition: Noise pollution is only one cause of stress.
III. Modern people are subjected to more stress than ever before.
     A. Work-related stress contributes to nervous disorders.
        Statistics: Calabrese
     B. The day-to-day stress of modern living contributes to
        circulatory diseases.
        Internal summary: What to do about it.
Conclusion
  I. Review the problem.
 II. Review what we can do about it.
III. One final thought.
     Quotation: Michael Smith on the pleasures of good health.

BIBLIOGRAPHY

Bergsman, Jurrit. *Health Care: Its Psychosocial Dimensions.* Atlantic Highlands, N.J.: Humanities Press, 1985.

Calabrese, Edward J., and Michael W. Dorsey. "How to Insure Your Health in a Dangerous World." *Redbook* 162 (January 1987): 94.

Kissick, William L. "Health Care in the 80's: Changes, Consequences, and Choices." *Vital Speeches of the Day* 52 (January 15, 1987): 213.

(continued)

Organization and Support

Figure 12–2
continued

Leonard, George B. "Ultimate Fitness: *Esquire's* 10 keys to High-Level Health and Athletic Performance." *Esquire* 101 (May 1987): 87.

Smith, Michael J. Personal interview on September 22, 1989. At Illinois State University.

Survey on Health Habits conducted at Illinois State University on September 24, 1989.

given. Finally, in speech classes, outlines are often used by the instructor to analyze student speeches.

SPEAKING NOTES   Like your working outline, your speaking notes are a personal device, so the format is up to you. Many teachers suggest that speaking notes should be in the form of a brief key-word outline, with just enough information listed to jog your memory but not enough to get lost in.

Many teachers also suggest that you fit your notes on one side of one 3-by-5-inch card. Other teachers recommend that you also have your introduction and conclusion on note cards, and still others suggest that your references and quotations be written out on them. Your speaking notes for a speech on modern illness might look like the ones in Figure 12–3.

◆ PRINCIPLES OF OUTLINING

Over the years, a series of rules or principles for the construction of outlines have evolved. These rules are based on the use of the standard symbols and format discussed below.

Standard Symbols

A speech outline generally uses the following symbols:

I. Main point (Roman numeral)
  A. Subpoint (capital letter)
    1. Sub-subpoint (standard number)
      a. Sub-subsubpoint (lowercase letter)

The major divisions of the speech—introduction, body, and conclusion—are not given symbols. They are listed by name, and the Roman numerals for their main points begin anew in each division.

Standard Format

In the sample outlines in this chapter, notice that each symbol is indented around five spaces from the symbol above it. Besides keeping the outline neat,

FIGURE 12–3
Speaking Notes

the indentation of different-order ideas is actually the key to the technique of outlining; it enables you to coordinate and order ideas in the form in which they are most comprehensible to the human mind.[2] If the standard format is used in your working outline, it will help you create a well-organized speech. If it is used in speaking notes, it will help you remember everything you want to say.

Proper outline form is based on a few rules and guidelines, the first of which is the rule of division.

The Rule of Division

In formal outlines main points and subpoints always represent a division of a whole. Because it is impossible to divide something into fewer than two parts, you always have at least two main points for every topic. Then, if your main points are divided, you will always have at least two subpoints, and so on. Thus, the rule for formal outlines is, never a "I" without a "II," never an "A" without a "B," and so on.

Organization and Support

Three to five is considered to be the ideal number of main points. It is also considered best to divide those main points into three to five subpoints, whenever possible.

If you were speaking on the topic "The Causes of Modern Illness," you might divide the body of your topic as shown in Figure 12–2.

The Rule of Parallel Wording

Your main points should be worded in a similar, or "parallel" manner. For example, if you are developing a speech against capital punishment, your main points might look like this:

I. Capital punishment is not effective: It is not a deterrent to crime.
II. Capital punishment is not constitutional: It does not comply with the Eighth Amendment.
III. Capital punishment is not civilized: It does not allow for a reverence for life.

Whenever possible, subpoints should also be worded in a parallel manner. For your points to be worded in a parallel manner, they should each contain one, and only one, idea. (After all, they can't really be parallel if one is longer or contains more ideas than the others.) This will enable you to completely develop one idea before moving on to another one in your speech. If you were discussing cures for indigestion, your topic might be divided incorrectly if your main points looked like this:

I. "Preventive cures" help you before eating.
II. "Participation cures" help you during and after eating.

You might actually have three ideas there and thus three main points:

I. Preventive cures (before eating).
II. Participation cures (during eating).
III. Postparticipation cures (after eating).

Organizing Your Points in a Logical Order

An outline should reflect a logical order for your points. You might arrange them from newest to oldest, largest to smallest, best to worst, or in a number of other ways that follow. The organizing pattern you choose ought to be the one that best develops your thesis.

TIME PATTERNS Arrangement according to periods of time, or chronology, is one of the most common patterns of organization. The period of time could be anything from centuries to seconds. The "cures for indigestion" example given earlier is an example of a **time pattern.** In a speech on the history of the ASPCA, a time pattern might look like this:

I. Early attempts by the city to control animals, 1900–1920.
II. The ASPCA takes over: 1920–present.
III. The outlook for the future.

Arranging points according to the steps that make up a process is another form of time patterning. The topic "Getting That Big Date" might use this type of patterning:

I. The first step: Choosing an appropriate person.
II. The second step: Breaking the ice.
III. The third step: Asking for the date.

SPACE PATTERNS   **Space patterns** are organized according to area. The area could be stated in terms of continents or centimeters or anything in between.

If you were discussing the ecology of the Great Lakes, you could arrange them from West to East:

I. Superior
II. Michigan
III. Huron
IV. Erie
V. Ontario

TOPIC PATTERNS   A topical arrangement or **topic pattern** is based on types or categories. These categories could be either well-known or original; both have their advantages. For example, a division of college students according to well-known categories might look like this:

I. Liberal arts majors
II. Science majors
III. Social science majors
IV. Preprofessional majors

Well-known categories are advantageous because audiences are generally more receptive to ideas that they can associate with their present knowledge. But familiarity also has its drawbacks. One disadvantage is the "Oh, this again" syndrome. If members of an audience feel they have nothing new to learn about the components of your topic, they might not listen to you. To avoid this, you could invent original categories that freshen up some topics by suggesting an original analysis. For example, original categories for "college students" might look like this:

I. Grinds—the students who go to every class and read every assignment before it is due and who are usually seen in dormitories telling everyone to turn their stereos down.
II. Renaissance students—the students who find a satisfying blend of scholarly and social pursuits. They go to most of their classes and do most of their assignments, but they don't let school get in the way of their social life.
III. Burnouts—the students who have a difficult time finding the classroom, let alone doing the work.

Organization and Support

345

Sometimes topics are arranged in the order that will be easiest for your audience to remember. To return to our Great Lakes example, the lakes could be arranged so their first letters spell the word "HOMES."

PROBLEM-SOLUTION PATTERNS   The **problem-solution pattern,** as you might guess from its no-nonsense title, describes what's wrong and proposes a way to make things better. It is usually (but not always) divisible into these two distinct parts:

I. The problem: Addiction (which could then be broken down into addiction to cigarettes, alcohol, prescribed drugs, and street drugs).
II. The solution: A National Addiction Institute (which would study the root causes of addiction as the National Cancer Institute studies the root causes of cancer).

MOTIVATED SEQUENCE   One variation of the problem-solution arrangement contains five steps and has come to be known as Monroe's Motivated Sequence,[3] after Alan Monroe, its originator:

I. THE ATTENTION STEP draws attention to your subject. (For example, "Have you ever gotten all dressed up to go out for a meal in a nice restaurant and then been choked by smoke from the table next to you?")
II. THE NEED STEP establishes the problem. ("Ambient smoke—that is, smoke from someone else's cigarette, cigar, or pipe—is a threat to your health as well as a general nuisance.")
III. THE SATISFACTION STEP proposes a solution. ("The State Clean Air Act will provide for separate smoking and nonsmoking areas in restaurants.")
IV. THE VISUALIZATION STEP describes the results of the solution. ("Imagine—clean air in every public place, without denying smokers their rights in any way.")
V. THE ACTION STEP is a direct appeal for the audience to do something. ("Sign this petition, and you will have done your part.")

CAUSE-EFFECT PATTERNS   **Cause-effect patterns** are similar to problem-solution patterns in that they are basically two-part patterns: First you discuss something that happened; then you discuss its effects. For example, many speakers feel that the topic of inflation is amenable to this pattern because the reason people tend to misunderstand inflation is that they confuse causes with effects. These speakers would organize a speech on inflation as follows:

I. Causes
   A. Government budget deficits
   B. Increase in money supply
II. Effects
   A. Rising prices
   B. Rising wages

A variation of this pattern is reversing the order and presenting the effects first and then the causes. Effect-to-cause patterns would work well with a topic such as "the terrorism crisis"; the audience would presumably already be interested in, and knowledgeable about, the effects, and discussing them first might increase interest in your analysis of the causes.

CLIMAX PATTERNS **Climax patterns** are used to create suspense. For example, if you wanted to create suspense in a speech about military intervention, you could chronologically trace the steps that eventually led us into World War II or the wars in Korea or Vietnam in such a way that you build up your audience's curiosity. If you told of these steps through the eyes of a soldier who was drafted into military service right before one of those wars, you would be building suspense as your audience wonders what will become of him.

This pattern can also be reversed. When it is, it is called *anticlimactic* organization. If you started your military intervention speech by telling the audience that you were going to explain why so-and-so was killed in such-and-such a war and then you went on to explain the things that caused him to become involved in that war, you would be using anticlimactic organization. This pattern is helpful when you have an essentially uninterested audience and you need to build interest early in your speech to get them to listen to the rest of it.

For practice in organizing ideas, divide each of the following into subcategories:

a. Transportation
b. Careers
c. U. S. Government
d. The National Park System
e. Balanced diets
f. Television programs

Listing Supporting Material

Supporting material, which we will cover in more depth in a moment, is also listed on a speech outline, but is not given one of the standard symbols. It is identified by type:

Definition:

Example:

Visual Aid:

Quotation:

Because supporting points are not divided into ideas, it *is* possible to have only one of them under a particular point. (See Figure 12–2.)

Organization and Support

Listing Connectives

Internal previews, reviews, and transitions might also appear on formal outlines. They also are not given standard symbols. Like supporting points, these connectives are not divisions of an idea, so it is possible to have only one of them under a point. (See Figure 12–2.)

Transitions keep your message moving forward. They perform the following functions:

◆ They tell how the introduction relates to the body of the speech.

◆ They tell how one main point relates to the next main point.

◆ They tell how your subpoints relate to the points they are part of.

◆ They tell how your supporting points relate to the points they support.

Transitions, to be effective, should refer to the previous point and to the upcoming point, showing how they relate to one another and to the thesis. They usually sound something like this:

> "...Like (*previous point*), another important consideration in (*topic*) is (*upcoming point*).

> "...But _____ isn't the only thing we have to worry about. _____ is even more potentially dangerous."

> "...Yes, the problem is obvious. But what are the solutions? Well, one possible solution is..."

Sometimes a transition includes an internal review, a preview of upcoming points, or both:

> "...So far we've discussed _____, _____, and _____. Our next points are _____, _____, and _____."

Other Parts of the Speech Outline

Many instructors require formal speech outlines to be full-sentence outlines. Speech outlines also often list the purpose, the thesis, and the topic or title. (It may be a good idea to title your speech, since a title often helps your audience understand your approach.) Most instructors also require a bibliography of sources at the end of the outline. The bibliography should include full research citations, the correct form for which can be found in any style guide, such as Kate Turabian's *Student's Guide for Writing College Papers*.[4] With all of the extra components added, a formal outline handed in for the speech on modern illness might look like the one in Figure 12–2 on page 341.

◆ BEGINNING AND ENDING THE SPEECH

◆ **The beginning is the most important part of the work.**

Plato

The **introduction** and **conclusion** of a speech are vitally important although they usually will occupy less than 20 percent of your speaking time. Listeners form their impressions of a speaker early, and they remember what they hear last; it is, therefore, vital to make those few moments at the beginning and end of a speech work to your advantage.

Plan an introduction and conclusion to speeches on each of the following topics (after devising a specific purpose and thesis statement).

a. Buying U. S. vs. imported cars
b. A history of circumcision
c. The aging of the population
d. Phobias
e. Television evangelism

The Introduction

As you have already read, the first part of your introduction should capture the attention of your listeners. There are several ways to get an audience's attention. The following discussion shows how some of these ways might be used in a speech entitled "Communication Between Plants and Humans."

REFER TO THE AUDIENCE The technique of referring to the audience is especially effective if it is complimentary, as "After the great class discussion last week on how animals communicate, I really looked forward to talking to you today about a related topic. . . ."

REFER TO THE OCCASION A reference to the occasion could be a reference to the event of your speech, as "We are gathered here today, as we are on every Tuesday and Thursday at this time, to examine the phenomenon of human communication. . . ." This might also be a reference to the date, as "On this date, just five years ago, a little-known botanist made a breakthrough that set the scientific world on its ear. . . ."

REFER TO THE RELATIONSHIP BETWEEN THE AUDIENCE AND THE SUBJECT "My topic, 'Communicating with Plants,' ties right in with our study of human communication. We can gain several insights into our communication with one another by examining our interactions with our little green friends."

REFER TO SOMETHING FAMILIAR TO THE AUDIENCE The technique of referring to something familiar to the audience is especially effective if you are discussing a topic that might seem new or strange to the audience. Audience attention will be attracted to the familiar among the new in much the same way that we are able to pick out a friend's face in a crowd of strangers. For example, "See that lilac bush outside the window? At this very moment it might be reacting to the joys and anxieties that you are experiencing in this classroom."

Organization and Support

CITE A STARTLING FACT OR OPINION   A statement that surprises an audience is bound to make them sit up and listen. This is true even for a topic that the audience considers old hat; if the audience members think they've heard it all before about plant-human communication, you might mention, "There is now actual scientific evidence that plants appreciate human company, kind words, and classical music."

ASK A QUESTION   A rhetorical question is one that causes your audience to think rather than to answer out loud. "Have you ever wondered why some people seem to be able to grow beautiful, healthy plants effortlessly whereas others couldn't make a weed grow in the best soil you could get?" This question is designed to make the audience respond mentally, "Yeah, why is that?"

TELL AN ANECDOTE   A personal story perks up audience interest because it shows the human side of what might otherwise be dry, boring information. "The other night, while taking a walk in the country, I happened on a small garden that was rich with lush vegetation. But it wasn't the lushness of the vegetation that caught my eye at first. There, in the middle of the garden, was a man who was talking quite animatedly to a giant sunflower."

USE A QUOTATION   Quotable quotes sometimes have a precise, memorable wording that would be difficult for you to say as well. Also, they allow you to

THE FAR SIDE   By GARY LARSON

Reprinted by permission of Chronicle Features, San Francisco, CA.

borrow from the credibility of the quoted source. For example, "Thorne Bacon, the naturalist, recently said about the possibility of plants and humans communicating, 'Personally, I cannot imagine a world so dull, so satiated, that it should reject out of hand arresting new ideas which may be as old as the first amino acid in the chain of life on earth.'"

TELL A JOKE   If you happen to know or can find a joke that is appropriate to your subject and occasion, it can help you build audience interest: "We once worried about people who talked to plants, but that's no longer the case. Now we only worry if the plants talk back." Be sure, though, that the joke is appropriate to the audience, as well as to the occasion and to you as a speaker.

After you capture the attention of the audience, an effective introduction will almost always state the speaker's thesis and give the listeners an idea of the upcoming main points. Katherine Graham, the chairperson of the board of the Washington Post Company, addressed a group of businessmen and their wives in this way:

> I am delighted to be here. It is a privilege to address you. And I am especially glad the rules have been bent for tonight, allowing so many of you to bring along your husbands. I think it's nice for them to get out once in a while and see how the other half lives. Gentlemen, we welcome you.
>
> Actually, I have other reasons for appreciating this chance to talk with you tonight. It gives me an opportunity to address some current questions about the press and its responsibilities—whom we are responsible to, what we are responsible for, and generally how responsible our performance has been.[5]

Thus, Mrs. Graham previewed her main points:

1. To explain whom the press is responsible to.
2. To explain what the press is responsible for.
3. To explain how responsible the press has been.

Sometimes your preview of main points will be even more straightforward:

"I have three points to discuss: They are _____, _____, and _____.

Sometimes you will not want to refer directly to your main points in your introduction. Your reasons might be based on a plan calling for suspense, humorous effect, or stalling for time to win over a hostile audience. In that case, you might preview only your thesis:

"I am going to say a few words about _____."
"Did you ever wonder about _____?"
"_____ is one of the most important issues facing us today."

The attention-getter and preview of every speech should accomplish two functions in addition to their stated purposes:

SETTING THE MOOD AND TONE OF YOUR SPEECH Notice, in the example just given, how Katherine Graham began her speech by joking with her audience. She was speaking before an all-male organization; the only women in the audience were the members' wives. That is why Mrs. Graham felt it necessary to put her audience members at ease by joking with them

Public Communication

about women's traditional role in society. By beginning in this manner, she assured the men that she would not berate them for the sexist bylaws of their organization. She also showed them that she was going to approach her topic with wit and intelligence. Thus, she set the mood and tone for her entire speech. Imagine how different that mood and tone would have been if she had begun this way:

> Before I start today, I would just like to say that I would never have accepted your invitation to speak here had I known that your organization does not accept women as members. Just where do you Cro-Magnons get off, excluding more than half the human race from your little club?

DEMONSTRATING THE IMPORTANCE OF YOUR TOPIC TO YOUR AUDIENCE Your audience will listen to you more carefully if your speech relates to them as individuals. Based on your audience analysis, you should state directly *why* your topic is of importance to your audience. This importance should be related as closely as possible to their specific needs at that specific time. For example, if you were speaking to your class about why they should help support the Red Cross, you might begin like this:

> Lives have been lost in the time it takes an ambulance or doctor to reach the victim of accidents. Too many people have died from accidentally severed veins or arteries, drowning, choking on food, or swallowing iodine, plant-spray, arsenic, or other poisons.
>
> If someone on the scene had known what emergency measures to take, tragedy could have been averted.
>
> The Red Cross, with vast experience in the latest, most successful lifesaving techniques, has put together a handy, easy-to-follow manual, *Standard First Aid and Personal Safety.* The information it contains could save your life—or that of someone dear to you. This book is available only through the Red Cross, and we'd like to send it to you *free.*[6]

This introduction establishes an immediate importance: The audience members don't have to wait until they need blood or until an emergency or a disaster strikes. Acquiring the free booklet is something that is important to them right now as healthy, reasonably secure members of a college class.

The Conclusion

The conclusion, like the introduction, is an especially important part of your speech. Your audience will have a tendency to listen carefully as your speech draws to a close; they will also have a tendency to consider what you say at the end of your speech as important. Because of this, the conclusion has two essential functions: to review the thesis and to leave the audience remembering your speech by using effective final remarks. You can review your thesis either through direct repetition or by paraphrasing it in different words. Either way your conclusion should include a short summary statement:

> And so, after listening to what I had to say this afternoon, I hope you agree with me that the city cannot afford to lose the services of the ASPCA.

◆ **Begin at the beginning and go on till you come to the end; then stop.**

The King, in *Alice in Wonderland*

◆ **A speech is like a love affair. Any fool can start it, but to end it requires considerable skill.**

Lord Mancroft

Organization and Support

You might also want to review your main points. This can be done directly: "I made three main points about the ASPCA today. They are..."

The review of your main points can also be done artistically. For example, first look back at that example of an introduction by Katherine Graham; then read her conclusion to that speech:

> ...So instead of seeking flat and absolute answers to the kinds of problems I have discussed tonight, what we should be trying to foster is respect for one another's conception of where duty lies, and understanding of the real worlds in which we try to do our best. And we should be hoping for the energy and sense to keep on arguing and questioning, because there is no better sign that our society is still healthy and strong.[7]

Let's take a closer look at how and why this conclusion was effective. Mrs. Graham posed three questions in her introduction. She dealt with those questions in her speech and reminded her audience, in her conclusion, that she had answered the questions.

PREVIEW

1. To whom is the press responsible?

2. What is the press responsible for?

3. How responsible has the press been?

REVIEW

1. To its own conception of where its duty lies.

2. For doing its best in the "real world."

3. It has done its best.

Your final remarks are important because they are the last words your audience will hear from you in the speech. You can make them most effective by avoiding the following mistakes:

DO NOT END ABRUPTLY   Make sure that your conclusion accomplishes everything it is supposed to accomplish. Develop it fully. You might want to use a "pointer phrase" such as "and now, in conclusion..." or "to sum up what we've been talking about here..." to let your audience know that you have reached the conclusion of the speech.

BUT DON'T RAMBLE EITHER   Prepare a definite conclusion, and never, never end by mumbling something like "Well, I guess that's about all I wanted to say..."

DON'T INTRODUCE NEW POINTS   The worst kind of rambling is "Oh, yes, and something I forgot to mention is..."

DON'T APOLOGIZE   Don't say, "I'm sorry I couldn't tell you more about this" or "I'm sorry I didn't have more time to research this subject" or any of those sad songs. They will only highlight the possible weaknesses of your speech, and there's a good chance those weaknesses were far more apparent to you than to your audience.

Instead, it is best to end strong. You can use any of the attention-getters suggested for the introduction to make the conclusion memorable. In fact, one kind of effective closing is to refer to the attention-getter you used in your introduction and remind your audience how it applies to the points you made in your speech.

You can use elements of surprise or suspense to make a point memorable; you can also use mnemonic devices, which are often formulated as collections of meaningful letters:

> Think of recycling in the same terms as you think of gas mileage: MPG. Only, in recycling, MPG stands for *metals, paper,* and *glass,* the three materials you stand to conserve.

Whatever device you use, end with a flourish, as John F. Kennedy did when he said, "Ask not what your country can do for you; ask what you can do for your country," or as General MacArthur did when he said, "Old soldiers never die; they just fade away."

TABLE 12–1 Checklist for Organizing a Speech

Develop Main Points

Properly Divided?
- ☐ Three to five main points?
- ☐ At least two divisions of each main point?
- ☐ Parallel wording?
- ☐ One, and only one idea in each point?

Order (Are the main points arranged in the most logical way?)
- ☐ Time
- ☐ Space
- ☐ Topic
- ☐ Problem-solution
- ☐ Cause-effect
- ☐ Climax
- ☐ Other

Plan the Introduction
- ☐ Do the opening remarks gain the attention of the audience?
- ☐ Does the introduction preview the thesis and main point?
- ☐ Do the introductory remarks set the proper tone for the topic and occasion?
- ☐ Does the introduction demonstrate the importance of the topic to the audience?

Plan the Conclusion
- ☐ Do you restate the thesis and review main points?
- ☐ Do you close the speech with strong, memorable remarks?

Develop Transitions
- ☐ Do transitions occur between the introduction and body, between the main points within the body, and between the body and conclusion?
- ☐ Does each transition refer to the previous and upcoming points, showing how they relate to one another and to the thesis?

Organization and Support

It is important to organize ideas clearly and logically. But clarity and logic by themselves won't guarantee that you'll interest or persuade others; these functions call for the use of supporting materials. These materials—the facts and information that back up and prove your ideas and opinions—are the flesh that fills out the skeleton of your speech.

Functions of Supporting Material

There are four purposes for supporting material:

TO CLARIFY As explained in Chapter 3, people of different backgrounds tend to attach different meanings to words. For example, if you were talking about recycling, every member of your audience could have a different idea about what you meant. To some, recycling refers just to aluminum beer cans; to others, the term means reusing everything that is normally thrown away as refuse. You could use supporting material to clarify this idea:

> The type of recycling I'm talking about here involves separating from the rest of your trash all glass, metals, newspapers, and magazines. The papers and magazines must be bundled, and containers must be uncapped and washed, and labels must be removed from the cans. The material is then placed in a separate container for removal once a week to a municipal recycling center.

TO MAKE INTERESTING A second use of support is to make an idea interesting or to catch your audience's attention. The audience might know what you mean by "recycling" but still not care. Supporting material could be used to bolster their interest in your topic:

> Outside New York City, where waste material has been dumped into the ocean for years, a large mass of thick, life-choking sludge is slowly inching its way toward the shore. It might be too late for New York, but we can avoid the same problem here, if we take action now.

TO MAKE MEMORABLE A third purpose of supporting materials, related to the preceding one, is to make a point memorable. We have already mentioned the importance of "memorable" statements in a speech conclusion; use of supporting material in the introduction and body of the speech provides another way to help your audience retain important information.

The most common way to make a point memorable is to use supporting material that is impressive because it stresses the importance of the point. For example:

> The State Environmental Protection Agency recently measured the air in this area, and what they found suggests that each and every one of us, at this moment, are breathing poisons into our systems. These are cumulative, carcinogenic, chemical toxins; and they are caused by our township incinerator's burning garbage that could just as easily be sold and reused.

TO PROVE Finally, supporting material can be used as evidence, to prove the truth of what you are saying. For example, if you said, "The way our local landfill area is filling up, it might have to be closed in a year or so," your audience would find it easy to disagree with you. But supporting material makes it less easy to disagree:

> According to Tom Murray, our village chief sanitation engineer and the man in charge of landfill areas, all our landfills will be filled to capacity and closed within one year. This means, in no uncertain terms, that we are not going to have anywhere to put our garbage.

Types of Support

As you may have noted, each function of support could be fulfilled by several different types of material. An examination of these different types of supporting material follows.

DEFINITIONS It's a good idea to give your audience definitions of your key terms, especially if those terms are unfamiliar to them or are being used in an unusual way. A good definition is simple and concise and is stated in such a way that no other terms within the definition need to be defined.

Dictionary definitions are a handy way of determining the most acceptable meaning for a word, but you should be careful about using them to define terms in your speech. Your own carefully chosen words are usually more interesting and clearer than a dictionary definition. Dictionaries are written for very general audiences. If you were speaking on the abortion issue and relying on a dictionary definition, you might be stuck with:

> By abortion I mean the expulsion of a nonviable fetus . . .

This might be an accurate definition, but it is probably too clinical for a college audience. It might be clearer to say:

> By abortion I mean the termination of pregnancy before the twelfth week of gestation . . .

if that's what you mean.

One other problem with dictionaries is that they sometimes give you a definition that includes the term itself and that will sometimes make it seem as if you are clarifying an idea when you actually aren't:

> By abortion, I mean the abortion of a fetus . . .

There are two types of definitions: traditional and operational. A traditional definition places something in a class and tells how it is different from other things in that class. The classic example of this is proposed by Aristotle: "Man [or "woman," we might add] is a featherless biped." Humans are, therefore, defined as belonging to a class (bipeds) but different from that class in that they do not have feathers. (For Aristotle, fur was a type of "feathers.")

To cite a more modern example, if you needed to define "the pancreas" for a speech on the causes of cancer, you could tell your audience that it is the gland that secretes digestive juice into the small intestine. Thus the pancreas

◆ **You raise your voice when you should reinforce your argument.**

Samuel Johnson

Organization and Support

is placed in a class (glands) and distinguished from other members of that class (it is the one that . . .).

Operational definitions tell what you would have to do to experience the thing being described. We could use an operational definition to define recycling: First you separate glass, metals, newspapers, and magazines from the rest of your trash, and so on. Operational definitions for the term *man* might sound something like this:

> You want to know what a man is? Go down to the graduation ceremonies for marine boot camp. Now *those* are men.

or,

> You want to know what a man is? Go to the state school for the retarded, and watch the men who work with those kids every day with compassion and unfailing patience. Those are men.

DETAILED DESCRIPTION   A description is a "word picture," a direct rendering of the details that summarize an idea from your perspective. Martin Luther King, Jr., used description in his famous "I Have a Dream" speech, when he described the plight of the black American:

> There are those who are asking the devotees of civil rights, "When will you be satisfied?" We can never be satisfied as long as our bodies, heavy with the fatigue of travel, cannot gain lodging in the motels of the highways and the hotels of the cities. We cannot be satisfied as long as the Negro's basic mobility is from a smaller ghetto to a larger one. We can never be satisfied as long as our children are stripped of their selfhood and robbed of their dignity by signs stating "for whites only."[8]

Dr. King's description helps us to imagine pain and fatigue as well as the sight of a sign that says "for whites only." These things can be truly perceived only through the senses, but he manages to give us an image of them by capturing their essence in a few words. In his description, as in all good description, it is the choice of details that makes the difference.

ANALOGIES/COMPARISON-CONTRAST   We use **analogies,** or comparisons, all the time, often in the form of figures of speech such as similes and metaphors. A simile is a direct comparison that usually uses *like* or *as* whereas a metaphor is an implied comparison that does not use *like* or *as.* So if you said that the rush of refugees from communist countries to the West was "like a tidal wave," you would be using a simile. If you used the expression "a tidal wave of refugees," you would be using a metaphor because you have only implied the comparison.

> For practice in formulating analogies, provide one for each of the following: deficit spending, inflation, shopping, studying, infatuation, true love, and a job interview. These particular terms are not essential to the exercise. Use any terms you like, but try to make them original. It was a good use of analogy when Vince Lombardi said that tying a football game was like "kissing your sister," but just to dredge up an analogy like that from your memory is less useful in this exercise than making up one of your own.

Analogies are extended metaphors. We run across analogies all the time. Here, for example, is the way Ingmar Bergman describes old age:

> Old age is like climbing a mountain. You climb from ledge to ledge. The higher you get, the more tired and breathless you become, but your view becomes much more extensive.

Here's the way Carl Sagan explains the age of the universe through analogy:

> The most instructive way I know to express this cosmic chronology is to imagine the fifteen-billion-year lifetime of the universe (or at least its present incarnation since the Big Bang) compressed into the span of a single year. . . . It is disconcerting to find that in such a cosmic year the Earth does not condense out of interstellar matter until early September: Dinosaurs emerge on Christmas Eve; flowers arise on December 28th; and men and women originate at 10:30 P.M. on New Year's Eve. All of recorded history occupies the last ten seconds of December 31; and the time from the waning of the Middle Ages to the present occupies little more than one second.[9]

Here's how a newspaper reporter pointed out how relatively inexpensive bike lanes can be:

> The proposed four-mile long freeway in New York City at $1.6 billion could finance 100,000 miles of rural bikeways. Or, alternatively, ribbon bikeways could be built paralleling the whole 40,000-mile national Interstate System of highways.[10]

Analogies can be used to compare or contrast an unknown concept with a known one. For example, if you had difficulty explaining to a public speaking class composed mostly of music majors why they should practice their speeches out loud, you might use this analogy:

> We all realize that great masters often can compose music in their heads; Beethoven, for example, composed his greatest masterpieces after he had gone deaf and couldn't even hear the instruments play out his ideas. However, beginners have to sit down at a piano or some other instrument and play their pieces as they create them. It is much the same way for beginning public speakers. When composing their speeches, they need to use their instruments—their voices—to hear how their ideas sound.

For an audience of music majors, this analogy might clarify the concept of practicing a speech. For a class of electrical engineers who may not know Mozart from Madonna, this analogy might confuse rather than clarify. It is important to remember to make your analogies appropriate to your audience.

ANECDOTES An **anecdote** is a brief story with a point, often (but not always) based on personal experience. (The word *anecdote* comes from the Greek meaning "unpublished item.") Anecdotes can add a lively, personal touch to your explanation.

President Reagan was famous for his use of anecdotes. In his Farewell Address, when he wanted to make the point that America stood as a symbol of freedom to people in other lands, he used the following anecdote:

> It was back in the early Eighties, at the height of the boat people, and the sailor was hard at work on the carrier Midway, which was patrolling the South China Sea. The

Organization and Support

sailor, like most American servicemen, was young, smart and fiercely observant. The crew spied on the horizon a leaky little boat—and crammed inside were refugees from Indochina hoping to get to America. The Midway sent a small launch to bring them to the ship, and safety. As the refugees made their way through the choppy seas, one spied the sailor on deck, and stood up and called out to him. He yelled, "Hello American sailor—Hello Freedom Man."

A small moment with a big meaning, a moment the sailor, who wrote it in a letter, couldn't get out of his mind. And, when I saw it, neither could I.[11]

> For practice in using anecdotes, try the following list: first, identify an anecdote to prove a point of your choice ("college is a rewarding experience," for example, or "power corrupts" or "love is blind"). Whatever point you choose, make sure you start with the point first and then think up the anecdote to support it. Then reverse the exercise: Think of one of your favorite stories or personal experiences, and then identify a point that the story could be used to support.

EXAMPLES   An **example** is a specific case that is used to demonstrate a general idea. Examples can be either factual or hypothetical, personal or borrowed. They can also be combined with other types of support.

One student used examples to begin her speech on the possible dangers of Nutrasweet:

> Jason Domingo was experiencing unprovoked fits of violence, very unusual for a 4-year-old boy. Fifty-year-old Dr. James Bowen's speech was slurred. Along with this, his movements were very uncoordinated. Joellen Embry, 28, was suffering from very severe headaches, a bloated feeling, and her periods were coming much later or being skipped altogether.
>
> What is the recurring factor in each of these situations? The fact that each of these victims had consumed an artificially sweetened beverage containing aspartame, more commonly known as Nutrasweet.[12]

Hypothetical examples can be often more powerful than factual examples, because hypothetical examples ask the audience to imagine something—thus causing them to become active participants in the thought. If you were speaking on the subject of euthanasia (mercy killing), you might ask your audience to imagine that someone they loved was suffering and being kept alive by a machine. If you were dealing with street crime, you might begin by saying, "Imagine you're walking down a dark street and you hear footsteps..." One way to generate a hypothetical example is to consider the possible consequences of some current trend or occurrence.

> For practice in using examples to support points, team up with someone else, and take turns supplying examples for points each of you identify. These points could be well-established truisms ("cheaters never prosper," "better safe than sorry") or more specific ideas ("Robert DeNiro is a great actor," "the Bermuda Triangle is a dangerous place"). Take note of those examples that combine with other forms of support.

This is how Robert J. Aaronson, the president of the Air Transport Association, used a hypothetical example in his speech before the American Bar Association:

> The case I have chosen is that of an airport construction worker named Charlie. He is finishing work for the day on the last airport expansion project paid for from the trust fund. He is aware of the OSHA* rule against leaving loose materials on a scaffold overnight. So when he notices some loose bricks on his scaffold, he grabs an empty barrel, hoists it up on the scaffold with a rope and pulley and puts the bricks inside of it.
>
> Back on the ground, Charlie proceeds to lower the load. He has no trouble swinging the barrel free of the scaffolding. But the barrel, filled with bricks, is heavier than he is. So the barrel goes down, Charlie goes up, and along the way they collide, giving Charlie a severe bump on the head.
>
> Charlie somehow manages to hold on, but when he reaches the top, his fingers get mangled in the pulley, just as the barrel crashes to the ground and breaks open. With the bricks now disgorged, Charlie outweighs the barrel. So he goes down, the barrel goes up. Again they collide. This time Charlie breaks a few ribs. He hits the ground. He's stunned, and he lets go of the rope.
>
> You probably can guess how this sorry tale ends. The barrel, no longer connected to Charlie, falls a second time. It lands on Charlie, and it breaks his leg. We all have our ups and downs in life, but certainly this falls in the category of a very bad day at the office.
>
> I am sure all of you have identified the central legal question here: Does Charlie sue the airport, the construction firm, the brick company or the barrel maker? The answer, of course, is all four, PLUS the first grade teacher who made it possible for Charlie to read the OSHA handbook in the first place![13]

Examples can be effective in clarifying information and making it interesting and memorable. Strictly speaking, however, they do not prove a point because they refer only to isolated instances that might not be representative. To prove an idea with examples, you have to collect a number of them; at that point they become statistics.

QUANTIFICATION AND STATISTICS   **Quantification** is the use of numbers to clarify a concept, to make it more specific. One example of quantification comes from a lecture given by a professor at Columbia University. He wanted to develop the idea that inflation lowers the value of paper currency, so he used quantification (developed in an anecdote) in the following way:

> Some time ago, I found a postcard which I had written to my father on November 23, 1923, while I was attending a boarding school in Germany. The card asked that my father send the bursar "immediately 1.2 trillion marks. If the tuition is not paid by the end of the month, you will have to pay four gold marks."
>
> Those two figures—1.2 trillion paper and four gold marks—illustrate the catastrophic fraud of the great German inflation which resulted in a revolutionary change in the economic and above all the social order of the country.[14]

Statistics are numbers that are arranged or organized to show how a fact or principle is true for a large number of cases. Statistics are actually collections of examples, which is why they are often more effective as proof

*Occupational Safety and Health Act

Organization and Support

than are isolated examples. If you wanted to develop the idea that American youths are not well informed about the American economic system, the following example would be insufficient proof:

> I asked my younger brother the other day if he knew the difference between collectivism and a free-enterprise society, and he had no idea. He didn't even know that the U. S. economy is based on free enterprise.

For practice in quantifying vague statements, try supporting statements such as the following with specific numbers:

"Servicing your own car saves money."

"It takes a lot of time to write a good speech."

"Local housing is very expensive."

"That's the gist of what I want to say. Now get me some statistics to base it on."

To practice using statistics, dig up a copy of this year's *Information Please Almanac, Statistical Abstract of the United States, World Almanac and Book of Facts*, or any other statistical yearbook or almanac. Then support or refute these statements statistically:

a. There are a lot of people out of work today.
b. The United States imports a lot of oil.
c. A lot of people die of heart attacks.
d. Crime is on the rise.
e. More and more people are getting divorced these days.
f. There are a lot of people on welfare these days.

Proof based on *lots* of people's younger siblings would be more effective:

A 1989 study by the Joint Council on Economic Education showed that 50 percent of high school students could not distinguish between collectivism and a free-enterprise society, and 50 percent did not know the U. S. economy was based on free enterprise.

Because statistics are potentially powerful proof, you have the ethical responsibility to cite them exactly as they were published or tabulated. It's usually all right to "round off" a percentage or other figure, but it's considered bad form to manipulate your statistics so they sound better than they are. For example, the term *average* is often used to manipulate statistics. As there are actually three measures of central tendency, or "averages" (mean, median, and mode), it is important to be clear about which one you mean. Imagine that you had the following list of annual incomes for a group of five people:

1. $0
2. $0
3. $500
4. $750
5. $23,750

The mode (most frequent value) for that group would be $0, the mean (arithmetic average) would be $5,000, and the median (the point at which 50 percent of the values are greater and 50 percent are less) would be $500. Any of these could be cited as the "average" by an unscrupulous speaker.

Another responsibility calls for you to cite the complete source of your statistic along with any other information that would have a bearing on its validity. Established professional pollsters such as Gallup, Roper, and Harris, as well as the best magazines and newspapers, have reputations for accuracy. If you cite them, your audience can be relatively sure that your statistics are reliable. Sometimes the source of a statistic will cause it to be suspect, as when, years ago, a cigarette company mailed cartons of cigarettes to doctors and then sent those same doctors a questionnaire asking which brand of cigarettes they were then smoking. Shortly afterward, advertising for the company stated that seven out of ten doctors reported smoking that brand.[15]

Organization and Support

A third rule about the use of statistics is based on effectiveness rather than ethics. You should reduce the statistic to a concrete image if possible. For example, $1 billion in $100 bills would be about the same height as a sixty-story building. Using concrete images such as this will make your statistics more than "just numbers" when you use them.

QUOTATION/TESTIMONY   Using a familiar, artistically stated saying will enable you to take advantage of someone else's memorable wording. For example, if you were giving a speech on personal integrity, you might quote Mark Twain, who said, "Always do right. This will gratify some people, and astonish the rest." A quotation like that fits Alexander Pope's definition of "true wit": "What was often thought, but ne'er so well expressed."

You can also use quotations as **testimony,** to prove a point by using the support of someone who is more authoritative or experienced on the subject than you. Theresa Clinkenbeard, a student at Regis College in Colorado, used quotation for this purpose in her speech entitled "The Loss of Childhood":

> "As a distinctive childhood culture wastes away, we watch with fascination and dismay." This insight of Neil Postman, author of *The Disappearance of Childhood,* raised a poignant point. Childhood in America is vanishing. Gradually, subtly, and to many, almost imperceptibly.... As Postman stated it, "The language, games, tastes, sexuality and clothing of our children and adults are becoming indistinguishable." During a recent ABC News report, it was stated that "one of the major reasons children are turning to alcohol, drugs, early sexual activity and suicide is to alleviate the pressures to grow up fast."[16]

You can usually signal to your audience that you are using a quotation simply by pausing or by changing your pace or inflection slightly. If you want to be more formal, you can preface the quotation with some variation of "And I quote..." and end it with some variation of "end of quote" although that technique becomes tiresome if used too often.

For practice in recognizing the functions of support, identify three instances of support in each of the speeches at the end of Chapters 14 and 15. Explain the function of each instance of support. (Keep in mind that any instance of support *could* perform more than one function.)

◆ VISUAL AIDS

Visual aids serve several purposes. They can show how things look (photos of your trek to Nepal or the effects of malnutrition). They can show how things work (demonstration of a new ski binding, a diagram of how seawater is made drinkable). Visual aids can also show how things relate to one another (a graph showing the relationship between gender, education, and income). Finally, visual aids can show important information clearly (steps in filing a claim in the small-claims court, symptoms of anemia).

Types of Visual Aids

OBJECTS AND MODELS   Sometimes the most effective visual aid is the actual thing you are talking about. This is true when the thing you are talking about is portable enough to carry and simple enough to use during a demonstration before an audience: a piece of sports equipment such as a jai-alai racket or a small piece of weight-training equipment. **Models** are scaled representations of the object you are discussing and are used when that object is too large (the new medical center) or too small (a DNA molecule) or simply doesn't exist anymore (a *Tyrannosaurus rex*).

PHOTOGRAPHS   When blown up large enough for the entire audience to see, photographs can be particularly striking. Photographs have the advantage over actual objects when those objects might be dangerous to an audience, as in a speech about poisonous plants or wild animals. They can also add an artistic touch to a speech, as when you show the portrait of the person you are discussing.

DIAGRAMS   A **diagram** is any kind of line drawing that shows the most important properties of an object. Diagrams do not try to show everything but just those parts of a thing that the audience most needs to be aware of and understand. Blueprints and architectural plans are common types of diagrams as are maps and organizational charts. A diagram is most appropriate when you need to simplify a complex object and make it more understandable to the audience. The diagram in Figure 12–4 is a flowchart showing the steps in producing a record album.

WORD AND NUMBER CHARTS   **Word charts** and **number charts** are visual depictions of key facts or statistics. Shown visually, these facts and numbers will be understood and retained better than if you just talked about

◆ **Be sure of it; give me the ocular proof.**

Shakespeare
Othello

FIGURE 12–4
Flowchart: Production of a Record Album

FIGURE 12–5
Word Chart

AVERAGE SENTENCE LENGTH, IN YEARS	
Murder	20.4
Rape	9.4
Robbery	8.0
Arson	6.7
Fraud	3.9

them. Many speakers arrange the main points of their speech, often in outline form, as a word chart. Many other speakers list their main statistics. (See Figure 12–5.)

PIE CHARTS AND PICTOGRAPHS **Pie charts** are shaped as circles with wedges cut into them. They are used to show divisions of any whole: where your tax dollars go, the percentage of the population involved in various occupations, and so on. Pie charts are always made up of percentages that add up to 100 percent. Usually, the wedges of the pie are organized from largest to smallest, with the largest beginning top center at twelve o'clock. The pie chart in Figure 12–6 represents the reasons a sample of students gave for enrolling in a communication course.

Pictographs are artistic modifications of graphs or charts, designed to make information interesting. Figure 12–7 is a pictograph representing how a typical broadcast hour is divided at a radio station.

FIGURE 12–6
Pie Chart

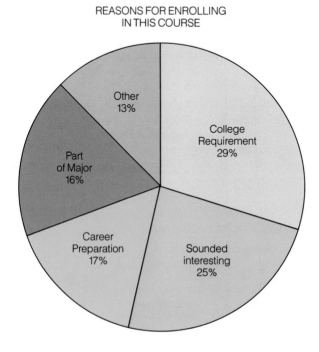

REASONS FOR ENROLLING
IN THIS COURSE

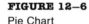

Music and
Talk
(33 min.)

Commercials
(13 min.)

News and
Information
(12 min.)

Odds and
Ends
(2 min.)

BAR AND COLUMN CHARTS **Bar charts,** such as the one shown in
Figure 12–8, compare two or more values by stretching them out in the form of
horizontal rectangles. **Column charts,** such as the ones shown in Figure 12–9
and 12–10, perform the same function as bar charts but use vertical

HAVES VS. HAVE NOTS

BRAZIL — 67%
2%

MEXICO — 58%
3%

ARGENTINA — 50%
4%

U.S. — 40%
5%

JAPAN — 38%
9%

The portion of total household income held by the richest
20% ([   ]) and the poorest 20% ([   ]) of
each country.

**Organization and
Support**

FIGURE 12–9
Simple Column Chart

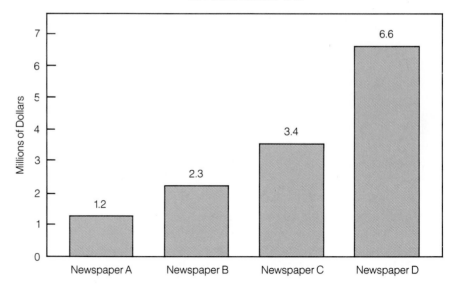

ANNUAL PROFITS
OF FOUR NEWSPAPERS

FIGURE 12–10
Divided Column Chart

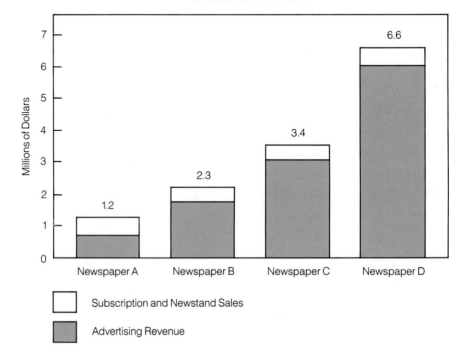

ANNUAL PROFITS DIVIDED
BY SOURCE OF INCOME

Public Communication

rectangles. These charts can be simple (like the column chart in Figure 12–9, which compares the annual profits of four newspapers), or subdivided (like the column chart in Figure 12–10, which compares the annual profits of four newspapers, divided by their source of income.

LINE CHARTS   A **line chart** maps out the direction of a moving point; it is ideally suited for showing changes over time. The time element is usually placed on the horizontal axis so that the line visually represents the trend over time. A soaring increase in AIDS in a community, for example, could be represented in the line chart in Figure 12–11.

Media for the Presentation of Visual Aids

CHALKBOARD   The major advantages of chalkboards are availability and spontaneity: They can be found in any classroom, and with them you can create your visual aid as you go, including items generated from audience responses. The major disadvantages of chalkboards (in addition to that squeaking sound that hurts your teeth) is the difficulty of preparing visual aids on them in advance, especially if several speeches are scheduled in the same room at the same hour.

POLYMER MARKING SURFACES   Available in most bookstores and art supply shops, polymer marking surfaces can be brought in and applied to any wall. These can be written on with special colored markers that wipe off easily with a dry cloth, and they can also be used as a projector screen.

FLIP PADS AND POSTER BOARD   Flip pads are like oversized writing tablets attached to a portable easel. As the name suggests, you reveal visuals

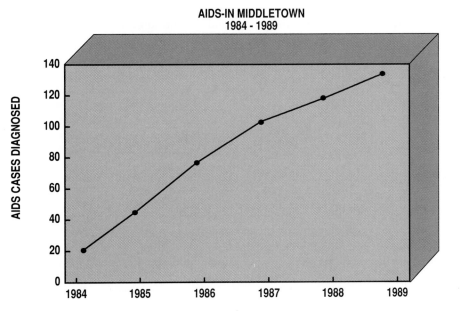

AIDS-IN MIDDLETOWN
1984 - 1989

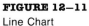

FIGURE 12–11
Line Chart

Organization and Support

on a flip pad one at a time by turning pages. Flip pads enable you to combine the spontaneity of the chalkboard (you can write on them as you go) with the portability that enables you to prepare them in advance. If you plan to use your visuals more than once or if you don't need to write on them, you can prepare them in advance on rigid poster board, and display them on the same type of easel.

PROJECTORS Overhead projectors use transparencies—large, clear sheets of acetate—to cast an image on a screen. Opaque projectors are the same general type of device except that with them you can use sheets of paper, including pages from books, as your image to be projected. If you have enough time to take a photograph of your visual aid with slide film, you can use a slide projector for an especially effective presentation. All three of these types of projectors can be used with an audience that is too large to see a flip pad all at once.

HANDOUTS The major advantage of handouts is that the audience takes these visuals with them. They are, therefore, excellent memory and reference aids. The major disadvantage is that they are distracting when handed out during a speech; first, there is the distraction of passing them around, and then there is the distraction of having them in front of the audience members while you have gone on to something else. It's best, therefore, to pass them out at the end of the speech.

Aids that extend senses other than sight are also effective in some circumstances. If you were speaking about perfume, skunks, or the effects of a chemical plant on a community, actually producing the appropriate smells might help explain your point. If you were talking about baking brownies, or brewing beer, a taste probably wouldn't hurt. And you could incorporate something to touch if you were speaking about the texture of a substance or how it feels.

Audio aids such as tape recordings and records can supply information that could not be presented any other way (comparing musical styles, for example, or demonstrating the differences in the sounds of gas and diesel engines), but in most cases you should use them sparingly. Remember that your presentation already relies heavily on your audience's sense of hearing; it's better to use a visual aid, if possible, than to overwork the audio. Of course, there are audio-visual aids, including films, videotapes, and sound-on-slide. These should also be used sparingly, however, because they allow the audience members to receive information passively, thus relieving them of the responsibility of becoming active participants in the presentation.

Rules for Using Visual Aids

It's easy to see that each type of visual aid and each medium for its presentation have their own unique advantages and disadvantages. No matter which type you use, however, there are a few rules that you should keep in mind.

SIMPLICITY   Keep your visual aids simple. Your goal is to clarify, not confuse. Use only key words or phrases, not sentences. Use eight or fewer lines of text, each with twenty-five or fewer characters. Keep all printing horizontal. Omit all nonessential details.

SIZE   Visual aids should be large enough for your entire audience to see them at one time but portable enough so you can get them out of the way when they no longer pertain to the point you are making.

ATTRACTIVENESS   Visual aids should be visually interesting and as neat as possible. If you don't have the necessary skills, try to get help from a friend or at the audiovisual center on your campus.

APPROPRIATENESS   Visuals must be appropriate to all the components of the speaking situation—you, the audience, and your topic—and they must emphasize the point you are trying to make. Often a speaker will grab a visual aid that has *something* to do with the topic and use it even though it is not directly related—such as showing a map of a city transit system while talking about the condition of the individual cars.

RELIABILITY   You must be in control of your visual aid at all times. Wild animals, chemical reactions, and gimmicks meant to shock a crowd are often too likely to backfire.

When it comes time for you to *use* the visual aid, remember one more point: Talk to your audience, not to your visual aid. Some speakers become so wrapped up in their props that they turn their backs on their audience and sacrifice all their eye contact.

Ray Helle cartoon copyright 1978 by Saturday Review, Inc.

"It's just something the kids scratched out, but for some reason I feel good when I look at it."

Organization and Support

◆ SAMPLE SPEECH

The sample speech for this chapter was presented by Jenny Clanton, a student at Southeastern Illinois College. With this speech, Jenny won the 1988 Interstate Oratorical Association Annual Contest. Her speech is organized in a problem-solution pattern, with two main points devoted to explaining the problem and one main point devoted to the solution. As you read, notice how her supporting material is chosen and worded so as to interest her audience and make her ideas memorable, and not just to "prove" her arguments to her own satisfaction. Notice how her introduction, body and conclusion fulfill their purposes as discussed in this chapter. Comments on the organization and supporting material appear in the margin; an outline of the speech accompanies it.

The Outline

Introduction
  I. Attention-getter: The Challenger Disaster (1–3)
     A. The Challenger astronauts did not die in vain.
     B. If the disaster had occurred on the next scheduled launch . . .
        Quotation/testimony: Dr. Gofman, Dr. Caldicott
 II. Preview of Main Points (4, 5)
Body

  I. Plutonium is hazardous. (6–9)
     A. Plutonium causes cancer.
     B. Plutonium 238 is 300 times more radioactive than the atomic bomb isotope.
        Testimony: Dr. Webb, Dr. Gofman
 II. NASA's safety plan is flawed. (10–14)
     A. The safety plan is based on three factors:
        1. The launch vehicle is safe.
        2. The iridium cannister is safe.
        3. The oxide pellets are safe.
     B. The launch vehicle might not be as safe as expected.
     C. The iridium cannister might not be as safe as expected.
     D. The oxide pellets might not be as safe as expected.

III. We can help. (15–19)
   A. Why hasn't Congress done anything?
   B. What should be done?
   C. What can we do to help?
      Interview: Congressman Markey

Conclusion (20)
   I. Review: main point
      Plutonium 238 is still NASA's fuel of choice.
   II. Final Remarks
      quotation/testimony: Dr. Bennett, "...a degree of risk."

A Degree of Risk[17]

JENNY CLANTON, Southeastern Illinois College

1. On January 28, 1986, the American Space Program suffered the worst disaster in its more than thirty year history. The entire world was shocked when the space shuttle Challenger exploded seconds after lift-off, claiming the lives of seven brave astronauts and crippling our entire space agenda. I suppose the oldest cliché in our culture, spoken on battlegrounds and indeed virtually anywhere Americans die, is "We must press forward so we can say they did not die in vain." Rest assured. They didn't. The deaths of our seven astronauts probably saved the lives of untold thousands of Americans.

2. For, you see, if the O-rings had not failed on January 28, 1986, but rather on May 20, 1987, the next scheduled shuttle launch, in the words of Dr. John Gofman, Professor Emeritus at the University of California at Berkeley, you could have "kissed Florida good-bye."

3. Because the next shuttle, the one that was to have explored the atmosphere of Jupiter, was to carry 47 pounds of Plutonium 238, which is, again, according to Dr. Gofman, the most toxic substance on the face of the earth. Dr. Helen Caldicott corroborates Dr. Gofman's claim in her book, *Nuclear Madness,* when she cites studies estimating one ounce of widely dispersed Plutonium 238 particles as having the toxicity to induce lung cancer in every person on earth.

4. Today, when you leave this room, I want you to fully understand just what impact NASA's plans could have on this planet. I want you to become cynical. I want you to be a little scared. I want you to become angry. But most of all, I want you to begin to demand some answers.

5. To move you in this direction I would first like to explore with you just what plutonium is and what could happen if it were released in our atmosphere. Second, let's consider NASA's argument for the safety of the plutonium as used in the shuttle program. And finally, I want to convince you that NASA's conclusions are flawed.

---

1. Jenny catches our attention with the first words of her introduction, and builds our interest as she begins to explain her topic.

2. Testimony on the severity of the problem helps the introduction set the mood and tone of this speech.

3. Testimony from a second expert, which includes a chilling statistic.

4. Previews main points to be covered.

5. Two points to establish the problem, the final point to present the solution.

6. The body of the speech begins with the development of the first main point. Jenny uses a traditional definition, an operational definition, a description, and one statistic.

6. So now, let's turn our attention to the nature of plutonium. Plutonium is a man-made radioactive element which is produced in large quantities in nuclear reactors from uranium. Plutonium is a chemically reactive metal which, if exposed to air, ignites spontaneously and produces fine particles of plutonium dioxide. These particles, when dispersed by wind and inhaled by living organisms, lodge in the lungs. Lung cancer will follow—sooner or later. Once inside the human body, plutonium rests in bone tissue, causing bone cancer. Plutonium 238 is so poisonous that less than one *millionth* of a gram is a carcinogenic dose.

7. By carefully establishing the credibility of her source, Jenny builds her own credibility with her audience. We'll have more to say about credibility in Chapter 15.

7. Last July, *Common Cause* magazine contacted Dr. Gofman at Berkeley and asked him to place Plutonium 238 in perspective. Before I share Dr. Gofman's assessment, please understand he's no poster-carrying "anti-nuke." Dr. Gofman was co-discoverer of Uranium 233, and he isolated the isotope first used in nuclear bombs. Dr. Gofman told Karl Grossman, author of the article "Redtape and Radio-activity" that Plutonium 238 is 300 times more radioactive than Plutonium 239, which is the isotope used in atomic bombs.

8. Analogy and quantification.

8. Dr. Richard Webb, a Nuclear Physicist and author of *The Accident Hazards of Nuclear Power Plants,* said in a similar interview that sending 46.7 pounds of Plutonium 238 into space would be the equivalent of sending five nuclear reactors up—and then hoping they wouldn't crash or explode.

9. Preview of second main point.

9. Dr. Gofman's final assessment? It's a crazy idea, unless shuttle launches are 100 percent perfect. Which is just about what NASA would have liked us to believe, and at first glance NASA's guarantees are pretty convincing.

10. Begins her second main point by analyzing a statistical counterargument.

10. NASA estimates the chance of releasing Plutonium into the environment, because of the possibility of a malfunction of the space shuttle, at .002%—that's not quite 100% perfect, but it's awfully close. NASA and the Department of Energy base their reliability figures on three factors: 1) the Titan 34D launch vehicle and its high success rate, 2) Energy Department officials in the March 10th *Aviation Week and Space Technology* magazine explain that the Plutonium would be safely contained in an unbreakable, quarter-inch thick iridium cannister which would withstand pressures of over 2,000 pounds per square inch, and 3) in that same article, NASA explains there is "little public danger" because the Plutonium on board would be in the form of oxide pellets, each one-inch in diameter. If you'll remember, the danger of Plutonium is in fine particles.

11. She now presents her own statistical argument. (Notice how carefully she explains the statistics that are the main planks of her argument; here she uses testimony, analogy, and quantification.)

11. Now, let's take a second glance. One month later, the April 28th issue of *Aviation Week and Space Technology* reported that two of the last nine Titans launched have blown up. Two failures in nine trips is great in baseball, but not when we're dealing with nuclear payloads. That same article estimates loss of orbiter and crew, not at .002% but at 1 in 25.

12. With odds on the launch vehicle reduced to 1 in 25, the dual question arises: just how breach-proof is that cannister and, in a worst case scenario, what could happen if the pellets of 238 were released? For the answers to those questions we go to Dr. Gary Bennett, former Director of Safety and Nuclear Operations, who not only answers those questions, but also explains why NASA is so insistent on using Plutonium.

13. Last July, Dr. Bennett told *Common Cause* that there is concern within NASA and the Department of Energy that an explosion aboard the Galileo spacecraft, a Titan or other rocket, would, in turn, set off an explosion of the booster rockets. Bennett admitted that government tests in 1984 and 1985 determined that if the shuttle exploded, and then the booster rockets exploded, there would be a likelihood of breaching the iridium cannister. The Plutonium would then be vaporized and released into the environment; and there goes Florida.

14. But why would NASA take such a risk? It's really quite simple. On the one hand, Plutonium 238 is the one fuel that would enable space exploration beyond the limit of Mars. Without it, distant space exploration must wait for research to develop an equally effective, safe fuel. On the other hand, a worst case scenario would create the worst nuclear accident in history. In short, NASA weighed exploration now against the chances for disaster and opted to take the risk. The only problem is, I really don't like the idea of someone risking my life without consulting me—and I hope you don't either. By the way, there is evidence that NASA and the Department of Energy have projected some pretty horrible figures. Under the Freedom of Information Act rules, Karl Grossman was able to obtain agencies' estimates for the number of lives lost in a major accident. The only problem there is, every reference to the number of people affected is blanked out with liquid paper and the term Exempt #1 is written over the deletion. James Lombardo of the Energy Department explains the white-outs were necessary for—you've got it—national security reasons. I would contend the national security would be threatened by mass anger over the callousness of the Energy Department, and justifiably so. Representative Edward Markey agrees, and when he was head of the House subcommittee on Energy, Conservation and Power, he uncovered most of the information I share with you today.

15. In a telephone interview last August, I asked Congressman Markey three questions. Why hasn't Congress done anything? What should be done? What can we do to help?

16. His answer to the first question was quite interesting. You may remember that shortly after the shuttle exploded and just when Congress was showing some interest in a thorough investigation of the space program, another larger, even more dramatic accident occurred—Chernobyl. The attention to Chernobyl as it related to our own power industry captured not only the attention of most Americans, but of Congress as well. Consequently, most of our nuclear experts are involved in working with Congress and the nuclear power industry.

17. And while Congress is focusing on one facet of the nuclear question, NASA and the Department of Energy are receiving much less attention. Which is why Congressman Markey helped found Space Watch.

12. Previewing the next two subpoints and establishing the credibility of the next source of testimony.

13. More testimony backs up her argument.

14. Internal review of her argument so far.

15. Previews the subpoints that support her final main point. This section demonstrates the effectiveness of interviewing as a form of research, as discussed in Chapter 11.

16. Testimony from interview.

18. More testimony.

18. Representative Markey is of the opinion that hysteria accomplishes nothing, but that all space flight should be halted until either Plutonium 238 can be made safe, which is highly unlikely, or until an alternative fuel can be found. The burden of proof should be on NASA to prove a fuel safe, and not on the public to prove it dangerous.

19. Last subpoint of last main point.

19. This is where you and I come in. First, if by now you are sufficiently scared or angry, contact Space Watch through Representative Markey's office. Then, keep abreast of developments and exert pressure through your elected officials if Congress does nothing to interfere with NASA's plans. Send your objections not only to your own legislators, but to Representative Markey as well. Allow him to walk into the House with mailbag after mailbag of letters in opposition to NASA's unbridled desire to go to Jupiter. We have a friend in Congress who solicits help. The least we can do is give it to him.

20. The conclusion: Reviews the main idea, and ends with a memory aid in the form of a striking quotation.

20. One last thought; as of November, Plutonium 238 is *still* NASA's and the Department of Energy's fuel of choice. Dr. Bennett's last words in that July interview were, "I think you should understand there's a degree of risk with any kind of launch vehicle." But isn't that the point?

◆ SUMMARY

This chapter dealt with speech organization and supporting material. Speech organization is a process that begins with the formulation of a thesis statement to express the central idea of a speech. The thesis is established in the introduction, developed in the body, and reviewed in the conclusion of a structured speech. The introduction will also gain the audience's attention, set the mood and tone of the speech, and demonstrate the importance of the topic to the audience.

Organizing the body of the speech will begin with a list of points you might want to make in your speech. These points are then organized according to the principles of outlining. They are divided, coordinated, and placed in a logical order. Transitions from point to point help make this order apparent to your audience.

Organization follows a pattern such as that of time, space, topic, problem-solution, cause-effect, and climax arrangements. Along with reviewing your thesis or main points or both, the conclusion also supplies the audience with a memory aid.

Supporting materials are the facts and information you use to back up what you say. Supporting material has four purposes: to clarify, to make interesting, to make memorable, and to prove. Any piece of support could perform any or all of these functions, and any of the functions could be fulfilled by any of the types of support.

Types of support include *definitions,* which can be either *traditional* or *operational; detailed descriptions,* which create word pictures that enable an audience to visualize an idea; *analogies,* which compare or contrast an

Public Communication

unknown or unfamiliar concept with a known or familiar one; *anecdotes,* which add a lively, personal touch; *examples,* which can be either real or hypothetical; *quantification,* which makes an idea more specific; *statistics,* which show that a fact or principle is true for a large number of cases; *quotations,* which are used for memorable wording as well as testimony from a well-known or authoritative source; and *visual aids,* which help clarify complicated points and keep an audience informed on where you are in the general scheme of things. Any piece of support might combine two or more of these types.

◆ NOTES

1. See, for example, L. Stern, *The Structures and Strategies of Human Memory* (Homewood, Ill.: The Dorsey Press, 1985). See also Christopher Turner, "Organizing Information: Principles and Practices," *Library Journal* (June 15, 1987).

2. See, for example, George A. Miller, "The Magical Number Seven, Plus or Minus Two: Some Limits on Our Capacity for Processing Information," in Richard C. Anderson and David P. Ausubel (eds.), *Readings in the Psychology of Cognition* (New York: Holt, Rinehart and Winston, 1965), pp. 242–267.

3. Alan H. Monroe, *Principles and Types of Speech* (Glenview, Ill.: Scott, Foresman, 1935).

4. Kate L. Turabian, *Student's Guide for Writing College Papers* (Chicago: University of Chicago Press, 1976).

5. Katherine Graham, "The Press and Its Responsibilities," *Vital Speeches of the Day* 42 (April 15, 1976).

6. From Red Cross fund-raising material.

7. Katherine Graham, op. cit.

8. Martin Luther King, Jr., "I Have a Dream," speech at civil rights rally, Washington, D. C., August 28, 1963. See James C. McCroskey, *An Introduction to Rhetorical Communication* (Englewood Cliffs, N.J.: Prentice-Hall, 1968), pp. 248–249, for transcript.

9. Carl Sagan, *The Dragons of Eden: Speculations on the Evolution of Human Intelligence* (New York: Ballantine, 1978), pp. 13–17.

10. Bob Burgess, "Hiking/Biking," *Santa Barbara News Press* (February 25, 1978).

11. Ronald Reagan, "President's Farewell Address to the American People," *Vital Speeches of the Day* (February 1, 1989): 226.

12. Lori VanOverbeke, "Nutrasweet," *Winning Orations, 1986* (Interstate Oratorical Association, 1986), p. 56.

13. Robert J. Aaronson, "Air Transportation: What Is Safe and Needed," *Vital Speeches of the Day* (July 15, 1989): 592.

14. G. C. Wiegand, "Inflation," *Vital Speeches of the Day* 43 (June 15, 1978).

15. Bert E. Bradley, *Fundamentals of Speech Communication: The Credibility of Ideas* (Dubuque, Iowa: William C. Brown, 1974), p. 157.

16. Theresa Clinkenbeard, "The Loss of Childhood," *Winning Orations, 1984* (Interstate Oratorical Association, 1984), p. 4.

17. Jenny Clanton, "A Degree of Risk," *Winning Orations, 1988* (Interstate Oratorical Association, 1988), pp. 24–27. The Galileo Jupiter launch that was originally scheduled for May 20, 1987, finally took off in October of 1989—without incident, but after court challenges by environmental groups and civil protests concerning the safety of its plutonium fuel.

After reading this chapter, you should understand the following:

1. The differences among the various types of delivery.

2. The visual and auditory aspects of delivery that help you choose the best type of delivery for a particular speech.

3. The difference between facilitative and debilitative stage fright.

4. The sources of debilitative stage fright.

You should be able to do the following:

1. Choose the most effective type of delivery for a particular speech.

2. Follow the guidelines for effective extemporaneous, impromptu, manuscript, and memorized speeches.

3. Overcome debilitative stage fright.

4. Offer constructive criticism of others' presentations.

KEY TERMS

addition
articulation
debilitative stage fright
deletion
extemporaneous speeches
facilitative stage fright
fallacy of approval
fallacy of catastrophic failure
fallacy of overgeneralization

fallacy of perfection
imaging
impromptu speeches
irrational thinking
manuscript speeches
memorized speeches
pitch
rate
slurring
substitution
visualization

Presenting Your Message

"So far, so good," you may be thinking to yourself. You've developed a purpose; you've chosen and researched a topic that suits your own interests, your audience, and the occasion. You feel confident about your ability to organize your ideas in a logical, effective way, and you've built up a healthy reserve of supporting material.

But then comes a problem: When you think about the actual act of standing before a group, your self-confidence begins to erode. How will you act? Should you be formal or casual? Should you memorize your remarks, read from a script, or use notes? How loudly should you speak, and how quickly? And what about your nerves? The prospect of talking to an audience probably seems much more threatening than expressing yourself in a blue book or even mixing chemicals in a laboratory.

Because the act of speaking before a group of listeners may be a relatively new one for you, we'll look at the process now. The purpose of this chapter is to make you feel more confident about yourself as a speaker and to give you a clearer idea of how to behave before an audience. The first thing to consider in this area is the style of delivery you choose.

◆ TYPES OF DELIVERY

There are four basic types of delivery—extemporaneous, impromptu, manuscript, and memorized. Each type creates a different impression and is appropriate under different conditions. Any speech may incorporate more than one of these types of delivery. For purposes of discussion, however, it is best to consider them separately.

Extemporaneous Speeches

An **extemporaneous speech** is planned in advance but presented in a direct, spontaneous manner. Extemporaneous speeches are conversational in tone, which means that they give the audience members the impression that you are talking to them, directly and honestly, without the artificiality that an obvious "prepared statement" has. Extemporaneous speeches *are* carefully prepared, but they are prepared in such a way that they create what actors call "the illusion of the first time"—in other words, the audience hears your remarks as though they were brand-new. This style of speaking is generally accepted to be the most effective, especially for a college class. In a classroom you generally speak before a small audience (five to fifty people) made up of people with diverse backgrounds. Spontaneity is essential with this type of audience, but so is careful message planning. Extemporaneous speaking allows you to benefit from both careful planning and spontaneous delivery. A speech presented extemporaneously will be researched, organized, and practiced in advance, but the exact wording of the entire speech will not be memorized or otherwise predetermined. Because you speak from only brief, unobtrusive notes, you are able to move and maintain eye contact with your audience. Extemporaneous speaking is not only the most effective type of

"I found the old format much more exciting."

delivery for a classroom speech, but it is also the most common type of delivery in the "outside" world. Most of those involved in communication-oriented careers find that the majority of their public speaking is done before audiences that, in terms of size and diversity of interests represented, resemble those found in a college classroom. Professional public speakers recognize the advisability of both careful planning and spontaneity with such an audience.

The extemporaneous speech does have some disadvantages. It is difficult to keep exact time limits, to be exact in wording, or to be grammatically perfect with an extemporaneous speech. Therefore, if you are speaking as part of a radio or television broadcast or if your speech will be reproduced "for the record," you might want to use a manuscript or to memorize your speech. Also, an extemporaneous speech requires time to prepare. If you don't have that time, an impromptu speech might be more appropriate.

Impromptu Speeches

An **impromptu speech** is given off the top of one's head, without preparation. An impromptu speech is often given in an emergency, such as when a scheduled speaker becomes ill and you are suddenly called upon:

> Grunt Johnson couldn't make it this evening, folks, but I notice in our audience another Sioux U student leader who I am sure would be glad to say a few words . . .

Presenting Your Message

> Identify at least one type of speech you have seen that represented each type of delivery: extemporaneous, impromptu, manuscript, and memorized. For each speech, decide whether the style of delivery was most effective for the topic, speaker, and situation. If the delivery style was not effective, explain why and suggest a more appropriate style.
>
> Now identify at least one situation in which each style of delivery might be appropriate for you to use.

◆ **It usually takes me more than three weeks to prepare a good impromptu speech.**

Mark Twain

Impromptu speeches are sometimes given when speakers forget they are scheduled for extemporaneous speeches. In fact, a certain amount of confusion exists between the terms *extemporaneous* and *impromptu*.

The problem with an impromptu speech is that it is given on the spur of the moment and, as more than one expert has pointed out, "Too often the 'moment' arrives without the necessary informed and inspired 'spur.' "[1] There are, however, advantages to impromptu speaking. For one thing, an impromptu speech is by definition spontaneous. It is the delivery style necessary for informal talks, group discussions, and comments on others' speeches. It also can be an effective training aid; it can teach you to think on your feet and organize your thoughts quickly. To take full advantage of an impromptu speaking opportunity, remember the following points:

1. Take advantage of the time between being called on to speak and actually speaking. Even if you have only a minute, you can still scribble a few brief notes to protect against mental blocks.
2. Don't be afraid to be original; you don't have to remember what every other expert says about your topic—what do *you* say about it? Review your personal experiences and use them. If nothing else, consider questions such as "Who? What? When? Where? How?" and formulate a plan to answer one or more of them.
3. Observe what is going on around you, and respond to it. If there were other speakers, you might agree or disagree with what they said. You can comment on the audience and the occasion, too, as well as on your topic.
4. Keep a positive attitude. Remember that audience expectations are low. They know you haven't prepared in advance, and they don't expect you to be Patrick Henry.
5. Finally, and perhaps most important, keep your comments brief. Especially, do not prolong your conclusion. If you have said everything you want to say or everything you can remember, wrap it up as neatly as possible and sit down. If you forgot something, it probably wasn't important anyway. If it was, the audience will ask you about it afterward.

Manuscript Speeches

Manuscript speeches are read "word for word" from a prepared text. They are necessary when you are speaking "for the record," as at legal proceedings or when presenting scientific findings. The greatest disadvantage of a manuscript speech is the lack of spontaneity that may result. Manuscript readers have even been known to read their directions by mistake: "And so, let me say in conclusion, look at the audience with great sincerity . . . oops!" Needless to say, this can lead to extreme embarrassment.

Manuscript speeches are difficult and cumbersome, but they are sometimes necessary. If you find occasion to use one, here are some guidelines:

1. When writing the speech, recognize the differences between written essays and speeches. Speeches are usually less formal, more repetitive, and more personal than written messages.[2] They use more adverbs, adjectives, and circumlocutions such as "well" and "as you can see." As one expert points out, "Speeches use more words per square thought than well-written essays or reports."[3]
2. Use short paragraphs. They are easier to return to after establishing eye contact with your audience.
3. Type the manuscript triple-spaced, in capital letters, with a dark ribbon. Underline the words you want to emphasize. (See Figure 13–1.)
4. Use stiff paper so that it won't fold up or fly away during the speech. Type on only one side, and number the pages by hand with large, circled numbers.
5. Rehearse until you can "read" whole lines without looking at the manuscript.
6. Take your time, vary your speed, and try to concentrate on ideas rather than words.

Memorized Speeches

Memorized speeches—those that are learned "by heart"—are the most difficult and often the least effective. They usually seem excessively formal. They tend to make you think of words rather than ideas. However, like manuscript speeches, they are sometimes necessary. They are used in oratory contests and on very formal occasions such as eulogies or church rituals. They are used as training devices for memory. They are also used in some political situations. For example, in the 1988 presidential debates, George Bush and Michael Dukakis were allowed to make prepared speeches, but they were not allowed to use notes. Thus, they had to memorize precise, "for-the-record" wording.

There is only one guideline for a memorized speech: Practice. The speech won't be effective until you have practiced it so you can present it with that "illusion of the first time" that we mentioned previously.

◆ PRACTICING THE SPEECH

Once you choose the appropriate delivery style for the type of speech you are giving, the best way to make sure that you are on your way to an effective

◆ **The late Senator Alben W. Barkley once told the story of how he had used a manuscript, instead of notes, for a talk. After he sat down, he turned to a friend and asked, "What did you think of it?"**

"Well," came the answer, "I have only three criticisms. First, you read it. Second, you read it poorly. Third, it wasn't worth reading."

Jacob Braude

TO SUMMARIZE, WE ARE IN THE EARLY STAGE OF DEVELOPMENTS IN

THE SCIENCE AND TECHNOLOGY OF INFORMATION PROCESSING THAT WILL

TRULY REVOLUTIONIZE OUR SOCIETY. ADVANCES ARE OCCURRING AT SUCH

A FAST PACE THAT RECENT EXPERIENCE IS NOT ALWAYS A GOOD GUIDE TO

THE FUTURE. IN THE PAST 30 YEARS, COMPUTER COMPUTATIONS HAVE

GONE FROM A FEW INSTRUCTIONS PER SECOND AT A COST OF SEVERAL

DOLLARS TO MILLIONS OF INSTRUCTIONS PER SECOND AT A COST OF LESS

THAN 1 CENT. BUT SUCH DRAMATIC INDICATORS OF PROGRESS DO NOT

MEASURE THE FULL IMPACT OF WHAT IS TAKING PLACE OR WHAT IS LIKELY

TO OCCUR IN THE NEXT 30 YEARS. THERE CAN BE LITTLE DOUBT THAT

THESE CHANGES WILL ALTER THE WAY PEOPLE LIVE AND EARN A LIVING,

AND THE WAY THEY PERCEIVE THEMSELVES AND RELATE TO ONE ANOTHER.

FIGURE 13—1
Sample Page from
Manuscript Speech

delivery is to practice your speech repeatedly and systematically. One way to do that is to go through as many of the following five steps as possible:

1. First, present the speech to yourself. "Talk through" the entire speech, including your examples and forms of support. In other words, don't just say, "This is where I present my statistics" or "This is where I explain about photosynthesis."
2. Tape-record the speech, and listen to it. Because we hear our own voices partially through our cranial bone structure, we are sometimes surprised at what we sound like to others.
3. Present the speech in front of the mirror, and watch your physical mannerisms.

Public Communication

4. Present the speech in front of a small group of friends or relatives or both.
5. Present the speech to at least one listener in the same room (or, if that room is not available, a similar room) that you will present the final speech in.

◆ GUIDELINES FOR DELIVERY

The best way to consider guidelines for delivery is through an examination of the nonverbal aspects of presenting a speech. As you read in Chapter 5, nonverbal messages can change the meaning assigned to the spoken word and, in some cases, can contradict that meaning entirely. In fact, if the audience wants to interpret how you *feel* about something, they are likely to trust your nonverbal communication more than the words you speak. If you tell an audience, "It's good to be here today," but you stand before them slouched over with your hands in your pockets and an expression on your face as if you were about to be shot, they are likely to discount what you say. This might cause your audience to react negatively to your speech, and their negative reaction might make you even more nervous. This cycle of speaker and audience reinforcing each other's feelings can work *for* you, though, if you approach a subject with genuine enthusiasm. Enthusiasm is shown through both the visual and auditory aspects of your delivery.

Visual Aspects of Delivery

Visual aspects of delivery include such things as appearance, movement, posture, facial expressions, and eye contact.

APPEARANCE   Appearance is not a presentation variable as much as a preparation variable. Some communication consultants suggest new clothes, new glasses, and new hairstyles for their clients. In case you consider any of these, be forewarned that you should be attractive to your audience but not flashy. Research suggests that audiences like speakers who are similar to them, but they prefer the similarity to be shown conservatively. For example, studies run in 1972, when long hair on males was becoming popular, showed that even long-haired listeners considered long-haired speakers less credible than shorter-haired speakers.[4]

MOVEMENT   Movement is an important visual aspect of delivery. The way you walk to the front of your audience, for example, will express your confidence and enthusiasm. And once you begin speaking, nervous energy can cause your body to shake and twitch, and that can be distressing both to you and to your audience. One way to control *involuntary* movement is to move *voluntarily* when you feel the need to move. Don't feel that you have to stand in one spot or that all your gestures need to be carefully planned. Simply get involved in your message, and let your involvement create the motivation for your movement. That way, when you move, you will emphasize what you are

◆ Gesture, but do not *make* gestures. Let your gestures spring from the impulse common to all expression through action.

James A. Winans

saying in the same way you would emphasize it if you were talking to a group of friends. If you move voluntarily, you will use up the same energy that would otherwise cause you to move involuntarily.

Movement can help you maintain contact with *all* members of your audience. Those closest to you will feel the greatest contact with you whereas the people who are less interested will have a tendency to sit farther away to begin with. This creates what is known as the "action zone" of audience members sitting in the front and center of the room. Movement enables you to extend this action zone, to include in it people who would otherwise remain uninvolved. Without overdoing it, you should feel free to move toward, away, or from side to side in front of your audience.

Remember: Move with the understanding that it will add to the meaning of the words you use. It is difficult to bang your fist on a podium or to take a step without conveying emphasis. Make the emphasis natural by allowing your message to create your motivation to move.

POSTURE   Generally speaking, good posture means standing with your spine relatively straight, your shoulders relatively squared off, and your feet angled out to keep your body from falling over sideways. In other words, rather than standing at military attention, you should be comfortably erect.

Of course, you shouldn't get *too* comfortable. There are speakers who are effective in spite of the fact that they sprawl on tabletops and slouch against blackboards, but their effectiveness is usually in spite of their posture rather than because of it. Sometimes speakers are so awesome in stature or reputation that they need an informal posture to encourage their audience to relax. In that case, sloppy posture is more or less justified. But because awesomeness is not usually a problem for beginning speakers, good posture should be the rule.

Good posture can help you control nervousness by allowing your breathing apparatus to work properly; when your brain receives enough oxygen, it's easier for you to think clearly. Good posture will also help you get a positive audience reaction because standing up straight makes you more visible. It also increases your audience contact because the audience members will feel that you are interested enough in them to stand formally, yet relaxed enough to be at ease with them.

FACIAL EXPRESSION   The expression on your face can be more meaningful to an audience than the words you say. Try it yourself with a mirror. Say, "College is neat," with a smirk, with a warm smile, deadpan, and then with a scowl. It just doesn't mean the same thing. When speaking, keep in mind that your face might be saying something in front of your back. Remember also that it is just about impossible to control facial expressions from the outside. Like your movement, your facial expressions will reflect your involvement with your message. Don't try to fake it. Just get involved in your message, and your face will take care of itself.

"When you quote a Presidential candidate, Gorman, you do
not—I repeat—do not roll your eyes."

EYE CONTACT Eye contact is perhaps the most important nonverbal facet
of delivery. Eye contact not only increases your direct contact with your
audience; it also should increase their interest in you by making you more
attractive. Eyes are beautiful things; much more beautiful than eyelids,
foreheads, or scalps. Furthermore, and contrary to popular opinion, eye
contact can be used to help you control your nervousness. Direct eye contact
is a form of reality testing. The most frightening aspect of speaking is the
unknown. How will the audience react? What will they think? Direct eye
contact allows you to test your perception of your audience as you speak.
Usually, especially in a college class, you will find that your audience is more
"with" you than you think. We found that out ourselves through personal
experience; when we first began teaching, we were terrified of the students
who would slither down in their chairs, doodle, and generally seem bored.
These students upset us so thoroughly that we usually would try *not* to look at
them. And that made matters worse. Eventually, by deliberately establishing
eye contact with the apparently bored students, we found that they often *were*
interested; they just weren't showing that interest because they didn't think
anyone was looking. Once these bored-looking students realized that someone
was actually looking at them, noticing their existence, they made their attention
more obvious by sitting up and looking back at us. The more eye contact they
received, the more interested they became. Because of this tendency, eye
contact could be viewed as a form of "audience control."

Presenting Your Message

◆ **I walked to the lectern. I hemmed. Then I hawed. I cleared my throat, then I said:**

"I shall give an illustrated lecture on the interior of the human mouth—the teeth, the tongue, the upper palate, the lower palate and other points of interest."

Then, to illustrate my lecture, I stuck my finger in my mouth, as if to point out the various things I was talking about, and for five solid minutes I spoke totally unintelligible gibberish, never removing the finger from my mouth and sometimes inserting my entire fist.

Alan Sherman
A Gift of Laughter

To maintain eye contact, you might try to meet the eyes of each member of your audience squarely at least once during any given presentation. Once you have made definite contact, move on to another audience member. You can learn to do this quickly, so you can visually latch onto every member of a good-sized class in a relatively short time.

The characteristics of appearance, movement, posture, facial expression, and eye contact are visual, nonverbal facets of delivery. Now consider the auditory, nonverbal messages that you might send during a presentation.

Auditory Aspects of Delivery

As you read in Chapter 5, the way you use your voice—your paralanguage—says a great deal about you—most notably about your sincerity and enthusiasm. In addition, using your voice well can help you control your nervousness. It's another cycle: Controlling your vocal characteristics will decrease your nervousness, which will enable you to control your voice even more. But this cycle can also work in the opposite direction. If your voice is out of control, your nerves will probably be in the same state. Controlling your voice is mostly a matter of recognizing and using appropriate *volume, rate, pitch,* and *articulation.*

VOLUME Volume—the loudness of your voice—is determined by the amount of air you push past the vocal folds in your throat. The key to controlling volume, then, is controlling the amount of air you use. The key to determining the *right* volume is audience contact. Your delivery should be loud enough so that your audience can hear everything you say but not so loud that they feel you are talking to someone in the next room. Too much volume is seldom the problem for beginning speakers. Usually, they either are not loud enough or have a tendency to fade off at the end of a thought. Sometimes, when they lose faith in an idea in midsentence, they compromise by mumbling the end of the sentence so that it isn't quite coherent. That's an unfortunate compromise, rather like changing your mind in the middle of a broad jump.

One contemporary speaker who has been criticized for inappropriate volume is Senator Edward M. Kennedy. One researcher pointed out that

"Kennedy tended to shout when an audience was small or uninterested or when he sensed he was losing them. Thus, his volume was often inappropriate to the time and place."[5] *Newsweek's* John Walcott observed, "When he had an unresponsive audience—300 Iowa farmers who were not jumping up on their chairs—he tended to shout more and it became more and more incongruous."[6]

> Speakers whose delivery is an act rarely succeed. It is far better to develop a natural speaking style that is effective. You can do this by recalling times when you have communicated a message most effectively to two or more people: in class, in your family, at church, on a team, and so on. How did you dress and move? What was your facial expression? How did you make eye contact with your listeners? How did your voice sound?
>
> Consider how you can use the same natural style that has worked for you in the past as you deliver prepared speeches.

RATE Rate is your speed in speaking. There is a range of personal differences in speaking rate. Daniel Webster, for example, is said to have spoken at around 90 words per minute whereas one actor who is known for his fast-talking commercials speaks at about 250. Normal speaking speed, however, is between 120 and 150 words per minute. If you talk much more slowly than that, you may tend to lull your audience to sleep. Faster speaking rates are stereotypically associated with speaker competence,[7] but if you talk too rapidly, you will tend to be unintelligible. Once again, your involvement in your message is the key to achieving an effective rate.

PITCH Pitch—the highness or lowness of your voice—is controlled by the frequency at which your vocal folds vibrate as you push air through them. Because taut vocal folds vibrate at a greater frequency, pitch is influenced by muscular tension. This explains why nervous speakers have a tendency occasionally to "squeak" whereas relaxed speakers seem to be more in control. Pitch will tend to follow rate and volume. As you speed up or become louder, your pitch will have a tendency to rise. If your range in pitch is too narrow, your voice will have a singsong quality. If it is too wide, you may sound overly dramatic. You should control your pitch so that your listeners believe you are talking *with* them rather than performing in front of them. Once again, your involvement in your message should take care of this naturally for you.

When considering volume, rate, and pitch, keep *emphasis* in mind. You have to use a variety of vocal characteristics to maintain audience interest, but remember that a change in volume, pitch, or rate will result in emphasis. If you pause or speed up, your rate will suggest emphasis. Words you whisper or scream will be emphasized by their volume. One of our students once provided an example of how volume can be used to emphasize an idea. He was speaking on how possessions like cars communicate things about their owners. "For example," he said, with normal volume, "a Cadillac says, 'I've got

Presenting Your Message

money!' But a Rolls-Royce says, *'I'VE GOT MONEY!'* " He blared out those last three words with such force the podium shook.

ARTICULATION   The final auditory nonverbal behavior, articulation, is perhaps the most important. For our purposes here, **articulation** means pronouncing all the parts of all the necessary words and nothing else.

It is not our purpose to condemn regional or ethnic dialects within this discussion. Native New Yorkers can continue to have their "hot dawgs" with their "cawfee," and Southerners can drawl as much as they-all please. You *should* know, however, that a considerable amount of research suggests that regional dialects can cause negative impressions.[8] But it is also true that an honest regional accent can work in your favor. For example, when Paul Volcker was president of the Federal Reserve Bank of New York, he used his accent to his benefit when he began a speech this way:

> Fellow New Yorkers: I am emboldened to use that simple salutation tonight for more than one reason. At the most personal level, I was reminded the other day where my own roots lay. I heard a tape recording of some remarks I had made. After spending three quarters of the past 16 years in Washington, I confess to being startled by what I heard—the full, rounded tones of a home-grown New York accent.[9]

The purpose of this discussion is to suggest *careful,* not standardized, articulation. Incorrect articulation is nothing more than careless articulation. It usually results in (1) leaving off parts of words (deletion), (2) replacing part of a word (substitution), (3) adding parts to words (addition), or (4) overlapping two or more words (slurring).

Deletion   The most common mistake in articulation is **deletion,** or leaving off part of a word. As you are thinking the complete word, it is often difficult to recognize that you are only saying part of it. The most common deletions occur at the end of words, especially *-ing* words. *Going, doing,* and *stopping* become *goin', doin',* and *stoppin'.* Parts of words can be left off in the middle, too, as in *natully* for *naturally* and *reg'lar* for *regular.*

Substitution   **Substitution** takes place when you replace part of a word with an incorrect sound. The ending *-th* is often replaced at the end of a word with a single *t,* as when *with* becomes *wit.* (This tendency is especially prevalent in many parts of the northeastern United States.) The *th-* sound is also a problem at the beginning of words, as *this, that,* and *those* have a tendency to become *dis, dat,* and *dose.*

Addition   The articulation problem of **addition** is caused by adding extra parts to words that are already perfectly adequate, such as *incentative* for *incentive, athalete* instead of *athlete,* and *orientated* instead of *oriented.* Sometimes this type of addition is caused by incorrect word choice, such as when *irregardless* (which is not a word) is used for *regardless.*

Another type of addition is the use of "tag questions," such as "you know?" or "you see?" or "right?" at the end of sentences. To have every other sentence punctuated with one of these barely audible superfluous phrases can be maddening.

He Talks Bawlamerese, Duddney?

BAWLAMER, Sept. 20—Following is a brief glossary of "Bawlamerese" compiled as a traveler's guide to the local patois by the Citizens' Planning and Housing Association of this city, which outsiders often mispronounce "BALT-i-more" and local residents pronounce "BAWL-uh-mer." The excerpts from the association's list are reproduced with its permission from its handbook, "Bawlamer":

AIG The thing with a yoke.
ARSH People from Arlin.
AWL Goes into the crankcase.
ARN What you do on an arnin board.
BLOW Opposite of above.
COLE RACE BEEF A favorite sandwich.
CALF LICK Protestant, Jewish and . . .
DRAFF Animal with the longest neck.
DRUCKSTEWER Drugstore.
DUDDNEY Doesn't he.
ELFIN Animal with a trunk.
ERF Planet on which we live.
FARN GIN Used for fighting fars.
FARST FARS Smokey Bear fights them.
GRANITE What you don't want to be taken for.
HOSKULL Where you went before cahwidge.
IGGLE Our national symbol.

JEET? Did you eat? Usually answered by "no, jew?"
LOBBLE Responsible for.
MERLIN The Free State.
MACELY Mostly.
MORALITY The race for mayor.
MEER What you look at in the morning.
MURIEL A large painting on a large wall.
NAPLIS The state capital.
OLTNO I don't know.
OLL What you walk down when you get married.
OLLIN A piece of land surrounded by water.
PO-LEECE A single police officer.
PLEECE Two or more po-leece.
PARAMOUR What your neighbor uses at 8 A.M. Sundays.
PHANE What you answer when it rings.
QUARR Sings in Church.
ROSTRUM Where the ladies go after dinner.
SORE Drainage area under streets.
TORST Tourist.
WARSHNIN Our nation's capital.
WRENCH Rinse, as in "wrench your hands in the zinc."
WOODER What you wrench your hands with.
YERP Europe.
ZOLLAFANE Xylophone.

Probably the worst type of addition, or at least the most common, is the use of *uh* and *anda* between words. *Anda* is often stuck between two words when *and* isn't even needed. If you find yourself doing that, you might want just to pause or swallow instead.[10]

Slurring Slurring is caused, in effect, by trying to say two or more words at once—or at least overlapping the end of one word with the beginning of the next. Word pairs ending with *of* are the worst offenders in this category. *Sort of* becomes *sorta, kind of* becomes *kinda,* and *because of* becomes *becausa.* Word combinations ending with *to* are often slurred, as when *want to* becomes *wanna.* Sometimes even more than two words are blended together, as when "that is the way" becomes "thatsaway." Careful articulation means using your lips, teeth, tongue, and jaw to bite off your words, cleanly and separately, one at a time.

Presenting Your Message

The general rule for articulation in extemporaneous speaking is to be both natural and clear. Be yourself, but be an understandable, intelligent-sounding version of yourself. The best way to achieve this goal is to accept your instructor's evaluation of whether you add, substitute, drop, or slur word sounds. Then you can, as Shakespeare had King Lear suggest, "Mend your speech a little, lest you may mar your fortune."

One cause of poor articulation is stage fright, a topic we will now attack in some detail.

◆ SPEAKING WITH CONFIDENCE

◆ **I have a slight inferiority complex still. I go into a room and have to talk myself into going up to people ... If I'm the epitome of a woman who is always confident and in control, don't ever believe it of anyone.**

Barbara Walters

The terror that strikes into the hearts of so many beginning speakers is called communication apprehension or speech anxiety by communication scholars, but it is more commonly known to those who experience it as stage fright.

Facilitative and Debilitative Stage Fright

Although stage fright is a very real problem for many speakers, it is a problem that can be overcome. Interestingly enough, the first step in feeling less apprehensive about speaking is to realize that a certain amount of nervousness is not only natural but facilitative. That is, **facilitative stage fright** is a factor that can help improve your performance. Just as totally relaxed athletes or musicians aren't likely to perform at the top of their potential, speakers think more rapidly and express themselves more energetically when their level of tension is moderate.

It is only when the level of anxiety is intense that it becomes **debilitative,** inhibiting effective self-expression. Intense fear causes trouble in two ways. First, the strong emotion keeps you from thinking clearly. Second, intense fear leads to an urge to do something, anything, to make the problem go away. This urge to escape often causes a speaker to speed up delivery, which results in a rapid, almost machine-gun style. As you can imagine, this boost in speaking rate leads to even more mistakes, which only adds to the speaker's anxiety. Thus, a relatively small amount of nervousness can begin to feed on itself until it grows into a serious problem.

Sources of Debilitative Stage Fright

Before we describe how to manage **debilitative stage fright,** it might be helpful to look at some reasons people are afflicted with the problem.[11]

PREVIOUS NEGATIVE EXPERIENCE   One reason people feel apprehensive about speech giving is because of unpleasant past experiences. Most of us are uncomfortable doing *anything* in public, especially if it is a form of performance that puts our talents and abilities "on the line." An unpleasant experience in one type of performance can cause you to expect that a future similar situation will also be unpleasant. These expectations can be realized

Public Communication

through the self-fulfilling prophecies discussed in Chapter 2.[12] A traumatic failure at an earlier speech or low self-esteem from critical parents during childhood are common examples of experiences that can cause later stage fright.

You might object to the idea that past experiences cause stage fright. After all, not everyone who has bungled a speech or had critical parents is debilitated in the future. To understand why some people are affected more strongly than others by past experiences, we need to consider another cause of speech anxiety.

IRRATIONAL THINKING   Cognitive psychologists argue that it is not events that cause people to feel nervous but rather the beliefs they have about those events.[13] Certain irrational beliefs leave people feeling unnecessarily apprehensive. Psychologist Albert Ellis lists several such beliefs, or examples of **irrational thinking,** which we will call "fallacies" because of their illogical nature.[14]

1. **Catastrophic Failure.** People who succumb to the **fallacy of catastrophic failure** operate on the assumption that if something bad can happen, it probably will. Their thoughts before and during a speech resemble these:

   "As soon as I stand up to speak, I'll forget everything I wanted to say."

   "Everyone will think my ideas are stupid."

   "Somebody will probably laugh at me."

   Although it is naïve to imagine that all your speeches will be totally successful, it is equally wrong to assume they will all fail miserably. One way to escape from the fallacy of catastrophic failure is to take a more realistic look at the situation. Would your audience really hoot you off the stage? Will they really think your ideas are stupid? Even if you did forget your remarks for a moment, would the results be a genuine disaster? It helps to remember that nervousness is more apparent to the speaker than to the audience.[15]

2. **Perfection.** Speakers who succumb to the **fallacy of perfection** expect themselves to behave flawlessly. Whereas such a standard of perfection might serve as a target and a source of inspiration (rather like making a hole-in-one for a golfer), it is totally unrealistic to expect that you will write and deliver a perfect speech—especially as a beginner. It helps to remember that audiences don't expect you to be perfect.[16]

3. **Approval.** The mistaken belief called the **fallacy of approval** is based on the idea that it is vital—not just desirable—to gain the approval of everyone in the audience. It is rare that even the best speakers please everyone, especially on topics that are at all controversial. To paraphrase Abraham Lincoln, you can't please all the people all the time . . . and it is irrational to expect you will.

4. **Overgeneralization.** The **fallacy of overgeneralization** might also be labeled the fallacy of exaggeration, for it occurs when a person blows one poor experience out of proportion. Consider these examples:

◆ A man is hurt not so much by what happens as by his opinion of what happens.

Montaigne

◆ I never was what you would call a fancy skater—and while I seldom actually fell, it might have been more impressive if I had. A good resounding fall is no disgrace. It is the fantastic writhing to avoid a fall which destroys any illusion of being a gentleman. How like life that is, after all!

Robert Benchley

"I'm so stupid! I mispronounced that word."

"I completely blew it—I forgot one of my supporting points."

"My hands were shaking. The audience must have thought I was a complete idiot."

A second type of exaggeration occurs when a speaker treats occasional lapses as if they were the rule rather than the exception. This sort of mistake usually involves extreme labels such as "always" and "never."

"I *always* forget what I want to say."

"I can *never* come up with a good topic."

"I can't do *anything* right."

To become better at understanding how your thoughts shape your feelings about speechmaking, think about the following situations, and list two opposite ways you could interpret each situation. Take note of the feelings that would follow from each interpretation.

a. While researching your topic you find it difficult to find material.
b. While organizing your ideas, you come to one that all the experts agree on but that you're not too sure about.
c. When you get up to give your speech, someone giggles.
d. In the middle of an important point you're making, one audience member yawns emphatically.
e. Toward the end of your presentation, you notice an attractive person staring at you and smiling.

Overcoming Stage Fright

There are four fairly simple ways to overcome debilitative stage fright. The first, as suggested earlier, is to be rational about the beliefs that cause your stage fright. The other three are to be receiver-oriented, positive, and prepared.

1. **Be Rational.** Listen to your thought processes, your internal voice, and try to figure out if the basis for your stage fright is rational. Then dispute any irrational beliefs. Use the list of fallacies given earlier to discover which of your internal statements are based on mistaken thinking.
2. **Be Receiver-oriented.** Concentrate on your audience rather than on yourself. Worry about whether they are interested, about whether they understand, and about whether or not you are maintaining human contact with them.
3. **Be Positive.** It is important to build and maintain a positive attitude toward your audience, your speech, and yourself as a speaker. Some communication consultants suggest that public speakers should concentrate on three statements immediately before speaking. The three statements are:

"I'm glad I'm here."

"I know my topic."

"I care about you" ("you," of course, being the audience).

Keeping these ideas in mind is supposed to help you maintain a positive attitude.

Another technique for building a positive attitude is known as **imaging** or **visualization.** This technique has been used successfully with athletes. It requires you to visualize the successful completion of a specific speech assignment.[17] Visualization can help the "self-fulfilling prophecy" mentioned earlier work in your favor.

4. **Be Prepared.** If you are fully prepared, your speech will represent less of a threat. Devote enough time to each step of message preparation so that you can feel secure. Devote an extra amount of time and effort to the introduction so that you can "break the ice" and develop audience rapport early. Be sure to leave enough time to *practice* your presentation thoroughly. As a guide, you might consult the checklist for delivery presented in Table 13–1. And when it comes time to give your presentation, keep in mind that nervousness is normal. Expect it, and remember that its symptoms—even shaky knees and trembling hands—are more obvious to you than they are to the audience. Beginning public speakers, when congratulated for their poise during a speech, are apt to make such remarks as "Are you kidding? I was *dying* up there."

Remember also some of the tips mentioned earlier: Stand with good posture so that you can breathe well. In fact, it usually helps to take one or two deep breaths before you begin. And use one or two effective visual aids; they

◆ **In speaking to the Winnipeg Rotary Club, I arrived a little early for the meeting and was greeted by an attractive lady who asked, "What are you doing here?"**

She looked a little familiar. I thought perhaps I had met her at a convention two years earlier. "I'm here to give a speech to the Rotary Club," I replied.

"Do you do this often?" she asked.

"Quite often," I said.

"Are you nervous before you talk?" she demanded.

"I don't think so," I replied.

She retorted, "Then what are you doing in the ladies' washroom?"

Ross Smyth

give you something to do with your hands, and they distract attention away from yourself.

These four guidelines will enable most speakers to control their stage fright to the point where it will be facilitative rather than debilitative. Speakers who find these methods inadequate have two other options: They might enlist the

TABLE 13–1   Checklist for Delivery

Choose Best Style of Delivery
_____extemporaneous
_____impromptu
_____manuscript
_____memorized

Practice the Speech
_____alone
_____tape-recorded
_____in front of a mirror
_____in front of a small group of friends
_____in the room where the final speech will take place

Analyze Effectiveness of Delivery
Visual aspects
_____appearance
_____movement
_____posture
_____facial expressions
_____eye contact

Auditory aspects
_____volume
_____rate
_____pitch
_____articulation

help of a professional counselor (these services are often provided free by colleges), or they could research a more extensive procedure for themselves, such as systematic desensitization. Ron Adler's book *Confidence in Communication: A Guide to Assertive and Social Skills*[18] outlines several procedures for managing communication anxiety.

> To analyze your own reaction to stage fright, think back to your last public speech, and rate yourself on how rational, receiver-oriented, positive, and prepared you were. How did these attributes affect your anxiety level?

◆ OFFERING CONSTRUCTIVE CRITICISM

As we hinted earlier, one of the most important examples of impromptu speaking is your criticism of a classmate's speech. It is important to make this criticism constructive, which means that it will be designed to help the speaker improve. To be constructive, your criticism has to be *substantive*.

1. Be Complete. The first element of substantive criticism is to criticize *what* was said as well as *how* it was said; in other words, to not concentrate on

"Must you use those three-by-five cards every time we have a discussion?"

Drawing by Joseph Farris; © 1986 The New Yorker Magazine, Inc.

Presenting Your Message

delivery traits to the point where you lose track of the speaker's ideas.[19]

2. Be Specific. The second aspect of substance is to be specific: Rather than just saying, "I liked this" or "I didn't like that," you should provide a detailed explanation of your reasons for liking or disliking parts of the speech.

3. Be Positive. Perhaps the most important guideline in offering criticism, however, is to point out what is *right* with the speech as well as what is *wrong* with it. Otherwise, you run the risk of extinguishing the *positive* aspects of the speaker's behavior. In fact, negative criticism unaccompanied by positive criticism is often useless because the speaker might become defensive and block out your criticism completely. It is a good idea, therefore, to offer your positive criticism first and then tactfully offer your suggestions for improvement. For example, rather than saying, "Your ideas about the psychological aspects of diabetes were completely unclear and unsupported," you might say, "I found your explanation of the physical aspects of diabetes to be clearly stated and well backed up with details and examples. However, your explanation of the psychological aspects of the disease left me a little confused. It might be my own fault, but it just did not seem to be as well supported as the rest of your speech."

To encourage this type of criticism, many instructors have their students use a speech evaluation form like the ones in Chapters 14 and 15 (pp. 419 and 417). Notice especially the first two open-ended questions on these forms: "What did you especially like?" comes before "In your opinion, how could the speech be improved?"

Your instructor might prefer a different evaluation form, or you might want to amend the one in Chapter 14 or 15 to your own liking. Whatever type of form you choose, make sure it allows for substantive, positive criticism.

◆ **SUMMARY**

There are four types of delivery: extemporaneous, impromptu, manuscript, and memorized. In each type, the speaker must be concerned with both visual and auditory aspects of the presentation. Visual aspects include appearance, movement, posture, facial expressions, and eye contact. Auditory aspects include volume, rate, pitch, and articulation. The four most common articulation problems are deletion, substitution, addition, and slurring of word sounds.

One of the most serious delivery problems is debilitative (as opposed to facilitative) stage fright. Sources of debilitative stage fright include irrational thinking, which might include a belief in one or more of the following fallacies: the fallacy of perfection (a good speaker never does anything wrong), the fallacy of absolute approval (*everyone* has to like you), the fallacy of overgeneralization (you *always* mess up speeches), and the fallacy of catastrophic failure (all is lost if this speech bombs).

There are several methods of overcoming speech anxiety. The first is to refute the irrational fallacies just listed. The others include being receiver-oriented, positive, and prepared.

Effective delivery is aided through the constructive criticism of speeches presented in class. Your criticism should be substantive, which means that it should address what was said as well as how it was said, it should be specific, and it should include positive as well as negative aspects of the speaker's behavior.

◆ NOTES

1. Alan H. Monroe and Douglas Ehninger, *Principles and Types of Speech Communication,* 7th ed. (Glenview, Ill.: Scott, Foresman, 1974), p. 142.

2. An interesting study in this area is Donald P. Hayes' "Speaking and Writing: Distinct Patterns of Word Choice," *Journal of Memory and Language* 27 (October 1988): 572–585. This extensive study of written/spoken language differences found these differences so pronounced that "conversations between college graduates more closely resemble a preschool child's speech to its parents than texts from newspapers." Earlier studies pertaining to the differences between written and spoken language are reviewed in John F. Wilson and Carroll C. Arnold, *Dimensions of Public Communication* (Boston: Allyn & Bacon, 1976), pp. 195–198.

3. Jerry Tarver, "Can't Nobody Here Use This Language? Function and Quality in Choosing Words," *Vital Speeches of the Day* (May 1, 1979): 420–423.

4. These studies are reviewed in Lawrence R. Rosenfeld and Jean M. Civikly, *With Words Unspoken* (New York: Holt, Rinehart and Winston, 1976), p. 62. Also see Shelly Chaiken, "Communicator Physical Attractiveness and Persuasion," *Journal of Personality and Social Psychology* 37 (1979): 1387–1397.

5. L. Patric Devlin, "An Analysis of Kennedy's Communication in the 1980 Campaign," *Quarterly Journal of Speech* 68 (November 1982): 397–417.

6. Ibid.

7. A study demonstrating this stereotype is Richard L. Street, Jr., and Robert M. Brady, "Speech Rate Acceptance Ranges as a Function of Evaluative Domain, Listener Speech Rate, and Communication Context," *Speech Monographs* 49 (December 1982): 290–308.

8. See, for example, Anthony Mulac and Mary Jo Rudd, "Effects of Selected American Regional Dialects upon Regional Audience Members," *Communication Mono-graphs* 44 (1977): 184–195. Some research, however, suggests that nonstandard dialects do not have the detrimental effects on listeners that were once believed. See, for example, Fern L. Johnson and Richard Buttny, "White Listener's Responses to 'Sounding Black' and 'Sounding White': The Effects of Message Content on Judgments about Language," *Communication Monographs* 49 (March 1982): 33–39.

9. Paul A. Volcker, "The Dilemmas of Monetary Policy," *Vital Speeches of the Day* 42 (January 15, 1976).

10. One study that looked at the effect of additions such as "uh" and "anda" was Lawrence A. Hosman and John W. Wright II, "The Effects of Hedges and Hesitations on Impression Formation in a Simulated Courtroom Context," *Western Journal of Speech Communication* 51 (Spring 1987): 173–188. What they found, basically, was that hedges and hesitations produced low perceptions of authoritativeness and attractiveness, and also made the speaker look guilty.

11. A substantial body of research literature on communication apprehension and anxiety has accumulated. See James C. McCroskey, "Oral Communication Apprehension: A Summary of Recent Theory and Research," *Human Communication Research* 4 (1977): 78–96. Or see James C. McCroskey, "Oral Communication Apprehension: A Reconceptualization," in Michael Burgoon (ed.), *Communication Yearbook* 6 (Beverly Hills, Calif.: Sage, 1982), pp. 136–170.

12. Expectations are a significant predictor of communication apprehension. See, for example, John O. Greene and Glenn G. Sparks, "The Role of Outcome Expectations in the Experience of a State of Communication Apprehension," *Communication Quarterly* 31 (Summer 1983): 212–219.

13. See John O. Greene and Glenn G. Sparks, "Explication and Test of a Cognitive Model of Communication Apprehension: A New Look at an Old Construct," *Human Communication Research* 9 (Summer 1983):

349–366. See also Ralph R. Behnke and Michael J. Beatty, "A Cognitive-Physiological Model of Speech Anxiety," *Communication Monographs* 48 (June 1981): 158–163.

14. Adapted from Albert Ellis, *A New Guide to Rational Living* (North Hollywood, Calif.: Wilshire Books, 1977).

15. Ralph R. Behnke, Chris R. Sawyer, and Paul E. King, "The Communication of Public Speaking Anxiety," *Communication Education* 36 (April 1987): 138–141. Indicates that audiences perceive speaker anxiety levels to be lower during performance than the speakers themselves report.

16. Joe Ayres, "Perception of Speaking Ability; An Explanation for Stage Fright," *Communication Education* 35 (July 1986): 275–287. Argues that stage fright is a function of the speaker's mistaken perception that ability falls short of audience expectation.

17. Joe Ayres and Theodore S. Hopf, "Visualization: A Means of Reducing Speech Anxiety," *Communication Education* 34 (October 1985): 318–323.

18. Ronald B. Adler, *Confidence in Communication: A Guide to Assertive and Social Skills* (New York: Holt, Rinehart and Winston, 1977).

19. We will not, at this point, get into the age-old argument of the relative importance of substance (what you say) and style (how you say it). Suffice it to say that this question is as old as the study of public speaking. See, for example, Barbara Warnick, "The Quarrel Between the Ancients and the Moderns," *Communication Monographs* 49 (December 1982): 263–276. One recent study pointed out that media commentators viewed substance as *less* important than delivery, appearance, and manner in the 1980 presidential debates. See Goodwin F. Berquist and James L. Goldin, "Media Rhetoric, Criticism, and the Public Perception of the 1980 Presidential Debates," *Quarterly Journal of Speech* 67 (May 1981): 125–137.

After reading this chapter, you should understand the following:

1. The importance of having a specific informative purpose.
2. The importance of creating information hunger.
3. The importance of using clear language.
4. The importance of generating audience involvement.

You should be able to do the following:

1. Formulate an effective informative purpose statement.
2. Create "information hunger" by stressing the relevance of your material to your listeners' needs.
3. Emphasize important points in your speech.
4. Generate audience involvement.

KEY TERMS

audience involvement
audience participation
general needs
information hunger

informative purpose
  statement
signpost
specific needs

Informative Speaking

Informative speaking is especially important in the dawning "age of information," in which transmitting knowledge will account for most of the work we do and, in a large part, for the quality of our lives. Although much of the information of the future will be transmitted by machines—computers and electronic media—the spoken word will continue to be the best way to reach small audiences with messages tailored specifically for them. At least some of these messages will be designed to help people make sense of the glut of information that surrounds them.

Informative speaking seeks to increase the knowledge and understanding of an audience. This type of speaking goes on all around you: in your professors' lectures, in news reports on radio and TV, in a mechanic's explanation of how to keep your car from breaking down. All demonstrations and explanations are forms of informative speaking. You engage in this type of speaking often whether you realize it or not. Sometimes it is formal as when you are giving a report in class. At other times, it is more casual, as when you are telling a friend how to prepare your favorite dish. It is often this everyday, informal type of informative speaking that we find most frustrating. One of the objectives of this chapter is to give you the skills that can help relieve that frustration. Another objective is to apply some general principles from earlier chapters to the specific task of informative speaking.

◆ TECHNIQUES OF INFORMATIVE SPEAKING

Define a Specific Informative Purpose

As Chapter 12 explained, any speech must be based on a purpose statement that is audience-oriented, precise, and attainable. When you are preparing an informative speech, it is especially important to define in advance, for yourself, a clear informative purpose. An **informative purpose statement** will generally be worded to stress audience knowledge or ability or both:

> After listening to my speech, my audience will be able to identify the four basic principles of aerodynamics.

> After listening to my speech, my audience will be able to discuss the idea of dramatic structure.

> After listening to my speech, my audience will be able to list six basic machines and explain their functions.

For practice in defining informative speech purposes, reword the following statements so they specifically point out what the audience will be able to do after hearing the speech.

a. My purpose is to tell my audience about Hitler's rise to power.
b. I am going to talk about internal combustion engines.
c. My speech is about the causes and cures of premature baldness.

Notice that in each of these purpose statements a specific verb such as *to identify, to discuss,* or *to list* points out the kind of thing the audience will be able to do after hearing the speech. Other key verbs for informative purpose statements include these:

analyze	contrast	integrate	recall	summarize
apply	describe	list	recognize	support
compare	explain	name	review	

A clear purpose statement will lead to a clear thesis statement. As you'll remember from Chapter 11, a thesis statement presents the central idea of your speech. Sometimes your thesis statement for an informative speech will just preview that central idea:

Understanding the laws of aerodynamics could help save your life some day.

Every effective form of storytelling conforms to the rules of dramatic structure.

Every machine, no matter how complex, is made up of some combination or variation of six basic machines

Other times, the thesis statement for an informative speech will delineate the main points of that speech:

The four basic principles of aerodynamics—lift, thrust, drag, and gravity—make it clear how an airplane flies.

Five components of dramatic structure—conflict, rising tension, climax, resolution, and denouement—are found in every effective form of storytelling.

All machines are made up of some combination or variation of the lever, the wheel and axle, the pulley, the inclined plane, the wedge, and the screw.

Setting a clear informative purpose will help keep you focused as you prepare and present your speech. Now that you have a purpose in speaking, you must give your audience a purpose in listening:

Create "Information Hunger"

In informative speaking, you must create **information hunger:** a reason for your audience to want to listen to and learn from your speech. The most effective way to do that is to respond in some way to their needs—either general needs that all human beings feel or specific needs that are unique to your audience.

GENERAL NEEDS To relate your speech to **general needs,** you can use Maslow's analysis, discussed in Chapter 1, as a guide. You could tap *physical needs* by relating your topic to your audience's survival or to the improvement of their living conditions. If you gave a speech on food (eating it, cooking it, or shopping for it), you would probably be dealing with that basic need. If you

Consider your classmates as an audience. How does Maslow's analysis of needs relate to these people? What other, more specific needs do they have? How could you relate the following speech topics to these needs?

a. The Changing Climate of the United States
b. Civil Rights
c. Gun Control
d. U.S. Foreign Policy

gave a speech on water pollution, you could relate it to physical needs by listing the pollutants in one of your local lakes and explaining what each one could do to a human body. In the same way, you could meet *safety needs* by relating your topic to your audience's security; you could touch on *esteem needs* by showing your audience how to be respected—or simply by showing them that *you* respect them. You can appeal to *self-actualization needs,* those based on the need to accomplish as much as possible with our lives, by showing your audience some way to improve themselves.

One speaker tapped a variety of audience needs in his speech "Waking Up the Right Lobe":

> My text is drawn from an exciting book by Julian Jaynes, called *The Origin of Consciousness in the Breakdown of the Bicameral Mind.* You must read it or else you will not be aware of some of the most exciting stuff that's going on in the scientific and academic search for how we came to be, who we are now, and what we are becoming.
>
> We don't have to generalize about these discoveries or speak in the abstract. You can apply these ideas right now, right here.
>
> The ultimate goal is to be fully alive—to your family, your work, and to yourself— to use your full brain! You will never possess anything in your life that is more valuable to you or will give you more thrills and excitement and pleasure than your mind![1]

This speaker is creating information hunger mostly by touching on self-actualization needs, but he also taps all the other needs Maslow outlined. Being "fully alive" is a physiological need, "family" is a social need, and the world of "work" involves both security and esteem needs.

SPECIFIC NEEDS   Maslow's analysis of needs should be kept in mind for all audiences, for all human beings share them. Yet the closer you can come to the **specific needs** of your audience, the more information hunger you will generate. For example, sleeping problems are universal. Everyone has a physiological need for sleep, but you could adapt this problem for a particular audience:

> Tonight, 50 million American adults will crawl into bed, draw up the covers, lay their heads down on their pillows, and then, try as they might, they will not be able to find restful sleep. You may very well be one of them. In fact, many college students suffer from sleep disorders that are particularly harmful to their academic and social

success. And the chances are very good that the disorder will hit the night before a big test, just when you need your sleep more than ever. In just one month, we will all be involved in final exams. How many of us will get lower grades than we might have, simply because we couldn't get to sleep the night before?

Emphasize Important Points

Along with defining a specific informative purpose and creating information hunger, you should stress the important points in your speech through *repetition* and *"signposts."*

REPETITION Chapter 12 discusses ways that you can emphasize material through clear organization: limiting your speech to three to five main points; dividing, coordinating, and ordering those main points; using a strong introduction that previews your ideas; using a conclusion that reviews them and makes them memorable; and using lots of transitions, internal summaries, and internal previews. Strong organization, in effect, provides your listeners with a repetition of important points, and that repetition will help them understand and remember those points.

You can also be repetitive stylistically by saying the same thing in more than one way, by restating an important idea:

It is a known fact that jogging is good for your heart; medical research is unequivocal in supporting the fact that jogging builds up heart muscle by increasing the flow of blood that nourishes the muscular tissue of the heart itself.

This is the type of repetition that one speaker used when she wanted to emphasize, without *sounding* redundant, the number of people killed by drunk drivers:

◆ **Because information can change society, and because the amount of information doubles every fifteen years, our culture, if it is to become enriched and improved by its information, needs speakers to digest and assimilate this information and present it with clarity.**

Otis Walter
Speaking to Inform and Persuade

Each year in the U.S., about 25,000 people are killed in alcohol-related crashes. In the past 10 years more than 250,000 have been killed nationwide and millions have been injured—many crippled or impaired for life.[2]

Twenty-five thousand a year is the same as 250,000 every ten years, but, stated in this way, the point does not sound redundant. Notice also that this speaker adds new information to her repetition of this important point. This expansion is another technique for making the second statement of a point "fresh."

Redundancy is no fault when you are using it to emphasize important points; it is only a fault when (1) you are redundant with obvious, trivial, or boring points; or (2) you run an important point into the ground. There is no sure rule for making certain you have not overemphasized a point. You just have to use your own best judgment to make sure that you have stated the point enough that your audience "gets" it without repeating it so often that they want to give it back.

SIGNPOSTS   Another way to emphasize important material is by using **signposts:** words or phrases that emphasize the importance of what you are about to say. You can state, simply enough, "What I'm about to say is important"; or you can use some variation of that statement: "But listen to this . . . ," or "The most important thing to remember is . . . ," or "The three keys to this situation are . . . ," and so on.

Use Clear Informative Organization and Structure

The following principles of organization from Chapter 12 become especially important in the *introduction* of an informative speech:

1. Establish the importance of your topic to your audience.
2. Preview the thesis, the one central idea you want your audience to remember.
3. If possible, preview your main points.

This is the way Kim Perry, a student at the University of Northern Iowa, organized the introduction of her speech on "Effortless Exercise":

It matters not whether one is young or old, male or female, black or white. The victim is obsessed with single-minded purpose and will do almost anything to reach his [or her] goal. I know, I've suffered from this affliction, and I'm sure that you have or know of someone who has, also.

I'm talking about the new American obsession—becoming "fit and trim." Yes, it's great that we're more aware of the importance of exercise and fitness, but, unfortunately, we're also seeking lazy alternatives for our overweight and out-of-shape bodies.

Passive exercise is one of the fastest-growing gimmicks offering quick fixes to our body bulges. The main promotion involving passive exercise is EMS, electrical muscle stimulators . . . . I'd like to explain what EMS is, the potential dangers associated with it, why little is currently being done, and what measures should be taken to forestall further problems.[3]

In the *body* of an informative speech, the following organizational principles take on special importance:

1. Use only three to five main points.
2. Limit your division of main points to three to five subpoints.
3. Use transitions, internal summaries, and internal previews.
4. Order your points in the way that they will be most easy to understand and remember.

Kim Perry followed these rules to organize the body of her speech on "Effortless Exercise" (see Figure 14–1).

Organizational principles are also important in the *conclusion* of an informative speech:

1. Review your main points.
2. Remind your audience of the importance of your topic to them.
3. Provide your audience with a memory aid.

For example, here is the way Kim Perry concluded her speech on "Effortless Exercise":

> I hope you now have a clearer understanding of what EMS is, its definitive hazards, and steps which the FDA, the state legislators, and we can take to stop such hazards from arising. Most of you know the only way you can fit back into your size 9 dress or your favorite blue jeans is by proper diet and exercise. Yet it's clear that the problems we've seen to date are merely "early warning signals" and will multiply with the growth in use of EMS. So if you're tempted to be an armchair jogger, maybe it's time to get out of your chair and into your jogging suit, or even your swimsuit. Who knows, you may find it "stimulating!"[4]

Use Supporting Material Effectively

The fifth technique for effective informative speaking has to do with the supporting material discussed in Chapter 12. Three of the purposes of support (to clarify, to make interesting, and to make memorable) are essential to informative speaking. Therefore, you should be careful to support your thesis in every way possible.

Use *examples,* lots of them. Often, if you cannot think of an example to support your idea, then there is something wrong with the idea. It might be a little misstated or undeveloped. Either way it is going to be confusing to your audience. Susan Martinez, a student at Bethany College in West Virginia, used examples to good effect when she began her speech on the importance of learning a foreign language with three of them:

◆ When General Motors advertised its "Body by Fisher" car in Belgium, the slogan was described in Flemish as "corpse by Fisher."

◆ In Spanish-speaking countries, car buyers avoided the Chevrolet Nova because "No va" in Spanish means "It doesn't go."

◆ And at the 1981 economic summit meeting held in Canada, President Reagan had to ask Canadian Prime Minister Pierre Trudeau for a translation when world leaders began chatting informally in French.[5]

FIGURE 14—1
Body of Informative Speech
Outlined

I. Electrical Muscle Stimulators (EMS) are devices that contract muscles involuntarily by delivering an electrical current through electrodes attached to the skin.
   A. They can be used as physical therapy under proper medical supervision.
   B. Individuals are turning to EMS to replace exercise.
   Internal preview So what are the complications associated with EMS? At least three can be identified: no significant muscle improvement, no cardiovascular benefits, and health hazards caused by improper use.
II. Electrical Muscle Stimulators are potentially dangerous.
   A. The "muscle toning effects" from EMS devices are basically worthless.
   Transition Not only does EMS fail to strengthen muscles; it may also indirectly contribute to reduced cardiovascular fitness.
   B. People are being lulled into a false sense of fitness, which could stop them from performing the muscle-strengthening types of exercise required in a balanced exercise routine.
   Internal Summary and Preview And aside from the fact that EMS does not really improve muscle strength or promote cardiovascular fitness, many hazards are associated with its misuse.
   C. Improper use results in electrical shocks and burns.
   Transition So in consideration of the intended uses and actual abuses of EMS, why isn't something being done to stop these multimillion-dollar industries from flourishing at the expense of our pocketbooks and our health?
III. Why isn't more being done to control EMS?
   A. The Food and Drug Administration (FDA) has limited authority.
      1. FDA has the authority to seize but not to ban.
      2. FDA funding is limited.
      3. FDA authority is fraught with legal loopholes.
   B. Uninformed consumers are lulled into accepting EMS devices.
      1. Advertisements offer "money-back guarantees."
      2. Consumers avoid expensive lawsuits.
      3. Some consumers see an improvement because of a "placebo effect."
   Internal Summary and Preview Tens of thousands of untrained consumers are continually buying EMS devices. How can we stop this growing epidemic?
IV. Measures should be taken to control EMS.
   A. Sales to the general public should be forbidden.
   B. Operation should be restricted to licensed practitioners.

Provide *detailed descriptions* to increase audience involvement in the information you are presenting. Here is the description David Whitt, a student at Wayne State College in Nebraska, used to begin his speech on "The Homeless Mentally Ill":

> Bill Jamison was a quiet, unobtrusive figure as he watched the unfamiliar landscape pass by. Occasionally his eyes would focus on a specific object and reflect a somewhat passive interest. Just as quickly, the interest would fade and he would continue his gaze. Bill was suffering from a psychotic disorder characterized by loss of contact with the environment and by disintegration of personality known as schizophrenia. His medical records indicate that, at 37, he had spent twenty years institutionalized with little to no hope of improvement. Now he was on a bus and traveling to a new life awaiting him hundreds of miles away. Bill didn't fully realize it, but he was deliberately being shipped to another city in a distant state. He was an unwilling participant in what has become known as "Greyhound Therapy"—the practice of providing mentally ill persons with one-way bus tickets out of town.[6]

Define your key terms if there is any chance that the audience might be confused by them. Here is the way David Whitt defined his key term in "The Homeless Mentally Ill":

> Cities and towns are becoming besieged by swelling ranks of homeless people, who are defined by the Alcohol Drug Abuse and Mental Health Administration as "anyone who lacks adequate shelter, resources and community ties."[7]

Use *analogies* to enable your audience to view your information from a different perspective. One student's speech on the false testing of medicines was built around the analogy of poison:

> The falsifying of tests in laboratories does exist, and the harm that can and does come of it has turned it into a deadly poison. There are antidotes, but they're useless unless they're injected into the system. . . .[8]

Use *quantification and statistics* to make your information more authoritative and accurate. One student used quantification and statistics when explaining the dangers of boxing:

> Since 1945, 339 professional fighters have died in the ring, 53 of those deaths since 1970. . . . This figure includes only professional fighters, so you must include injury and death among the estimated 10,000 10- to 15-year-old amateurs, the estimated 12,500 golden-glove boxers, and innumerable contestants in "tough-man" contests.[9]

Use *anecdotes* to make your information more interesting and memorable. Here is how one student used an anecdote in her speech about the importance of speech education in public schools:

> As I was working my way through the public school system, I, like my peers, believed that I was receiving a fine education. I could read and write, and add and subtract—yes, all of the essentials were there. At least that's what I thought. And then, the boom lowered: "Attention class—your next assignment is to present an oral report of your paper in front of the class next week." My heart stopped. Panic began to rise up

inside. Me? In front of thirty other fourth-graders giving a speech? For the next five days I lived in dreaded anticipation of the forthcoming event. When the day finally arrived, I stayed home. It seemed at the time to be the perfect solution to a very scary and very real problem. Up to that time, I had never been asked to say a word in front of anyone, and, more importantly, had never been taught anything about verbal communication skills.[10]

Any time you can make your ideas visual in an informative speech, do so. Sometimes one *visual aid* can grab your audience's attention and keep them attuned to your topic throughout your speech. This is how Hydee Harris, a student at Oakland University in Michigan, used a visual aid in the introduction of her speech on how to read product labels:

> I hope you don't mind, but I've brought in a plate of Oreo cookies to share. I'm going to have one myself . . .
>
> Wait a minute, what is that they say: a kid will eat the middle of an Oreo first and save the chocolate cookie outside for last. I wonder what makes this creamy white stuff so appealing? Let's see; says here that creamy white stuff is made with sugar and animal shortening. Animal shortening! That's lard. That can't be. I mean *Webster's Dictionary* defines lard as "the clarified fat of swine."
>
> So I guess the kid will eat the middle of an Oreo first to get to sugar and clarified swine fat.
>
> I'll understand if you've lost your appetite . . . [11]

Demonstrations can be particularly effective in creating impact and understanding. One physics major wanted to give a speech with the following purpose:

> After listening to my speech, my audience will understand the total independence of contiguous motions that are directed along mutually perpendicular axes.

When he gave his speech, the class did not know what he was talking about; so he tried clarifying his purpose somewhat and included a demonstration. (See Figure 14–2.) This time, his purpose was the following:

> After listening to my speech, my audience will understand that to predict trajectory, you have to take two different perpendicular motions into consideration.

Believe it or not, his speech fulfilled his purpose because it included the following demonstration:

Apparatus:
toy crossbow, teddy bear

Procedure:
1. Hang teddy from coatrack.
2. Secure crossbow, and aim directly at teddy.
3. Explain that both y motion and x motion must be taken into consideration to shoot teddy out of tree (place diagram on board).
4. With help of volunteer, release arrow and teddy simultaneously.
5. Because of the interaction of x motion and y motion, arrow will drop at the same rate as teddy, and you will score a bull's-eye every time!

DIAGRAM

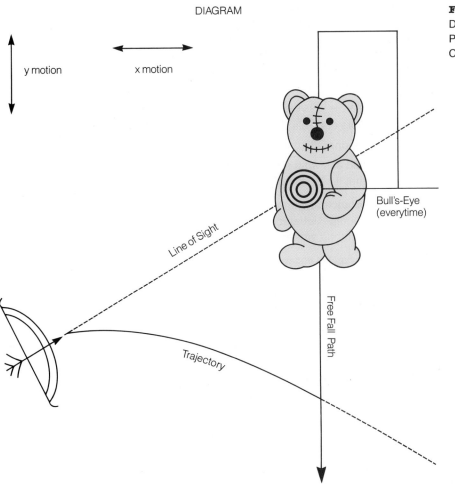

y motion

x motion

Line of Sight

Bull's-Eye
(everytime)

Free Fall Path

Trajectory

Use Clear Language

Another technique for effective informative speaking is to use clear language—which means using precise, vivid, simple wording and providing
definitions for obscure but necessary terms.

PRECISE VOCABULARY   When planning an informative speech, you have
to be a wordsmith, an artisan just like a silversmith or a watchsmith, only with
words as your raw materials and dictionaries (or even a thesaurus, which is
really just a dictionary of synonyms) as your tools. You should use these tools
to find the most precise word to say what you want to say. If you have any
doubt about the clarity of something you are saying, then you should devise
several different ways of saying it and choose the best way. Most of the

Informative Speaking

413

memorable phrases that are so familiar to us now started off in some different form and were then refined by the speaker. Consider the following expressions and see if they ring a bell:

"Friends, Romans, Countrymen: May I have your attention, please?"

"Eighty-seven years ago, our fathers brought forth on this continent..."

"Don't fire until they get right up next to you."

"Old soldiers don't die; they just leave."

"Why, I'd sooner die than not have liberty."

"You should ask what services you can perform for your country rather than asking what it can do for you."

The importance of careful rewriting to attain precise language can be seen in the way Thomas Jefferson reworked George Mason's "Declaration of Rights." Mason had written,

All men are created equally free and independent, and have certain inherent natural rights, of which they cannot, by any compact, deprive or divest their posterity; among which are the enjoyment of life and liberty...happiness and safety...all power is by God and Nature vested in, and consequently derives from the people.[12]

Jefferson reworded Mason's declaration until he had the Declaration of Independence that we are all familiar with today. Jefferson's declaration reads, in part:

We hold these truths to be self-evident, that all men are created equal, that they are endowed by their Creator with certain unalienable rights, that among these are life, liberty and the pursuit of happiness....

VIVID LANGUAGE   You should make your language "come alive" through devices such as action-oriented vocabulary and varied sentence structure. This is how H. Keith Brodie, president of Duke University, worded the idea "people are becoming less tolerant these days":

A shadow has fallen on our educational community—indeed, this shadow has swept across our nation. It is not new, but as our community has become increasingly more diverse, the shadow has darkened. I refer, of course, to the shadow of intolerance.[13]

SIMPLE VOCABULARY   Using the right word, the most precise word, seldom means using a word that is difficult to find. In fact, just the opposite is true. Important ideas do not have to sound complicated. Consider the following passage:

Objective considerations of contemporary phenomena compel the conclusion that success or failure in competitive activities exhibits no tendency to be commensurate with innate capacity, but that a considerable element of the unpredictable must invariably be taken into account.[14]

That is George Orwell's satirical idea of how a biblical passage would be written in twentieth-century jargon. The original verse, from the King James

◆ **My father was a man of great intellectual energy. My best training came from him. I carried to him everything I wrote. He would make me read it aloud. Every now and then he would stop me: "What do you mean by that?" he'd ask. I would tell him, and of course in doing so would express myself more simply than I had on paper. "Why don't you say so?" he would go on. "Don't shoot at your meaning with birdshot and hit the whole countryside; shoot with a rifle at the thing you have to say."**

Woodrow Wilson

---

translation of Ecclesiastes, reads:

> The race is not to the swift, nor the battle to the strong, neither yet bread to the wise, nor yet riches to men of understanding, nor yet favor to men of skill; but time and chance happeneth to them all.

DEFINE OBSCURE BUT NECESSARY TERMS It is a good idea to define key terms that you use; it is also a good idea to define any words that might be obscure or misunderstood in the context in which they are used. This is especially necessary if the word you're using qualifies as jargon, which is a word of a specialized nature that is used, and therefore understood, only by specific groups of people. Educators, for example, talk of "empirically validated learning" and "multimode curricula" and rather than saying that a child can do better, they say that "academic achievement is not commensurate with abilities." Doctors and military strategists are famous for their use of jargon also. A heart attack is a "coronary thrombosis" or a "cardiovascular accident" for doctors whereas air raids are "routine limited duration protective reactions" for military folks. Business people, religious groups, sports enthusiasts, lawyers, and many other groups have semiprivate vocabularies that are clearly understood only by those who use them regularly. When speaking to an outsider, jargon should probably be avoided; if it turns out to be absolutely necessary, it should be defined.

For practice in using clear language, select an article from any issue of a professional journal in your major field. Using the suggestions in this chapter, rewrite a paragraph from the article so that it will be clear and interesting to the layperson.

Generate Audience Involvement

The final technique for effective informative speaking is to get your audience involved in your speech. Educational psychologists have long known that the best way to *teach* people something is to have them *do* it; social psychologists have added to this rule by proving, in many studies, that involvement in a message increases audience comprehension of, and agreement with, that message.

There are many ways to encourage **audience involvement** in your speech. One way is by following the rules for good delivery by maintaining enthusiasm, energy, eye contact, and so on. Other techniques include audience participation, the use of volunteers, and a question-and-answer period.

AUDIENCE PARTICIPATION   One way to increase audience involvement is to have the audience members actually *do* something during your speech, that is, bring about **audience participation.** For example, if you were giving a demonstration on isometric exercises (which don't require too much room for movement), you could have the entire audience stand up and do one or two sample exercises. (Exercise not only involves them psychologically; it also keeps them more alert physically by increasing the flow of blood and adrenalin in their systems.) If you were explaining how to fill out a federal income-tax long form, you could give each class member a sample form to fill out as you explain it. Outlines and checklists could be used in a similar manner for just about *any* speech.

Here's how one student organization used audience participation to demonstrate the various restrictions that were once placed on voting rights:

Voting is something that a lot of us may take for granted. Today, the only requirements for voting are that you are a US citizen aged 18 or older who has lived in the same place for at least 30 days—and that you have registered. But it hasn't always been that way. Americans have had to struggle for the right to vote. I'd like to illustrate this by asking everyone to please stand. (Wait, prod class to stand.) I'm going to ask some questions. If you answer no to any question, please sit down.

Do you have at least $2 in your pocket right now? If not, sit down. Up until 1964, poll taxes existed in many states.

Have you resided at the same address for at least 1 year? If not, sit down. Residency requirements of more than 30 days weren't abolished until 1970.

Are you white? If not, sit down. The 15th amendment gave non-whites the right to vote in 1870 but many states didn't enforce it until the late 1960's.

Are you male? If not, sit down. The 19th amendment gave women the right to vote in 1920.

Are you at least 21 years old? If not, sit down. It wasn't until 1971 that 18 year olds gained the right to vote.

Do you own property? If not, sit down. Through the mid-1800's only property owners could vote.

Are you Protestant? If not, sit down. That's right. Religious requirements existed in the early days throughout the country.[15]

VOLUNTEERS   If the action you are demonstrating is too expensive or intricate to allow all the class members to take part in it, you can select one or two volunteers from the audience to help you out. You will increase the psychological involvement of all the members, because they will tend to identify with the volunteers.

QUESTION-AND-ANSWER PERIOD   One way to increase audience involvement that is nearly *always* appropriate if time allows is to answer questions at the end of your speech. You should encourage your audience to ask questions. Solicit questions and be patient waiting for the first one. Often no one wants to ask the first question. When the questions do start coming, the following suggestions might increase your effectiveness in answering them:

1. **Listen to the Substance of the Question.** Don't zero in on irrelevant details; listen for the big picture—the basic, overall question that is being asked. If you're not really sure *what* the substance of a question is, ask the questioner to paraphrase it. Don't be afraid to let the questioners do their share of the work.
2. **Paraphrase Confusing Questions.** Use the active listening skills described in Chapter 4. You can paraphrase the question in just a few words: "If I understand your question, you are asking _____. Is that right?"
3. **Avoid Defensive Reactions to Questions.** Even if the questioner seems to be calling you a liar or stupid or biased, try to listen to the substance of the question and not to the possible personality attack.
4. **Answer the Question as Briefly as Possible.** Then check the questioner's comprehension of your answer. Sometimes you can simply check his or her nonverbal response—if he or she seems at all confused, you can ask, "Does that answer your question?"

To analyze an informative speech, you go through it and point out where the speaker used effective techniques; if necessary, you point out places where effective techniques are still needed, making specific suggestions for improvement. To hone your skills in recognizing effective informative speaking, try one of the following analyses:

Informative Speaking

> **a.** Go over the analysis of the sample speech on pages 418–422. See which points you agree or disagree with, or both, and tell why. What would you add to the analysis?
>
> **b.** Select an informative speech from *Vital Speeches of the Day, Representative American Speeches*, a newspaper, or any other source. Analyze this speech in terms of its effectiveness as an informative message. Use our analysis of the sample speech as a model.
>
> **c.** Perform your analysis on your own informative speech, as delivered or to be delivered in class.

The importance of audience involvement, as well as the other techniques mentioned earlier in this chapter, is reflected in the sample speech evaluation form in Figure 14–3.

◆ SAMPLE SPEECH

The following speech was presented by Jerry Tarver, Professor of Speech Communication at the University of Richmond in Richmond, Virginia. The speech was delivered to a group of professional speech writers in 1988. It happens to deal with a topic of great interest to the reader of this book: the differences between written and spoken language.

If Professor Tarver were to write out a purpose statement, it might read as follows:

> After listening to my speech, my audience will understand three ways that spoken language differs from written language.

And his thesis statement might sound like this:

> Spoken language is subject to the dictates of time, which requires the speaker to be more expansive, to pay careful heed to word order, and to observe the rhythm of language.

The speech, in other words, conforms to a tight three-point organization.

Words in Time
Some Reflections on the Language of Speech[16]

JERRY TARVER
University of Richmond

1–2. To increase audience involvement, the introduction refers directly to the group and to the member who introduced the speaker.

1. Thank you, Steve. And thank you for inviting me to address the Forum. I am flattered to be your guest on your first anniversary.

2. I understand that Steve Hallmark formed this organization because of the isolation that seems so often a part of the speech writer's fate. My friend Ed Shiver says isolation is one of the chief hazards of his work in writing speeches. And he points to the power that isolation has to demoralize and

FIGURE 14–3
Evaluation Form for an
Informative Speech

SPEECH EVALUATION FORM

Informative Speech

Name _____   Topic _____

Assignment # _____   Date _____

What did you especially like? _____

_____

In your opinion, how could the speech be improved? _____

_____

Please comment on the following areas:

Did the speaker seem to have a clear informative purpose?

Was "information hunger" created?

Were important points emphasized?

Was the speech clearly organized and structured?

   Did the introduction—
      establish importance of topic to audience?
      preview thesis?
      preview main points?
   Did the body of the speech—
      contain three to five main points?
      contain three to five subpoints per main point?
      contain transitions, internal summaries, interal previews?
      contain points ordered to be easy to understand and remember?
   Did the conclusion of the speech—
      review main points?
      remind audience of the importance of the topic to them?
      provide audience with a memory aid?

Was supporting material used effectively?

Was the language clear?

Did the speaker seek to involve the audience?

depress by reminding us that prisons use it to punish unruly criminals—by putting them in solitary confinement.

3. I have found that when speech writers do get together and talk about their work, a lot of creative sparks are generated. Some of the most lively discussions I've heard center on distinctions between the written and the spoken word. And I have become increasingly convinced that the most significant

2–3. Building "information hunger": tapping into audience needs, based on their attendance at this conference.

3. Explanation of main idea.

consideration in the differences between language in writing and language in speaking may well be the role played by time—a word in print is frozen and free from time constraints while the spoken word is fleeting and subject to the dictates of time.

4. "Sign post" tells us the number of main points to listen for.

4. Let's look for a few minutes at three of the ways time affects the spoken word.

5. First of all, time imposes a need for expansion. All rules have exceptions, of course, but I offer you Tarver's Law of Conciseness: It takes more words per square idea to say something than to write it.

6. Definition of key term.

6. I define conciseness the same way you do. Using no more words than necessary to express an idea well. It just happens that it takes more words to express an idea well in a speech than it does in an article.

7. Testimony and example. The text referred to is *Speech Communication: A Contemporary Introduction* by Simmerman, Owen, and Seibert.

7. One speech textbook estimates that "all human languages, as they are spoken naturally, are approximately 50 percent redundant." In other words, about half the words we use would serve to carry our information. To cut the previous sentence by 50 percent: So, half our words carry our information. This book reminds us that one function of redundancy is "to give interpreters *time* to process the information in ordinary speech."

8. A clever turn of phrase makes this idea memorable.

8. The great orators from Cicero to Churchill have understood this concept though they have paid a price for it in being called at best verbose or at worst windbags.

9. Transition to second main point.

9. But time does more than merely control the number of words we use in speaking. A second effect is to determine in many cases the order in which ideas must be arranged in a sentence.

10. Example, repetition.

10. I recently read in a newspaper column a spirited defense of a public figure. The last line of the column was, "For that he should be congratulated, not chastised." Well and good. The reader gobbles up the line in an instant and digests the contrast between congratulations and chastisement. But when we speak the line we feed it to a listener morsel by morsel. And the last two words prove to be rather bland. We need to *hear* "For that he should not be chastised, he should be congratulated." More words; but more important, a different order.

11. Analogy.

11. In speech the words are received at a *slower rate* than they are when the eye picks them up in silent reading. The rapid pace of silent reading blends words and phrases somewhat in the way that the movie projector flashes discrete still pictures before our eyes so fast that we see motion rather than individual frames. In the slower pace of speech, individual words stand out more, and thus *time* accords a special emphasis to the last idea, the climactic idea in the sentence.

12–13. Repetition, two more examples.

12. As a rule, then, the stronger, more impressive idea should be saved for the end. And it will often be the case that the punch comes from a positive rather than a negative thought. In John Kennedy's "ask not" line, the balanced sentence structure and the irregular word order hide the fact that part of Kennedy's eloquence resulted from placing the more powerful idea—the positive idea—at the end of the line. Even if we keep all of Kennedy's rhetorical flourishes, we can emasculate his statement by simply inverting his ideas:

13.   "Ask what you can do for your country, ask not what your country can do for you." Or we can make Patrick Henry sound a bit petulant with, "Give me liberty or give me death; I know not what course others may take."

14. The three examples I have just cited have been presented in what we might call increasing degrees of obviousness. By the time we get to the Patrick Henry example, the line is not even fit for print.

14. Internal review.

15. But the written word nevertheless places less stringent demands than does the spoken word on the need for attention to order of ideas. The eye and the ear do not process information the same way. To approximate the effect of time on the listener, a reader would have to see the text of a book fed out on a ticker tape—one . . . word . . . at . . . a . . . time.

15. Analogy.

16. Again I want to stress that we are not talking about mere differences in style among writers and editors; we are talking about basic differences in language imposed by time. For one final example, I ask you to look at the way dialogue is written. In print the "he said's" and "she said's" appear in the middle of a quoted line or at the end of the line as often as at the beginning.

16. Repetition.

17. Let me again turn to a newspaper column. An excellent writer reported a joke President Reagan told a young couple at a White House reception. It seems that an 80-year-old man's golf game was hampered by poor eyesight. He could hit the ball well but he couldn't see where it went. So his doctor teamed him up with a 90-year-old man who had perfect eyesight and was willing to go along to serve as a spotter. Here's how the columnist reported the dialogue after the 80-year-old man hit the first ball and asked his companion if he saw where it landed:

17. Example, in the form of a joke.

"Yep," said the 90-year-old.
"Where did it go?" the 80-year-old demanded.
"I don't remember," the 90-year-old replied.

18. In spoken language this conventional writing order is nothing less than absurd. In normal speech, time would impose a reversed order to tell us who is talking before we hear what the person says. As a bonus, this approach avoids "stepping on" the punch line of the joke.

18. Further explanation, to make sure that audience understands the point of the example.

19. This brings us to a third effect of time. The beat or flow or rhythm of the syllables is more important in words written to be heard than in words written to be seen.

19. Third main point.

20. Extended analogy; four examples.

20. Let's consider verse and song—which are essentially oral and are generally written down only as a matter of convenience. Words in verse and song demonstrate the power of rhythm to make language stick in the memory. No doubt there are people in this room who occasionally dredge up a bit of useful data by reciting, "Thirty days hath September..." Of course, memory gets assistance not only from rhythm but from repetition, from rhyme, and—in the case of songs—from melody. But rhythm is the key when rhyme and melody are absent as in "Stop, Look, and Listen" or "Remember Pearl Harbor." Some rhythmic slogans seem in fact merely incomplete verse. My dentist has a sign on his wall that reads:

> "You don't have to floss all your teeth,
> Just the ones you want to keep."

21. Internal review of a sub-point.

21. An echo of poetic rhythm, then, can easily find its way into spoken prose as an aid to memory, although a speaker may be happy to settle for a passage with a much shorter life span than would please a poet, a songwriter, or a sloganeer.

22. The next subpoint, with example.

22. But rhythm in speech can have an even more significant effect. It enhances the emotional impact of a speaker's words. A beat loosely borrowed from poetry elevates an idea. Preachers who copy the stately flow of the King James Bible invest their words with special power.

23. Another subpoint previewed.

23. Where does the power of rhythm come from? Russell Baker thinks that as children we learn rhythm from lullabies and nursery rhymes. And we never outgrow them deep down inside. There may indeed be some primal force in the human pulse that vibrates to a good beat. To speak or hear a rough, irregular sentence goes against our grain.

24. Example.

24. Let me ask you to recall the famous quote from Hamlet where he is holding Yorick's skull. You remember the line begins, "Alas, poor Yorick!" If this is a typical audience about half of you will go on to finish the line incorrectly as "I knew him *well.*" There is no "well" in the line. It reads, "Alas, poor Yorick! I knew him, Horatio. A fellow of infinite jest." We misquote the line in its abbreviated form because to end with "Horatio" produces an unsatisfactory rhythm which that "primal force" causes us to "correct."

25. Example.

25. Let me return to Patrick Henry's line which I often use to illustrate this point. There is an obvious redundancy in his repetition of the phrase "give me." So let's take one of them out:

> "I know not what course
> Others may take.
> But as for me,
> Give me liberty
> Or death...."

I trust you feel the vague and unpleasing effect of that deletion.

26. Conclusion begins: First main point is reviewed.

26. When spoken words lack a proper beat, listeners smell the odor of the ink. They detect the intrusion of writing into the realm of speaking.

27. That intrusion may also occur when the writers of speeches neglect the importance of either climactic order or an appropriately expanded style.

27. Second and third main points reviewed.

28. Let me conclude by reminding you that when you are writing your best, you only appear to be composing words for the page; in reality you are composing words in time.

28. A memory aid, based on thesis.

◆ SUMMARY

This chapter suggested techniques for effective informative speaking. These suggestions include the use of a specific informative purpose, the creation of "information hunger" by tapping both general and specific audience needs, the emphasis of important points through repetition and "signposts," the use of clear informative organization and structure, the use of effective supporting material, the use of clear language (language that incorporates precise, vivid, simple vocabulary), and the involvement of the audience.

◆ NOTES

1. Porter Crow, "Waking Up the Right Lobe," *Vital Speeches of the Day* (July 15, 1984): 600–601.
2. Candy Lightner, "Mothers Against Drunk Drivers," in George Rodman, *Public Speaking,* 3d ed. (New York: Holt, Rinehart and Winston, 1986), p. 10.
3. Kim Perry, "Effortless Exercise," *Winning Orations, 1984* (Interstate Oratorical Association, 1984), pp. 27–28.
4. Ibid., p. 30.
5. Susan Martinez, "Sorry . . . We Only Speak English," *Winning Orations, 1983* (Interstate Oratorical Association, 1983), p. 82.
6. David Whitt, "The Homeless Mentally Ill," *Winning Orations, 1987* (Interstate Oratorical Association, 1987), pp. 78–79.
7. Ibid., p. 79.
8. Veda M. Backman, "Science's Internal Poison," *Winning Orations, 1984* (Interstate Oratorical Association, 1984), p. 21.
9. Keith Murphy, "The Shadows of Boxing," *Winning Orations, 1984* (Interstate Oratorical Association, 1984), p. 34.
10. Marcie Groover, "Learning to Communicate: The Importance of Speech Education in Public Schools," *Winning Orations, 1984* (Interstate Oratorical Association, 1984), p. 7.
11. Hydee Harris, "A Labeling Problem," *Winning Orations, 1988* (Interstate Oratorical Association, 1988), pp. 56–57.
12. Cited in Kathleen Hall Jamieson, *Eloquence in an Electronic Age* (New York: Oxford University Press, 1988), p. 92.
13. H. Keith Brodie, address welcoming Duke students, Fall, 1989. Reprinted in *The Chronicle of Higher Education* (September 27, 1989): 83.
14. George Orwell, "Politics and the English Language," in *Shooting an Elephant and Other Essays* (New York: Harcourt Brace Jovanovich, 1945).
15. New York Public Interest Research Group, Brooklyn College Chapter, 1989 Voter Registration Report.
16. Jerry Tarver, "Words in Time: Some Reflections on the Language of Speech," *Vital Speeches of the Day* (April 15, 1988): 410–412.

15

After reading this chapter, you should understand the following:

1. That persuasion involves important ethical questions.
2. The difference between questions of fact, value, and policy.
3. The difference between the goals of convincing and actuating.
4. The difference between direct and indirect approaches.
5. The basic idea of a persuasive strategy.
6. The importance of setting a clear persuasive purpose.
7. The importance of analyzing and adapting to your audience.
8. The components of personal credibility.

You should be able to do the following:

1. Formulate an effective persuasive strategy to convince or actuate an audience.
2. Formulate your persuasive strategy based on ethical guidelines.
3. Bolster your credibility as a speaker by enhancing your competence, character, and charisma.
4. Build persuasive arguments with common ground, solid evidence, and careful reasoning.
5. Organize a persuasive speech for greatest audience effect.

KEY TERMS

actuating
causal reasoning
character
charisma
common ground
competence
convincing
credibility
deduction
direct persuasion
emotional evidence
enthymeme
ethical persuasion
evidence

indirect persuasion
induction
motivated sequence
persuasion
question of fact
question of policy
question of value
reasoning by analogy
sign reasoning
strategy to actuate
strategy to convince
syllogisms
target audience

Persuasive Speaking

Persuasion is the act of motivating someone, through communication, to change a particular belief, attitude, or behavior. You can appreciate the importance of this skill by imagining how your life would be without the ability to persuade others. Your choice would be limited either to accepting people as they were or to coercing them to comply.

This last point is worth further comment, for persuasion is not the same thing as coercion. If you held a gun to someone's head and said, "Do this or I'll shoot," you would be acting coercively. Besides being illegal, this approach would be ineffective. Once you took the gun away, the person would probably stop following your demands.

The failure of coercion to achieve lasting results is apparent in less dramatic circumstances. Children whose parents are coercive often rebel as soon as they can; students who perform from fear of an instructor's threats rarely appreciate the subject matter; and employees who work for abusive and demanding employers are often unproductive and eager to switch jobs as soon as possible. Persuasion, on the other hand, makes a listener *want* to think or act differently.

Even when they understand the difference between persuasion and coercion, some students are still uncomfortable with the idea of persuasive speaking. They see it as the work of high-pressure hucksters: salespeople with their feet stuck in the door, unscrupulous politicians taking advantage of beleaguered taxpayers, and so on. Indeed, many of the principles we are about to discuss have been used by unethical speakers for unethical purposes, but that is not what all—or even most—persuasion is about. Ethical persuasion plays a necessary and worthwhile role in everyone's life.

It is through ethical persuasion that we influence others' lives in worthwhile ways. The person who says, "I do not want to influence other people," is really saying. "I do not want to get involved with other people," and that is an abandoning of one's responsibilities as a human being. Look at the good you can accomplish through persuasion: You can convince a loved one to give up smoking or to give up some other destructive habit; you can get members of your community to conserve energy or to join together in some other beneficial action; you can persuade an employer to hire you for a job where your own talents, interests, and abilities will be put to their best use.

Persuasion is considered ethical if it conforms to accepted standards. What standards are accepted today? Whose opinion should you accept for what is good or bad? If your plan is selfish and not in the best interest of your audience—but you are honest about your motives—is that ethical? If your plan *is* in the best interest of your audience, yet you lie to them to get them to accept the plan, is *that* ethical? Philosophers and rhetoricians have argued endlessly over questions like these.[1]

> ◆ He that complies
> against his will
> Is of his own opinion
> still.
>
> Samuel Butler

> ◆ The heart of the wise
> teaches his mouth, and
> adds persuasiveness to
> his lips.
>
> Proverbs 16:23

> ◆ Honesty is one part of
> eloquence. We persuade
> others by being in ear-
> nest ourselves.
>
> William Hazlitt

Identify an advertisement, editorial, or sales pitch with which you are familiar. Is this message, in your opinion, ethical or unethical? Does it conform to the definition of ethical persuasion given in this chapter?

Public Communication

There are many ways to define **ethical persuasion.**[2] For our purpose, we will consider it as *communication in the best interest of the audience that does not depend on false or misleading information to change an audience's attitude or behavior.* The best way to appreciate the value of this simple definition is to consider the many strategies listed in Table 15–1 that do not fit it. For example, faking enthusiasm about a speech topic, plagiarizing material from another source and passing it off as your own, or making up statistics to support your case are clearly unethical.[3]

Besides being wrong on moral grounds, unethical attempts at persuasion have a major practical disadvantage: If your deception is uncovered, your credibility will suffer. If, for example, prospective buyers uncover your attempt to withhold a mechanical flaw in the used car you are trying to sell, they will

TABLE 15–1   Unethical Communication Behaviors

I. Failing to Prepare Adequately
   A. Insufficient research (speaker does not know what he or she is talking about)
   B. Not meeting logical standards of proof

II. Sacrificing Convictions in Adapting to an Audience
   A. In propositions endorsed
   B. In style of presentation (for example, clothing)

III. Appearing to Be What One Is Not; Insincerity
   A. In words, saying what one does not mean or believe
   B. In delivery (for example, feigning enthusiasm)

IV. Withholding Information; Suppression
   A. About self (speaker); not disclosing private motives or special interests
   B. About speech purpose
   C. About sources (not revealing sources; plagiarism)
   D. About evidence; omission of certain evidence (card-stacking)
   E. About opposing arguments; presenting only one side

V. Relaying False Information
   A. Deliberate lying
   B. Ignorant misstatement
   C. Deliberate distortion and suppression of material
   D. Using fallacious reasoning to misrepresent truth

VI. Using Motivational Appeals to Hinder Truth
   A. Using emotional appeals as a substitute or cover-up for a lack of sound reasoning and valid evidence
   B. Failing to use balanced appeals

VII. Plagiarism
   A. Claiming someone else's ideas as your own.
   B. Quoting without citing the source.

Adapted from Mary Klaaren Andersen, "An Analysis of the Treatment of Ethos in Selected Speech Communication Textbooks" (unpublished dissertation, University of Michigan, 1979), pp. 244–247.

Persuasive Speaking

probably suspect that the car has other hidden problems. Likewise, if your speech instructor suspects you are lifting material from other sources without giving credit, your entire presentation will be suspect. One unethical act can cast doubt on future truthful statements. Thus, for pragmatic as well as moral reasons, honesty really *is* the best policy.

◆ TYPES OF PERSUASION

There are several ways to categorize the kinds of persuasive attempts you will make as a speaker. What kinds of subjects will you focus on? What results will you be seeking? How will you go about getting those results? In the following pages we will look at each of these questions.

Types of Questions

All persuasive topics fall into one of three categories: questions of fact, questions of value, and questions of policy.

QUESTIONS OF FACT   Some persuasive messages focus on **questions of fact**: issues in which there are two or more sides with conflicting evidence, where listeners are required to choose the truth for themselves. Some questions of fact are these:

> A "nuclear winter" is likely (unlikely) after even a small nuclear war.
>
> Experience shows that rent control will (will not) make housing more available for tenants.
>
> People who live in communist countries are (are not) generally dissatisfied with their style of government.*

These examples show that many questions of fact can't be settled with a simple yes or no or with an objective piece of information. Rather, they are open to debate, and answering them requires careful examination and interpretation of evidence, usually collected from a variety of sources. That's why it's possible to debate questions of fact, and that's why these questions form the basis of persuasive speeches, and not of informative ones.

QUESTIONS OF VALUE   **Questions of value** go beyond issues of truth or falsity and explore the worth of some idea, person, or object. Questions of value include the following:

> The use of laboratory animals for many scientific experiments is (is not) cruel and immoral.

*Despite their label, the "questions" of fact, value, and policy described in the following pages are usually phrased as statements in a speech in order to strengthen the speaker's argument. They are called "questions" because they can be answered in more than one way. For example, the three questions in this example could be worded thus:

> "Is a 'nuclear winter' likely after even a small nuclear war?"
>
> "Will rent control make housing more available for tenants?"
>
> "Are people who live in communist countries generally dissatisfied with their style of government?"

Pledging allegience to the flag is (is not) an appropriate way to demonstrate patriotism.

Magazines such as *Playboy* and *Cosmopolitan* are (are not) sexist.

In order to answer most questions of value, you will first need to answer one or more questions of fact. For example, you won't be able to debate whether the experimental use of animals in research is often immoral—a question of value—until you have dealt with several fundamental questions of fact such as whether lab animals suffer during experiments and whether such experiments are necessary.

QUESTIONS OF POLICY   **Questions of policy** go one step beyond questions of fact or value; they recommend a specific course of action (a "policy") for the audience. Some questions of policy are these:

The United States should (should not) withdraw its support from any government that uses torture.

College athletes should (should not) be paid in cash for their talents.

Flag burning should be made illegal.

One student made the following suggestions for a specific course of action against frivolous lawsuits:

First of all, we must define the term *frivolous case* so that judges can rule immediately on whether or not a case is justified. . . .Another solution lies in awarding adequate compensation to victims of frivolous lawsuits. . . .Finally, we must try to settle our minor problems outside the courtroom.[4]

Looking at persuasion according to "type of question" is a convenient way to generate topics for a persuasive speech. However, fully developed persuasive speeches are likely to develop all three types of questions within their arguments. For example, one student outlined his persuasive argument against high insurance premiums this way:

To insure ourselves against this out-of-control industry, I am filing a claim that, first, these rising premiums are a problem for all of us; and, second, I will investigate who is liable for this dilemma; and, finally, I will offer a protection plan to safeguard us from further and future damage.[5]

This speaker dealt first with a question of value, then with a question of fact, and finally with a question of policy.

Desired Outcome

We can also divide persuasion according to two major outcomes: **convincing** and **actuating.**

CONVINCING   When you set about to convince an audience, you want to change the way they think. When we say that convincing an audience changes the way they think, we do not mean that you have to swing them from one belief or attitude to a completely different one. Sometimes an audience will already think the way you want them to, but they will not be firmly enough

◆ **If it is urged that an abuse of the rhetorical faculty can work great mischief, the same charge can be brought against all good things such as strength, health, wealth, and military skill. Rightly employed, they work the greatest blessing; and wrongly employed, they work the utmost harm.**

Aristotle

committed to that way of thinking. When that is the case, you *reinforce,* or strengthen, their opinions. For example, if your audience already believed that the federal budget should be balanced but did not consider the idea important, your job would be to reinforce their current beliefs. Reinforcing is still a type of change, however, because you are causing an audience to adhere more strongly to a belief or attitude. In other cases, convincing will *begin* to shift attitudes without bringing about a total change of thinking. For example, an effective speech to convince might get a group of skeptics to *consider the possibility* that bilingual education is (isn't) a good idea.

ACTUATING   When you set about to actuate an audience, you want to move them to a specific behavior. Whereas a speech to convince might move an audience to action based on the ideas you've convinced them about, it won't be any specific action that you've recommended. In a speech to actuate, you do recommend that specific action.

There are two types of action you can ask for—*adoption* or *discontinuance.* The former asks an audience to engage in a new behavior; the latter asks them to stop behaving in an established way. If you gave a speech for a political candidate and then asked for contributions to that candidate's campaign, you would be asking your audience to adopt a new behavior. If you gave a speech against smoking and then asked your audience to sign a pledge to quit, you would be asking them to discontinue an established behavior.

Directness of Approach

We can also categorize persuasion according to the directness of approach employed by the speaker.

DIRECT PERSUASION   **Direct persuasion** is that which does not try to disguise the speaker's persuasive purpose in any way. In direct persuasion the speaker will make his or her purpose clear, usually by stating it outright early in the speech. This is the best strategy to use with a friendly audience, especially when you are asking for a response that the audience is reasonably likely to give you:

> I'm here today to let you know why you should take part in the Red Cross blood drive. . . .

> Have you ever wished that students had more rights and power? They can, if they organize effectively. I'm here today to show you how to do just that. . . .

> I'm going to try to convince you today that Candy Tate is the best choice for city council and that she needs your vote. . . .

Direct persuasion is the kind we hear in most academic situations. One student, speaking on the FDA's proposal to allow the irradiation of food and vegetables, announced her intent to persuade:

> Today I would like to urge you to recognize the startling lack of safety of this proposal and to help you see how unnecessary the "Federal Food Irradiation Development and Control Act" is.[6]

◆ **The credit goes to the person who convinces the world, not to the one to whom the idea first occurs.**

Sir Francis Darwin

Another student chose a direct approach in her speech on the importance of wills:

> My purpose today is to convince each of you that having a will is important by discussing why people avoid writing a will; what a will is and why we need one; and, finally, how we can obtain a will.[7]

Find a current political speech in *Vital Speeches of the Day*, *The New York Times* on microfilm, or some other source. Which type of persuasive strategy is used in the speech, direct or indirect? Is the strategy used effectively? Why or why not?

INDIRECT PERSUASION   **Indirect persuasion** disguises or de-emphasizes the speaker's persuasive purpose in some way. The question "Is a season ticket to the symphony worth the money?" (when you intend to prove that it is) is based on indirect persuasion, as is any strategy that does not express the speaker's purpose at the outset.

Indirect persuasion is sometimes easy to spot. A television commercial that shows us a handsome young man and a beautiful young woman romping in the surf on a beautiful day and then flashes the product name on the screen is pretty indisputably indirect persuasion. Political oratory is sometimes indirect persuasion, also, and it is sometimes more difficult to identify as such. A political hopeful might be ostensibly speaking on some great social issue when the real persuasive message is "Please—remember my name, and vote for me in the next election."

In public speaking, indirect persuasion is usually disguised as informative speech. For example, a supposedly informative speech could be given on AIDS, which actually has the intent of persuading audience members to remain celibate before marriage, and monogamous after marriage. Persuasive intent has also been known to appear in the guise of special occasion speaking. This is best exemplified in Shakespeare's version of Marc Antony's funeral oration for Julius Caesar.[8] Brutus, one of Caesar's assassins, has just finished speaking, convincing the crowd that Caesar's murder was just and honorable. Antony has to appear cordial toward the assassins so they will allow him to speak over Caesar's body in the forum. Antony begins by saying that he has "come to bury Caesar, not to praise him," but he slowly works his crowd back to an appreciation of their murdered leader and rage against those who killed them.

Indirect persuasion is the approach to use when your audience is hostile to either you or your topic. It is also often necessary to use the indirect approach to get a hearing from listeners who would tune you out if you took a more direct approach. Under such circumstances, you might want to ease into your speech slowly.[9] You might take some time to make your audience feel good about you or the social action you are advocating. If you are speaking in favor of Candy Tate for city council, but Tate is in favor of a tax increase and your audience is not, you might talk for a while about the benefits of that increase. You might even want to change your desired audience response. Rather than trying to

Persuasive Speaking

get them to rush out to vote for Tate, you might want them simply to read a recent newspaper article about her or attend a speech she will be giving. The one thing you cannot do in this instance is to begin by saying, "I'm not here to speak in support of Candy Tate"—that would be a false statement. It is more than indirect; it is unethical.

Indirect persuasion *can* be ethical, however. The test of the ethicality of an indirect approach would be whether you *would* express your persuasive purpose directly if asked to do so. In other words, if someone in the audience stopped you and asked, "Aren't you supporting Candy Tate for city council?" if you were ethical, you would admit to it rather than deny your true purpose.

As one example of a situation in which indirect persuasion might be ethical and fruitful, imagine that certain books—books like *Huckleberry Finn, To Kill a Mockingbird,* or *Romeo and Juliet* are being removed from the shelves of your local library because of pressure from groups who believe that these books promote "un-American" values.[10] If you chose to speak to the citizens of your town about this matter, you would be well advised to begin your speech by assuring them that you share most of the same values they do: You want the children of your town to grow up honest and healthy; you want them to be levelheaded about drugs, sex, and alternative life-styles. You want them to be civilized and humane, and you want them to be active members of American democracy. You would agree with your listeners that obscenity and pornography degrade humanity, that they are devoid of human sentiments and ideals.

Only after you have established these mutual values would you try to persuade them that the censorship of works of literature is not the best way to achieve their objectives. You might then point out the dangers of artistic repression and the impracticality of trying to "legislate morality." You might then point out that works of literature are not instruction manuals, and readers are not destined to imitate the events portrayed in the book. You might wind up with the idea that, as one speaker pointed out, the censorship of books undermines the more vital function of education, which is to help students cope with life by exploring with them the realities and ambiguities expressed in recognized literary works.[11]

◆ **PERSUASIVE STRATEGY**

Whether you choose a direct or an indirect approach to reaching your goal, your approach when persuading an audience should follow the same basic strategy, outlined in Table 15–2. In many ways, this strategy is similar to the approach you would use in an informative speech: You have to explain your topic to your audience before you persuade them. In fact, a persuasive speech will actually contain two or three different informative ones. First, you will have to explain the problem. Next, you will describe the solution. Finally, if your goal is to actuate the audience, you will inform the audience members about the part they can play in bringing about the solution. Let's look at each of these steps more closely.

Public Communication

TABLE 15-2   Strategy for a Persuasive Speech

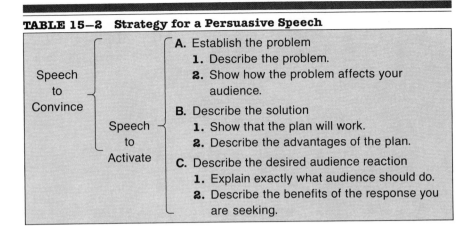

Speech to Convince	Speech to Activate	A. Establish the problem
		   1. Describe the problem.
		   2. Show how the problem affects your audience.
		B. Describe the solution
		   1. Show that the plan will work.
		   2. Describe the advantages of the plan.
		C. Describe the desired audience reaction
		   1. Explain exactly what audience should do.
		   2. Describe the benefits of the response you are seeking.

Study the sample speech at the end of this chapter. Has the speaker explained the problem, the solution, and the audience's role in the solution adequately? Can you suggest any changes that might have improved her presentation?

Define the Problem

In order to convince an audience that something needs to be changed, you have to show them that a problem exists. After all, if your listeners don't recognize the problem, they won't find your arguments for a solution very important. An effective definition of the problem will answer two questions, either directly or indirectly.

WHAT IS THE NATURE OF THE PROBLEM?   Your audience might not recognize that the topic you are discussing is a problem at all, so your first task is to convince them that there is something wrong with the present state of affairs. For example, if your thesis was "This town needs a shelter for homeless families," you would need to show that there are, indeed, homeless families and that the plight of these homeless families is serious.

Your approach to defining your problem will depend largely upon your audience analysis, as discussed in Chapter 11. If your prespeech analysis shows that your audience may not feel sympathetic to your topic, you will need to explain why your topic is, indeed, a problem that your listeners should recognize. In a speech about the plight of the homeless, you might need to establish that most homeless people are not lazy, able-bodied drifters who choose to panhandle and steal instead of working. You could cite respected authorities, give examples, and maybe even show photographs to demonstrate that some homeless people are hardworking but unlucky parents and innocent children who lack shelter owing to forces beyond their control.

HOW DOES THE PROBLEM AFFECT YOUR AUDIENCE? It's not enough to prove that a problem exists. Your next challenge is to show your listeners that the problem affects them in some way. This is relatively easy in some cases: the high cost of tuition, the lack of convenient parking near campus, and so on. In other cases, you will need to spell out the impact to your listeners more clearly.

This is how former First Lady Nancy Reagan established the importance of the drug abuse problem to audiences across the nation:

> I want to talk about the battle against drugs.
>
> Now before any of you can think to yourself, "Well, drug abuse really doesn't concern me," let me say it does concern you. It concerns you if you have a family because drugs can unexpectedly tear a family to pieces—even the most loving families.
>
> It concerns you as an employer because drugs cost billions in illness, accidents, lost productivity, and corruption.
>
> It concerns you as a citizen because there's a direct and undeniable link between crime and drugs. Law enforcement officers are being murdered in their effort to protect our society from those who would destroy it with drugs.
>
> And, furthermore, it concerns you as an individual of conscience because the tragedy and pain drugs cause are staggering.
>
> Ladies and gentlemen, there's a drug and alcohol epidemic in this country and no one is safe from its consequences—not you, not me, and certainly not our children. Drugs are a very powerful force in America, and we cannot ignore them.[12]

For practice in formulating persuasive strategies, choose one of the following topics, and develop it according to the approaches outlined in Table 15–2.

a. Parole should (should not) be abolished.
b. Standardized tests should (should not) be used as the main criteria for college admissions.
c. The capital of the United States should (should not) be moved to a more central location.
d. Police should (should not) be required to carry nonlethal weapons only.
e. Capital punishment should (should not) be abolished.
f. Bilingual education should (should not) be required for all schools serving bilingual students.

Define the Solution

Your next step in persuading your audience is to convince them that there is an answer to the problem you have just introduced. In other words, you need to propose a solution—a plan to correct this problem. Just describing your solution isn't enough. You have to answer two questions about this solution before your audience is likely to accept it.

WILL THE PLAN WORK? A skeptical audience might agree with the desirability of your solution but still not believe that it has a chance of succeeding. Suppose your thesis is "The United States should immediately begin reducing the number of its own nuclear weapons, in order to encourage the USSR to do likewise." As many of your listeners might brush off this idea as too idealistic to work, you'll need to offer some evidence that unilateral disarmament has a chance of succeeding. In the homeless speech we have been discussing, you would need to prove that establishment of a shelter can help unlucky families get back on their feet—especially if your audience analysis shows that some listeners might view such a shelter as a way of coddling people who are too lazy to work.

WHAT ADVANTAGES WILL RESULT FROM YOUR PLAN? You need to describe in specific terms how your plan will lead to desired changes. This is the step where you will paint a vivid picture of the benefits of your proposal. In the speech proposing a shelter for homeless families, the benefits you describe would probably include these:

1. Families will have a safe place to stay, free of the dangers of living on the street.
2. Parents will have the resources that will help them find jobs: an address, telephone, clothes washers, and showers.
3. The police won't have to apply antivagrancy laws (such as prohibitions against sleeping in cars) to people who aren't the intended target of those laws.
4. The community (including your listeners) won't need to feel guilty about ignoring the plight of unfortunate citizens.

Describe the Desired Audience Response

You should follow the previous steps of describing the problem and outlining your solution in all persuasive speeches. When you want to go beyond simply a **strategy to convince** your audience and use a **strategy to actuate** them to follow your plan, you need to describe exactly what you want them to do (see Table 15–2). This action step, like the previous ones, should answer two questions.

WHAT CAN THE AUDIENCE DO TO PUT YOUR PLAN INTO ACTION? Make the behavior you are asking your audience to adopt as clear and simple as possible for them. If you want them to vote in a referendum, tell them when and where to go to vote and how to go about registering, if necessary. (Some activists even provide transportation.) If you're asking them to support a legislative change, don't expect them to write their congressional representative. *You* write the letter or draft a petition, and ask them to sign it. If you're asking for donations, pass the hat at the conclusion of your speech, or give each audience member a stamped, addressed envelope and simple forms that they can return easily.

FRANK AND ERNEST by Bob Thaves

THANK YOU FOR NOT SINNING

LOOK, I KNOW THESE PEOPLE ... YOU'RE GOING TO HAVE TO BE TOUGHER THAN THIS!

THAVES 2-3

WHAT ARE THE DIRECT REWARDS OF THIS RESPONSE? Your solution might be important to society, but your audience will be most likely to adopt it if you can show that they will get a personal payoff. Show that supporting legislation to reduce acid rain will produce a wide range of benefits from reduced lung damage to healthier forests to longer life for their car's paint. Explain that saying no to a second drink before driving will not only save lives but also help your listeners avoid expensive court costs, keep their insurance rates low, and prevent personal humiliation. Show how helping to establish and staff a homeless shelter can lead to personal feelings of satisfaction and provide an impressive demonstration of community service on a job-seeking résumé.

Adapting the Basic Persuasive Strategy

Establishing the problem and defining the solution make up the basic strategy for any persuasive speech. However, you don't have to analyze too many successful persuasive speeches to realize that the best of them do far more than the basic minimum. One way to augment the basic persuasive strategy is to use the organization suggested by Alan Monroe in his **Motivated Sequence,**[13] which we mentioned briefly in Chapter 11. To recap, it suggests that a successful persuasive speech should contain the following steps:

1. The Attention Step: Generally, the introduction of the persuasive speech grabs the audience's attention and makes them aware of the problem. This is the way Michael Stolts, a student at the University of Wisconsin, Eau Claire, used the attention step in his speech on preventing childhood obesity:[14]

   Camp Kingsmont is in many ways very much like any other summer camp. Children have rowboat races, swim and shortsheet their counselors' beds. But they also endure extensive calisthenics classes and three-mile jogs, attend group sessions on how to balance their nutritional needs and struggle through a strict, reduced-calorie diet. Camp Kingsmont is an adolescent weight loss camp, and all 350 of its yearly clientele are obese children.

2. The Need Step establishes the problem. Here's how Michael used it in his speech:

Obesity is rapidly becoming a serious problem, diminishing the lives of millions of American children. Children who are 20% over their ideal weight are considered medically obese and in need of help. John C. McCable, Chairman of Blue Cross and Blue Shield of Michigan says, "Obesity is challenging malnutrition as a major American health problem, and fat children become fat adults."

3. The Satisfaction Step proposes a solution that can be used to solve the problem. Here's how it sounded in Michael's speech:

The key to stopping childhood obesity is preventing it from ever occurring. This can be done by seeing that children do get enough exercise and that they don't eat too much.

4. The Visualization Step describes the results of the solution in a way that allows the audience to "see" it. Again, in Michael's speech:

Healthy, fit children face an excellent chance of remaining healthy and fit all their lives. For today, freedom from obesity means children can run, jump and play as they ought, and summer camps, like Camp Kingsmont, can concentrate not on dieting and exercising, but on swimming, boating and prankstering, the fun parts of summer camp.

5. The Action Step is a direct appeal for the audience to do something. In Michael's speech, part of the action step sounded like this:

We as parents or future parents must be involved in preventing obesity. Dr. Leonard Epstein suggests in *Consumer's Research Magazine* that we incorporate exercise into children's daily activities. Where safe, children should walk to school instead of being driven. He also says, "Don't reward good behavior with food; use parent/child activities instead." Doing things with children will cut out some calories, burn more and strengthen family bonds.

◆ TECHNIQUES FOR EFFECTIVE PERSUASIVE SPEAKING

The preceding discussion suggests several techniques for effective persuasion. Let us focus on a few important techniques.

Set a Clear Persuasive Purpose

Remember that your objective in a persuasive speech is to move the audience to a specific, attainable attitude or behavior. In a speech to convince, the purpose statement will probably stress an attitude:

After listening to my speech, my audience members will *agree* that steps should be taken to save whales from extinction.

In a speech to actuate, the purpose statement will stress a behavior:

After listening to my speech, the audience members will *sign* my petition to the United Nations.

As we explained in Chapter 11, your purpose statement should always be specific, attainable, and worded from the audience's point of view. "The purpose of my speech is to save the whales" is not a well-thought-out purpose statement.

A clear, specific purpose statement will help you stay on track throughout all the stages of speech preparation. Because the main purpose of your speech is to have an effect on your audience, you have a continual test that you can use for every idea, every piece of evidence, and every organizational structure that you think of using. The question you ask is, "Will this help me to get the audience members to think/feel/behave in the manner I have described in my purpose statement?" If the answer is yes, you forge ahead.

Of course, to *affect* your audience you have to *know* your audience, which brings us to our second persuasive technique.

Analyze and Adapt to Your Audience

It is important to know as much as possible about your audience for a persuasive speech. For one thing, you should appeal to the values of your audience whenever possible even if they are not *your* strongest values. This advice does not mean you should pretend to believe in something. According to our definition of ethical persuasion, pretense is against the rules. It does mean, however, that you have to stress those values that are felt most forcefully by the members of your audience.[15]

Also, you should analyze your audience carefully to predict the type of response you will get. Sometimes you have to pick out one part of your audience—a **target audience,** the subgroup you MUST persuade to reach your goal—and aim your speech mostly at them. Some of your audience members might be so opposed to what you are advocating that you have no hope of reaching them. Still others might already agree with you, so they do not need to be persuaded. A middle portion of your audience might be undecided or uncommitted, and they would be the most productive target for your appeals.

Of course, you need not ignore that portion of your audience that does not fit your target. For example, if you were giving a speech against smoking, your target audience might be the smokers in your class. Your main purpose would be to get them to quit, but at the same time, you could convince the non-smokers not to start.

All the methods of audience analysis described in Chapter 11—surveys, observation, interviews, and research—are valuable in collecting information about your audience for a persuasive speech.

Once you know who you're talking to, you can use that knowledge to build your credibility—our next technique.

From your experiences hearing or reading persuasive messages about social or political issues, how well do you think the advice for planning a strategy to convince is followed? If you think such advice is *not* heeded, what steps or components of the process are most often ignored or slighted?

◆ **He Was a Sincere But Friendly Presbyterian**

He was a sincere but friendly Presbyterian—and so
If he was talking to a Presbyterian,
He was for Presbyterianism.
If he was talking to a Lutheran,
He was for Protestantism.
If he was talking to a Catholic,
He was for Christianity.
If he was talking to a Jew,
He was for God.
If he was talking to a theosophist,
He was for religion.
If he was talking to an agnostic,
He was for scientific caution.
If he was talking to an atheist,
He was for mankind.
And if he was talking to a socialist,
   communist, labor leader, missiles
   expert, or businessman,
He was for
   PROGRESS.

Kenneth Burke
Collected Poems

Build Your Personal Credibility

Credibility refers to the believability of a speaker. Credibility isn't an objective quality; rather, it is a *perception* in the minds of the audience. In a class such as the one you're taking now, students often wonder how they can build their credibility. After all, the members of the class tend to know each other pretty well by the time the speech assignments roll around. It is important to realize, therefore, that credibility has a tendency to change during a speaking event. In fact, researchers speak in terms of *initial credibility* (what you have when you first get up to speak), *derived credibility* (what you acquire while speaking), and *terminal credibility* (what you have after you finish speaking). It is not uncommon for a student with low initial credibility to earn increased credibility while speaking, and finish with much higher terminal credibility.

Credibility is perhaps the most important ingredient in persuading an audience. Without it you won't be able to convince your listeners that your ideas are worth accepting even if your material is outstanding. On the other hand, if you can develop a high degree of credibility in the eyes of your listeners, they will be likely to open up to ideas they wouldn't otherwise accept.

An audience forms judgments about the credibility of a speaker based on their perception of many characteristics, the most important of which might be called the "Three C's" of credibility: *competence, character,* and *charisma.*[16]

Persuasive Speaking

Reprinted by permission of the Interstate Oratorical Association.

"WHAT I DO IS BELIEVE ⅕ OF WHAT THE CONVICTED PERJURERS SAY, ⅖ OF WHAT THE SUSPECTED PERJURERS SAY, AND ⅗ OF WHAT ANYONE ELSE SAYS."

COMPETENCE   **Competence** refers to the speaker's expertise on the topic. Sometimes this competence can come from *personal experience* that will lead your audience to regard you as an authority on the topic you are discussing. If everyone in the audience knows you've earned big profits in the stock market, they'll probably take your investment advice seriously. If you tell them you lost twenty-five pounds from a diet-and-exercise program, they'll almost certainly respect your opinions on weight loss.

The other way to be seen as competent is to be well prepared for speaking. A speech that is well researched, organized, written, and presented will greatly increase the audience's perception of the speaker's competence.

CHARACTER   All the expertise in the world won't generate enough credibility unless your audience trusts you enough to believe what you are saying. **Character** involves the audience's perception of at least two ingredients: honesty and impartiality. You should try to find ways to talk about yourself (without boasting, of course) that demonstrate your integrity. You might describe how much time you spent researching the subject or demonstrate your open-mindedness by telling them that you changed your mind after your investigation. For example, if you were giving a speech arguing against a proposed tax cut in your community, you might begin this way:

> You might say I'm an expert in the municipal services of this town. As a lifelong resident, I owe a debt to its schools and recreation programs. I've been protected by its police and fire fighters and served by its hospitals, roads, and sanitation crews.

Public Communication

As I'm also a taxpayer who's on a tight budget, when I first heard about the tax cut that's been proposed, I liked the idea. But then I did some in-depth investigation into the possible effects. I looked into our municipal expenses and into the expenses of similar communities where tax cuts have been mandated by law . . .

In addition to demonstrating your sincerity, you can also boost your credibility by proving that you are impartial. One way to do so is to mention both sides of the issue you are discussing. You could also quote sources who could be expected to oppose the issue you're advocating. A Republican's praise for the local Democratic candidate would be more effective than a fellow Democrat's, for instance.

> Based on your viewing of television news, identify three highly credible speakers and three with low credibility. Which of the factors in this chapter contribute to the trustworthiness of each speaker?

CHARISMA **Charisma** is a combination of a speaker's enthusiasm and likability. Audiences are more likely to be persuaded by a charismatic speaker than by a less charismatic one who delivers the same information.

Enthusiasm is sometimes termed "dynamism" by communication scholars. Your enthusiasm will mostly be perceived from *how* you deliver your remarks, not from *what* you say. The nonverbal parts of your speech will show that you believe in what you are saying far better than your words. Is your voice animated and sincere? Do your gestures reflect your enthusiasm? Do your facial expression and eye contact show you care about your audience?

You can boost your likability in two ways. First, you can show that you like and respect your audience. Insincere flattery will boomerang, of course, but if you can find a way to give your listeners a genuine compliment, they'll be more receptive to your ideas.

You can also increase your likability by emphasizing the similarities between you and your listeners. This is known as establishing **common ground**, which is our next technique for effective persuasion.

Establish "Common Ground"

It helps to stress as many similarities as possible between yourself and your audience. This technique helps prove that you understand them: If not, why should they listen to you? Also, if you share a lot of common ground, it shows you agree on many things; therefore, it should be easy to settle one disagreement—the one related to the attitude or behavior you would like them to change.

The manager of public affairs for *Playboy* magazine gave a good demonstration of establishing common ground when he reminded a group of Southern Baptists that they shared some important values with him:

> I am sure we are all aware of the seeming incongruity of a representative of *Playboy* magazine speaking to an assemblage of representatives of the Southern Baptist Convention. I was intrigued by the invitation when it came last fall, though I was not

◆ **Every production of genius must be the production of enthusiasm.**

Benjamin Disraeli

surprised. I am grateful for your genuine and warm hospitality, and I am flattered (although again not surprised) by the implication that I would have something to say that could have meaning to you people. Both *Playboy* and the Baptists have indeed been considering many of the same issues and ethical problems; and even if we have not arrived at the same conclusions, I am impressed and gratified by your openness and willingness to listen to our views.[17]

No matter how much you bolster your personal credibility and establish common ground, it is always a good idea to choose your **evidence** carefully, which brings us to our next technique.

Use Solid Evidence

All of the forms of support discussed in Chapter 12 can be used to back up your persuasive arguments.[18] For example, this is how one student used statistics to bolster her arguments about children with AIDS:

Since 1983 there have been 563 documented cases of children who have died of pediatric AIDS alone. Estimates made by pediatricians and AIDS specialists at a recent AIDS conference have predicted that by the year 1991 the number of children under the age of 13 showing symptoms of this disease will reach 10,000, and *could* reach as high as 20,000.[19]

This is how another student used testimony, definition, statistics, and examples to bolster his arguments about the agricultural herbicide 2–4–D.

According to Richard Jones, a former employee of the Dawson County, Nebraska Weed Control District, 2–4–D is an amine herbicide. It's a chemical that kills broadleaf plants by mimicking natural growth compounds, causing the plant to use up stored reserves of energy and literally grow itself to death. On one level 2–4–D is by definition a cancer: It kills plants by forcing them to grow more unwanted cells than they can support.

And 2–4–D is a popular cancer. The *Boston Globe* called it the nation's 4th most common pesticide, and according to the *Washington Post,* "More than 60 million pounds of 2–4–D are applied yearly as a weed control for a wide variety of crops. . . ." In addition to being used in huge quantities, 2–4–D is used in a wide variety of applications from agricultural and municipal spraying to home lawn care use and golf course maintenance. In fact, according to the *New York Times,* 2–4–D is sold over-the-counter in American hardware stores in more than 1500 products, under familiar brand names like Trimec and Ortho Weed-B-Gon.[20]

When determining which evidence is appropriate to your argument, do not discount **emotional evidence.** We have known since the ancient Greeks that human beings are not strictly logical. They are instead *psychological,* which means that they respond strongly to emotional proofs. As Clarence Darrow once pointed out, "You don't have to give reasons to the jury. Make them *want* to acquit your client, and they'll find their own reasons."

One expert in persuasive communication gives the following example of emotional evidence:

Not long ago, the minister of my local congregation was making a point about human neglect. He wished to show that neglecting others is a fault that is often costly to us, so he related a story about a family whose son phoned them on his return from

Vietnam, just prior to his discharge. He wondered if he could bring home a friend who had nowhere to go except a Veteran's hospital—the friend had no family and was severely disabled, having lost an eye, an arm, and a leg in battle. After some discussion, the parents called their son back at his hotel and told him that taking care of a person with these disabilities would prove too difficult for any extended time, so although their son's comrade was welcome for a short stay, his best interests would be served by his staying in the Veteran's hospital. The next day, the parents were informed that their son had killed himself by jumping from the hotel window soon after their call. His remains were shipped home. The grief-stricken parents went to the railroad station to identify their son's body. When the casket was opened, they discovered that their son was missing one eye, one arm, and one leg.[21]

Solid evidence has to be part of a well-reasoned argument. This brings us to our next technique.

Use Careful Reasoning

In its purest form, logical reasoning provides an audience with a series of statements, all of which are true, that lead to the conclusion the speaker is trying to establish. The most common forms of logical reasoning are *deduction* and *induction.*

DEDUCTION   **Deduction** is reasoning from a general rule to a specific conclusion. Deductive reasoning can be demonstrated in **syllogisms,** which are arguments made up of two premises (a major premise and a minor premise) and a conclusion. The classic syllogism is:

> All men are mortal.
> Socrates is a man.
> Therefore, Socrates is mortal.

◆ **To say that it is possible to persuade without speaking to the passions is but at best a kind of specious nonsense.**

George Campbell

Persuasive Speaking

This is the way one student used deduction to argue one of her points in a speech on the problem of illiteracy:

> We come into the picture as taxpayers, especially in welfare and unemployment costs. According to *U.S. News and World Report,* 75 percent of the unemployed lack the skills necessary in reading and communication. Welfare is the answer for those illiterates who can't work. This costs us $6 billion per year.[22]

This argument might be phrased in the following syllogism:

> Unemployment costs us plenty.
> Illiteracy causes unemployment.
> Therefore, illiteracy costs us plenty.

If all logical appeals were expressed as complete syllogisms, people could examine the major and minor premises and decide if the conclusions drawn from those premises were valid. This method would make most arguments cumbersome, so we generally use *enthymemes* for logical appeals.[23] An **enthymeme** is a compressed version of a syllogism in which the underlying premises are concealed, as in:

> Because Socrates is a man, he is mortal.

Enthymemes become dangerous when they disguise faulty premises. Some of the best examples of this type of enthymeme are provided in the form of arbitrary rules. For example, take the rule enforced by some college-town landlords: "Because Joe Schmidlap is a college student, he will have to pay a damage deposit before he can rent an apartment." This rule is based on an enthymeme that is based on the following syllogism:

> All college students wreck apartments.
> Joe Schmidlap is a college student.
> Therefore, Joe Schmidlap will wreck this apartment.

The conclusion, "Joe Schmidlap will wreck this apartment," is based on an untrue, unstated premise: "All college students wreck apartments."

College students often run up against this type of reasoning from landlords and utility companies. Even if they can supply letters of reference from former landlords and receipts for utility bills paid on time, they are still told, "I'm sorry, we don't rent to college students. It's a rule we have," or "I'm sorry, we require a deposit of $75 to turn on your electricity. It's a rule," or "There's no sense arguing. We don't need to give you a *reason*. It's a rule."

The frustration you feel when you are subjected to illogical rules is the same frustration that an audience feels when it is subjected to an argument that does not supply valid reasons. That is why we take this close look at deductive reasoning: To make sure that the reasons we use in deduction are valid, we examine the underlying premises of our argument.

Of course, formal logic does not explain all of human reasoning.[24] As we pointed out earlier, humans are not inherently logical or illogical; they are instead "psychological," which means that their reasoning processes are far more complex than any set of rules, no matter how elaborate, could encompass. However, formal logic does have at least one specific use besides being a standard for testing arguments. People who reason fallaciously are generally able to recognize their reasoning as fallacious when confronted with their errors through formal proofs. Therefore, we use formal logic to point out errors in reasoning.[25]

INDUCTION   **Induction** is reasoning from specific evidence to a general conclusion. In induction we observe that something is true for a specific sample. From this evidence we reason that it is *generally* true.

The student speaking against illiteracy used induction to argue that it is a serious problem:

> Nonreading adults have innumerable problems because of their hand-
> icap....Illiterates can't read maps or signs, bills or bank statements. They have
> problems telling the difference between, for example, dog food and beef stew
> because they can't read the labels....In one case, an illiterate worker at a
> construction company was killed because he couldn't read a warning sign....[26]

Induction would be the appropriate type of reasoning to use with a skeptical or hostile audience when you do not want to state an unpopular claim right away. If you are seeking to prove that your local government is generally corrupt, for example, you might build your case with specific examples: The mayor has been convicted of bribery, the building inspector has resigned after being charged with extortion, the fire chief has been indicted for running the station's Dalmation at the track, and the chief of police has admitted to keeping his infant nephew on the police department's payroll. If you used these specific instances to conclude that most of your local officials are corrupt, you would be using induction.

Although induction and deduction are the most common types of logical reasoning, there are other forms. These forms include reasoning by sign, causal reasoning, and reasoning by analogy. Often these forms are combined with induction and deduction.

Reasoning by Sign   **Sign reasoning** is reasoning from specific evidence to a specific conclusion without explaining how the evidence and conclusion are related. The classic example of sign reasoning is, "It is snowing outside, therefore it must be winter." Sign reasoning is used when the argument will be easily accepted by the audience. For example, an audience would probably accept the claim that an increase in bank robberies is a sign that a community is becoming more dangerous to live in. We would not need to go into a long, logical explanation of our reasoning in that case, and the time we save could be used to develop more important aspects of the argument. For example, we might want to go on to claim a particular *cause* for the rash of bank robberies. That would require causal reasoning.

Causal Reasoning   **Causal reasoning,** like sign reasoning, is reasoning from one specific to another specific. However, in causal reasoning you go on to prove that something happened or will happen *because* of something else. If you claimed that the increase in bank robberies in your community was caused by a decrease in police personnel, you would be involved in causal reasoning. In fact, you would be using effect-to-cause reasoning, which is based on the organizational pattern of the same name discussed in Chapter 12. Effect-to-cause reasoning is used when you are talking about something that has already happened. If you were arguing about something that *will* happen (for example, the probability of future bank robberies because the police have cut the size of their force or the hours they patrol), you would be using cause-to-effect reasoning.

Reasoning by Analogy   **Reasoning by analogy** is reasoning from specific evidence to a specific conclusion by claiming that something is *like* something else. Although this type of reasoning could not be used for legal proof, it can help prove a point to an audience. For example, if you were arguing that the methods of law enforcement that curbed bank robbery in a nearby city would also work in your city, you would have to argue that your city is similar to that nearby city in all the respects that are important to your argument—number of banks, size of banks, size of police department, and so on. Thus, if you could argue that the two cities are alike except in one respect—the size of their police forces—you could argue that this is what makes the difference in the incidence of bank robbery. If you did so, you would be arguing by analogy.

There are two types of analogy—*literal* and *figurative.* The analogy of the two cities is a literal analogy because it compares two things that are really (literally) alike. A figurative analogy compares two things that are essentially different. If you argued that bank robberies are like a disease that must be treated to keep it from spreading, you would be using a figurative analogy.

The perceived logic of your argument will be affected by how it is organized. This brings us to our final persuasive technique.

Organize According to the Expected Response   It is much easier to get an audience to agree with you if they have already agreed with you on a previous point. Therefore, you should arrange your points in a persuasive speech so you develop a "yes" response. In effect, you get your audience into the habit of agreeing with you. For example, if you were giving a speech on the donation of body organs, you might begin by asking the audience if they would like to be able to get a kidney if they needed one. Then you might ask them if they would like to have "a major role in curbing tragic and needless dying." The presumed answer to both questions is yes. It is only when you have built a pattern of "yes" responses that you would ask the audience to sign organ donor cards.

An example of a speaker who was careful to organize material according to expected audience response was the late Robert Kennedy. Kennedy, when speaking on civil rights before a group of South Africans who believed in racial discrimination, arranged his ideas so that he spoke first on values that he and his audience shared—values like independence and freedom.[27]

If an audience is already basically in agreement with you, you can organize your material to reinforce their attitudes quickly and then spend most of your time convincing them to take a specific course of action. If, on the other hand, they are hostile to your ideas, you have to spend more time getting the first "yes" out of them.

> Examine an everyday appeal of your own choosing. This appeal might be one made by a child to a parent, by one friend to another, by a student to a teacher, or by anyone else who is trying to change someone else's attitude or behavior or both. Decide which elements of this appeal are based on logic, which elements are based on emotion, and which are based on credibility.

◆ SAMPLE SPEECH

Our sample speech was given by Susanne Landowski, a student at St. Cloud State University in Minnesota.[28] With it, she reached the semifinals at the

SPEECH EVALUATION FORM

Persuasive Speech

Name _____ Topic _____

Assignment # _____ Date _____

What did you especially like? _____

_____

In your opinion, how could the speech be improved? _____

_____

Please comment on the following areas:

Did speaker formulate an effective persuasive strategy?

Did speaker establish own credibility?

Did speaker establish credibility of material used?

Were logical appeals well reasoned?

Were emotional appeals effective?

Did speaker analyze and adapt to audience?

Did speaker appear to have a clear persuasive purpose?

Did speaker establish "common ground"?

Did speaker organize according to expected response?

Did speaker use a variety of appeals and supporting materials effectively?

FIGURE 15—1
This evaluation form—or some adaption of it—might be handy as a guide for your own persuasive speeches, as well as for your evaluation of others' speeches.

Interstate Oratorical Association annual tournament in 1988. She was coached by Kenneth Haught. Susanne's speech deals with a question of policy. Her purpose statement could be expressed as follows:

> After listening to my speech, my audience members will help spread the word about the importance of student lab safety.

Susanne's basic persuasive strategy is structured as follows (numbers in parenthesis represent numbered paragraphs in text):

Persuasive Strategy

  I. Establish the problem (4–16)
  II. Establish the solution (17–21)
  III. The desired audience behavior (22)

Some comments concerning persuasive techniques appear in the margin.

Academic Laboratories: Risking Life and Limb for Credit

SUSANNE LANDOWSKI
St. Cloud State University, Minnesota

1. Introduction grabs attention...

1 For Ramsey Bittar, a typical day involves private nursing, physical therapy sessions and communicating simple messages such as "hello" or "mom" on his computer keyboard. Ironically, however, three years ago Bittar was a gifted chemistry student. What happened? An accident that could and should have been prevented. Three years ago Bittar was performing a dangerous chemistry experiment when his flask exploded and an artery in his neck was severed. Before paramedics were summoned, he had lost enough blood to cause serious brain damage.

2. Introduces the problem...

2 Ramsey Bittar is just one example of a shocking lack of safety in student chemical labs. Academic laboratories. We're all familiar with them, from taking a lab class ourselves or knowing someone who did. Academic labs in high schools or universities are where curious students fearlessly learn about acids and bases or watch photos develop. The thrill of mixing a few millimeters of this with a few millimeters of that, however, easily becomes pain when a lab accident occurs.

3. And previews main points.

3 Today, I will show you just how unsafe student labs are and convince you that steps must be taken to improve their safety. I'll begin by examining the extent and seriousness of unsafe student labs nationwide. Next I'll examine the causes behind this lack of safety. Finally, I'll discuss a three-part solution that must be implemented to protect anyone who has to work in a student laboratory.

4 Most universities and colleges have education requirements that require students to take at least one course involving some laboratory work. The *Journal of Chemical Education* released the results of a survey conducted to

Public Communication

determine the number of people involved in student labs over a recent four-year period. Two hundred and fifty schools reported approximately 800,000 undergraduates involved. When you add the number of faculty, graduate students and support personnel and the number of schools that did not respond, the number of people involved in student labs, in one way or another, is significant.

5 Many chemical accidents involving these students go unreported for many reasons, thus their exact number is not known. The survey released by the *Journal of Chemical Education* estimates that approximately 60 percent of the students received some type of injury during that four-year period.

6 Now we can assume that some of them were nothing more severe than cuts from a broken test tube, treatable with a Band-Aid. Some of them, however, were severe enough to cause permanent disability or death.

7 For example, in late September of 1987, five high school students and a teacher were rushed to the emergency room with lacerations and burns when a test tube of alcohol exploded during a routine lab procedure.

8 In 1982, an undergraduate student in a freshman lab received third-degree burns when a Bunsen burner accidentally ignited his hair.

9 In 1979, a Southern Massachusetts University graduate student died in an explosion after an attempt to distill a dangerous chemical.

10 Now you may think that any dangerous activity must tolerate some accidents. I agree. However, academic labs have tolerated too much. According to the Occupational Safety and Health Administration, or OSHA, the rate of injury in a student lab is as much as 50 times higher than in the chemical industry. That means for every one accident in industry, 50 occur in academic labs, a difference we can no longer ignore.

11 Lab accidents are also not limited to Chemistry Departments. Many non-science departments, such as art, anthropology and photography have poor student safety records. Students in art classes routinely mix paints containing chemicals known to cause nasal, lung and skin cancer. Photography students work with chemicals that can cause kidney damage and nervous system disorders. Harry Teitelbaum, a Biochemist at the EPA states, "Teachers in these areas aren't trained to handle hazardous chemicals safely. In one instance, the National Institute for Occupational Safety and Health, or NIOSH, found that poor ventilation at Columbia College was the cause of skin, eye and respiratory inflammations among students in a photography class in 1981. The instructor didn't realize how toxic the fumes would be in an enclosed area.

12 People who have no connection to student labs must also be concerned about their safety, because just being in the same building that houses a

4. Statistics as evidence: A great number of people use student labs. This is the beginning of the inductive argument proving that student labs are a problem.

5. Statistics and testimony build the inductive argument: A high percentage of students receive some type of injury during lab work.

6. Presenting "both sides" of the evidence helps to build credibility.

7–9. Specific examples; building her argument through inductive reasoning.

10. She responds to the expected audience response at this point.

11. Testimony: Lab accidents occur in nonscience departments, also.

Persuasive Speaking

12. Example: Other people on campus are also at risk.

laboratory is dangerous. In 1987, at my own university, the Physics, Geology and, interestingly, the Speech Departments had to evacuate their building when the bomb squad was called to remove dangerous chemicals from the Chemistry Department.

13. Testimony: Safety measures are inadequate.

13 Given the number of persons involved in student chemical labs, one would assume that safety measures would be at their finest. However, just the opposite seems to be true. Dr. James Kaufman, a former Research Chemist for Dow Chemical and current Director of the Laboratory Safety Workshop at Curry College has investigated over 1,000 chemical accidents in educational institutions. He states, "Schools and colleges are notoriously poor in terms of safety performance. There's a tremendous difference in terms of what's considered good sense and practice at a major chemical company versus a school."

14 Unsafe student labs result from two interrelated causes: unsafe laboratory conditions and poor safety instruction. NIOSH states that even in the best of labs, they routinely turn up poor housekeeping, unsafe chemicals and insufficient safety measures. Chemicals are improperly labeled and do not have disposal information on them. Without this information it becomes very easy for a chemical to be disposed of incorrectly, stored improperly or accidentally combined with another chemical, causing a dangerous accident. In 1981 a student at the University of Pennsylvania lost an eye, suffered a punctured ear drum and received lacerations when a chemical exploded during an experiment. The label on the chemical didn't explain that it explodes when exposed to air.

15. Personal experience enhances credibility.

15 In addition to the unsafe lab situations, there is also a serious lack of safety instruction. John Leach, Head of the Safety Management Program at the National Institute of Health, states, "The lack of safety consciousness among many teachers is practically criminal. Because of their poor awareness of lab hazards, safety plays a very minor part in the instructional process." This is devastating, because instructors represent the primary method of teaching students safety. Think back to a chemistry, photograph or art class you may have taken. Was your safety instruction as thorough as it could have been? If you can answer yes, consider yourself one of the fortunate few. When I took a chemistry class several years ago, the instructor did not show the class the proper method for smelling a chemical—waving the fumes to your nose instead of directly inhaling them—and I almost cost myself my sense of smell.

16 In another instance, a student in California spilled a flask of phenol. Not knowing the proper emergency procedure, she mopped up the spill with paper towels. Unfortunately, phenol is toxic when ingested, inhaled or absorbed by the skin and the student became seriously ill.

17 Student labs are an experiment in poor safety. Having heard about the lack of safety, you might be wondering: Isn't there a law that mandates student safety? The simple answer is no. Even though legislation exists that protects

employees who work with hazardous chemicals, there is no regulation that applies to academic institutions. Students are left at the hands of their instructors, who are supposed to teach them safety. The accidents I've discussed suggest that such instruction is not enough. Further, because no national standard exists for regulating lab safety, insurance companies can only regulate schools on the basis of their own standards, which may or may not be accurate.

18 One part of a solution to this problem is an extension of existing OSHA legislation to educational institutions. Extending such legislation could do a great deal to improve student safety. Ramsey Bittar's accident, which I referred to earlier, could have been prevented. Dr. Kaufman states that had he been performing the same experiment at Dow Chemical, federal guidelines would have required that it be performed under a shield. Also, the lab lacked a phone, posted emergency telephone numbers and required first aid training. Such measures would be required if federal regulations were extended to include students.

19 The funding for such legislation would not have to be extensive. I talked to the Chairperson of the Chemistry Department at my university and he asserted that the schools, insurance companies and accrediting agencies, such as the American Chemical Society, could do a great deal to monitor student labs. All that is needed is a national standard, a standard that is already found in existing legislation.

20 A second part of the solution to unsafe labs would be for schools to develop a comprehensive safety program. Basically, a safety program ensures that relevant information reaches the people who need it. A good safety program addresses the hazards associated with all departmental activities and materials in use, the process for training students to work in labs, the monitoring of labs and the procedures to be followed in the event of an emergency. The best part of a safety program is that it can be tailored to the needs of each school. The University of California at Irvine implemented just such a safety program in every department that used chemicals in 1986. According to Ron Kolb, the Director of News and Communication for Irvine, in the two years since, the accident rate has fallen by 25 percent.

21 A final solution involves our own actions. There is a safe way to perform most lab work. We have to make sure we know that method. The book *Safety in Academic Laboratories,* produced by the American Chemical Society, recommends the following as rules for all students in any lab:

— If your instructor does not discuss each experiment and possible hazards, ask before you begin so you know what could happen

— never work alone

— wear eye protection at all times

— wash face and hands before leaving the lab to make sure all traces of chemicals are gone

17. No law requiring safety standards at educational institutions.

18. One part of solution: extending OSHA legislation to educational institutions.

19. Answering the question, is this part of the solution practical?

20. Second part of solution: for schools to develop a comprehensive safety program. Answering the question, will the solution work?

21. Final solution: personal actions.

Persuasive Speaking

22. Desired audience behavior: Spread the word.

22 It's also important just to know that this problem exists. Some of us may never have had a lab class and may never have one. In the past few moments I've told you about the problem of unsafe student labs. As listeners, you can now take the information I've given you and give it to your friends and people you know who are taking lab classes, so they can take every precaution available to them. After all, I can't give my speech to everyone, but you can help.

23. Conclusion reviews main ideas.

23 Student laboratories across the country are needlessly unsafe, exposing students, faculty and bystanders to unnecessary dangers. Both minor and serious accidents occur because of a lack of safety in labs and insufficient safety instruction. A solution to this problem is threefold: existing legislation must be extended to include students, schools must develop comprehensive safety programs and we ourselves must take every available precaution. Student labs have been unsafe long enough. They must be improved before more people risk life and limb for credit.

◆ SUMMARY

Persuasion—the act of moving someone, through communication, toward a belief, attitude, or behavior—can be both worthwhile and ethical. Ethical persuasion requires that the speaker be sincere and honest and avoid such behaviors as poor preparation and plagiarism. It also requires that the persuasion be in the best interest of the audience.

Persuasion can be categorized according to the type of question (fact, value, or policy), approach (direct or indirect), or its outcome (convincing or actuating). A typical strategy for a speech to convince requires you to explain what the problem is and then propose a solution. For a speech to actuate, you also have to ask for a desired audience response. The basic three-pronged strategy can be adapted to more elaborate persuasive plans, but the basic components will remain a part of any persuasive strategy. For each of these components, you need to analyze the arguments your audience will have against accepting what you say and then answer those arguments.

A persuasive strategy is put into effect through the use of several techniques. These include setting a specific, clear persuasive purpose, analyzing and adapting to your target audience, building your personal credibility, establishing "common ground," using solid evidence (including emotional evidence), using careful reasoning, and organizing in such a way that you can expect a "yes" response along each step of your persuasive plan.

1. For an incisive look into the problem of deception, see Robert Hopper and Robert H. Bell, "Broadening the Deception Construct," *Quarterly Journal of Speech* 67:3 (August 1984): 288–302. These authors found six different types of deception: fictions, playings, lies, crimes, masks, and unlies. Another recent analysis is Michael Osborne, "The Abuses of Argument," *Southern Speech Communication Journal* 49:1 (Fall 1983): 1–11. Osborne lists six major abuses.

2. For a research perspective on ethical guidelines, see Ronald Arnett, "The Status of Communication Ethics Scholarship in Speech Communication Journals from 1915 to 1985," *Central States Speech Journal* 38:1 (Spring 1987): 44–61. See also James A. Jaska and Michael S. Pritchard, *Communication Ethics: Methods of Analysis* (Belmont, Calif.: Wadsworth, 1988).

3. Robert L. Frank, "The Abuse of Evidence in Persuasive Speaking," *National Forensic Journal* 1 (Fall 1983): 97–107. Discusses three ethical problems with the use of evidence by student finalists in the Persuasion Section of the 1981 National Forensic Association's "Individual Events Nationals": (1) fabrication of sources and data; (2) source deception; and (3) plagiarism.

4. Greg Robinson, "The Frivolous Fever," *Winning Orations, 1986* (Interstate Oratorical Association, 1986), p. 65.

5. Matthew J. Solomon, "A Case of Liable," *Winning Orations, 1986* (Interstate Oratorical Association, 1986), p. 23.

6. Samantha L. Hubbard, "Irradiation of Food," *Winning Orations, 1986* (Interstate Oratorical Association, 1986), p. 1.

7. Laurel Johnson, "Where There's a Will There's a Way," *Winning Orations, 1986* (Interstate Oratorical Association, 1986), p. 59.

8. William Shakespeare, *Julius Caesar,* Act III, Scene ii.

9. Some research findings suggest that audiences may perceive a direct strategy as a threat to their "freedom" to form their own opinions. This perception hampers persuasion. See J. W. Brehm, *A Theory of Psychological Reactance* (New York: Academic Press, 1966). There also exists considerable evidence to suggest that announcing an intent to persuade in the introduction can reduce a message's effectiveness. Sample studies on this matter include J. Allyn and L. Festinger, "The Effectiveness of Unanticipated Persuasive Communications," *Journal of Abnormal and Social Psychol-*

ogy 62 (1961): 35–40; C. A. Kiesler and S. B. Kiesler, "Role of Forewarning in Persuasive Communications," *Journal of Abnormal and Social Psychology* 18 (1971): 210–221.

10. Battles over this type of censorship continue to be fought. See, for example, Seth Mydans, "In a Small Town, a Battle over a Book," *New York Times,* September 3, 1989, p.21.

11. Jerzy Kosinsky, "Against Book Censorship," in George Rodman (ed.) *Mass Media Issues: Analysis and Debate* (Chicago: SRA, 1984), p. 21.

12. Nancy Reagan, "The Battle Against Drugs: What Can You Do?" *Vital Speeches of the Day* (August 15, 1986): 645.

13. Alan H. Monroe, *Principles and Types of Speech* (Glenview, Ill.: Scott, Foresman, 1935).

14. Michael D. Stolts, "An Ounce Worth Pounds," *Winning Orations, 1987* (Interstate Oratorical Association, 1987), pp. 127–130.

15. For an examination of how one politician adapted to his audience's attitudes, see David Zarefsky, "Subordinating the Civil Rights Issue: Lyndon Johnson in 1964," *Southern Speech Communication Journal* 48 (Winter 1983): 103–118.

16. Joseph A. DeVito, *The Communication Handbook: A Dictionary* (New York: Harper & Row, 1986), pp. 84–86.

17. Anson Mount, speech before Southern Baptist Convention, in Wil A. Linkugel, R.R. Allen, and Richard Johannessen (eds.), *Contemporary American Speeches,* 3d ed. (Belmont, Calif.: Wadsworth, 1973).

18 For an excellent review of the effects of evidence, see John C. Reinard, "The Empirical Study of the Persuasive Effects of Evidence: The Status After Fifty Years of Research," *Human Communication Research* (Fall 1988): pp 3–59.

19. Katie Siplon, "Children with AIDS," *Winning Orations, 1988* (Interstate Oratorical Association, 1988), p. 21.

20. Cam Jones, persuasive speech presented at the 1989 national finals of the National Forensics Association.

21. Charles U. Larson, *Persuasion: Reception and Responsibility,* 4th ed. (Belmont, Calif.: Wadsworth, 1986), p. 147.

22. Joan Braaten, "It's English," *Winning Orations, 1984* (Interstate Oratorical Association, 1984), p. 64.

23. Aristotle once stated, "Everyone who persuades by proof in fact uses either enthymemes or examples. There is no other way" (*The Rhetoric*, op. cit., 1.2,

356b 5–7). An excellent modern look at the 1356b 5–7). An excellent modern look at the enthymeme and the nature of argument is Thomas M. Conley, "The 300.6/33.6x13.11Enthymeme in Perspective," *Quarterly Journal of Speech* 70:2 (May 1984): 168.

24. An explanation of two theories of why reasoning breaks down is provided in Sally Jackson, "Two Methods of Syllogistic Reasoning: An Empirical Comparison," *Communication Monographs* 49 (September 1982).

25. P. C. Wason and P. N. Johnson-Laird, *Psychology of Reasoning: Structure and Content* (Cambridge, Mass.: Harvard University Press, 1972), p. 2.

26. Joan Braaten, op. cit.

27. Harriet J. Rudolf, "Robert F. Kennedy at Stellenbosch University," *Communication Quarterly* 31 (Summer 1983): 205–211.

28. Susanne Landowski, "Academic Laboratories: Risking Life and Limb for Credit," *Winning Orations, 1988* (Interstate Oratorical Association, 1988), pp. 64–67.

GLOSSARY

Abstract language   Language that lacks specificity, that fails to refer to observable behavior or other sense data. *See also* Behavioral description.

Abstraction ladder   A range of more-to-less abstract terms describing an event or object.

Actuating   *See* Strategy to actuate.

Addition   The articulation error that involves adding extra parts to words.

Advising response   A helping response in which the receiver offers suggestions about how the speaker should deal with a problem.

Affect blend   The combination of two or more expressions, each showing a different emotion.

Affection   The social need to care for others and know that one is cared for.

All-channel network   A communication network in which all parties have equal access to one another.

Ambiguous response   A disconfirming response with more than one meaning, leaving the other party unsure of the responder's position.

Ambushing   A style in which the receiver listens carefully to gather information to use in an attack on the speaker.

Analogy   An extended comparison that can be used as supporting material in a speech.

Analyzing response   A helping style in which the listener offers an interpretation of a speaker's message.

Anecdote   A brief personal story, used to illustrate or support a point in a speech.

Articulation   The process of pronouncing all the necessary parts of a word.

Assertion   A direct expression of the sender's needs, thoughts, or feelings, delivered in a way that does not attack the receiver's dignity.

Attending   The process of focusing on certain stimuli from the environment. *See also* Selection.

Attitude   A predisposition to respond to an idea, person, or thing favorably or unfavorably.

Audience analysis   A consideration of characteristics including the type, goals, demographics, beliefs, attitudes, and values of your listeners.

Authoritarian leadership style   A leadership style in which the designated leader uses legitimate, coercive, and reward power to dictate the group's actions.

Bar chart   A visual aid that compares two or more values by showing them as elongated horizontal rectangles.

Basic speech structure   The division of a speech into introduction, body, and conclusion.

Behavioral description   An account that refers only to observable phenomena.

Belief   An underlying conviction about the truth of an idea, often based on cultural training.

Brainstorming   A method for creatively generating ideas in groups by minimizing criticism and encouraging a large quantity of ideas without regard to their workability or ownership by individual members.

Causal reasoning   *See* Cause-effect pattern.

Cause-effect pattern   Organizing plan for a speech that demonstrates how one or more events result in another event or events.

Certainty   Messages that dogmatically imply that the speaker's position is correct and that the other person's ideas are not worth considering. Likely to generate a defensive response.

Chain network   A communication network in which information passes sequentially from one member to another.

Channel   The medium through which a message passes from sender to receiver.

Charisma   The dimension of credibility that is a combination of a speaker's enthusiasm and likability.

Chronemics   The study of how humans use and structure time.

Cliché   A ritualized, stock response to a social situation.

Climax pattern   Organizing plan for a speech that builds ideas to the point of maximum interest or tension.

Closed question   Interview question that can be answered in a few words.

Coercive power   The power to influence others by the threat or imposition of unpleasant consequences.

Cohesiveness   The totality of forces that causes members to feel themselves part of a group and makes them want to remain in that group.

Column chart   Visual aid that compares two or more values by showing them as elongated vertical rectangles.

Common ground A persuasive strategy stressing similarities between speaker and audience.

Communication A continuous, irreversible, transactive process involving communicators who occupy different but overlapping environments and are simultaneously senders and receivers of messages, many of which are distorted by physical and psychological noise.

Communication climate The emotional tone of a relationship as it is expressed in the messages that the partners send and receive.

Communication networks Systems of stable person-to-person relationships through which information flows in an organization.

Conclusion(of a speech) The final structural unit of a speech, in which the main points are reviewed and final remarks are made to motivate the audience to act or help listeners remember key ideas.

Confirming response A message that expresses caring or respect for another person.

Conflict An expressed struggle between at least two interdependent parties who perceive incompatible goals, scarce rewards, and interference from the other party in achieving their goals.

Conflict stage A stage in problem-solving groups when members openly defend their positions and question those of others.

Connotation The emotional associations of a term.

Consensus Agreement between group members about a decision.

Content message A message that communicates information about the subject being discussed. *See also* Relational message.

Control The social need to influence others.

Controlling communication Messages in which the sender tries to impose some sort of outcome on the receiver, usually resulting in a defensive reaction.

Convincing A speech goal that aims at changing audience members' beliefs, values, or attitudes. *See also* Strategy to actuate.

Crazymaking Passive aggressive messages sent in indirect ways that frustrate and confuse the recipient.

Credibility The believability of a speaker or other source of information.

Debilitative stage fright Intense level of anxiety about speaking before an audience, resulting in poor performance.

Decoding The process in which a receiver attaches meaning to a message.

Deduction Reasoning from a generality to a specific conclusion.

Defensive listening A response style in which the receiver perceives a speaker's comments as an attack.

Democratic leadership style A style in which the nominal leader invites the group's participation in decision making.

Demographics Audience characteristics that can be analyzed statistically, such as age, gender, education, group membership, and so on.

Denotation The objective, emotion-free meaning of a term. *See also* Connotation.

Descriptive communication Messages that describe the speaker's position without evaluating others. Synonymous with "I" language.

Diagram A line drawing that shows the most important components of an object.

Direct aggression An expression of the sender's thoughts or feelings or both that attacks the position and dignity of the receiver.

Direct persuasion Persuasion that does not try to hide or disguise the speaker's persuasive purpose.

Direct question Interview question that makes a straightforward request for information.

Disconfirming response A message that expresses a lack of caring or respect for another person.

Disfluency A nonlinguistic verbalization, for example, *um, er, ah.*

Downward communication Communication from superior to one or more subordinates.

Dyad A two-person unit.

Dysfunctional roles Individual roles played by group members that inhibit the group's effective operation. *See also* Functional roles.

Emblems Deliberate nonverbal behaviors with precise meanings, known to virtually all members of a cultural group.

Emergence phase A stage in problem-solving when the group moves from conflict toward a single solution.

Emotional evidence Evidence that arouses emotional reactions in an audience.

Emotive language Language that conveys the sender's attitude rather than simply offering an objective description.

Empathic listening Listening in which the goal is to help the speaker solve a problem.

Empathy The ability to project oneself into another person's point of view, so as to experience the other's thoughts and feelings.

Encoding The process of putting thoughts into symbols, most commonly words.

Enthymeme Compressed version of a syllogism in which the underlying premises are not stated.

Environment   Both the physical setting in which communication occurs and the personal perspectives of the parties involved.

Equality   A type of supportive communication described by Gibb, suggesting that the sender regards the receiver as worthy of respect.

Equivocal words   Words that have more than one dictionary definition.

Ethical persuasion   Persuasion in an audience's best interest that does not depend on false or misleading information to induce change in that audience.

Euphemism   A pleasant-sounding term used in place of a more direct but less pleasant one.

Evaluative communication   Messages in which the sender judges the receiver in some way, usually resulting in a defensive response.

Evaluative listening   Listening in which the goal is to judge the quality or accuracy of the speaker's remarks.

Evidence   Material used to prove a point, such as testimony, statistics, and examples.

Example   A specific case that is used to demonstrate a general idea.

Expected response   The audience reaction predicted on the basis of audience analysis; used in planning a speech.

Expert power   The ability to influence others by virtue of one's perceived expertise on the subject in question. *See also* Information power.

Expressive communication   Communication of emotional information. *See also* Instrumental communication.

Extemporaneous speech   A speech that is planned in advance but presented in a direct, conversational manner.

External noise   Factors outside the receiver that interfere with the accurate reception of a message.

Facilitative stage fright   A moderate level of anxiety about speaking before an audience that helps improve the speaker's performance.

Factual question   Interview question that investigates matters of fact. *See also* Opinion question.

Factual statement   A statement based on direct observation of sense data.

Fallacy of approval   The irrational belief that it is vital to win the approval of virtually every person a communicator deals with.

Fallacy of catastrophic expectations   The irrational belief that the worst possible outcome will probably occur.

Fallacy of overgeneralization   Irrational beliefs in which (1) conclusions (usually negative) are based on limited evidence or (2) communicators exaggerate their shortcomings.

Fallacy of perfection   The irrational belief that a worthwhile communicator should be able to handle every situation with complete confidence and skill.

Flowchart   A graphic representation of the communication that needs to take place in order to accomplish an organizational task. *See also* Formal communication networks.

Force field analysis   A method of problem analysis that identifies the forces contributing to resolution of the problem and the forces that inhibit its resolution.

Formal communication networks   Management's idea of who should talk with whom in order to accomplish the organization's mission.

Formal outline   A consistent format and set of symbols used to identify the structure of ideas. *See also* Speech structure.

Forum   A discussion format in which audience members are invited to add their comments to those of the official discussants.

Functional roles   Member roles (usually unstated) that must be carried out if the group is to accomplish its task-related goals. *See also* Task functions; Maintenance functions.

General needs   Needs that are shared by all humans. *See also* Maslow's needs.

General purpose   One of three basic ways a speaker seeks to affect an audience: to entertain, inform, or persuade.

Gibb categories   Six sets of contrasting styles of verbal and nonverbal behavior. Each set describes a communication style that is likely to arouse defensiveness and a contrasting style that is likely to prevent or reduce it. Developed by Jack Gibb.

Group   A small collection of people who interact with each other, usually face-to-face, over time in order to reach goals.

Group goals   Goals that a group collectively seeks to accomplish. *See also* Individual goals.

Growth group   A group whose goal is to help members learn more about themselves.

Hearing   The process wherein sound waves strike the eardrum and cause vibrations that are transmitted to the brain.

Hidden agendas   Individual goals that group members are unwilling to reveal.

Homeostasis   A form of equilibrium that keeps a system following its established standards of behavior.

Horizontal communication   Communication between people who are not connected vertically on an organization chart.

Hypothetical example   Example that asks an audience to imagine an object or event.

"I" language   Language that describes the speaker's position without evaluating others. Synonymous with *description*.

Illustrators   Nonverbal behaviors that accompany and support verbal messages.

Imaging   Technique for behavior rehearsal (for example, for a speech) that involves visualization of the successful completion of the task.

Impersonal communication   Behavior that treats others as objects rather than as individuals. *See also* Interpersonal communication.

Impersonal response   A disconfirming response that is superficial or trite.

Impervious response   A disconfirming response that ignores another person's attempt to communicate.

Impromptu speech   A speech given "off the top of one's head," without preparation.

Inclusion   The social need to feel a sense of belonging in some relationship with others.

Incongruous response   A disconfirming response in which two messages, one of which is usually nonverbal, contradict one another.

Indirect communication   Hinting at a message instead of expressing thoughts and feelings directly. *See also* Passive aggression and Assertion.

Indirect question   Interview question that does not directly request the information being sought. *See also* Direct question.

Individual goals   The motives of individual members that influence their behavior in groups. *See also* Group goals.

Induction   Reasoning from specific evidence to a general conclusion.

Inferential statement   A statement based on interpretation of sense data.

Informal communication networks   Patterns of interaction that are not described on organization or flow charts.

Informational interview   An interview intended to collect facts and opinions from the respondent.

Informational listening   Listening in which the goal is to receive accurately the same thoughts the speaker is trying to convey.

Information hunger   An audience's desire to learn information. Created by a speaker.

Information power   The ability to influence others by virtue of the otherwise obscure information one possesses. *See also* Expert power.

Insensitive listening   Failure to recognize the thoughts or feelings that are not directly expressed by a speaker, instead accepting the speaker's words at face value.

Instrumental communication   Communication of functional, practical information. *See also* Expressive communication.

Insulated listening   A style in which the receiver ignores undesirable information.

Interactive communication model   A characterization of communication as a two-way event in which sender and receiver exchange messages in response to one another.

Interpersonal communication   Communication in which the parties consider one another as unique individuals rather than as objects. It is characterized by minimal use of stereotyped labels; unique, idiosyncratic social rules; and a high degree of information exchange.

Interpersonal relationship   An association in which the parties meet each other's social needs to some degree.

Interpretation   The act of attaching meaning to a set of stimuli.

Interrupting response   A disconfirming response in which one communicator interrupts another.

Interview   A structured form of oral communication involving two parties, at least one of whom communicates in ways designed to achieve a preconceived purpose.

Intimate distance   One of Hall's four distance zones, ranging from skin contact to eighteen inches.

Intrapersonal communication   Communication that occurs within a single person.

Introduction(of a speech)   The first structural unit of a speech, in which the speaker captures the audience's attention and previews the main points to be covered.

Irrational thinking   Beliefs that have no basis in reality or logic; one source of debilitative stage fright.

Irrelevant response   A disconfirming response in which one communicator's comments bear no relationship to the previous speaker's ideas.

Johari Window   A model that describes the relationship between self-disclosure and self-awareness.

Judging response   A reaction in which the receiver evaluates the sender's message either favorably or unfavorably.

Kinesics   The study of body movement, gesture, and posture.

Laissez-faire leadership style   A style in which the designated leader gives up his or her formal role, transforming the group into a leaderless collection of individuals.

Language   A collection of symbols, governed by rules, and used to convey messages between individuals.

Leader   *See* Nominal leader.

Leadership   The ability to influence the behavior of others in a group.

Learning group   A group whose goal is to expand their knowledge about some topic other than itself or its individual members. *See also* Growth group.

Legitimate power   The ability to influence a group owing to one's position in a group. *See also* Nominal leader.

Linear communication model   A characterization of communication as a one-way event in which a message flows from sender to receiver.

Line chart   A visual aid consisting of a grid that maps out the direction of a trend by plotting a series of points.

Listening   The process wherein the brain reconstructs electrochemical impulses generated by hearing into representations of the original sound and gives them meaning.

Lose-lose problem-solving   An approach to conflict resolution in which neither party achieves its goals.

Maintenance functions   *See* Social functions.

Managerial Grid   A two-dimensional model that describes the various combinations of a leader's concern with task-related and relational goals.

Manipulators   Movements in which one part of the body grooms, massages, rubs, holds, fidgets, pinches, picks, or otherwise manipulates another part.

Manuscript speech   A speech that is read word-for-word from a prepared text.

Maslow's needs   A hierarchy of needs that motivate humans, that is, physical, safety, social, self-esteem, and self-actualization needs in that order.

Memorized speech   A speech that is learned and delivered by rote without a written text.

Message   A sender's planned and unplanned words and nonverbal behaviors.

Metacommunication   Messages (usually relational) that refer to other messages: Communication about communication.

Mixed messages   Contradiction between a verbal message and one or more nonverbal cues.

Model   A simplified representation of some process or object.

Motivated sequence   A five-step plan used in persuasive speaking; also known as "Monroe's Motivated Sequence."

Negotiation   A process in which two or more parties discuss specific proposals in order to find a mutually acceptable agreement.

Networks   Patterns that individual channels of communication form between group members.

Neutrality   A defense-arousing behavior described by Gibb in which the sender expresses indifference toward a receiver.

Noise   External, physiological, and psychological distractions that interfere with the accurate transmission and reception of a message.

Nominal leader   The person who is identified by title as the leader of a group.

Nonassertion   The inability or unwillingness to express one's thoughts or feelings when necessary.

Nonverbal communication   Messages expressed by other than linguistic means.

Norms   Shared values, beliefs, behaviors, and procedures that govern a group's operation.

Number chart   Visual aid that lists numbers in tabular form in order to clarify information.

One-way communication   Communication in which a receiver provides no feedback to a sender.

Open question   Interview question that requires the interviewee to respond in detail. *See also* Closed question.

Open system   A system that is influenced by the environment in which it operates.

Opinion question   Interview question seeking the interviewee's opinion. *See also* Factual question.

Organization   The act of arranging perceived data in some manner.

Organization chart   Charts that describe lines of authority within an organization.

Orientation stage   A stage in problem-solving groups when members become familiar with one another's positions and tentatively volunteer their own.

Panel discussion   A discussion format in which participants consider a topic more or less conversationally, without formal procedural rules. Panel discussions may be facilitated by a moderator.

Paralanguage   Nonlinguistic means of vocal expression: rate, pitch, tone, and so on.

Parallel relationship   One in which the balance of power shifts from one party to the other according to the situation.

Paraphrasing   Feedback in which the receiver rewords the speaker's thoughts and feelings. Can be used to verify understanding, demonstrate empathy, and help others solve their problems.

Parliamentary procedure   A problem-solving method in which specific rules govern the way issues may be discussed and decisions made.

Participative decision making   Development of solutions with input by the people who will be affected.

Passive aggression   An indirect expression of aggression, delivered in a way that allows the sender to maintain a facade of kindness.

Perception checking   A three-part method for verifying the accuracy of interpretations, including a description of the sense data, two possible interpretations, and a request for confirmation of the interpretations.

Performance appraisal interview   An interview intended to acknowledge good performance, identify areas where problems exist, resolve problems, improve productivity, and help develop the employee's talents.

Personal distance   One of Hall's four distance zones, ranging from eighteen inches to four feet.

Personality   A relatively consistent set of traits a person exhibits across a variety of situations.

Persuasion   The act of motivating a listener, through communication, to change a particular belief, attitude, value, or behavior.

Phonological rules   Linguistic rules governing how sounds are combined to form words.

Physical need   Identified by Maslow as the most fundamental type of human need. Includes sufficient food, air, rest, and the ability to reproduce as a species.

Physiological noise   Biological factors in the receiver that interfere with accurate reception of a message.

Pictograph   A visual aid that artistically modifies a chart or graph in order to make it more interesting.

Pie chart   A visual aid that divides a circle into wedges, representing percentages of the whole.

Pitch   The highness or lowness of one's voice.

Primary question   The first question asked to elicit information on an interview topic. *See also* Secondary question.

Probative question   An open question used to analyze a problem by encouraging exploratory thinking.

Probe   *See* Secondary question.

Problem orientation   A supportive style of communication described by Gibb in which the communicators focus on working together to solve their problems instead of trying to impose their own solutions on one another.

Problem-solution pattern   Organizing pattern for a speech that describes an unsatisfactory state of affairs and then proposes a plan to remedy the problem.

Problem-solving group   A task-related group whose goal is to resolve a mutual concern of its members.

Procedural norms   Norms that describe rules for the group's operation. *See also* Task norms; Social norms.

Prod   Word or phrase that encourages a speaker to continue talking.

Provisionalism   A supportive style of communication described by Gibb in which the sender expresses a willingness to consider the other person's position.

Proxemics   The study of how people and animals use space.

Pseudolistening   An imitation of true listening in which the receiver's mind is elsewhere.

Psychological noise   Forces within a communicator that interfere with the ability to express or understand a message accurately.

Public communication   Communication that occurs when a group becomes too large for all members to contribute. It is characterized by an unequal amount of speaking and by limited verbal feedback.

Public distance   One of Hall's four distance zones, extending outward from twelve feet.

Punctuation   The perceptual process in which the causal relationship between two events is determined.

Purpose statement   A complete sentence that describes precisely what a speaker wants to accomplish.

Quantification   The use of numbers to clarify a concept.

Questioning   Feedback that usually requests the speaker to supply additional information in order to clarify or expand the receiver's understanding. Also, a style of helping in which the receiver seeks additional information from the sender. Some questioning responses are really disguised advice.

Question of fact   Issue in which there are two or more sides of conflicting factual evidence.

Question of policy   Issue that involves adopting or rejecting a specific course of action.

Question of value   Issue involving the worth of some idea, person, or object.

Rate   The speed at which a speaker utters words.

Reasoning by analogy   An argument based on the similarity between two ideas.

Receiver   One who notices and attends to a message.

Referent power   The ability to influence others by virtue of the degree to which one is liked or respected.

Reflected appraisal   The theory that a person's self-concept matches the way the person believes others regard him or her.

Regulative rules   Linguistic rules that govern what interpretation of a message is appropriate in a given context.

Reinforcement stage   A stage in problem-solving groups when members endorse the decision they have made.

Relational message   A message that expresses the social relationship between two or more individuals.

Relationship   *See* Interpersonal relationship.

Relative words   Words that gain their meaning by comparison.

Remembering   The act of recalling previously introduced information. Recall drops off in two phases: short- and long-term.

Residual message   The part of a message a receiver can recall after short- and long-term memory loss.

Reward power   The ability to influence others by the granting or promise of desirable consequences.

Roles   The patterns of behavior expected of group members.

Rule   Explicit, officially stated guideline that governs group functions and member behavior.

Safety need   Identified by Maslow as protection from threats to an individual's well-being.

Secondary question   Follow-up question used in an interview to elicit information not revealed by a primary question.

Selection   The act of attending to stimuli from the environment.

Selective listening   A listening style in which the receiver responds only to messages that interest him or her.

Self-actualization   One of five of Maslow's needs. The desire to reach one's maximum potential.

Self-concept   The relatively stable set of perceptions each individual holds of himself or herself.

Self-disclosure   The process of deliberately revealing information about oneself that is significant and that would not normally be known by others.

Self-esteem   The degree of regard a person holds for himself or herself.

Self-fulfilling prophecy   A prediction or expectation of an event that makes the outcome more likely to occur than would otherwise have been the case.

Semantic rules   Rules that govern the meaning of language as opposed to its structure. *See also* Syntactic rules.

Sender   The creator of a message.

Sex role   The social orientation that governs behavior, in contrast to a person's biological gender.

Significant other   A person whose opinion is important enough to affect one's self-concept strongly.

Signpost   A phrase that emphasizes the importance of upcoming material in a speech.

Sign reasoning   Reasoning from specific evidence to a specific conclusion without explaining how the evidence and conclusion are related.

Situational leadership   A theory that argues that the most effective leadership style varies according to leader-member relations, the nominal leader's power, and the task structure.

Slurring   The articulation error that involves overlapping the end of one word with the beginning of the next.

Small group   A group of a size such that every person can participate actively with the other members.

Social distance   One of Hall's distance zones, ranging from four to twelve feet.

Social functions   Functional roles concerned with maintaining smooth personal relationships among group members. Also termed "Maintenance functions." *See also* Task functions.

Social goals   Motives of individual group members related to satisfying their social needs, for example, inclusion, control, affection. *See also* Task-related goals.

Social group   A group whose goal is to meet the social needs of its members rather than to meet task-related goals.

Social needs   Identified by Maslow as needs associated with one's interpersonal relationships. *See also* Inclusion; Control; Affection.

Social norms   Norms that govern the relationship of group members to each other. *See also* Task norms; Procedural norms.

Social role   Emotional roles concerned with maintaining smooth personal relationships among group members. Also termed "Maintenance functions." *See also* Task functions.

Sociogram   Graphic representation of the interaction patterns in a group.

Space pattern   Organizing plan in a speech that arranges points according to their physical location.

Specific needs   The needs of a particular audience as opposed to "general needs."

Specific purpose   The precise effect that the speaker wants to have on an audience. Expressed in the form of a *purpose statement.*

Spontaneity   A supportive communication behavior described by Gibb in which the sender expresses a message without any attempt to manipulate the receiver.

Stage hogging   A listening style in which the receiver is more concerned with making his or her own point than in understanding the speaker.

Statistic   Numbers arranged or organized to show how a fact or principle is true for a large number of cases.

Strategy   A defense-arousing style of communication described by Gibb in which the sender tries to manipulate or trick a receiver; also the general term for any type of plan, as in the plan for a persuasive speech.

Strategy to actuate   Persuasive plan that seeks to move an audience to immediate action.

Strategy to convince   Persuasive strategy that seeks to change the way an audience thinks. *See also* Actuating.

Substitution   The articulation error that involves replacing part of a word with an incorrect sound.

Superiority   A defense-arousing style of communication described by Gibb in which the sender states or implies that the receiver is not worthy of respect.

Supporting response   A response style in which the receiver reassures, comforts, or distracts the person seeking help.

Survey research   Information gathering in which the responses of a sample of a population are collected to disclose information about the larger group.

Syllogism   Arguments made up of two premises and a conclusion.

Symbol   An arbitrary sign used to represent a thing, person, idea, event, or relationship in ways that make communication possible.

Symposium   A discussion format in which participants divide the topic in a manner that allows each member to deliver in-depth information without interruption.

Syntactic rules   Rules that govern the ways symbols can be arranged as opposed to the meanings of those symbols. *See also* Semantic rules.

System   A group of people who interact with one another to form a whole greater than the sum of its parts.

Tangential response   A disconfirming response that uses the speaker's remark as a starting point for a shift to a new topic.

Target audience   That part of an audience that must be influenced in order to achieve a persuasive goal.

Task functions   Functional roles of group members concerned with accomplishing the group's stated task. *See also* Maintenance functions.

Task norms   Norms that focus on how a group should achieve its goal. *See also* Social norms; Procedural norms.

Task-related goals   Goals related to accomplishing the group's stated purpose for operating.

Territory   Fixed space that an individual assumes some right to occupy.

Testimony   Supporting material that proves or illustrates a point by citing an authoritative source.

Thesis statement   A complete sentence describing the central idea of a speech.

Topic pattern   Organizing scheme for a speech that arranges points according to logical types or categories.

Trait theories of leadership   The belief that it is possible to identify leaders by personal traits, such as intelligence, appearance, or sociability.

Transactional communication model   A characterization of communication as the simultaneous sending and receiving of messages in an ongoing, irreversible process.

Transition   Phrase that connects ideas in a speech by showing how one relates to the other.

Two-way communication   An exchange of information in which the receiver deliberately provides feedback to a sender.

Understanding   The act of interpreting a message by following grammatical and semantic rules.

Upward communication   Communication from one or more subordinates to a superior.

Value   A deeply rooted belief about a concept's inherent worth.

Visual aid   Graphic devices used in a speech to illustrate or support ideas.

Visualization   The technique for self-improvement that involves one's imagining the successful completion of a task.

Wheel network   A communication network in which a gatekeeper regulates the flow of information from between all other members.

Whorf-Sapir hypothesis   The theory that the structure of a language shapes the worldview of its users.

Win-lose problem-solving   An approach to conflict resolution in which one party reaches its goal at the expense of the other.

Win-win problem-solving   An approach to conflict resolution in which the parties work together to satisfy all their goals.

Word chart   Visual aid that lists words or terms in tabular form in order to clarify information.

Y network   A communication network in which a gatekeeper conveys information from one member to all other members.

"You" language   Language that judges another person, increasing the likelihood of a defensive reaction. *See also* Evaluative communication.

INDEX

COPYRIGHT ACKNOWLEDGMENTS

Literary Credits

Chapter 7   202 From "The Death of the Hired Man" from *The Poetry of Robert Frost*, edited by Edward Connery Lathem. Reprinted by permission of Henry Holt and Company, Inc. **205** Excerpt from the *Playboy* Interview: Kurt Vonnegut, *Playboy* Magazine, (July 1973). Interview conducted by David Standish. **213** Drawing by Ziegler; ©1988 The New Yorker Magazine, Inc.

Chapter 8   225 "Far Side" copyright 1987 Universal Press Syndicate. Reprinted with permission. All rights reserved. **232** Reprinted by permission from *Communication in Small Group Discussion*, Second Edition by John F. Cragan and David W. Wright; Copyright ©1986 by West Publishing Company. All rights reserved. **233** Reprinted by permission of Faber and Faber Ltd. and The Putnam Publishing Group from *Lord of the Flies* by William Golding. **237** From John K. Brilhart and Gloria J. Galanes, *Effective Group Discussion*, 6th ed., p. 174. Copyright ©1989 Wm C. Brown Publishers, Dubuque, Iowa. All Rights Reserved. Reprinted by permission.

Chapter 9   248 Reprinted by permission of Thomas V. DiBacco. **253** "B.C." reprinted by permission of Johnny Hart and Creators Syndicate. **255** "Frank and Ernest" reprinted by permission of NEA, Inc. **257** From John K. Brilhart and Gloria J. Galanes, *Effective Group Discussion*, (6th ed. Copyright ©1989 Wm C. Brown Publishers, Dubuque, Iowa. All Rights Reserved. Reprinted by permission.) **263** Reprinted from *Pasadena Weekly*. Author unknown. **265** Drawing by Leo Cullum; ©1986 The New Yorker Magazine, Inc. **268** The Managerial Grid figure from *The Managerial Grid III: The Key to Leadership Excellence*, by Robert R. Blake and Jane Srygley Mouton. Houston: Gulf Publishing Company, Copyright ©1985, page 12. Reproduced by permission. **269** Situational Leadership® model reprinted by permission of Paul Hersey, Leadership Studies, Inc. All rights reserved. **271** "Far Side" copyright 1988 Universal Press Syndicate. Reprinted with permission. All rights reserved.

Chapter 10   287 Drawing by Woodman; ©1981 The New Yorker Magazine, Inc. **295** Drawing by H. Martin; ©1981 The New Yorker Magazine, Inc. **297** Reprinted with permission of The Free Press, a Division of Macmillan, Inc. from *Communication in Organizations* by Everett M. Rogers and Rehka Agarwala-Rogers. Copyright ©1976 by The Free Press. **302** "Peanuts" reprinted by permission of UFS, Inc.

Chapter 11   309 Shana Alexander, *Life Magazine* ©1967 Time, Inc. **321** Reprinted by permission of Richard Armour. **329** ACADEMIC INDEX™ printout copyright 1989, Information Access Company, Foster City, California 94404. **333** Reprinted by permission of the Interstate Oratorical Association.

Chapter 12   350 "The Far Side" cartoon by Gary Larson is reprinted by permission of Chronicle Features, San Francisco, CA. **352** Copyright 1980 Universal Press Syndicate. All rights reserved. Reprinted by permission of Jerry Marcus. **362** Drawing by Joe Mirachi; ©1977 The New Yorker Magazine, Inc.

COPYRIGHT ACKNOWLEDGMENTS

Photo Credits